Tracing the Visual Language of Raphael's Circle to 1527

Brill's Studies in Intellectual History

VOLUME 313

Brill's Studies on Art, Art History, and Intellectual History

VOLUME 46

The titles published in this series are listed at *brill.com/bsai*

Tracing the Visual Language of Raphael's Circle to 1527

By

Alexis R. Culotta

BRILL

LEIDEN | BOSTON

The Library of Congress Cataloging-in-Publication Data is available online at http://catalog.loc.gov
LC record available at http://lccn.loc.gov/2020011997

Typeface for the Latin, Greek, and Cyrillic scripts: "Brill". See and download: brill.com/brill-typeface.

ISSN 0920-8607
ISBN 978-90-04-43014-3 (hardback)
ISBN 978-90-04-43048-8 (e-book)

This book is printed on acid-free paper and produced in a sustainable manner.

Printed by Printforce, the Netherlands

Contents

Acknowledgements

For all of the individuals who have helped in the development of this book:

For all of the faculty on my doctoral advisory committee at the University of Washington who helped to encourage a space for scholarly inquiry that helped me to think of Raphael from new perspectives.

For the additional institutions, including the American Academy in Rome, the Archivio di Stato di Roma, the Accademia dei Lincei, the Bibliotheca Hertziana, the Istituto Luigi Sturzo as well as the Newberry Library and Art Institute of Chicago, who have afforded me access to invaluable resources to advance my arguments.

For those in my scholarly community and my personal life who have offered their valuable critique and insight into my observations. Most importantly, my family, including my husband, Aron, and my children, Luca and Livia, who have been both patient and enthusiastic since the very beginning of this research.

For all of these individuals, this book is for you. Thank you.

Illustrations

Introduction

> You too, Raphael, have moved the jealousy of the gods, while restoring Rome, her whole corpse dilapidated, with your miraculous art, and recalling to life and pristine glory the remains of a city maimed by arms, fire and age; as you did so, death's indignation was aroused by your gift of returning to life what had long been extinct, and of renewing once more, disdaining the way of all flesh, what the long days of time had slowly taken away.
>
> BALDASSARRE CASTIGLIONE, *De morte Raphaelis pictoris*, 1520[1]

On 6 April, 1520, as church bells rang across Rome to commemorate Good Friday, Raffaello Sanzio took his final breath.[2] His rise to artistic success in Rome in the early years of the sixteenth century, combined with his early demise at the age of 37, transformed the artist into a mythic character who, in the words of Rona Goffen, "[*lived*] as a prince and [*died*] as a god."[3] His seemingly effortless talent exemplified *sprezzatura*, a notion coined by his associate Baldassarre Castiglione, and scholars have since exalted Raphael's roles in projects across Rome as epitomizing the best of early *cinquecento* artistic production. His work in the Vatican's *Stanza della Segnatura*, for example, has been lauded as "the apogee of High Renaissance painting in Rome,"[4] and his designs for the unfinished Villa Madama on the suburban Monte Mario have been hailed as "the most ambitious villa-garden complex planned for post-classical Rome."[5] Such laudatory praise is not isolated to the modern day but rather reflects the

1 As published in: V. Golzio, *Raffaello: nei documenti nelle testimonianze dei contemporanei e nella letteratura del suo secolo* (Città del Vaticano: Pontificia insigne Accademia Artistica dei Virtuosi al Pantheon, 1936), 232.

2 Raphael's death date is derived from a letter written by Marcantonio Michiel. For full text, see: J.K.G. Shearman, *Raphael in Early Modern Sources* (New Haven: Yale University Press, 2003), I: 572.

3 R. Goffen, "Raphael's Designer Labels: From the Virgin Mary to La Fornarina," *Artibus et Historiae*, 24 (4) (2003), 123.

4 C.L. Joost-Gaugier, *Raphael's Stanza della Segnatura* (NY: Cambridge University Press, 2002), 1.

5 D.R. Coffin, "The Plans of the Villa Madama." *The Art Bulletin*, Vol. 49 (2) (Jun., 1967), 111.

 | DOI:10.1163/9789004430488_002

pervasive mythologization of the artist that has endured since Raphael's era. From Baldassarre Castiglione's eulogizing praise of Raphael's purported ability to revive the lost splendor of Rome (as reflected in this chapter's opening quotation) to Giorgio Vasari's graceful accounts of the artist's accomplishments—"for in truth we have from him art, colouring, and invention harmonized and brought to such a pitch of perfection as could scarcely be hoped for; nor may any intellect ever think to surpass him"—Raphael enjoyed a rather rapid apotheosis to the pantheon of lost artistic masters.[6]

Accordingly, the level of mourning resulting from Raphael's departure would have led most to believe that the brilliance of the Roman Renaissance died with him. Indeed, Raphael's death did coincidentally foreshadow the imminent demise of the artistic *largesse* that defined the first decades of the *cinquecento*. Agostino Chigi (1466–1520), for instance, the flamboyant and exorbitantly wealthy patron who had secured Raphael's iconic Roman status with his extensive commissions at his villa (now known as the Villa Farnesina), died only five days after Raphael at the age of 54.[7] Months later, on 1 December, 1521, Pope Leo X (1475–1521), a pivotal patron of the arts, proponent of humanism, and past promoter of Raphael, also met his end. Leo's successor, Adrian VI (1522–1523), did little to further his predecessor's commitment to the arts, nor did the subsequent Pope Clement VII who assumed the papacy in 1523.[8] Then, on 6 May 1527, seven years after Raphael's death, the hostile troops of Holy Roman Emperor Charles V descended upon the Eternal City, laying siege to its streets, savagely plundering palaces and churches, and sending Pope Clement VII into hiding.[9]

Dramatized in a print series, "The Victories of Charles V," engraved by Dirck Volkertszoon Coornhort (1522–1590) after drawings by Maarten van Heemskerck (1498–1547) (Fig. 1), the catastrophic cascade of events was also documented in the diaries of Benvenuto Cellini (1500–1571).

6 G. Vasari, *Lives of the Painters, Sculptors and Architects*, trans. by Gaston du C. de Vere (NY: Alfred Knopf, 1996), I: 746.

7 For more see: F. Gilbert, *The Pope, His Banker, and Venice* (Cambridge, MA: Harvard University Press, 1980), 95.

8 For a complete account of Clement VII's patronage, see: S. Reiss and K. Gouwens, eds., *The Pontificate of Clement VII: History, Politics, Culture* (London: Routledge, 2017).

9 For more, see: A. Chastel, *The Sack of Rome, 1527. The A.W. Mellon Lectures in the Fine Arts, 1977, The National Gallery of Art, Washington. D.C.* trans. by Beth Archer (Princeton, NJ: Princeton University Press, 1983). For the humanist perspectives on these atrocities, see: K. Gouwens, *Remembering the Renaissance: Humanist Narrative of the Sack of Rome* (Leiden, Netherlands: Brill, 1998).

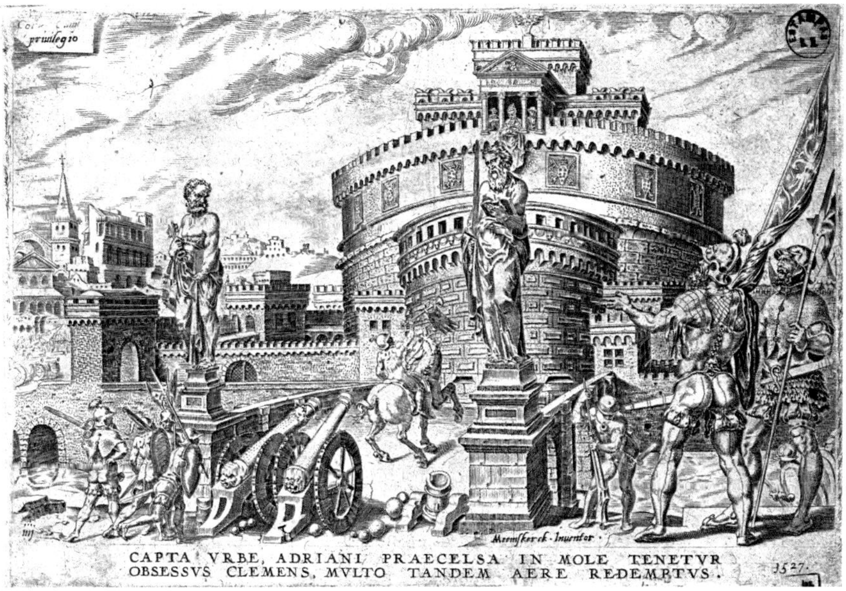

FIGURE 1 Dirck Volkertszoon Coornhort after Maarten van Heemskerck, *Pope Clement VII Besieged in the Castel Sant'Angelo in 1527*, 1555; Engraving
BIBLIOTECA NACIONAL, MADRID, SPAIN/ALAMY

> At this moment the whole world was in arms. Pope Clement had sent to Giovanni de' Medici to ask for troops. But when they came to Rome, they were so unruly that it was not sage to be in public shops (…) Pope Clement … disbanded the five companies sent him by my lord Giovanni, … [and] Bourbon, knowing that Rome was unprotected, forced on his army with all speed to our gates. Then all Rome rushed to arms.[10]

Though order would return in a matter of months, the Sack of Rome nevertheless served as a more permanent cultural breaking point as it sent artistic masters fleeing to the far reaches the Italian peninsula, halted many projects, and caused archaeology, as defined by Raphael and espoused by Leo X, to vanish.[11]

10 B. Cellini, *The Autobiography of Benvenuto Cellini*, trans. by A. MacDonell (New York: Everyman's Library, 2010), 65; for a more on this print series, see: B. Rosier, "The Victories of Charles V: A Series of Prints by Maarten van Heemskerke, 1555–1556." *Simiolus: Netherlands Quarterly for the History of Art* 20 (1) (1990–1991), 24–38.

11 For more on Raphael and the definition of archaeology, see: A. Nesselrath, "Raphael's Archaeological Method," in André Chastel, ed., *Raffaello a Rome: Il Covegno del 1983* (Rome:

What thrived, though, in this transitional era, were those who had emerged from Raphael's shadow: the members and associates of his workshop. This time between the chronological bookends of Raphael's death in 1520 and the Sack of Rome in 1527 reveals a remarkable—yet often overlooked—moment of artistic production that was spurred on in part by the artistic relationships that had been fostered during Raphael's lifetime. This book explores the origins of these relationships and traces their development through the visual production of a generation of artists once key players in Raphael's orbit. It examines how this style took root in Raphael's final years, as he engaged in both competitive and collaborative endeavors, and will then transition to discussion of the key figures of and projects associated with this workshop with the aim to deepen understanding of how these artists capitalized upon novel means of artistic exchange in the recombined forms of a shared visual language.

1 Reclaiming Raphael's Workshop

Despite the millions of words that have been lavished upon the study of Raphael from the days of Castiglione and Vasari to the critical eyes of contemporary scholars, there is still space to investigate the artist and his methodologies particularly as they related to the management of his workshop team. This book aims to tap into this space by focusing on the exchange between Raphael and his workshop and how it revolutionized the nature of artistic production in early *cinquecento* Rome. Since the days of John Shearman's landmark 1983 essay, "The Organization of Raphael's Workshop," numerous scholars have grappled with the ways in which Raphael's workshop functioned and, more broadly, how the concept of the workshop mentality evolved during the era.[12] Michael Cole and Mary Pardo's 2005 edited volume, *Inventions of the Studio, Renaissance to Romanticism*, for example, dissected the various aspects of the artist's studio development and noted the essential transformation in the Renaissance moment of the workshop into a space where artistic identity was formed.[13] This identity, though, was paradoxical in nature, as it established a

Edizioni dell'Elefante, 1986), 369; also see: G. Morolli, *"Le Belle Forme degli Edifici Antichi": Raffaello e il Progetto del Primo Trattato Rinascimentale sulle Antichità di Roma* (Florence: Alinea, 1984), 33.

12 J.K.G. Shearman, "The Organization of Raphael's Workshop," *Art Institute of Chicago Museum Studies*, 10 (1983), 40–57.

13 M. Cole and M. Pardo, eds., *Inventions of the Studio, Renaissance to Romanticism* (Chapel Hill, NC: University of North Carolina Press, 2005).

scenario in which the output of a studio teeming with artists would come to signify one artistic identity to the outside world of patrons.

This, in essence, was the space that Raphael succeeded in creating, one in which working relationships are to be optimized for success in order to maintain the integrity of that artistic identity. Raphael's final years in Rome were incredibly busy, so much so that his need for a strong team of artists—those who understood and could uphold his "brand"—became only more crucial as the months passed. Shearman notes in his pivotal essay the novelty in Raphael's reliance on his team members and their ability to maintain a remarkable level of consistency in their execution, so much so that discerning the authorship of preparatory drawings across Raphael's major projects can prove challenging. Since Shearman's interpretation of this studio's practices, scholars have generally agreed that Raphael's workshop was not only novel in its structure—in that it gave participants an unprecedented autonomy—but was also essential to Raphael's success. What is still missing, though, is a deeper understanding of the novelty in Raphael's approach and how this novelty was absorbed and adapted by the members of Raphael's artistic entourage.

Achim Gnann has suggested that these associated artists were spurred on by their "enthusiasm, because they … could develop their skills to the full. … They knew that they were contributing to something new and unique that could only come to fruition with their help and under the leadership of their brilliant master."[14] While Gnann paints a rather rosy picture, so to speak, of the workshop's motivations, his rationale recalls one of the perennial issues associated with the study of this network, that which positions Raphael as the supreme genius and subsequently pegs his workshop artists as devotees so mesmerized by Raphael's abilities that they simply took Raphael's orders and churned out works in his style. This same sentiment, for instance, was implied by Paul Joannides in his contributions to the symposium proceedings for the Prado Museum's *Late Raphael* exhibition: "by the end of Raphael's life, his workshop's methods were drilled in and—broadly—its members' artistic personalities were subsumed into the collective … but this unity did not long survive the master."[15] This claim on the one hand reinforces the need for collective thinking within a successful workshop space; on the other hand, though,

14 A. Gnann, "Raphael's Workshop in Rome," in A. Gnann and M.C. Plomp, *Raphael and his School* (Haarlem: Teylers Museum, 2012), 19.

15 T. Henry and P. Joannides, "Raphael and his workshop between 1513 and 1525: 'per la mano di maestro Rafaello e Joanne Francesco e Giulio sui discepoli,'" in T. Henry and P. Joannides, eds., *Late Raphael* (UK: Thames & Hudson, 2013), 20.

it suggests that Raphael's workshop members were mere minions following a regimented set of protocols handed down by Raphael and thus discounts any important legacy of visual exchange that might radiate from Raphael's workshop. It also implies that the professional relationships fostered within Raphael's workshop were quickly abandoned following the master's death, as if the freedom from Raphael's grasp led them to favor the exaltation of their own individual genius.

Also missing in the critical assessment thus far of Raphael's engagements is his association with Baldassarre Peruzzi (1481–1536) who, though never officially a member of the workshop, was nevertheless an enduring collaborator with Raphael and continued to work closely with many of the workshop artists during the 1520s. Peruzzi's work and his role in Rome as artist, architect, and student of the antique has gained increased scholarly attention in recent years. Since Mark Wilson Jones's seminal article "Palazzo Massimo and Baldassarre Peruzzi's Approach to Architectural Design" (1998), which highlighted Peruzzi's study of antiquity in the creation of two of his chief architectural projects there, Ann Huppert has done much to expand our understanding of Peruzzi from both an architectural and artistic perspective.[16] Her recent book, *Becoming an Architect in Renaissance Italy* (2015), showcases the various threads of Peruzzi's career in unprecedented detail.[17] Still other recent work has revealed a revived interest in Peruzzi's forays into theatrical scenography, an emerging field in the early years of the sixteenth century.[18] This book adds to this growing field of investigation by considering how Peruzzi's career intersected with that of Raphael and his circle in an effort to both shed more light on Peruzzi and also to underscore his pivotal role as an essential voice in this artistic chorus of Renaissance Rome.

As this book argues, Raphael was not the singularly divine artist whose skill surpassed all those around him to the extent that others obsequiously followed his artistic orders. Instead, his genius lies in the way in which he reconceptualized the practice of painting through a means of recombining visual form. He happened upon a cohort in Rome that could share in that vision—

16 M.W. Jones, "Palazzo Massimo and Baldassarre Peruzzi's Approach to Architectural Design." *Architectural History*, Vol. 31 (1998), 59–106.

17 A. Huppert, *Becoming an Architect in Renaissance Italy: Art, Science, and the Career of Baldassarre Peruzzi* (New Haven, CT: Yale, 2015).

18 For a recent essay on this topic, see: M.Y. Hara, "Capturing eyes and moving souls: Peruzzi's perspective set for La Calandria and the performative agency of architectural bodies." *Renaissance Studies* (October 2016), 586–607; also see: J. Berzal de Dios, *Visual Experiences in Cinquecento Theaters* (Toronto: University of Toronto Press, 2019).

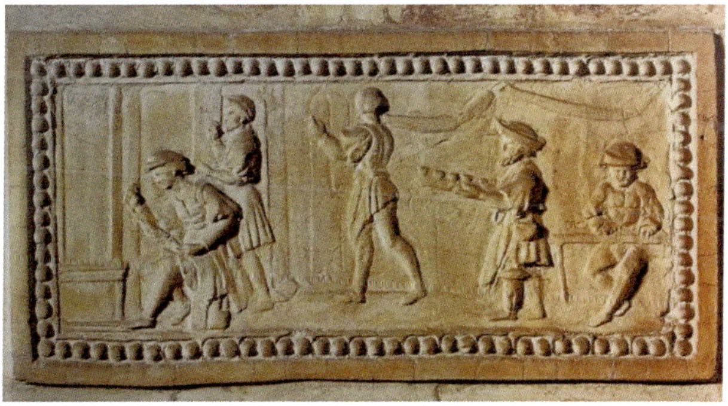

FIGURE 2 Giovanni da Udine, *Studio Assistants at Work*, Stucco relief; Loggia of Leo x, Vatican Palace/Foto Musei Vaticani

Peruzzi and the associates of Raphael's workshop—and the result was a dynamic period of artistic production that redefined compositional development through the borrowing of sources. This borrowing of visual phrases and concepts was hence carried forth past his lifetime by these workshop figures as they continued to engage with one another. A review of the commissions enjoyed by these figures in the wake of Raphael's death, as will be examined in this book's later chapters, reveals echoes of this approach through the quotations of figures, motifs, and styles. These commissions will reveal that this borrowing was part of a more profound artistic contemplation that spoke to the influence of Raphael and a shared visual dialogue among peers that continued past his lifetime.

2 Mechanics of a Visual Language: Imitation/Emulation/Repetition/Recombination

What does it mean to rely upon a visual language? The premise, simply put, is to have visual components or phrases that are repurposed or reused across various works. These forms thus become a point of reference to adopt a variety of meanings—links, for example, between artists, themes, or epochs—that can enrich a composition's impact.

The very act of this borrowing—whether we term it imitation, emulation, repetition, or recombination—has a long history before the days of Raphael. Indeed, the very concept of recombination itself recalls the legacy of scholarly debate over the intricacies of imitation and emulation. While the origins of this debate can be traced to the fourteenth century, it became particularly pronounced in the subsequent *cinquecento*, with the writings of Pico della Mirandola and Pietro Bembo, who took two polarizing approaches to imitation and the associated emulation (from a literary perspective).[19]

Pico della Mirandola advocated for the study of a wide variety of sources, which allowed for imitation through the recombination of literary elements from these sources into a new work.[20] Bembo, however, argued that such seamless recombination was implausible, writing: "the activity of imitating is nothing other than translating the likeness of some other's style into one's own writings and to cultivate that very temperament present in him whom you have chosen as a master."[21] In short, Bembo envisioned imitation as a pure act of mindless mimicry. Bembo does applaud, however, one's ability to sample a theme in myriad different ways. He lauds Petrarch, for example, because "he composed several poems out of one little aspect or features of his subject, which he did many times, … [and] he went on varying in such a wonderful way that the more one reads and rereads them, the more one longs to read and reread them."[22] This practice becomes for Bembo what Robert Williams called "a demonstration of originality: it … allows both poet and reader to concentrate on what Bembo believes to be the essence of poetry."[23] It also implies space in Bembo's interpretation for imitation if it takes the form of identifiable components: terms or phrases that can remind the reader (or viewer) of another work.

In his 1992 book, *Only Connect …: Art and the Spectator in the Italian Renaissance*, Shearman revived the discussion of imitation and emulation from an art historical perspective and, in doing so, seemingly sides with Pico della Mirandola.[24] The process of emulation, or sophisticated imitation, as Shearman calls it, became essential to artistic careers such as Raphael's because it involved the artful extraction of recognizable visual references from other sources and the recombination of those references in a new context. His preliminary efforts to this end can be seen in his portraits, *Agnolo Doni* and *Maddalena Strozzi Doni* (1506), wherein he alluded to elements of Leonardo's *Mona Lisa* (1503–1506; Louvre Museum) to reinforce the impact of these portraits. The same could be said of Raphael's nearly simultaneous *The Marriage of the Virgin* (*Lo Sposalizio*) (1504; Pinacoteca di Brera, Milan), which, as many scholars have observed,

19 For more, see: T.M. Greene, *The Light In Troy: Imitation and Discovery in Renaissance Poetry* (New Haven: Yale University Press, 1982), 171.

20 Greene, 172–174.

21 P. Bembo, *Prose della volgar lingua*, ed. M. Marti (Padua: Liviana, 1955), 15: Greene, 174.

22 C. Dionisotti, ed., *Pietro Bembo: Prose e rime* (Turin, 1960), 171.

23 Williams, 60.

24 Shearman, *Only connect …: art and the spectator in the Italian Renaissance*. The A.W. Mellon Lectures in the Fine Arts, 1988 (Princeton, NJ: Princeton University Press, 1992), 232.

bears striking similarity to his master Perugino's painting of the same subject (1500–1504; Musée des Beaux Arts, Caen). In summary, Shearman identifies "Imitation" and "Emulation," or Imitation with intent, as key sources of creativity in Renaissance artistic practice with roots again in antiquity and inextricably linked to the study of sources.[25]

The practice of such imitation and repetition across sources, of course, was a popular practice before Raphael's day in the studios of *quattrocento* Florence. Lorenzo Ghiberti's quotation of a Classical nude torso in his famed bronze competition panel of *Abraham and Isaac* (1401; Museo del Opera del Duomo), for example, or Sandro Botticelli's borrowing of the antique form of *Venus pudica* in his execution of *The Birth of Venus* (1485–1486; Galleria degli Uffizi) are instances that immediately come to mind as illustrations of the ways in which artists in the fifteenth century incorporated antique phrases in their work. In addition, Marvin Trachtenberg has noted how Donatello's early marble *David* bears a posture recalling both the work of his mentor, Lorenzo Ghiberti, and an ancient bronze sculpture once held by the Medici family.[26] Then there were the tensions of collaboration in the lives of Donatello and Brunelleschi as noted in Vasari's biographies, wherein he fueled a rumor that the *Saint Peter* sculpted for Orsanmichele was a collaborative creation.[27] This pulling together of sources was indeed well-established in the early days of the Renaissance. It would seem, though, that by the days of Raphael, the ways in which this repetition and recombination were being used took on new meaning. Namely, it would seem that Raphael explored more extensively the potential of extracting visual elements from other artist's works and then using them as a foundation of a visual language that he could cultivate among his workshop as it began to grow.

This type of practice would have challenged the contemporaneous conceptualization of how one juxtaposed originality and repetition, but similar contemplations were also underway elsewhere in Italy. As an example, one can look to Maria Loh's analysis of the aims of repetition in the oeuvre of Venetian master Titian, a contemporary of Raphael. Highlighting the recurring form of

25 "One of the most 'Renaissance' things about Imitation was that it was well known to have been an enterprise operating effectively and complexly within the classics of the ancient world: Virgil visibly imitating Homer was only the most obvious case that came to the surface" (Shearman, *Only Connect*, 232).

26 M. Trachtenberg, "An Antique Model for Donatello's Marble David." *The Art Bulletin*, 50 (3) (Sep., 1968), 268–269.

27 For more on this relationship between Brunelleschi and Donatello, see: R. Tarr, "Brunelleschi and Donatello: Placement and Meaning in Sculpture." *Artibus et Historiae*, 16 (32) (1995), 101–140.

the reclining nude as captured in compositions like the *Venus of Urbino* (1534; Galleria degli Uffizi) and subsequently echoed in the work of later painters like Il Padovanino (e.g., his *Sleeping Venus*, circa 1625), Loh stresses that the act of repetition was a strategic one that even Titian employed.[28] One can look to the earlier *Sleeping Venus* (1510) in Dresden to see such a case. As Loh notes, in his subsequent *Venus of Urbino* "Titian remade an old favorite and opened up the hermeneutic possibilities of the genre by relocating the setting to the boudoir and redirecting the gaze of the female figure outward, addressing the implied viewer."[29] In other words, by reusing a strikingly similar form of a reclining female nude, Titian drew direct attention to the tensions between imitation, repetition, and novelty.

This same idea is echoed to some extent in the recent work of Stephen J. Campbell that argued for an artistic "grafting," evident in the work of Titian and the Venetian *poesie* painting tradition. Campbell argues that Titian's description of his later paintings as *poesie* was to imply the act of joining diverse elements into a cohesive whole, or verse, through allusion, simile and metaphor.[30] To illustrate this point, Campbell turns to Titian's Dresden *Sleeping Venus* (1510), a work whose earliest commentator, Marcantonio Michiel, shared the presence of two artistic hands: Giorgione, in the figure, and Titian, in the background landscape.[31] Campbell describes the deliberate disjunctions between figure and landscape that nevertheless play off of each other—he cites, for example, Venus' curves being echoed in the rolling background hills—implying the combined efforts of Giorgione and Titian to create visual metaphors as found poetry. Here too Campbell notes a sense of visual tension, established primarily by the fact that works such as the *Sleeping Venus* simultaneously visually engage but also limit. The viewer is drawn toward the reclining nude figure, who has been artfully propped to fully reveal herself to the viewer. At the same time, however, she is inaccessible. Her closed eyes and

28 M. Loh, *Titian Remade: Repetition and the Transformation of Early Modern Italian Art* (Los Angeles: Getty Research Institute, 2007), 17–20.

29 Loh, 26.

30 S.J. Campbell, "Naturalism and the Venetian 'Poesia': Grafting, Metaphor, and Embodiment in Giorgione, Titian, and the Campagnolas" in A. Nagel and L. Pericolo, eds., *Subject as Aporia in Early Modern Art* (VT: Ashgate, 2010), 115.

31 "In casa de M. Ieronimo Marcello A.S. Tomado, 1525: la tela della Venere nuda, che dorme in uno paese, con Cupidine, fu de mano de Zorzo da Castelfranco; ma lo paese e Cupidine furono finite da Tiziano" (M. Michiel, *Notizie d'opere di disegno nella prima metà del secolo XVI, esistenti in Padova, Cremona, Milano, Pavia, Bergamo, Crema e Venezia. Scritta da un anonimo di quello tempo. Pubblicata e illustrata da D. Iacopo Morelli* (Bassano, 1800), 66).

arm framing her head create distance that is amplified by the landscape to give her an air of artificiality, thereby disrupting the hermeneutic potential once again.

These tensions as seen in the work of Titian speak to the notion that Raphael was not alone in his generation in his use of repeated visual elements; however, what seems particularly significant in Raphael's case is both the array of references he was able to absorb into his style and the ability to exchange these concepts within his circle. Robert Williams made strides in tackling the first of these nuances in his recent renewed look at Raphael's workshop participants and their web of connections as he grappled with the elements of synthesis and imitation in Raphael's work. Noting Raphael's ability to weave together elements from his mentors and contemporaries, Williams positions Raphael's work as "meta-style," one that is not individual but rather reflects an entirely new way of thinking about the practice of painting itself.[32]

This book builds on this premise—breaking down Williams' notion of a meta-style into the component parts of a visual language—in an effort to offer new insights into how Raphael built this lexicon through borrowing and fostered its continuation in novel ways among his workshop associates. As will be seen, ample visual evidence exists to demonstrate that these artists partook in a shared set of visual concepts, wherein one's sketches became the source of another's compositions or wherein the ideas of one artist are recast and revived in another artist's work. This perspective transcends current scholarship in that it attempts to place greater emphasis on these associated figures themselves and the ways in which they, like Raphael, so artfully recombined these visual references in new displays of artistic virtuosity. A simple—albeit anachronistic—parallel would be that of the revolutionary quality of jazz music in the 1920s and the introduction of the ostinato, or "riff." These chord progressions, the building blocks of a given song's structure, could be borrowed and sampled as a means to recall an earlier song while developing a new, perhaps even better, composition. It is this riffing, in visual terms, that Raphael's workshop associates can be seen as performing particularly in the days following Raphael's death, not in an act of mindless imitation or of repetition for lack of other inspiration; rather, this visual riffing became the source for ongoing novelty. This approach pushes past the hermeneutic considerations Loh saw in Titian's work and adjusts from Williams' approach to give Raphael's workshop artists more agency in their enduring careers.

---

32 R. Williams, *Raphael and the Redefinition of Art in Renaissance Italy* (UK: Cambridge University Press, 2017), 7.

3 Recombination in Light of Competition and Collaboration

This sharing of visual components becomes more intriguing when accomplished within the context of competition and collaboration between artists. As will be discussed, prior to his arrival in Rome, Raphael seemingly enjoyed a rather fluid process of absorbing visual types as he began to construct his "meta-style," as Williams termed it. What happens, though, when this melding is interrupted with competition? Once in Rome, Raphael was confronted with outright rivalries with both Michelangelo and Sebastiano del Piombo, with whom relations eventually became so contentious that Sebastiano would imply Raphael had borrowed too much from the Venetian's work in the late 1510s.[33] Despite these later accusations, this borrowing from other artistic sources nevertheless continued, and perhaps even spurred greater innovation, in Raphael's aesthetic during his earlier Roman years.

The notion of competition, or rivalry, in the sixteenth century has proven a strong source of fascination in recent scholarship. Rona Goffen's *Renaissance Rivals* (2002), for instance, showcased how the landscape of exchange among the three most powerful voices of the early *cinquecento*—Leonardo, Michelangelo, and Raphael—was contoured by the nature of their competition with each other.[34] At the same time, others have focused on the nature of collaboration. For instance, in *Raphael, Dürer, and Marcantonio Raimondi: Copying and the Renaissance Print* (2004), Lisa Pon examines the subtleties of collaboration in the printmaking process as a means of determining the presence of and exchange between artists.[35]

These various studies have been pivotal in the continued development of our greater understanding of the nature of artistic exchange, but what they tend to discount are the intersections of the two realms of competition and collaboration; in other words, that two artists can be both competitors and collaborators, particularly within the relatively unpredictable world of artistic commissions.[36] The notion of competition was, of course, foundational to

33 As captured in: 2 July 1518 letter from Sebastiano to Michelangelo (Shearman, *Raphael in Early Modern Sources*, I: 352). Previous letters—dated 19 January 1517 and 26 September 1517 letter from Leonardo Sellaio in Rome to Michelangelo (Shearman, *Raphael in Early Modern Sources*, I: 280 and 299, respectively) speak of Sebastiano's acquisition of the *Raising of Lazarus* composition and his assured triumph over Raphael.

34 R. Goffen, *Renaissance Rivals: Michelangelo, Leonardo, Raphael, Titian* (New Haven: Yale University Press, 2002).

35 L. Pon. *Raphael, Dürer and Marcantonio Raimondi: copying and the Italian Renaissance print* (New Haven: Yale University Press, 2004).

36 For more on the sixteenth-century art market, see: M. Fantoni, L.C. Matthew, and

Renaissance ideology, in that the premise of the age—the "rebirth" of humanism and the ideals of the Greco-Roman world—was based in rivalry. Renaissance artists, architects, and intellectuals did not wish simply to revive these ideals but rather to embody them, perhaps even more fully than those in antiquity had done. Thus, as singular actors in such an artistic framework, competition was crucial for early sixteenth-century painters in Rome.

An explanation for this somewhat paradoxical response might be found in the concept of co-opetition, borrowed from the economics field of game theory and defined as a means of optimizing economic relationships through a blend of competition and collaboration. Introduced in John von Neumann and Oskar Morgenstern's landmark 1944 publication, *Theory of Games and Economic Behavior*, the theory suggests that when two competitive entities share congruent interests, working together to develop those shared characteristics will most likely allow those two entities to achieve a greater outcome or higher valuation than if they did not cooperate within those shared parameters.[37] In other words, when players in a given scenario are competitors, were they to collaborate they could accelerate their success to a greater degree than would have been possible on their own. Applying this term to the realm of art history, specifically to the work of Raphael, has its challenges and limitations (how, for instance, could we define this greater "success" without becoming mired once more in questions of "genius"?). It does help, nevertheless, to synthesize succinctly how Raphael's meta-style continued to curate a collection of visual forms from both collaborative and competitive sources that he then instilled among his workshop circle.

4 Revisiting Recombination within the Workshop

As already discussed, Raphael's workshop was atypical in that it sidestepped the traditional hierarchy of "master versus apprentice." Having such a hierarchy in place would eliminate a competitive framework, as within it the apprentice is tasked with only meeting the demands of the master. Without this hierarchy, then, competition—that is, who is "greatest"—can arise. This, however, did not occur in Raphael's space. Rather, the artists assumed an equal footing wherein individual mastery was encouraged and yet intense rivalries did not ensue. This

---

S.F. Matthews-Grieco. 2003. *The art market in Italy 15th–17th century = Il mercato dell'arte in Italia secc. XV–XVII* (Modena: Franco Cosimo Panini, 2003).

37 J. Von Neumann and O. Morgenstern, *Theory of Games and Economic Behavior* (Princeton: Princeton University Press, 1944; reprinted 1953).

model succeeded because Raphael seems to have grasped a co-opetitive model: alone they could thrive, but in sum they became a powerhouse.

The simple fact that Raphael formed his own workshop and allowed participants therein to engage with compositional design at its most embryonic stage illustrated his unique outlook. Other artists of his generation, like Leonardo and Michelangelo, perhaps avoided such a collaborative practice because of a belief in the primacy of *invenzione*, the unique trademark of the master.[38] Raphael, it would seem, envisioned a sense of *invenzione* that allowed for group participation. In such a model, one that stresses both *invenzione* and the individual, it makes sense that a visual language would be key. Amplifying the importance of such language was the fact that many of these workshop masters specialized in particular techniques or subjects. For example, as will be discussed, Raphael would give Giulio Romano (1499–1546) and Gianfrancesco Penni (1488/1496–1528) the kernels of a composition's plan and allow them to blend together motifs using their own artistic license. Giovanni da Udine (1487–1564) was expert in the art of the *grotteschi* and the emulation of ancient stucco, skills that Raphael would call upon not in an effort to outdo him but rather to assemble a more perfect decorative program. The same goes for Raphael's associations with Marcantonio Raimondi. Though discussion of their working relationship falls mainly outside the scope of this book, it is important to note briefly here that Raimondi became an invaluable vehicle in the extension of Raphael's reach to a larger audience through the pairing of Raphael's drafting skill and Raimondi's mastery of the techniques of printmaking. In any of these examples, the individual could not have accomplished such feats alone; whether it be the sheer volume of work required or the specialized skills involved, they required a meeting of minds, a shared visual or conceptual language, to transform what could be staunch competitors into collaborators to achieve a greater outcome. Employing such a shorthand championed by both master and the workshop circle would in many regards be ideal for business as it results in one singular identity (despite the input of many) and aesthetically raises the possibility that these shared elements can later be repurposed for continued innovation.

If such a visual language existed, one that allowed each artist to have his own voice while also coming together in visual harmony for each work by "Raphael," then his workshop was uniquely dynamic indeed. One can only imagine that

38 As Shearman noted, "neither Leonardo nor Michelangelo introduced assistants to any significant degree in the production of what passed for their own works; assistants were never involved in the preparatory drawings" (J.K.G. Shearman, "The Organization of Raphael's Workshop," 44).

a similar atmosphere most likely was fostered between Raphael and Peruzzi, given that several of Raphael's key workshop participants were also active in Peruzzi's studio and collaborated with him in the years following Raphael's death.

Accordingly, beyond an examination of key works by Raphael that demonstrate the use of this visual language, or the recombination of visual elements, equally important to this book is an analysis of how this same practice continues among these associates in the decade following Raphael's death. The identification of compositional parallels throughout these projects will hopefully reveal to the reader that these quotations are not acts of careless copying but rather deliberate experiments in the recombination of forms to expand upon the points of reference a composition can recall. By fostering this recombinative mindset among these artists, Raphael encouraged a new line of thinking that, as will be shown, carried on into the 1520s.

5 Continuing the Conversation

The quotation of another's artwork serves as an act of commentary; whether in homage, critique, collaboration, or competition, such visual reference inspires greater engagement on the part of the viewer by activating a cascade of interpretation. These quotations, when joined together, served as the foundations for a visual language that was Raphael's style. This language, in turn, proved foundational for his group of workshop associates as they continued to explore new ways to bring these visual elements together in instances of reference and revolution.

This book aims to examine the visual production of these key artists who emerged from or interacted within this ideological space from the late years of Raphael's lifetime and throughout the 1520s that followed. It will assess how these artists maintained an ongoing artistic conversation with Raphael by recalling and recombining visual elements in novel ways and thus consequently drove the overall nature of artistic exchange in Rome between 1520 and 1527. It will also reexamine a fundamental tension faced by Raphael's collaborators and followers: on the one hand, they borrowed visual sources as a means of advertising their artistic pedigree, while on the other hand, they sought to distinguish themselves from this same pedigree by showcasing their own creativity and virtuosity.

In doing so, this book aims to add to the growing understanding of the impact of Raphael's workshop practice even after his death by bringing together examples of the various ways in which his enduring workshop artists carried on. As such, this book hopes to explore a current void noted by Linda Wolk-Simon in a recent book chapter on the topic of Raphael's workshop: "though its cast of characters is well known, Raphael's workshop is well known, … no synthetic overview of this busy enterprise in all its complexity has yet been written."[39] This book attempts the beginnings of such a synthesis by tracing the elements of this recombinative artistic approach seen from the point of Raphael's arrival in Rome through the final days of the workshop and the transformative years of the 1520s. Throughout, the goal will be to seek out the various ways in which these artists continue to collaborate and to incorporate this central practice of recombination of this shared language in novel ways.

The goal of this book is not to exhaustively catalog every artist associated with Raphael's workshop. Little is said, in the end, of Maturino da Firenze (1490–1527); also missing are figures such as pupils Tommaso di Andrea Vincidor (1493–1536) and Pellegrino da Modena (1465–1523), who aided Raphael in his early days at the Vatican; sculptor Lorenzetto (1490–1541) who proved crucial to the realization of the Chigi Chapel in Santa Maria del Popolo; and Ugo da Carpi (circa 1480–1532) and Marcantonio Raimondi (1470/82–1527/34) who, as mentioned previously, aided in spreading the ideas of Raphael in print form. Nor does this book discuss all of the projects executed by the various surviving members of the workshop. Instead, it offers the framework for a larger reconsideration of this network through insightful discussion of landmark moments for the essential artists as they ventured beyond Raphael's era.

Thus, while Raphael features prominently in the following pages, his inclusion is not so much to celebrate his work but rather to examine the ingenuity of his working process and the parallel skill of those with whom he surrounded himself in absorbing and further developing that process. To that end, the premise in this book is twofold. First, it aims to examine the key influences on Raphael's emerging visual language after his arrival in Rome and how those adjustments both transformed the practice of painting and laid the groundwork for the development of his workshop artists. Second, it aims to reframe the discussion of the period 1520–1527 from the perspective of Raphael's surviving workshop members and colleagues as one not lost in the wake of Raphael's death but rather carrying forward the visual language and the art of recombination to their subsequent commissions.

39 L. Wolk-Simon, "Competition, Collaboration, and Specialization in the Roman Art World, 1521–1527." In S. Reiss and K. Gouwens, eds., *The Pontificate of Clement VII: History, Politics, Culture* (London: Routledge, 2017). Kindle edition, Chapter 14. As she continues: "Since little of a synthetic nature has been written, the overarching questions remain to be addressed."

The following chapters will outline this evolution to provide a greater understanding of workshop exchange in the pivotal 1520s, beginning with the advent of Raphael's recombinant style and its development once he arrived in Rome in 1508 up through the infiltration of the city by Charles V's troops in 1527. Chapter One, "The Origins of a Visual Language," begins at the macroscopic level to briefly contextualize Rome and the remarkably dynamic transformation it was experiencing in the early years of the sixteenth century in an effort to illustrate the dynamic atmosphere into which Raphael had plunged. The *renovatio urbis* instigated by Pope Julius II (1443–1513), instigated shortly after his ascendance to the papacy in 1503, resulted in a "new aesthetic of *romanitas*,"[40] a paradoxical civic renovation through antique revival that was carried forward by his successor, Pope Leo X.[41] This atmosphere was particularly receptive to both the blurring of social and professional roles as well as the resulting innovation, thereby fostering an environment ripe for ingenuity that was further fueled through the visual sourcebook provided by antiquity. To further set the stage for the discussions to come, also illuminated in this chapter will be a discussion of the foundations of Raphael's practice, established during his student days with Perugino, of borrowing and recombining concepts both from his contemporaries and from the past before his arrival in Rome. This will be laid out to underline how his subsequent rivalrous engagements with both Michelangelo and Sebastiano continued to fuel his innovation as he embarked upon his earliest work within the Vatican chambers.

Chapter Two, "Visual Language through the Lens of Competition at the Villa Farnesina," focuses primarily on Sebastiano's confrontation of Raphael in the creation of their paired scenes in the Loggia di Galatea at the villa of Agostino Chigi. His *villa suburbana* was one of the most remarkable of its day, both in its unorthodox melding of business and pleasure and in its groundbreaking exploration of *all'antica* themes. Marking the first encounter between two artists who would become staunch rivals, this early project at Chigi's villa is instruc-

40 K.E. Butler, "Reddita Lux Est: Raphael and the Pursuit of Sacred Eloquence in Leonine Rome." In S.J. Campbell and E.S. Welch, eds., *Artists at Court: Image-Making and Identity, 1300–1550* (2004), 135–142.

41 According to Leo X's biographer, Paolo Giovio: "Rome then flourished with outstanding talents and an abundance of everything, which explains why it was that Leo X … was said to have founded after many centuries an age of gold" (P. Giovio, *De Vita Leonis Decimi Pont. Ma. Libri IIII* (Florence, 1551); T.C.P. Zimmerman, *Paolo Giovo: The Historian and the Crisis of Sixteenth-Century Italy* (Princeton, NJ: Princeton University Press, 1995), 23; J. Burke, "Inventing the High Renaissance, from Winkelmann to Wikipedia: An Introductory Essay," in J. Burke, ed., *Rethinking the High Renaissance: The Culture of the Visual Arts in Early Sixteenth-Century Rome* (UK: Ashgate, 2012), 7).

tive in understanding the nuanced way in which Raphael approached such a project and how such competition further fueled the development of his burgeoning visual vocabulary.

Chapter Three, "Collaborative Practice and Emerging Workshop Mentalities," showcases the collaborative aspects of Raphael's time at Chigi's villa. It builds on the hints of exchange between Raphael and Peruzzi that were seen in their earliest projects for Chigi and reveals how both shared a similar mindset that valued collaboration—as will be discussed briefly through the lens of Raphael's architectural contributions to Chigi's property—as well as the reuse and recombination of visual elements to the final projects completed between 1517 and 1519. This like-mindedness will be showcased at the Villa Farnesina in spaces such as the Peruzzi's Sala delle Prospettive as well as the projects for the Loggia di Amore e Psiche and the frescoed *scaenae frons* façade, planned by Raphael and Peruzzi, respectively. These three spaces are highlighted specifically because they involved primarily the artists from Raphael and Peruzzi's workshops and thus illustrate how seamlessly these workshop figures absorbed and embodied the tenets of Raphael's approach while also foreshadowing the innovation to come. Also discussed will be the various Vatican projects in which Raphael's circle began to take on increasingly prominent roles during these late months of Raphael's life. This chapter incorporates examples from across these projects to showcase how the central members of Raphael's circle, including Romano, Penni, da Udine, and Polidoro da Caravaggio (1492–1543), continued this practice of recombination to carry Raphael's vision forward following the artist's death. Exploring the various references as seen in this suite of images, the chapter will help pave the way for the remainder of the book that will examine specific spaces designed and implemented by various combinations of members Raphael's circle after his death.

Chapter Four, for example, looks closely at the Palazzo Baldassini, designed by colleague Antonio da Sangallo (1484–1546) and whose interior visual program was envisioned by da Udine, Perino del Vaga (1501–1547), and Polidoro. Somewhat ravaged by history, these interior scenes nevertheless suggest that once again these colleagues were relying on a shared visual language to build a series of images, one of which continues to defy interpretation. Chapter Five looks similarly to the Villa Lante al Gianicolo, the first architectural project rendered by Giulio Romano in the wake of Raphael's death and a space packed with an array of frescoes referencing Raphael in both literal and figurative means. Though modifications to the villa throughout history make the reading of these images more challenging, the language of this visual recombination is clear.

Chapter Six examines the lingering artistic relationship between Polidoro, Peruzzi, and Maturino da Firenze, who became Polidoro's associate both in the crafting of the Fetti Chapel in San Silvestro al Quirinale and also, alongside Peruzzi, in the unique form of the frescoed façade. Juxtaposing these two practices, the chapter explores primarily how Polidoro was able to build upon the visual language surviving among Raphael's workshop members while also expanding that conversation into a more incisive exploration of landscape and perspective. The modes of representation that Polidoro explored in the Fetti Chapel serve as a segue into the eighth and concluding chapter that explores one of Peruzzi's final Roman commissions for the Church of Santa Maria della Pace, wherein an unusual compositional layout is re-envisioned as an homage of sorts to this recombinative language that dominated his career as well as the various figures in this larger artistic and architectural entourage.

CHAPTER 1

Origins of a Visual Language

To understand how a workshop model of artistic exchange based on a shared visual language could have thrived in early sixteenth-century Rome, it is essential to first step back and explore the early years of Raphael's career to see where the roots of such a practice took hold. Equally important is to consider the context of the city itself at the time of Raphael's approximate 1508 arrival, which, to borrow the words of Marcia Hall, was "already a massive construction site."[1] This construction was quite literal, as by this date Rome was in the midst of the massive *renovatio*, or renovation, encouraged by Pope Julius II (Fig. 3). At the same time, however, Roman culture was also undergoing reconstruction of a more metaphorical kind as it experienced the building of a new set of social constructs and values. It was this new cultural mindset, for example, that allowed imports such as Sienese banker Agostino Chigi to so skillfully insert himself into Roman society. It was also this same advancing ideology that allowed Raphael's enterprising personality not only to rapidly ascend to artistic celebrity but also to pursue significant innovations in art and architecture that would prove foundational for the visual language of his workshop.

1 The Prevalent Language of the Classical

The grandiose renovation that Pope Julius II envisioned for Rome was an attempt to restore a city that had been struggling, in essence, since the fall of the Roman Empire in the fifth century. By the eleventh century it had rebounded to fill a portion of the ancient *abitato*, yet two centuries later this district still tallied only 35,000 inhabitants.[2] This bustling town center, its skyline punctuated by baronial towers, was as much the center of commerce as it was the center of crime, disease, and ongoing skirmishes between land barons and the *Popolo*

1 M.B. Hall, "Introduction," In M.B. Hall, ed., *The Cambridge Companion to Raphael* (NY: Cambridge University Press, 2002), 4.

2 L. Pellechia, "The Contested City: Urban Form in Early Sixteenth-Century Rome." In M.B. Hall, ed., *The Cambridge Companion to Raphael* (NY: Cambridge University Press, 2005), 59–94; R. Brentano, *Rome Before Avignon: A Social History of Thirteenth Century Rome* (New York: Basic Books, 1914).

 | DOI:10.1163/9789004430488_003

Romano from which even the pope himself was not immune.[3] Though the process of papal reinvigoration progressed in fits and starts for a number of years, hope was renewed upon the reunion of the papacy in 1420, following the conclusion of the Great Schism. It was at that time that Pope Martin V launched his campaign of *Renovatio Romae* to rebuild the city, which coincidingly provided an unprecedented opportunity for archaeological excavation.[4] When materials could not be gathered from ancient remnants above ground (already spoliated for generations), license was given to excavate, and a cultural love affair began with all things antique. A preponderance of excavations yielded by century's end many important archaeological finds, such as the massive *Tiber* sculpture in the 1440s and the fragments of the colossal sculpture of *Constantine the Great* in 1486. As this push for renovation continued, and as more of the ancient world was unearthed, the importance of antiquity in Roman society grew.

While Rome's engagement with remnants of the antique world was renewed, it was by no means new. Petrarch's associate Giovanni Dondi, for example, was one of the first to chronicle Rome's monuments in 1375.[5] Noble Roman families of the twelfth and thirteenth centuries had also sensed the historical gravitas of antique inscriptions and fragments and thus appropriated them into their dwellings to imply an impressive (albeit often fabricated) historical lineage.[6] Ancient objects increasingly became more than a link to the Eternal City's past grandeur; they also gave hope that such glory could be rekindled. As more antique artifacts were unearthed—sixteenth-century antiquarian Pirro Ligorio described Rome as having "two populations, the one of living men and the other of marble statues"—contemporary understanding of the non-linearity of time began to blur the lines between ancient and modern.[7] This blurring of

3 As one instance: in 1504, a Papal envoy was murdered while attempting to arrest a fugitive holed up in the Orsini *monte* (Pellechia, "The Contested City," 67).

4 I. Campbell, "Rescue Archaeology in the Renaissance," in I. Bignamini, ed., *Archives & Excavations: Essays on the History of Archaeological Excavations in Rome and Southern Italy from the Renaissance to the Nineteenth Century* (London: British School at Rome, 2004), 14.

5 Ibid., 13.

6 A prime example of this was the residence of Lorenzo Manlio who, after "adopting" a noble lineage (and subsequently changing his name to "Manlius"), built in 1476 on the Piazza Guidea a house replete with fragments of antique and modern reliefs and inscriptions. As Christian comments: "with this immense bulletin board of *spolia* Manlius heralded his recent reinvention as a *nobilis vir*." (K. Christian, *Empire Without End: Antiquities Collections in Renaissance Rome, c. 1350–1527* (New Haven: Yale University Press, 2010), 65; 76).

7 E. Mandowsky and C. Mitchell, *Pirro Ligorio's Roman Antiquities: The Drawings in MS XIII. B 7 in the National Library of Naples* (London: Warburg Institute, University of London, 1963), 49–50; As Leonard Barkan suggests: "the unearthed object becomes the place of exchange not only between words and pictures but also between antiquity and modern times" (L. Barkan,

time resulted in a fluid environment in which antique artifacts and fragments could be repurposed with multiple resonances and could thus transcend time periods.[8] Take, for instance, the Torre delle Milizie: completed in the thirteenth century, the tower nevertheless was categorized as ancient, even earning the misnomer "Nero's Tower" for allegedly being the spot where the maniacal first-century Emperor purportedly watched his city burn.[9]

Such rooting in antiquity became increasingly popular by the early years of the *cinquecento*. Wealthy Romans scrutinized the location and design of their palaces to seek any and all ways to amplify their connection with the ancient world and establish ancient roots. In the 1480s, for example, Cardinal Raffaello Riario deliberately chose a location for his palazzo (the Palazzo della Cancelleria) that bore both historical and religious significance: not only was it sited in close proximity to the ancient Theater of Pompey, it also was the rumored location of the palace of Pope Saint Damasus (366–384 CE).[10] This interest in building on top of and on to—and the symbolic allusions it implied—created new demand for *all'antica* architecture that channeled the principles of the ancient while also contributing to the developing professional definition of "architect."

Simultaneous with such architectural integration with the past was the rise in *vigne*, or garden collections of antiquities, that served as a *locus amoenus* activated through historical reconstruction. These *vigne* became a showcase through which important individuals could display not only the wealth of their collection but also their knowledge of antiquity. A prime example is the *vigna* of Pomponio Leto. Having founded an academy in the 1460s to study Rome's ruins, Leto eventually built a home in the footprint of the Baths of Constantine on the Quirinal Hill.[11] The shrunken state of the city's population afforded Leto ample land for an adjacent garden, filled with exotic birds and foliage and cultivated following the principles of the ancients.[12] Throughout was an extensive

---

Unearthing the Past: Archaeology and Aesthetics in the making of Renaissance Culture (New Haven: Yale University Press, 2011), 4).

8 Barkan, *Unearthing the Past*, 61.

9 J.E. Packer, "Report from Rome: The Imperial Fora, A Retrospective." *American Journal of Archaeology*, Vol. 101 (2) (Apr., 1997), 320–321.

10 P. Giovo, *Pauli Iovii novocomensis episcopi nucerini Elogia virorum literis illustrium, quotquot vel nostra vel avorum memoria vixere* (Basel: Petri Pernae typographie, 1577), 79; Packer, "Report from Rome," 308; Christian, *Empire*, 142; H. Denard, "Virtuality and Perfomativity: Recreating Rome's Theatre of Pompey," *PAJ: A Journal of Performance and Art*, 24 (1) (Jan., 2002), 25–43.

11 Christian, *Empire*, 129–131; S. Magister, "Pomponio Leto collezionista di antichità: Note sulle tradizione manoscritta di una raccolta epigrafia nella Roma del tardo Quattrocento." *Xenia antiqua*, 7 (1998): 167–196.

12 Christian, *Empire*, 130.

collection of fragmentary ancient inscriptions, more of which were plastered into the walls of a central atrium for both appreciation and preservation. As Kathleen Christian comments, "at a time when inscriptions were still melted down in the kilns, building them into his house was a strong statement of the need to protect them from destruction and human invention, not only in Leto's own lifetime but over the *long durée*."[13] Other members of Roman humanist culture subsequently followed suit.

Cardinal Oliviero Carafa, for example, whose antiquarian inclinations had yielded his installation of the speaking statue, *Pasquino*, along the foundation of his rented *cinquecento* palace, also populated a suburban refuge on the Quirinal with antiquities. Carafa's villa and accompanying *vigna* grouped ancient inscriptions with statuary, such as an antique sculpture of *Flora* paired with a paraphrased excerpt from Francesco Colonna's *Hypernotomachia Poliphili*, to enhance an antiquarian atmosphere.[14] The same was conjured at the del Bufalo family dwelling built adjacent to the home and *vigna* of Angelo Colocci along the footprint of the Aqua Virgo aqueduct.[15] The del Bufalo garden was hailed by the 1520s as "one of the city's most impressive and scenographic arrangements of antiquities" and included a casino frescoed—fittingly, by Polidoro da Caravaggio and Maturino—with scenes from Ovid's *Metamorphosis*.[16]

2 The Visual Language of the Papacy

As more antiquities were unearthed toward the end of the fifteenth century, such private collections of ancient artifacts became signifiers of status.[17] As the new century dawned, the resonances of antiquity only intensified. This escalation was due in large part to the election of Giuliano della Rovere as Pope Julius II. Known as *il Papa terrible* for his tendency towards military force and for his grand plan to conquer the Italian peninsula in the name of the Catholic Church, Pope Julius II sought to renovate Rome to renew its former glory.

---

13 Ibid., 132.

14 K.M. Bentz, "Cardinal Cesi and His Garden: Antiquities, Landscape and Social Identity in Early Modern Rome." (Ph.D. Diss., The Pennsylvania State University, 2003), 3; Christian, *Empire*, 290–291.

15 Bentz, 3; R. Kultzen, "Die Malerei Polodoros da Caravaggio im Giardino del Bufalo in Rom," *Mitteilungen des Kunsthisorichen Institutes in Florenz*, 9 (2) (Feb. 1960), 119.

16 Christian, *Empire*, 281.

17 Ibid., 151.

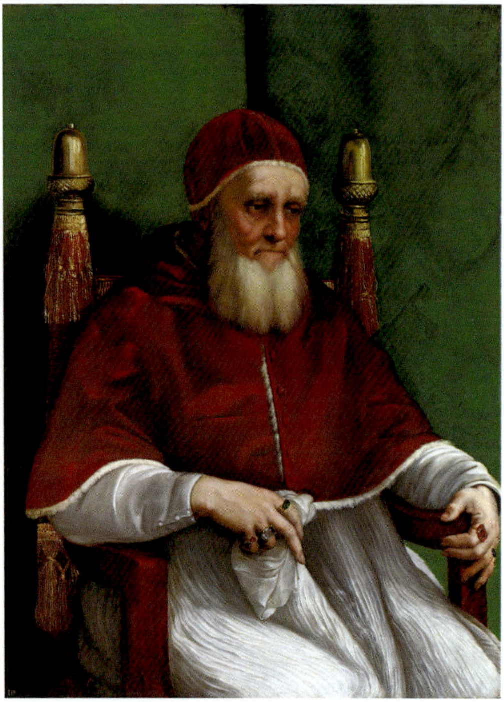

FIGURE 3 Raphael, *Pope Julius II*, 1511. Oil on poplar wood; 108.7 by 81 cm
THE NATIONAL GALLERY, LONDON (PD)

When he ascended the papacy on the first of November 1503, Julius II envisioned Rome as a gleaming beacon of Western civilization. In truth, however, the city was still in a rather decrepit state.[18] Julius nevertheless appeared undeterred to realize his vision. He combatted crime, for example, and took power from the land barons, whose territorial control of the city had contributed significantly to heightened violent outbreaks, by distancing the papacy from their domineering grasp.[19]

---

18 In the words of Ingrid Rowland, the city at the time of Julius' ascendancy "looked anything but eternal; time had treated it with cruel disdain" (I.D. Rowland, *The Roman Garden of Agostino Chigi: The Thirteenth Lecture Held in Memory of Horst Gerson (1907–1978) in the aula of the University of Groningen on the 17th of November 2005* (Groningen: Gerson, 2005), 5).

19 Rowland, *The Roman Garden*, 5. Julius's militaristic tendency led to both the creation in 1506 of the Swiss Guard and his storied retort to Michelangelo while designing his likeness in bronze, "give me a sword; I'm not a man of letters." As Nesselrath points out, though, Julius' campaigns were not all militaristic (A. Nesselrath, "Raphael and Pope Julius II,"

At the same time, Julius set out on a massive beautification campaign. Beyond plans to rebuild St. Peter's Basilica and renovate the Vatican Apartments and the Sistine Chapel, Julius II envisioned an even more overarching transformation of the city through the development and amplification of two main streets that flanked the Tiber River on the west (via della Lungara) and east (via Giulia) banks of the Tiber River to create "a fusion of the utopian and the practical."[20] Had his plan been fully realized, via della Lungara and via Giulia would have served as main thoroughfares along the Tiber's western and eastern banks, connected to the south by the Ponte Sisto and to the north by the planned Ponte Giulia, both bridges conveniently grounded in the footprint of ancient Roman ones.[21] Julius II's ultimate goal was to create a newly consolidated civic, legal, and administrative center that merged all major city functions into a closed circuit around the Tiber River adjacent to the Vatican.[22] Included in this plan was Donato Bramante's monumental Palazzo dei Tribunali, an impressive Hall of Justice that was to become the main law courts of Rome but which never materialized.

Julius II's vision for Rome's future was intrinsically rooted in the city's ancient past, connections that he also encouraged in various projects at the Vatican. In the midst of his renovations to the Vatican Apartments, for example, he called upon architect Donato Bramante to create a series of garden terraces that would connect the papal palace to the nearby Villa Belvedere. A veritable *vigna* writ large, this plan included a courtyard designed to showcase the Pope's impressive collection of antiquities.[23] Julius II's first major sculptural addition to this courtyard was the *Laocoön* in 1506, found in the vineyard

---

in H. Chapman, T. Henry, C. Piazotta, A. Nesselrath, and N. Penny, *Raphael: from Urbino to Rome* (London: National Gallery, 2004), 281). For more, see: L. Pellechia, "The Contested City," 64–67; C.L. Stinger, *The Renaissance in Rome* (Bloomington: Indiana University Press, 1998), 11.

20 Pellechia, "The Contested City," 64.

21 Pope Sixtus IV had (re)built the Ponte Sisto in 1475 to incorporate the remnants of the second-century CE Pons Aurelius, while the new Ponte Giulia would have shared foundations with the first-century CE Pons Triumphalis. This would have connected the Via Giulia directly to the Vatican. For illustration of this tentative location, see Pellechia's overlaid illustration on Giambattista Nolli's 1748 map of Rome (Pellechia, "The Contested City," 65). It was not until the nineteenth-century construction of the Ponte Vittorio Emmanuele II that the absence of the Ponte Giulia was remedied. (Pellechia, "The Contested City," 66).

22 Ibid., 66.

23 F. Haskell and N. Penny, *Taste and the Antique: The Lure of Classical Sculpture, 1500–1900* (New Haven: Yale University Press, 1981), 7.

of a Roman nobleman. Considered by Pliny as one of the prized treasures of the Roman Emperor Nero,[24] the *Laocoön* was soon joined by other impressive works, including the *Venus Felix* in 1509, the *Apollo* (*Belvedere*) in 1511, and the *Sleeping Nymph* in 1512. In no time, Julius II's courtyard collection was renowned across Europe.

These ambitious renovation plans for the city inspired by antiquity further heightened the fervor over the ancient world. The multiple valences the antique held—at once both a symbol of the old Rome and a herald of the new; a resonance of the Pagan world in the midst of the Christian—seemed to become even more significant. *All'antica* style pervaded artistic and architectural commissions and encouraged artists to seek increasingly novel applications of the antique in their works. This momentum only grew with the ascendance of Pope Leo X following Julius II's death in 1513. Leo encouraged the study of the antique world, incorporating similar references in his various commissions and even going so far as to initiate a full mapping of antique Rome, with significant structures revealed within their original context. For this task he turned to Raphael, who at the time was already overwhelmed with commissions but who nevertheless graciously accepted the endeavor.[25]

3 The Visual Language of Raphael

This dynamism of Rome in the early years of the sixteenth century was assuredly not lost on Raphael at his arrival. By that time (around 1508), he had both burgeoning acclaim to bolster him from his previous years spent in Florence and his own parallel practice of reconstruction, or recombination, cultivated therein.[26] In truth, such borrowing began during his days in Perugia while

24 Christian, *Empire*, 163.

25 Raphael is connected to this project through an anonymous letter penned by colleague Andrea Colocci to Pope Leo X, which reads: "havendomi Vostra Santità comandato che io ponessi in disegno Roma antichav, quanto cognosciersi si può per quello che oggidi si vede, con gli edifice che di sé dimostrano tal relique" (Munich Bayerische Staatsbibliotek, Cod. II. 37b).

26 Scholarship bookends Raphael's "Florentine Period" as the years 1504–1508, but Talvacchia reinforces the fact that this portion of Raphael's career was so defined for the technical, rather than geographic, influence. As Talvacchia comments: "the so-called 'Florentine Period' is better understood as a time when Raphael systematically acquired advanced techniques and opened himself to new models, rather than being defined as a stable geographical change of residence during a fixed period" (B. Talvacchia, *Raphael* (London: Phaidon, 2007), 52).

under the tutelage of Perugino, as noted by Vasari in his biography of Raphael and illustrated in Raphael's previously mentioned *Lo Spozalizio* (1504) when compared to Perugino's rendition of the same theme (1499–1503).[27] The striking similarities between two such compositions reveal Raphael's early ability to adopt the technique of his mentor and perhaps also indicates an impressively astute appreciation of the concept of artistic identity and branding even in these first years of his career. At the same time, these exchanges with Perugino mark only the first such instance of imitation in Raphael's career and, as time progressed, one can see where such imitation evolved into a broader practice of the recombination of borrowed elements.

Vasari mentions, for example, that in Raphael's youth he "imitated the style of his master Pietro Perugino," and, once having surpassed him, desired "to imitate the style of said Leonardo," to whom "Raphael did come close … rather more successfully than any other painter, and above all in the grace of colors."[28] This can also be seen in surviving examples from Raphael's Florentine years. In addition to Raphael's close quotation of Leonardo's *Mona Lisa* in drawings such as *Study for a Young Woman on a Balcony* (circa 1504; Louvre Museum, Paris), one can also consider *Portrait of a Young Woman with a Unicorn* (1506; Galleria Borghese, Rome) for its close quotations likely borrowed from Leonardo's iconic oil on canvas composition. These instances seem reflective of the same kind of imitation that Raphael performed in his absorption of Perugino's technique, however there is also evidence from this period that he was borrowing specific elements from the work of Leonardo in his generation of new works. David Alan Brown has noted, for example, that Raphael's *Small Cowper Madonna* (1505; National Gallery of Art, Washington, D.C.) reveals a pastiche of Leonardesque elements, from the swell of drapery akin to Leonardo's *Benois Madonna* to the Virgin's hand that has been linked to *Mona Lisa*.[29] This extrac-

27 Goffen declares Raphael's version as that which "redefined the relationship, [*declared*] his rivalry with Perugino—and [*asserted*] victory over him," (Goffen, *Renaissance Rivals*, 173), but this seems perhaps too strong an assertion given that some of this similarity was undoubtedly owed to the requests of the respective patrons. For more on these parallels between Perugino and Raphael, see: P. Rubin, "Il Contribuo di Raffaello allo sviluppo della Pala d'Altare Rinascimentale," *Arte Cristiana*, 737–738 (March-June, 1990), 173–174.

28 Vasari, "Life of Raphael," I: 743; A. Chastel, "Raffaello e Leonardo," in M.S. Hamoud and M.L. Strocchi, ed., *Studi su Raffaello: Atti del Congresso Internazionale di Studi (Urbino-Firenze, 1984)* (Urbino, 1987), I: 335–343.

29 For more, please see: D.A. Brown, "Raphael's 'Small Cowper Madonna' and 'Madonna of the Meadow': Their Technique and Leonardo Sources." *Artibus et Historiae*, 4 (8) (1983), 9–26.

tion of select visual elements—from the specificity of a limb's rendering to the more general borrowing of a fabric's drapery deliberate enough nevertheless to recall the work of another artist—seems to have become a key component of Raphael's working process even during these early days of his career. Whether or not this was intended as an act of rivalry, it would seem that when Raphael brought this practice to Rome it was quickly taken as such.

Meanwhile, Raphael was rising in artistic acclaim. His *Madonna del Cardellino* (1505–1506; Galleria degli Uffizi, Florence), commissioned by Lorenzo Nasi, marked one of his early successes, and he continued his ascent toward artistic acclaim by accepting his first large-scale commission, that for the altarpiece of the Dei family chapel in Santo Spirito, in 1507.[30] A few months later, however, Raphael suddenly quit Florence permanently for Rome, leaving the Dei altarpiece, the *Madonna del Baldacchino* (Fig. 4), incomplete.[31] He was no doubt aware of the flurry of artistic and architectural activity underway as part of Pope Julius II's *renovatio*, so when Bramante, rumored relative of Raphael, suggested that he come to Rome, Raphael acquiesced.[32]

With his attentions turned toward Rome, it would seem logical that he would continue to explore his novel conceptualization of such recombination in his practice as he came into more direct confrontation with Michelangelo. The meeting between Raphael and Michelangelo in Rome was not their first encounter with one another. Michelangelo's departure from Florence in 1505 for Rome meant a brief overlap with Raphael's time in the city (between 1504 and 1508), and it is clear that Raphael turned to the work of Michelan-

30 Ibid., 75.

31 S. Reiss, "Raphael and His Patrons: From the Court of Urbino to the Curia and Rome," in M.B. Hall, ed., *The Cambridge Companion to Raphael* (NY: Cambridge University Press, 2005), 47.

32 Vasari introduced the speculation that Bramante and Raphael were related, stating that Bramante reached out to Raphael "on account of his being distantly related to him and also his compatriot," (Vasari, *Lives*, I: 717), however there is little else to substantiate that claim. Talvacchia, *Raphael*, 80. Though consensus proposes Raphael's initial visit to Rome to coincided with his relocation there in 1508, John Shearman argued for earlier visits in 1502 and 1506 before Raphael's permanent relocation to the city (as outlined in: J.K.G. Shearman, "Raphael, Rome, and the Codex Escurialensis," *Master Drawings*, Vol. 15 (2) (Summer 1977), 107–146). Shearman's position is worth rekindling, as it helps to explain Raphael's desire for a Roman career: Rome might have allowed Raphael the opportunity to associate with and learn from Bramante, just as Raphael had done with Leonardo and Michelangelo in Florence. Raphael's installation in the city by the very latest in 1509 is without debate, as a contract for Raphael's payment for work completed in the Stanza della Segnatura that year survives (Shearman, *Raphael in Early Modern Sources*, I: 122; Golzio, 21).

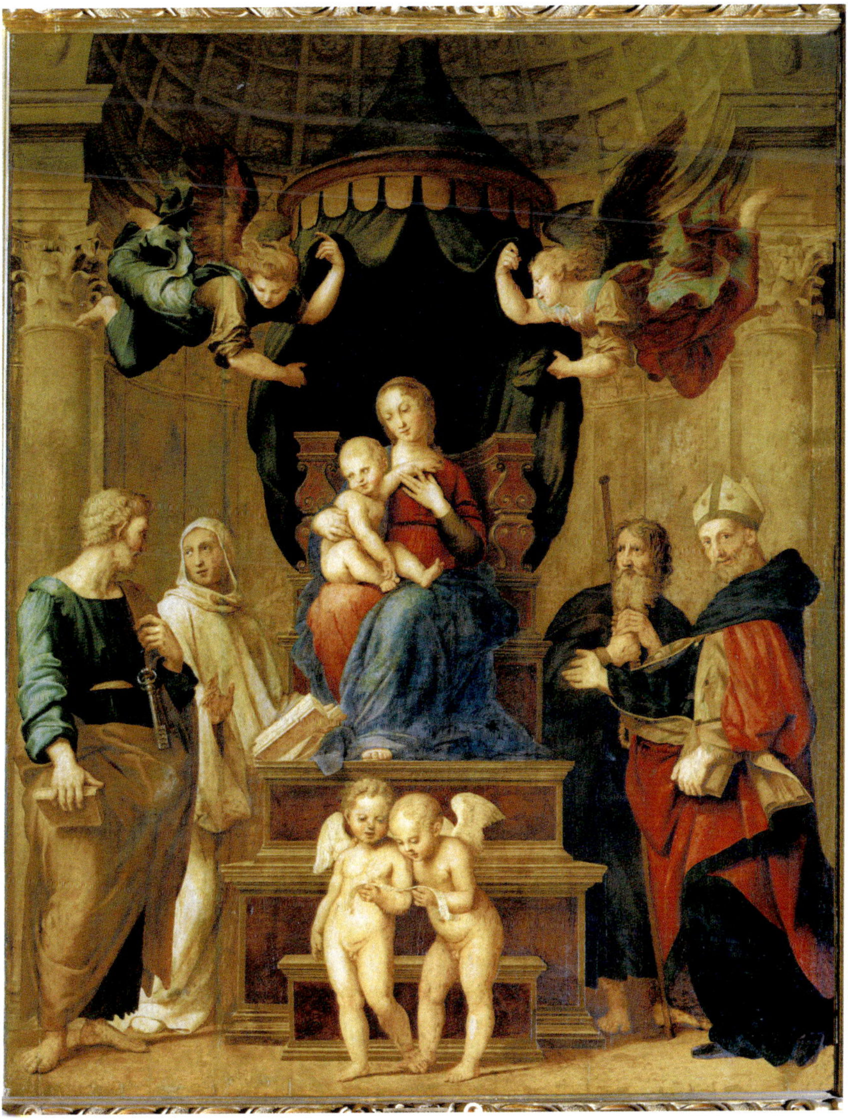

FIGURE 4 Raphael, *Madonna del Baldacchino*, 1507–1508. Oil on canvas; 108.6 by 88.1 cm
PALAZZO PITTI, FLORENCE/ALAMY

gelo as a source of inspiration, similarly to how he had treated the work of Leonardo. Sketched quotations of completed works—such as Raphael's drawing of *David* (1504–1508; British Museum, Pp. 1.68)—abound, as do similar studies of unfinished projects by Michelangelo.[33] For example, one can note

33 Underscoring the novelty in Raphael's study of Michelangelo's work, Goffen noted: "none

Raphael's drawing after Michelangelo's incomplete *Saint Matthew* (1507; British Museum, 1885,2.14.1*v*) or of nude torsos (1505–1506; British Museum, 1895,0915.624) that seem to have been inspired by Michelangelo's preparatory studies for the incomplete Florentine *Battle at Cascina*. This sharing, particularly of unrealized works in drawing form, suggests a rather friendly relationship between Raphael and Michelangelo—at least, such was the manner in which Bette Talvacchia characterized the "initial openness of the senior artist to his younger colleague."[34] As the narrative of art history is often put forward, though, any such amicability rapidly dissolved into animosity once the two met again in Rome once Raphael had insinuated himself into Julius II's ambitious plans to renovate his newly selected suite within the Vatican.

Having moved out of the traditional papal apartment, Julius II selected new rooms on the floor above and first tasked the aging Perugino with their decoration.[35] When Perugino declined the project, Julius II turned to Luca Signorelli; however, he soon realized that the scope of work to be completed required far more than one artist.[36] He thus amassed a team of painters, including Raphael, to embark on this space's renovation.[37] To be hired for such a commission was an honor, but it also undoubtedly fueled a competitive atmosphere.[38] Nesselrath surmised that this initial hire was not as designer but rather as contract painter, yet he soon transcended this role, as evidenced by his eventual receipt of twice the initial contract payment.[39] Surrounded with these talents, Raphael

---

of the three drawings after *David* reproduces the statue exactly, but rather presents a variation on Michelangelo's invention" (Goffen, *Renaissance Rivals*, 196).

34 Talvacchia, *Raphael*, 56.

35 C.L. Joost-Gaugier, *Raphael's Stanza della Segnatura: Meaning and Invention* (NY: Cambridge University Press, 2002), 9.

36 For Perugino's role, please see: Talvacchia, *Raphael*, 84; Joost-Gaugier, *Raphael's Stanza*, 10; For the transfer of commission to Signorelli, please see: Nesselrath, "Raphael and Pope Julius II," in H. Chapman et al., *Raphael: from Urbino to Rome* (London: National Gallery, 2004), 281–282.

37 Talvacchia suggests that Raphael's connection to Perugino "is another factor in the web of contacts that smoothed the way for the young artist's arrival in Rome and facilitated his introduction into the papal court for immediate entry into the highest levels of commission on offer." (Talvacchia, *Raphael*, 86).

38 I. Rowland, "The Vatican Stanze." In M.B. Hall, ed., *The Cambridge Companion to Raphael* (NY: Cambridge University Press, 2005), 97. Quinlan-McGrath suggests that Sodoma's employment by the Pope was orchestrated by Chigi's brother (Mary Quinlan-McGrath, "The Villa of Agostino Chigi: The Poems and The Paintings" (PhD Diss, University of Chicago, 1983), 38).

39 Nesselrath suggests that Raphael was a close associate of Signorelli's ("Raphael and Pope

nevertheless swiftly became the pope's preferred painter; many of the artists Raphael shut out, though, would return to his orbit soon after.[40]

4 The Language of Recombination in the Stanza della Segnatura

Regardless of whether it was by his talents as a painter or his various connections within the art world that secured Raphael's assumption of sole control of the Vatican commissions, what is noteworthy about this moment is that he used it as an opportunity to both introduce this practice of visual recombination within a setting as revered as the Papal chambers while also showcasing its development. Namely, his exchanges with Papal librarian Tommaso Inghirami, fellow Vatican favorite Michelangelo, and Venetian painter Lorenzo Lotto reveal the rather unique ways in which Raphael digested the ideas of others and seamlessly imported them into his visual lexicon.

Raphael was first tasked alongside Il Sodoma to work within the Stanza della Segnatura, which was designed to function as the pope's private library.[41] Hav-

Julius II", 282) and thus perhaps used this connection, in addition to his ties to Bramante, to secure his preliminary role in the Vatican commission. A testament to the challenge of joining this team is the fact that even with two personal connections and a letter of recommendation from Piero Soderini (Golzio, 19; Shearman, *Raphael in Early Modern Sources*, I: 113) Raphael was still only able to secure initially the most menial of painterly positions.

40 As Arnold Nesselrath comments, though Raphael's original contract stipulated payment equivalent to Sodoma and Ruysch of 50 ducats, in the end "Raphael was paid 100 ducats in his first installment, twice as much as Sodoma and Ruysch. He received the money on 13 January 1509, which suggests by then he had finished a significant part of the decoration in the Segnatura. He had also been given responsibility for painting the entire apartment, since Julius sent away all other artists working in the stanze." ("Raphael and Pope Julius II," 285; payment reiterated in: Shearman, *Raphael in Early Modern Sources*, 122). In October 1511, Julius II also bestows upon the young artist the post of *Scriptor Brevium* (Sherman, *Raphael in Early Modern Sources*, I: 150–152), which Frommel suggests was a perk for Raphael's completion of the *Disputa* (Frommel, *Die Farnesina und Peruzzis architektonisches Frühwerk (Berlin: W. de Gruyter, 1961)*, 116).

41 Sodoma was commissioned to work on the stanze in a letter dated 13 October 1508 following endorsement by Agostino Chigi's brother, Sigismondo (Shearman, *Raphael in Early Modern Sources*, I: 125; A. Hayum, *Giovanni Antonio Bazzi—"Il Sodoma"* (NY: Garland Publishing, 1976), 17–18); Sodoma was soon after joined by Flemish painter Johannes Ruysch (contracted in a letter dated 14 October 1508), and Lorenzo Lotto (in a contract dated 9 March 1509); Talvacchia, "Raphael's Workshop and the Development of a Managerial Style," in M.B. Hall, ed., *The Cambridge Companion to Raphael* (NY: Cambridge University Press, 2005), 172.

ing risen above the original team of artists assigned to work in the space to become the sole artist within a matter of months, Raphael had in the Stanza della Segnatura secured a commitment to these chambers that would endure to the very end of his life. From this point, though, it seems that Raphael embraced the evolution of these images as a meeting of minds rather than as a conflict of masters. This is illustrated by the revelation in recent analyses suggesting that Raphael was the artist, though not necessarily the source, of these frescoes' messages. Both Ingrid Rowland and Christiane Joost-Gaugier make the case that Raphael was guided by humanist colleague Tommaso Inghirami, who proved the true source of the chamber's iconography. Joost-Gaugier supports this observation by the simple fact that the humanist themes here were too complex for the young Raphael to have manifested on his own.[42] Rowland also notes the sheer influence of proximity: "If [the Stanza della Segnatura] was Julius' library and [Tommaso] was its librarian, it is not surprising that he and Raphael were thinking about the same ideas."[43] Regardless of the exact nature of ideological exchange, what this connection showcases is that even at the outset of his various Vatican projects Raphael embraced a strikingly collaborative mode for compositional development.

To further underscore the novelty of Raphael's approach in the Stanza della Segnatura, one can contrast it with the methods of Michelangelo who, at the time, was at work on the ceiling frescoes of the Sistine Chapel. There too the counsel of Inghirami potentially played a role, at least according to Matthias Wivel, who noted that Michelangelo's design was nevertheless of his own plan, "poetry wrought by hand, as personal in formulation and as universal in scope as that of Dante."[44] Such phrasing seems to reiterate the singular genius of Michelangelo—and perhaps also emphasizes the solitary nature of Michelangelo's generation of the monumental fresco cycle—but leaves little space for collaborative exchange between Inghirami and Michelangelo. In contrast, Raphael made apparent in his designs for the Stanza della Segnatura the visual potential of his recombinatory practice, not only in his exchanges with Inghirami but also in his specific references to Michelangelo's evolving Sistine Chapel imagery.

---

42 As Joost-Gaugier points out: "it is certain that the young artist newly arrived from Florence did not have the humanist education or dramaturgical experience appropriate to so important an undertaking, for which, in any case, planning had surely begun before his arrival in Rome in 1508." (C. Joost-Gaugier, *Raphael's Stanza della Segnatura: Meaning and Invention* (NY: Cambridge University Press, 2002), 17).

43 Rowland, *The Culture of the High Renaissance*, 165.

44 M. Wivel, *Michelangelo & Sebastiano* (New Haven: Yale University Press, 2017), 20.

Raphael completed two of the Stanza della Segnatura's monumental lunette frescoes within the first year of work (1508–1509), the result of which was imagery that commemorated the pillars of knowledge, venerated Pope Julius II, and sent a singular message of the power and importance of the principles of Christian faith.[45] The first scene completed was *The Disputation of the Sacrament* and featured as its focal point a gilded monstrance atop a decorated altar that thereby anchors the represented terrestrial and celestial realms through the vertical alignment with the Holy Trinity. The terrestrial register reveals portraits of important figures to theological history. This cast of characters begins with the founders of the Western Church enthroned closest to the altar and includes a portrait of Julius II, in the guise of Saint Gregory the Great, and Egidio da Viterbo, close papal associate and contributor to the Stanza's overall visual program, depicted as Saint Augustine. Portraits continue to radiate to the extremities of the composition, from Dante mingling among the right-hand figural cluster to a portrait of Bramante in the left lower foreground, below what is assumed to be a reference to the emerging Saint Peter's Basilica depicted in the distance.

Directly opposite from *The Disputation*, Raphael subsequently completed the so-called *School of Athens* (Fig. 5), thus juxtaposing philosophy with theology and revealing Raphael's rapidly accelerating interest in the antique. Designed, according to Rowland, to "reveal the Christian truth in ancient wisdom,"[46] the *School of Athens* echoed poet Battista Casali's 1508 proclamation of Rome as the "new Athens" by presenting a veritable stage play of philosophers throughout history.[47] Plato and Aristotle appear at center, surrounded by a plethora of great thinkers. Inghirami, for example, appears as Epicurus at left, his figure obscured behind a marble pedestal, and the cluster of figures at right have often been associated with colleagues of Raphael, including Baldassare Castiglione in the guise of Strabo and Bramante appearing as Euclid.[48]

45 As Rowland summarizes: "Raphael's design is a triumph of another kind, of ingenuity: in graphic form, he lays out the basic articles of Christian faith while suggesting at the same time that his art can communicate only an approximate idea of that faith's true glory" (Rowland, *The Culture of the High Renaissance*, 99).

46 Ibid., 104.

47 J. O'Malley, "The Vatican Library and the School of Athens, a Text of Battista Casali, 1508." *Journal of Medieval and Renaissance Studies*, Vol. 7 (1977), 271–287; Rowland, "The Vatican Stanze," 103. As Rowland summarizes this gathering, "from the sublime heights of Platonic theology to the personal foibles of ancient philosophers and contemporary artists, Raphael's *School of Athens* presents a portrait of Rome in the time of Julius II." (Ibid., 107).

48 For more, see: C.L. Joost-Gaugier, "Ptolemy and Strabo and Their Conversation with

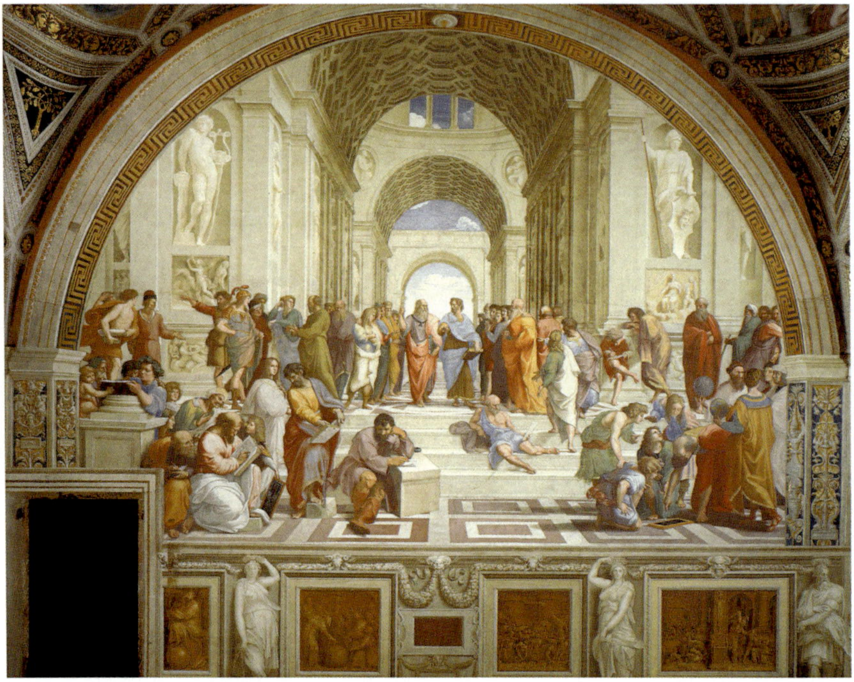

FIGURE 5 Raphael, *School of Athens*, circa 1510. Fresco; 670 cm
VATICAN PALACE (PD)

Among them, Raphael includes a self-portrait at the lower right-hand corner of the composition, gazing intently out at the viewer amidst a figural group otherwise wholly engaged within the scene.

What sets *School of Athens* apart from *The Disputation*, aside from subject, is Raphael's inclusion of an ornately articulated architectural backdrop. In place of the simplified landscape seen in *The Disputation*, Raphael here framed his gathering of philosophical figures within an architectural artifice not only derived directly from antique sources but also echoing contemporaneous plans for Saint Peter's. In this regard, the *School of Athens* represented what Arnold Nesselrath called "the most complete idea Julius II would ever have had of how his new basilica, finished long after his death, would eventually look."[49] Thus, though its central aim was to reinforce ecclesiastical principles, the *School of Athens* also revealed Raphael's burgeoning study of antiquity and architecture. Though these two interests would become central elements of his later career,

---

Appelles and Protogenes: Cosmography and Painting in Raphael's School of Athens." *Renaissance Quarterly*, 51 (3) (Autumn, 1998), 761–787.

49 Nesselrath, "Raphael and Pope Julius II," 284.

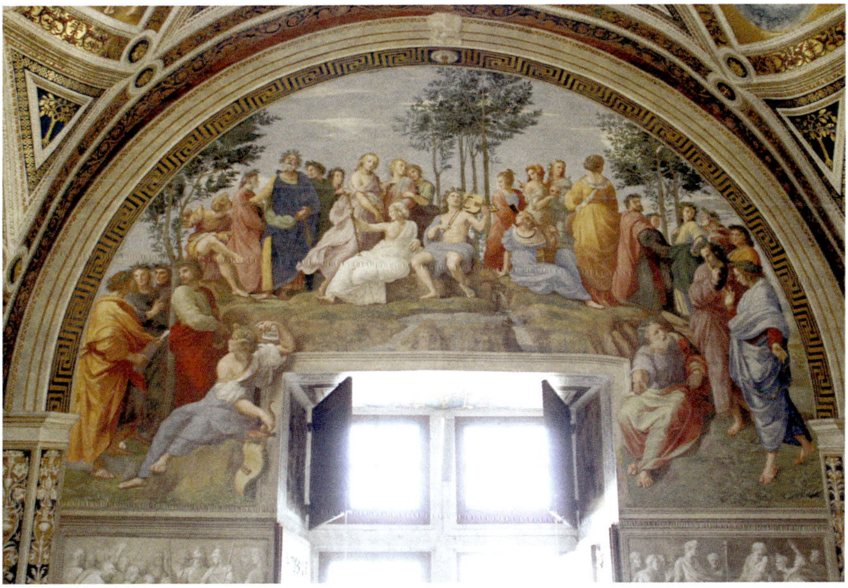

FIGURE 6 Raphael, *Parnassus*, 1511. Fresco; 670 cm
VATICAN PALACE—AUTHOR'S IMAGE

Raphael's initial efforts in these two compositions were sufficient to secure a sole commission from the pope to complete the remaining papal chambers.[50]

By 1511, Raphael had completed the third fresco, that of *Parnassus* (Fig. 6). This frescoed lunette was a testament to poetry, the literary form that Raphael, among others, considered the "most divinely inspired"[51] and thus a fitting counterpoint to the adjacent *School of Athens*. Taken together, the *School of Athens* and *Parnassus* became a veritable portrait of contemporary Rome through an ancient lens. *Parnassus*' central figure of Apollo was echoed in the monumental statue of the god inset in the left-hand niche within the *School of Athens* and revealed a similar melding of past and contemporary figures through the guises of poetry. Amid the Nine Muses and ancient Roman poets appear contemporary humanist scholars, including Jacopo Sannazaro and, once again, Inghirami.

What Raphael also incorporates into this third addition to the room were references to Michelangelo's Sistine series. As both Joannides and Wivel have noted, Raphael refers in *Parnassus* to Michelangelo's Adam from the *Creation*

50 Rowland, "The Vatican Stanze," 99.
51 Ibid., 106.

of Man in his rendering of the muse Euterpe adjacent to Apollo wearing white; he also incorporated an allusion to one of Michelangelo's *ignudi* that frames the *Creation of Man* in the posture of Sappho, whose figure drapes over the left-hand corner of the framed window opening below the center of the composition.[52] This borrowing of figures—specific compositional elements taken from their original context and adapted to align harmoniously with Raphael's *Parnassus*—implies that Raphael had indeed carried forward the same working process that he had begun to refine in his earlier years. In other words, just as he extracted elements from artists like Leonardo and Michelangelo while in Florence, so too was Raphael borrowing and reinterpreting visual fragments or phrases in the Stanza's emerging cycle.

While it is unclear whether Raphael's intention in such borrowing was to provoke Michelangelo—particularly given the proximity of their projects to one another—the borrowing of these visual elements would nevertheless prove to be the foundation of a long-standing rivalry between Raphael and Michelangelo, one that would culminate in Michelangelo's oft-cited rebuke that what Raphael "had from art, he had from me."[53] While this chiding quip, made so much later in Michelangelo's career and well beyond Raphael's lifetime such that perhaps it should be read simply as lingering animosity, it nevertheless might serve as some evidence of how Raphael's innovative approach was interpreted by other masters of his generation.

The novelty in the compositional design of *Parnassus* also suggests an evolution in Raphael's practice given the levels upon which its imagery can be read. At the same time that Raphael can be seen as quoting Michelangelo's work, one can also note that Raphael's *Parnassus* deliberately recalls ancient sculpture. An aspect that is often overlooked in discussions of this fresco, this use of antiquity as inspiration can be seen in his central figure of Apollo, for example, which bears echoes of the *Belvedere Torso* or *Jupiter Enthroned* (*Jupiter Ciampolini*), drawings of which have been firmly attributed to Raphael's hand.[54] In addition, his depiction of the Muse Euterpe to Apollo's right bears direct quotation

---

52 Joannides, *Drawings of Raphael*, 192; Wivel, 21.

53 Letter from Michelangelo to an anonymous recipient; documented in Poggi, Barocchi, and Ristori, *Il Carteggio di Michelangelo* (Florence: Sansoni, 1965–1983), IV: 155, no. 1001.

54 Bober suggests the *Torso Belvedere* was part of the Colonna collection on the Quirinal prior to its appropriation into the Vatican collection sometime between 1515, when a sketch identifies it as being located "in mo(n)te cavallo," and 1532–1535, when Martin van Heemskerck sketched it as part of the Vatican Belvedere (M. van Heemskerck, *Die römischen Skizzenbücher von Marten van Heemskerke*, I: f. 63; Bober and Rubenstein, 167). K.T. Parker attributed two views of the *Belvedere Torso* to Raphael's school (*Catalogue of the Collection of Drawings in the Ashmolean Museum, Volume II: The Italian Schools* (UK:

from the *Sleeping Ariadne*.[55] Both *Ariadne* and the *Torso Belvedere* would eventually make their way into Julius II's collection of antiquities and thus would add to the significance of such reference in Raphael's fresco, though neither of these pieces was yet installed within the Vatican walls at the time the pictorial program was conceived. What is perhaps most intriguing here, though, is that this figure of Euterpe can be visually compared to the art of both the past and its contemporaneous present. By quoting an antique sculpture that also bears reference to the work of Michelangelo, Raphael showcases the innovative power of his visual language in its ability to cross time so fluidly. Thus, while these quotations can be seen as signifiers of Raphael's already advancing study of antiquity, they also suggest that something even more dynamic is happening.

Though one wall (*Jurisprudence*) of the Stanza della Segnatura remained to be finished, the completion of *Parnassus* and its engagement with the *School of Athens* nevertheless sufficed to reveal Raphael's transformative approach to painting. The root subjects of these four scenes—Theology, Philosophy, Poetry, and Law, respectively—and their paired ceiling personifications—those of *Apollo and Marsyas*, the *Fall of Man*, the *Judgment of Solomon*, and *Astrology*—represented a powerful visual allegory for the pope and showcased Raphael's ability to translate visual schema into metaphorical message with the aid of Tommaso Inghirami, whose knowledge of humanist scholarship undoubtedly both engaged and encouraged Raphael's intellectual thinking and creative practice.[56]

On the one hand, Raphael's designs for the Stanza della Segnatura blended his burgeoning interest in both humanist ideology and antiquarianism with imagery in support of the Church.[57] This adoption of antique themes was, at the same time, a break with them. As much as it was a comment on the art

Oxford University Press, 1956), no. 625). Shearman notes Raphael's sketch of the *Jupiter Ciampolini* in the collection of Giovanni Ciampolini until his death in 1518. It also appeared in two of his contemporary paintings, the previously mentioned *Madonna del Baldacchino* (1508) and the *Madonna del Pesce* (circa 1514) (Bober, *Renaissance Artists*, 51–52, no. 1; Shearman, "Raphael, Rome," 130, no. 6).

55 The *Sleeping Ariadne* was a part of the Maffei collection in Rome prior to its appropriation into that of Julius II in 1512 (Bober, *Renaissance Artists*, 114, no. 79).

56 Talvacchia, *Raphael*, 86; Joost-Gaugier, *Raphael's Stanza*, 157–158; Rowland, "The Vatican Stanze," 98.

57 Joost-Gaugier nods to Raphael's abilities to craft pictorial allusions to Papal propaganda as seen through the lens of both humanist themes and his "new reverence for antiquity, now expressed in the rich conflation of setting and subject, … and the complex orchestration of theme and space, projects the entirely new ambition that became his in Rome" (Joost-Gaugier, *Raphael's Stanza*, 162).

of the past, so too did it comment on the art and architecture of contemporary Rome. The architectural framework of the *School of Athens*, as previously mentioned, bears hints of Bramante's designs for the crossing of Saint Peter's, and the triumphal arch at the furthest recesses of the scene reveals Raphael's already burgeoning interest in architecture. His carefully conjured *Parnassus*, replete with portraits of his contemporaries, also asserts his status as a blossoming intellect as he navigated the bounds between painting and poetry.[58] Thus, in the very fabric of these early Roman commissions, Raphael displayed his ability to weave these concepts of repetition and recombination throughout.

On the other hand, Raphael also made space for personal connections in his Stanze designs, as if to remind us that it was his ability to collaborate that brought this impressive program to life or perhaps to give a singular identity to an artist who had already capitalized on the innovations of many. Already mentioned in this regard was his self-portrait inserted into the lower right register of the *School of Athens*, where Raphael is one of the few figures to stare directly out of the composition as if to engage directly with his audience, who might question the appearance of painters in a scene otherwise teeming with philosophers.

If one keeps this figure in mind and then turns to *Parnassus*, one can identify a strikingly similar likeness that appears nestled between Apollo and his Muses and the nearby gathering of Homer, Virgil, and Dante. A comparison of this visage with that of Raphael in the *School of Athens*, as well as with that of his self-portrait of 1504–1506, reveals strikingly similar features, from the gentle cleft in his chin to his aquiline nose. Strengthening the identification of this figure as a self-portrait is the anonymous sketch held by the Ashmolean of Raphael's initial designs for *Parnassus*, in which this figure is conspicuously omitted.[59] It is also missing from Marcantonio Raimondi's engraving after a drawing of *Parnassus* (Metropolitan Museum of Art 17.37.150). Furthermore, in the documented preparatory sketches for these poet portraits, yet again this mysterious figure remains absent.[60] The repeated omission of this figure, particularly from Raphael's own preparatory drawings, suggests that this final portrait head was a relatively late inclusion, perhaps designed as much to fill a notable void in the composition as to applaud his own accomplishments. Such

58 A prime illustration of this meander between painting and poetry is his inclusion of a preparatory sketch for *Parnassus* next to several early sonnets he wrote between 1509–1510 (Shearman, *Raphael in Early Modern Sources*, I: 130).

59 As illustrated in: Joannides, *The Drawings*, plate 21, 84.

60 Joannides, *The Drawings*, 241v, 192.

a theory is supported by John Shearman's observation of the *putti* overhead, all of which hold laurel crowns to "reinforce the idea of inspiration in action, of *poesia* in the making."[61] In other words, simultaneous with Raphael's conjuring of the painted poetry with *Parnassus* is his conception of self as the painter-poet realized most literally with this self-portrait. It is intriguing is to consider the implications of this potential second self-portrait, particularly given the fact that this figure was most likely such a later addition.

Thus, while Raphael can be seen here to the very last adjusting his composition to reinforce the room's overall messaging, he might also be working between *School of Athens* and *Parnassus* to reinforce the role of the Painter—that is of the profession as well as Raphael himself—alongside that of the papacy as a testament to the successful collaboration between, in essence, painting and philosophy. That Raphael would depict himself as both philosopher and poet was indicative of his innovative spirit. He found inspiration not through singular art forms but rather considering parallels across them, in part because he found such essential connections between them. As Rowland comments, "this fundamental sense of the unity of human creative force explains why, in the end, Raphael refused to specialize as an artist, why he dabbled as a poet, and why he ultimately found himself deeply embroiled in archaeology for its own sake."[62] While the full intent of such self-portraits might never be uncovered, it seems not coincidental that they made an appearance wrapped up in a fresco cycle that was remarkably dynamic for its day and that launched one of the most prolific and experimental phases of Raphael's career.

By 1512, Raphael had embarked upon another exchange in the creation of the fourth and final contribution to the Vatican's Stanza della Segnatura: *Jurisprudence* (Fig. 7). This is a composition that is often overlooked, in part due to the fact that its decoration is less substantial relative to the other three walls (to account for a large window that looks southward toward Saint Peter's) and also because it is not wholly Raphael's work.[63] Nevertheless it merits further consideration, as it bears similar seeds of Raphael's growing interests in collaboration and recombination.

61 John Shearman, "Raphael's Unexecuted Projects for the Stanze," in G. Kauffmann et al., eds., *Walter Friedlaender zum 90. Geburtstag: Ein Festgabe seiner europäischen Schüler, Fruend und Veherer* (Berlin: De Gruyter, 1965), 159.

62 I.D. Rowland, "Raphael, Angelo Colocci and the Genesis of the Architectural Orders." *The Art Bulletin*, 76 (1) (March, 1994), 82.

63 Rowland, "The Vatican Stanze," 109; Nesselrath, "Lorenzo Lotto," 4–12.

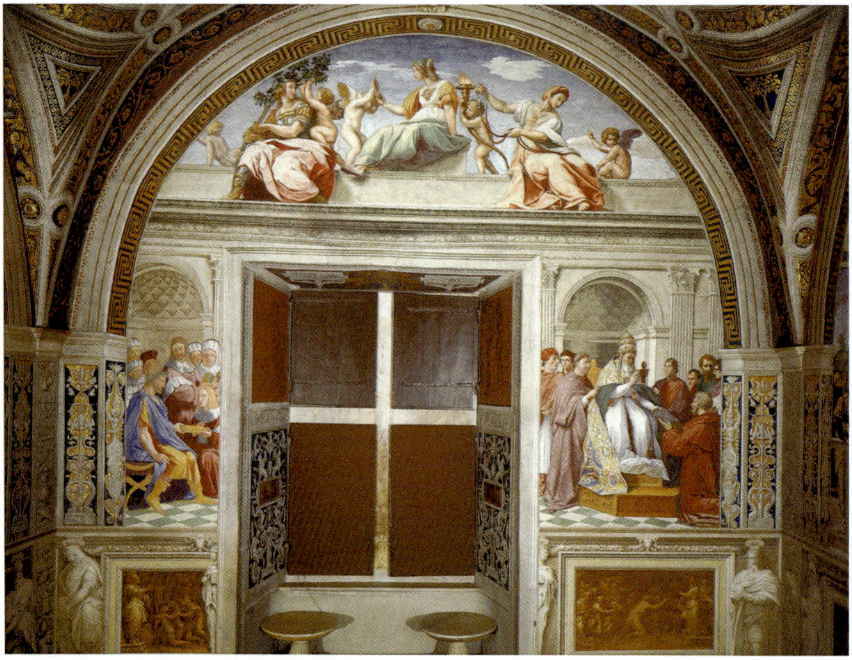

FIGURE 7 Raphael and Lorenzo Lotto, *Jurisprudence*, 1511–1512. Fresco, 660 cm
VATICAN PALACE (PD)

Jurisprudence consists of three narrative scenes: two lower rectangular zones on either side of the window topped by an accompanying lunette-shaped zone above. This upper lunette reveals personifications of Fortitude, Temperance, and Prudence, the essential qualities the philosopher Plato outlined in his theory of Justice in the fourth century BCE.[64] Each figure is matched with paired putti and an identifying attribute. At right, Temperance holds a bridle; at center Prudence has both a mirror and a "double face" to reflect her providence; and at left, Fortitude's strong grip bends a young black oak tree, a fitting inclusion that plays on both the Latin word for Fortitude or Strength, *robur*, and the pope's family name.[65] Below, the scene to the left of the window, completed by Lorenzo Lotto and titled by Nesselrath the *Presentation of the Pandects*, depicts sixth-century Emperor Justinian I as he receives a portion of his *Corpus Juris Civilis*, or civil law code, from Trebonianus, one of his officials.[66] Opposite this

64 For more on Plato's theories, please see: Plato, *The Republic*, Book II.
65 Rowland, "The Vatican Stanze," 110.
66 A. Nesselrath, "Lorenzo Lotto in the Stanza della Segnatura," *The Burlington Magazine*, 142

scene is a depiction of *Gregory IX Approving the Decretals*, which shows the thirteenth-century Pope Gregory as he hands a similar document of canon law to Saint Raimund. These two narrative scenes, united by the shared architectural recessed niches in the background and the entablature that extends across the entirety of the composition, bear notice for two reasons, both of which could be seen as precursors to Raphael's later works.

First, these two scenes stand out from all the rest in the room for having such a specific narrative. *The Disputation*, *School of Athens*, and *Parnassus* include identifiable figures and themes but nevertheless remain more universal and thus are freed from illustrating a specific moment in time. These two registers of Jurisprudence, however, tell a very direct story, and for that they become relatively conspicuous within the room for their more textual qualities. This contemplation foreshadowed an ongoing interest on Raphael's part in the intersections between text and image and, consequently, the realm of reproducibility in the burgeoning print age.[67]

Second, it is noteworthy that these scenes were the product of collaboration between Raphael and Venetian painter Lorenzo Lotto, an artistic relationship that would extend into the subsequent years of work within the Vatican stanze.[68] While Lotto faithfully produced Raphael's design for the *Presentation of the Pandects*, he nevertheless employed his own artistic style. As Nesselrath notes, Lotto's approach was to create figural volume and compositional depth through "the application of successive, fairly even layers of different tones one

(1162) (Jan., 2000), 4–12; A. Nagel and C. Wood, *Anachronic Renaissance*. (New York: Zone Books, 2010), 364.

67 Raimondi's engraving of Raphael's *Quos Ego* (1515–1516) has been similarly interpreted as emulating a book illustration. For more, see: C.K. Kleinbub, "Raphael's *Quos* Ego: forgotten document on the Renaissance *paragone*," *Word & Image*, 28 (3) (July-September 2012), 287–301. It also seems significant that this connection between literature and painting emerges in Raphael's career roughly around the same time Chigi returns from Venice, bringing with him both Sebastiano and Greek bookmaker/printer Zacharias Kallierges who, thanks to Chigi's patronage, was credited with having produced first Greek book printed in Rome. For more, please see: N. Barker, *Aldus Manutius and the Development of Greek Script & Type in the Fifteenth Century* (New York: Fordham University Press, 1992); A. Hobson, "The printer of the Greek editions 'in gymnasio mediceo ad Cabillinum montem'," in F. Barberi, G. de Gregori, and M. Valenti, *Studi di biblioteconomia e storia del libro in onore di Francesco Barberi* (Roma: Associazione italiana biblioteche, 1976), 331–335; E. Layton, *The Sixteenth-Century Greek Book in Italy: Printers and Publishers for the Greek World* (Venice: Istituto ellenico di studi bizantini e postbizantini di Venezia, 1994), 318–329.

68 For more on this ongoing collaboration between Raphael and Lotto, see: Nesselrath, "Lotto as Raphael's Collaborator in the Stanza di Eliodoro," *Burlington Magazine* 146 (1220, Raphael) (Nov. 2004), 732–741.

on top of the other."[69] The result was a colorfully rich yet visually distinct composition to that of Raphael's adjacent *Gregory IX Approving the Decretals*. Here Raphael matched vibrant color with masterful shadow and, as Nesselrath comments, "figures [that] show Raphael's virtuosity at portraiture."[70] Thus, while the two registers read together well, the distinction of styles was apparent and, arguably, deliberate. This close pairing of two distinct painterly styles hearkens back to Campbell's discussion of artistic grafting. Accordingly, perhaps one can propose that a similar meeting of styles occurred here, with Raphael absorbing Lotto's tonality while ensuring that the end visual result was adequately distinct to form a visual contrast or parallel.

This exchange between Raphael and Lotto can be seen as yet another case in which Raphael called upon the visual vocabulary or techniques of colleagues. In doing so, Raphael negotiated once again with the concept of artistic identity, as the two artists working together on *Jurisprudence*, though distinct in artistic heritage, were able to produce a work that, relatively speaking, reads as a harmonious whole. Another aspect of note here is that this creative process behind *Jurisprudence* reflects yet another way in which Raphael was growing his art of recombination. From the wholesale imitation of his prior days under the tutelage of Perugino to the artful distinctions between elements and techniques, this final Stanza della Segnatura scene showcases how rapidly Raphael's approach was developing as he found his footing in Rome. These themes embedded within the visual program of the Stanza della Segnatura primed the young artist for continued innovation. It seems not without coincidence, for example, that Raphael's *Madonna di Foligno*, commissioned in 1511 by Sigismondo di Conti for the high altar of Rome's Santa Maria in Aracoeli, bears hints of a more atmospheric approach to painting, perhaps owing to his early exposure to Lotto's technique.

Raphael's work in the Vatican Stanza della Segnatura revealed a new mode of artistic production, one that exalted the exploration of blending diverse themes and messages into a dynamic pictorial program. This innovation would be further encouraged upon Raphael's arrival at the villa of Agostino Chigi, wherein direct engagement with another Venetian, Sebastiano del Piombo, would serve as a further catalyst for Raphael's ideas and launch him into the most artistically dynamic period of his career. The years to follow would afford Raphael noteworthy opportunities for professional competition, collaboration, and exchange as he continued to develop his visual language to be share among what would become one of Rome's most thriving workshops.

69 Nesselrath, "Lorenzo Lotto," 5.

70 Ibid., 4.

CHAPTER 2

Visual Language through the Lens of Competition at the Villa Farnesina

As Raphael's work on the Vatican stanze progressed, his attentions were pulled to an increasing number of projects. One such space was the villa of Agostino Chigi (known today as the Villa Farnesina). It was Raphael's work for Chigi that would launch one of Raphael's most enduring rivalries—that with Venetian transplant Sebastiano del Piombo—but it was also the space where Raphael developed a connection with Baldassarre Peruzzi and continued to explore the potential within the recombination of forms. Thus, for as much as this splendid villa is a landmark for its beauty and opulence, it also reinforces the various themes that fed into the ongoing development of Raphael's artistic approach that would eventually be absorbed by his workshop colleagues.

1 Commissions from Agostino Chigi

Chigi, like Raphael, embraced the dynamic atmosphere of Rome, in part because it was the source of that atmosphere, Pope Julius II, who had prompted his arrival in the city. While the pope may have had a grand vision to transform Rome into the "Eternal City" through a revival of the ancient world, to do so was an expensive task. When Julius II took the papacy, the coffers of the Church had been nearly emptied.[1] Fortunately, Julius had Agostino Chigi, a banker whose financial backing was essential to the Pope's planned *renovatio*.

Descendant from a long lineage of affluent Sienese bankers that had already established a presence in Rome by 1440, Chigi himself began his banking career working for the Ghinucci bank of Siena before moving to Rome in 1487 to open his own bank at the remarkably young age of 21.[2] His rapid financial success allowed his purchase of the major alum mines at Porto Ercole for use in his trading business.[3] Meanwhile, as Chigi secured his family's status as banking

1 Pellechia, "The Contested City," 67.

2 For more, see: Rowland, *The Culture of the High Renaissance*, 73; R. Lanciani, *The Golden Days of the Renaissance in Rome: From the Pontificate of Julius II to that of Paul III*. (Boston and New York: Houghton Mifflin & Co., 1906).

3 So vast were Chigi's trade routes across the Mediterranean that he earned the moniker "the

 DOI:10.1163/9789004430488_004

barons, his brothers Angelo and Lorenzo fortified the familial connection to the Pope by entering the curial office of *scriptor*, under the eye of Pope Alexander VI Borgia (1492–1503).[4]

Agostino's first allegiance with the Papacy occurred in his joint lease of the papal alum mines in Tolfa in 1501 with Giulio and Antonio Spannocchi (heirs to Ambrogio Spannocchi, former head of the Apostolic Court).[5] This agreement with the papacy brothers proved particularly lucrative when the brothers were later driven to bankruptcy following the exorbitant expenses incurred for the installation of Pope Pius III Piccolomini (whose sudden death only twenty-six days after his installation dashed any hopes of repayment). When this development ruined the Spannocchi, Chigi emerged financially reinforced, and this security grew in step with his increasing fidelity to the Pope. This financial allegiance between Pope Julius II and Chigi quickly evolved into one of close friendship.[6]

This bond at times gave Chigi the upper hand, in negotiations of both business and pleasure. Julius II went so far as to adopt Agostino and his brother, Sigismondo, into the family of the della Rovere, an honor substantiated, among other instances, in the prose of Blosio Palladio's epigram, *Suburbanum Augustini Chisii* (1512).[7] These close ties to the Pope gave Chigi a unique position

---

Great Merchant of Christendom" from the Sultan in Constantinople (A. Majanlahti, *The Families Who Made Rome: A History and Guide*. (London: Chatto & Windus, 2005), 321.) According to Frommel, Chigi's investment in the alum mining industry was "la vera base della sua futura richezza," as attested to by the fact that his original investment of 34,000 ducats in 1500 had multiplied to a value of 300,000 ducats by the time of his death twenty years later (C.L. Frommel, "La Villa Farnesina," in C.L. Frommel, G. Caneva, and A. Angeli, *La villa Farnesina a Roma = The villa Farnesina in Rome*. Mirabilia Italiæ, 12 (Modena: F.C. Panini, 2003), 2: 10).

4 Unfortunately, Lorenzo Chigi met his demise when lightning from a thunderstorm on 29 June 1500 caused the roof of the Apostolic Palace to collapse; he was later buried in St. Peter's. (Rowland, *The Correspondence*, 14; Sigismondo Tizio, *Historiae Senenses*, Cod. Chigi G.II.36, fol. 322^{r}; A. Chigi, *The Correspondence of Agostino Chigi (1466–1520) in Cod. Chigi R.V.c.* Annotated by I.D. Rowland. (Città di Vaticano: Biblioteca Apostolica Vaticana, 2001), *Studi I Testi* 399, 8).

5 I. Rowland, "Render Unto Caesar the Things Which are Caesar's: Humanism and the Arts in the Patronage of Agostino Chigi." *Renaissance Quarterly*, Vol. 39 (4) (Winter, 1986), 678–680.

6 The two were so close in fact that when Julius II fell ill on a sojourn to Bologna in 1506, Chigi remained at his bedside until his condition improved. (G. Cugnoni, *Agostino Chigi il Magnifico* (Rome: A cura della Società Romana di Storia Patria, 1878), 36–37; Tizio, B.A.V. cod. Chigi, G. II: 37, fol. 25; Rowland, "Render Unto Caesar," 681).

7 Palladio not only includes the della Rovere name in the title of his epigram, but he also refers to the villa within the text as "the Suburban Estate of Agostino Chigi della Rovere of Siena." (Mary Quinlan-McGrath, "Blosius Palladius, *Suburbanum Augustini Chisii*. Introduction, Latin Text and English Translation." *Humanistica Lovaniensia*, Vol. 39 (1990), 116).

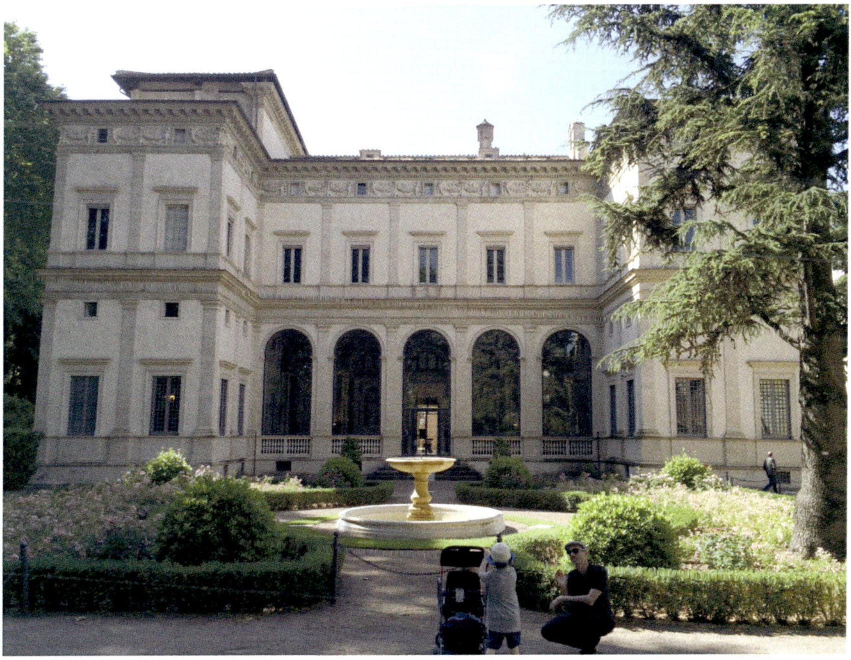

FIGURE 8 Baldassarre Peruzzi
VILLA CHIGI (VILLA FARNESINA), 1506–1510; ROME—AUTHOR'S IMAGE

in sixteenth-century Rome, one that no doubt contributed to the expressive nature of his artistic and architectural patronage. Added to this vision was Chigi's penchant for showmanship, all of which would be embodied in his villa, a space that initiated a collapse of time and a competition between art forms to yield a truly unique product of *cinquecento* Rome.

Having purchased a meagerly-priced parcel of overgrown land stretching along Pope Julius' new via della Lungara on the left bank of the Tiber in 1505, Chigi set out to build a pleasure residence, a place of business, and an entertainment venue.[8] Thus, this *villa suburbana* was at both an escape from and a functioning component within Roman civic functions that placed him squarely within Julius II's planned new civic center of Rome (Fig. 8).[9]

8 Frommel reports Chigi's purchase of this plot for a sum of 530 ducats (Frommel, "La Villa," 17); Pellechia, "The Contested City," 77. Following this purchase and through the construction process, Chigi continued to live in the original Banco Chigi structure on the Via dei Banchi, adjacent to the Palazzo Gaddi-Strozzi until the Farnesina was habitable (approximately 1511). (Frommel, "La Villa," 13).

9 Majanlahti, 684. A. Tagliolini, *I giardini di Roma: Folclore, poesia e storia della città attraverso*

Near the center of Chigi's oasis rose his lavish *rus in urbe* where business intermingled with pleasure.[10] Its original entrance was the open-air Loggia di Amore e Psiche, which ran along the northern façade of the building and opened onto a forecourt area defined in part by the U-shaped structure of the villa itself.[11] One could progress across this forecourt toward the riverfront gardens, interlaced with an enticing network of verdant pergolated walkways flanked by alternating apple and cedar trees, rare exotic plants, and an impressive collection of antiquities that recalled Rome both past and present.[12] The nexus of this intersection was an axial walkway that extended from the northernmost boundary of Chigi's property to its southernmost reaches, effectively parallel to the Tiber River. Going eastward along these paths, one would arrive at the riverfront casino and the shores of the Tiber River. Turning southward would instead mean aiming in the direction of the nearby Porta Settimiana. A stroll along this course would lead one along the eastern edge of the villa, which featured another open-air loggia known as the Loggia di Galatea, to eventually meet a new path network running through a continuation of the garden.

---

l'evoluzione delle isole verdi, la riscoperta di una rinascimentale bellezza in un'ideale sintesi tra natura e arte (Rome: Newton Compton, 1980), 108.

10 Pellechia, "The Contested City," 77.

11 D. Coffin, *The Villa in the Life of Renaissance Rome. Princeton monographs in art and archaeology*, 43 (Princeton, N.J.: Princeton University Press, 1979), 91.

12 E. Gerlini, *Giardino e Architettura nella Farnesina* (Rome: Reale Istituto di Studi Romani, 1942), 4. Chigi's collection was documented in inventories by Cornelio Benigno and Filippo Segrardi in 1520 as well as in accounts of Jacopo Mazzochi (1521), Pietro Aretino (1537), Ulisse Aldrovandi (1556), and Paolo Alessandro Maffei and Domenico de Rossi (1704). Benigno and Sergardi's inventory, conducted between November and December of 1520 following Chigi's death, revealed a vast collection of medals, gems, coral, cameos, and a wide array of antique objects so valuable that Alessandro Farnese stipulated their inclusion in his contract to purchase the property in 1579. This inventory was republished in full in: R. Bartalini, "Due Episodi del Mecenatismo di Agostino Chigi e le Antichità della Farnesina." *Prospettiva* 67 (1992), 25–34; it was also rexamined in: C. Barbieri, *Le "magnificenze" di Agostino Chigi: Collezionie e passioni antiquarie nella Villa Farnesina* (Rome: Sceince e Lettere Editore Commerciale, 2014). More on Chigi's collection can be found in: A. Cremona, *Felices Procerum Villulae*, 570–571; Archivio di Stato di Roma, Collegio di Notai Capitolini, Prosper Campanus, vol. 443, c. 40*v*; Fabio Chigi, *Chisiae Familiae Comentarij* (Biblioteca Vaticana, MS Chigi a. 1.1, 1618; Cugnoni, 63–65; Cremona, 567). Here Chigi references a letter written by Pietro Aretino in 1537, in which he mentions a "satiro di marmo che tenta di violare un fanciullo" (Pietro Aretino, letter to Battista Zatti da Brescia, 19 December, 1537, in *Tutte le opere di Pietro Aretino. Lettere. Il primo e secondo libro* (Milan: Arnoldo Mondatori, 1960), 399–400); J. Mazzochi, *Epigrammatica antiquae urbis* (Rome: Mazzochi, 1521); U. Aldrovandi, *Delle statue antiche di Roma* (Rome: 1556); D. de Rossi and P.A. Maffei, *Raccolta di statue antiche e moderne* (Rome: 1704).

To conjure this magnificent structure, Chigi called upon emerging Sienese architect Baldassarre Peruzzi, who would soon come to represent the new generation of architects dominating Rome. While little is known about Peruzzi, one can surmise that after training in Siena he departed for Rome around 1503 to launch his career as "architect."[13] It was during this time, thanks to the fervor for all things antique, that the profession emerged, simultaneous with the rebirth of the ancient architectural treatise that served as fodder for a new generation of theorists and authors.[14] The only surviving ancient architectural source was Vitruvius, and thus his first-century BCE principles as outlined in *De Architectura Libri Decem* (*Ten Books on Architecture*) became the sourcebook of ancient architectural practices for the fifteenth century.[15]

While Vitruvius was a watershed text, his writings were often confusing thanks to unusual turns of phrase and the lack of guiding illustrations.[16] Alberti tried to work around these hurdles, even choosing deliberately to exclude a section devoted to ancient architecture in his treatise, *De Re Aedificatoria*.[17] Others, such as Giuliano da Sangallo and Francesco di Giorgio Martini, attempted illustrations by seeking out ancient architectural remains to sketch as inspiration. This was in an effort not only to capture what was remained of antiquity in sixteenth-century Rome but also to grasp Vitruvian concepts and designs while making a more comprehensible manual of architectural principles.[18] Neither

13 Ann Huppert notes that: "Born in 1481, even his place of birth is a point of contention, … [*however*] the artist signed himself Baldassarre of Siena, his place of baptism." (Huppert, "The Archaeology of Baldassarre Peruzzi's Architectural Drawings." (Ph.D. Diss., University of Virginia, 2001), 1); C. Rowe and L. Satkowski, *Italian Architecture of the Sixteenth Century* (NY: Princeton Architectural Press, 2002), 136.

14 Günther, Hubertus, "The Renaissance of Antiquity," in H.A. Millon and V.M. Lampugnani, eds., *The Renaissance from Brunelleschi to Michelangelo: The Representation of Architecture* (NY: Rizzoli, 1997), 265.

15 Peter Fane-Saunders has also published an insightful look into the role of Pliny the Elder's writing in the formation of the role of the Renaissance architect. For his discussion please see: P. Fane-Saunders, *Pliny the Elder and the Emergence of Renaissance Architecture* (UK: Cambridge University Press, 2016). As Huppert comments, "Vitruvius' treatise had little influence during antiquity," relegating it to minimal dissemination, however it did survive in print through the Middle Ages. (Huppert, "The Archaeology," 25).

16 For more, please see: Huppert, "The Archaeology", 26–27.

17 R.J. Betts, "*Si come dice Vitruvio*: Images of Antiquity in Early Renaissance Theory of Architecture." In A. Payne, A. Kuttner and R. Smick, eds., *Antiquity and its Interpreters*. (Cambridge: Cambridge University Press, 2000), 251.

18 Betts, 253; Huppert echoes a similar sentiment: "Francesco di Giorgio stated elsewhere in his treatise, [it was] the art of *disegno* and *invenzione*." (Huppert, "The Archaeology," 39). Part of the motivation for some architects and artists to engage in such extensive sketch-

treatise, though, was ever published.[19] The growing interest in Vitruvius nevertheless fed into a flurry of *all'antica* architectural design across the Italian peninsula in the closing years of the fifteenth century.

Having trained with Francesco di Giorgio Martini, Peruzzi thus shared in his teacher's fascination with the antique, an element illustrated in some of Peruzzi's presumably early sketches depicting portions of the Baths of Caracalla (U323A*r* and A*v*).[20] These drawings share in an element noted by Huppert in Peruzzi's sketches from the Flavian amphitheater, namely a "fragmentary quality; rather than disjointed, however, together they create a comprehensive portrayal."[21] In these Baths of Caracalla scenes, Peruzzi juxtaposed portions of the bath complex's ground plan with a sketch of a rearing horse, thereby leaving his study of the ancient structure incomplete yet perhaps conflating what he saw as the most significant elements of the design.[22] This extraction of elemental components seems a direct parallel to Raphael's concurrently emerging meta-style of recombined visual elements, albeit in the realm of architecture rather than painting. That Peruzzi was also a trained painter—an element also evident in his meticulous study of architectural elements—and would later

---

ing was to chronicle the ever-deteriorating remnants of what once was the glory of Rome, as echoed in Raphael's iconic letter to Pope Leo X (F.P. di Teodoro, *Raffaello, Baldassar Castiglione e la Lettera a Leone X* (Bologna: Nuova, Alfa, 1994), 115).

19 The first illustrated edition of Vitruvius' *Ten Books* in Italian was not published until 1521 by Cesare Cesariano (C. Cesariano, *Di Lucio Vitruuio Pollione de architectura libri dece traducti de latino in vulgare affigurati: commentati: & con mirando ordine insigniti.* (Como: Gotardo da Ponte, 1521)).

20 There is no documentary proof that Peruzzi was a student of Francesco di Giorgio, yet as Francesco Paolo Fiore comments: "il legame tra le opera anche tarde di Baldassarre e le origini martiniane è tanto evidente da indicare che un influsso profondo prese corpo almeno attraverso la conoscenza o esercizi di copia dei *Trattati* [*di architettura civile e militare*] o di disegni e attraverso la practica architettonica almeno di maestri della sua scuola" (F.P. Fiore, "La Villa Chigi a 'Le Volte' e il linguaggio architettonico peruzziano nella tradizione di Francesco di Giorgio," in M. Fagiolo and M.L. Madonna, eds., *Baldassarre Peruzzi: Pitture, scena e architettura nel Cinquecento* (Rome: Istituto della Enciclopedia Italiana, 1987), 149). For more on the dating of this sketch to the late fifteenth century, see: H. Burns, "I disegni di Francesco di Giorgio agli Uffizi di Firenze." In F.P. Fiore and M. Tafuri, eds., *Francesco di Giorgio architetto* (Milan: Electa, 1993), 337.

21 A.C. Huppert, *Becoming an Architect in Renaissance Italy: Art, Science, and the Career of Baldassarre Peruzzi* (New Haven: Yale University Press, 2015), 51.

22 Indeed, Burns links this small sketch to Peruzzi by way of its similarity to another series of animal studies credited to his hand: "il cavallo assomiglia a quello disegnato da Peruzzi nell'U 336Av … che hanno stretti paralleli in schizzi che, sono senza dubbio di Peruzzi." (Burns, "I disegni," 337, 354).

combine these skills in his work in scenographic design, implies that Peruzzi was perhaps experimenting with a similar concept of compositional development as was Raphael at this point.

Peruzzi put these practices to use in his designs for Chigi's villa along the Tiber, which adopted a U-shaped structure with entryways positioned on the northern and southern facades (Fig. 8). Striking what Mark Wilson Jones termed a "harmonious balance between elegant symmetry and relaxed planning, between architectural and painted decoration," the design of the villa revealed Peruzzi's blending of the teachings of Francesco di Giorgio, Alberti, and Vitruvius.[23] Peruzzi also continued his patchwork quotation of antique sources in his designs. Perhaps most significant, from an *all'antica* perspective, was Peruzzi's design for the main entrance façade, which, save for slight deviations, complied with Vitruvius' suggested proportions.[24] Peruzzi's recreation of the ancient *scaenae frons* indicated how his own mastery of a recombinative practice could result in compositional (architectural) novelty, but it also marked a crucial moment for the developing field of *all'antica* architecture because such adherence to Vitruvian prescriptions for a theatrical space was, by all accounts, unprecedented in Renaissance Rome.[25]

Two encomiums published by Palladio and Egidio Gallo in the villa's (and by association Chigi's) honor between 1511–1512 illuminate the overall success of the villa's conjuring of this *all'antica* atmosphere and its blend of resonances. Translated from the Latin by Quinlan-McGrath,[26] Gallo's *De Viridario Augustini Chigii Vera Libellus* likens the idyllic oasis Chigi created to a haven for the myth-

23 J.W. Jones, "Palazzo Massimo and Baldassarre Peruzzi's Approach to Architectural Design." *Architectural History*, Vol. 31 (1998), 59. Tessari notes the placement of the inner staircase as a direct quotation of Francesco di Giorgio's approach (C. Tessari, *Baldassarre Peruzzi: il progetto dell'antico* (Milan: Electa, 1995), 27).

24 For discussion of Vitruvian proportions for the theater, see: Vitruvius, 5:6, in Rowland and Howe, *Vitruvius*, 68–69. For more on how closely this building's ratios aligned, see: Jones, "Palazzo Massimo," 82; and A. Culotta, "The Dramatic Side of Breaking Bad: Raphael, Peruzzi, and a Remarkable Revival of Vitruvius' *Scaenae Frons*." In J.C. Fischer, ed., *Breaking with Convention in Italian Art* (UK: Cambridge Scholars Publishing, 2017), 48–71.

25 Jones, "Palazzo Massimo," 60. The closest precedent occurred in 1473, when Cardinals Pietro Riario and Giuliano della Rovere (future Pope Julius II) had constructed a temporary theater structure that joined their two palazzi adjacent to the Church of Santissima Apostoli on the Quirinal to as part of the celebration of the impending marriage of Eleonora of Aragon and Ercole d'Este. This structure served as the locale for both banquets and plays but was dismantled following the retinue's departure; it also never attempted to Vitruvian proportions. (M. Licht, "Elysium: A Prelude to Renaissance Theater," *Renaissance Quarterly*, 49 (1) (Spring, 1996), 1–29).

26 First appearing in the appendices of: M. Quinlan-McGrath, "The Villa."

ical Venus so splendid that the goddess herself cannot discern between the earthly garden and her immortal dwelling.[27] Palladio's *Suburbanum Augustini Chisii*, meanwhile, borrows directly from first-century poets Statius and Martial by paraphrasing sections of their poetry such that it would seem as if Chigi's property was modeled directly from antique sources.[28] These words helped to mold the artful conflation of the old and new Rome for those who visited Chigi's villa, but the illusion succeeded in large part thanks to Peruzzi's novel revival of antique themes within a contemporary setting. In so doing, Peruzzi helped to create a haven for intellectual pondering and, from an artistic perspective, intense innovation.

2 Raphael, Sebastiano, and Competition

It was around the time that Palladio's and Gallo's encomiums were published that Raphael came to contribute to the carefully cultivated interior visual program headed by Peruzzi for the Loggia di Galatea (despite the fact that his work in the Vatican stanze was not yet completed). This eastern-facing loggia served as a transitional space along a visitor's trajectory as it connected the perpendicular Loggia di Amore e Psiche (recall, along the northern façade) with the outside gardens that ran to the river's edge. Visually speaking, though, these two rooms are separated by much more than a doorway: the frescoes in these two spaces represent both the beginning and the end of the villa's visual program, their creation having spanned almost ten years' time during which both Raphael and Peruzzi would evolve toward a similar mindset of visual exchange.

---

27 Coffin posits that Gallo's *De Viridario Augustini Chigii* serves as "a literary equivalent of the pictorial self-image" that is "modeled on the poem by the ancient Roman Claudian entitled the *Epithalamium of Honorius and Maria.*" (D. Coffin, *Magnificent Buildings, Splendid Gardens* (NJ: Princeton University Press, 2008), 92). For full text of Claudian's epithalamium, please see: Claudian, *Claudian*, ed. by M. Platnauer (London: W. Heinemann, 1922).

28 As Quinlan-McGrath comments, "Martial's picture of villa life, a serene overview of the marketplace, gives Blosius a classical precedent and excuse for dwelling at length on an overview of the ancient Roman ruins which can be viewed from Chigi's estates. This was a topic dear to his patron, and to the other members of the Roman Academy." (Quinlan-McGrath, "Blosius Palladius," 102). Quinlan-McGrath continues: "Chigi … had his private apartments in the northeast corner of the *piano nobile* (following the analysis of G. Cugnoni, "Agostino Chigi," 497–506 and Christoph Luitpold Frommel, *Die Farnesina*, 46–53.) [These chambers allowed] access to the rooftop loggia [*now lost*], from which one could survey the antiquities and vineyards, the city and the country." (Quinlan-McGrath, "Blosius Palladius," 103–104).

Adding fuel to the dynamism of Raphael's arrival was that he was not the only one to have recently joined the villa's artistic forces. In 1511, just before Raphael turned to work on *Galatea* in Chigi's loggia, and just as Peruzzi was nearing completion of Chigi's villa construction and had begun work on interior adornments, Chigi traveled to Venice following political negotiations for the Pope in the aftermath of Julius II's failed anti-Venetian League of Cambrai. When he returned, he brought with him Francesca Ordeaschi, his future wife and mother to his four children, and Sebastiano Luciani, better known as Sebastiano del Piombo. Many have speculated as to why he did so, but regardless of Chigi's motives, Sebastiano's arrival in Rome was a transformative one.[29] For Sebastiano, this relocation signaled his plunge into the epicenter of one of the most dynamic periods of Rome's history; for Raphael, Sebastiano's arrival would present the opportunity to challenge the bounds of his painterly practice as the duo worked to complete *Polyphemus* and *Galatea*, respectively, between 1511–1513.

By the time of Sebastiano's arrival, Peruzzi had already established a visual architecture for the Loggia di Galatea devoted at its apex to an elaborate astrological ceiling (executed between 1509–1511) commemorating the moment of Chigi's birth as centered around two *quadro riportato* panels revealing *The Constellation of Perseus with Fame* and *The Constellation of the Chariot* (Fig. 9).[30] Supporting this upper register of the room from below was to be a series of nine lunettes by Sebastiano depicting scenes from Ovid's *Metamorphoses*. Below these lunettes was to appear a series of frescoes encircling the room and framed by *trompe l'oeil* pilasters. Only two of these of lower frescoes were completed, that of *Polyphemus* and *Galatea*.[31] The fact, however, that the painted pilasters

29 Hirst suggests that Chigi desired Sebastiano to infuse his villa with the Venetian aesthetic of the day (M. Hirst, *Sebastiano del Piombo* (Oxford: Clarendon Press, 1981), 32). This hypothesis was echoed, by Costanza Barbieri: "when in Venice, Agostino could have looked at the decoration of the facades of Venetian palaces—like the Fondaco dei Tedeschi or Ca Soranzo at San Polo, painted by Giorgione ... with curiosity and admiration. The decision to bring Sebastiano, Giorgione's pupil, with him to Rome, could have stemmed from Chigi's fascination with Giorgione's frescoes." (Barbieri, "The Competition," 152). Interestingly, in this regard, Sebastiano is again serving as surrogate, a stand-in for the unattainable Giorgione.

30 For more on the astrological ceiling, see: Quinlan-McGrath, "The Villa"; and Quinlan-McGrath, "The Astrological Vault of the Villa Farnesina Agostino Chigi's Rising Sun." *Journal of the Warburg and Courtauld Institutes*, 47 (1984), 91–105.

31 The remaining decoration within this register seen today dates to the seventeenth century: "when Chigi died the loggia was open, all but two of the wall panels were white, and the *basamento* has some fascinating sketches in the *arriccio*" (Quinlan-McGrath, "The Villa," 236). In Alma Tantillo's analysis of the restorations on the room, she proposes that a scene

dividing these scenes date to the first decade of the sixteenth century suggests that Peruzzi was integral in the overall vision for the loggia.[32]

Peruzzi's astrological ceiling was not the first of its kind; Pinturicchio had accomplished something similar in both the Piccolomini Library of Siena and the Vatican's Room of the Prophets and Sibyls, while a similar program was rendered within a loggia of the Ville Le Volte, a project on which Peruzzi had worked and whose patron was none other than Chigi's father, Mariano, near Siena.[33] What stands out, however, in Peruzzi's ceiling is a pronounced element of recombination, labeled by Quinlan-McGrath as having a "heroic dimension, classical grace and decorative life" that "no one other than Raphael had ever combined … with such robust vigor."[34] This connection to Raphael's style bears further consideration, especially given Raphael's ties to the designs of Pinturicchio's Piccolomini Library (as established in his *modello* for *The Journey of Aeneas Silvius Piccolomini to the Count of Basel*, circa 1502).[35] Peruzzi also had the opportunity to study the work in the Piccolomini Library, as during the early years of the 1500s he was at work on ceiling fresco for the San Giovanni Chapel in the same church. Furthermore, Alessandro Angelini has offered evidence to suggest that Peruzzi, like Raphael, had also collaborated with Pinturicchio in the design of *The Coronation of Pius III*.[36] This collaborative aspect takes on new meaning when one considers the elements of elements of both theatricality and antiquity that are cleverly worked into in the finished visual program. The perspectival depth, for example, within this composition is arguably more accurate than that seen in the Piccolomini Library's interior.

---

of Acis was also once intended for one of these panels (A.M.M. Tantillo, "Restuari alla Farnesina," *Bolletino d'Arte*, 57 (1972), 41).

32 R. Varoli-Piazza, "Peruzzi e Beccafumi alla Farnesina," *Quaderni di Palazzo Venezia*, 1 (1981): 60–64.

33 Quinlan-McGrath, "The Villa," 245. An illustration of Peruzzi's frescoed ceiling for the studiolo of the Villa Le Volte, completed roughly by 1505 (illustrated in Francesco Scoppola, "Villa Chigi alle Volte," *Rilievi di fabbriche attribuite a Baldassarre Peruzzi* (Siena: Palazzo Pubblico, 1981), 361–433), reveals striking compositional similarity to that used at Chigi's villa in Rome. For comparison to Pinturrichio's Room of the Prophets and Sibyls, see: Quinlan-McGrath, "The Villa," 248–249.

34 Ibid., 251.

35 Talvacchia, *Raphael*, 48. Specifically she notes the similarity between Raphael's *modello* (Uffizi 520E) for and Pinturrichio's final fresco depicting *The Journey of Aeneas Silvius Piccolomini to the Council of Basel*, circa 1502–1508, a point echoed by earlier scholars, including Joannides (*The Drawings*, cat. no. 56, 48).

36 Documented payment to Peruzzi for the San Giovanni ceiling frescoes dates to 1501, and Angelini proposes that Peruzzi perhaps worked with Pinturicchio between 1503 and 1504 (A. Angelini, "Francesco di Giorgio e l'architettura dipinta a Siena alla fine del Quattrocento," *Bolletino Senese di Storia Patria*, 109 (2002); 124; 140).

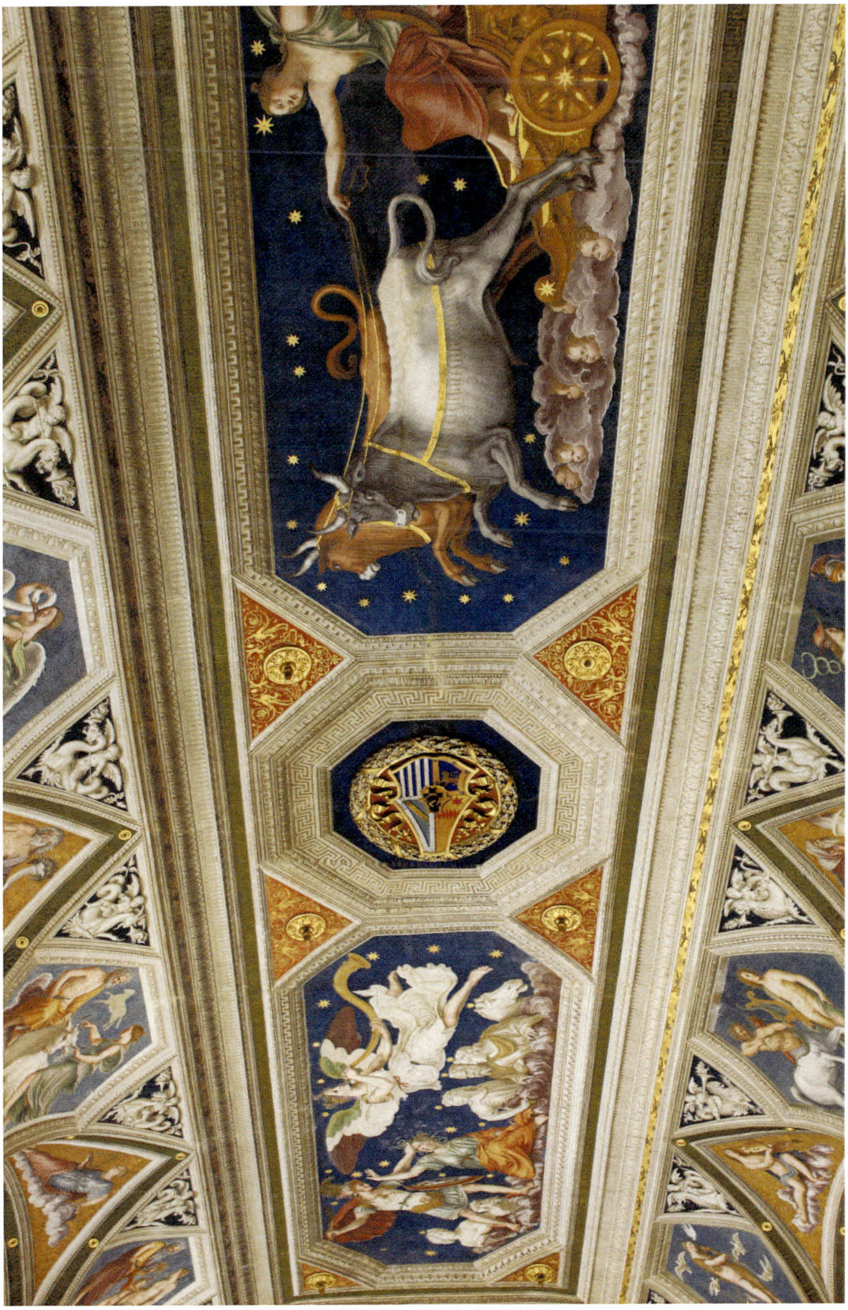

FIGURE 9 Baldassarre Peruzzi, ceiling of the Sala di Galatea
VILLA FARNESINA, 1510–1511; ROME—AUTHOR'S IMAGE

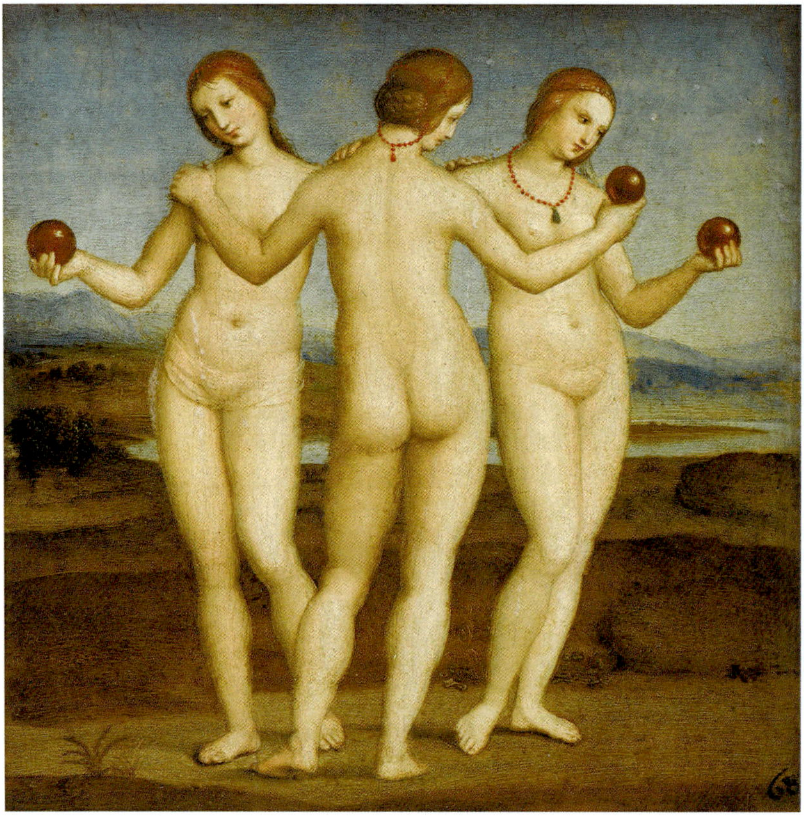

FIGURE 10 Raphael, *The Three Graces*, 1504. Oil on panel; 17 by 17 cm
MUSÉE CONDÉ, CHANTILLY (PD)

Also significant is the inclusion of a quotation of an ancient relief below the central composition inscription. This relief panel, which depicts a maritime battle between Tritons and sea nymphs, is significant because it is the only panel in the entire Library decorative program to so directly link with antiquity. Accordingly, it creates a historical bond with *The Three Graces*, a sculpture from antiquity that was part of Cardinal Francesco Piccolomini's collection and was on prominent display within the Piccolomini Library from 1502 onward. Raphael also studied from *The Three Graces*, resulting in his painted rendition of these three handmaidens of Venus around 1504 (Fig. 10). Peruzzi carries this practice a bit further by extracting one of these maidens to use as his source in his depiction of *Venus in Capricorn* for Chigi's astrological ceiling, one of the hexagonal spandrel images on the western wall of the Loggia di Galatea. Here Peruzzi cites the right-most handmaiden from the antique triad, making only slight adjustments to accommodate his vision of Venus set against the common reductive blue background shared by these hexagonal scenes. As such, this example illustrates Peruzzi's ability, like that of Raphael, to harvest elements simultaneously from the antique and the contemporary and recombine them into an expressive part of a much larger pictorial narrative.

These references seem to suggest that, in addition to Peruzzi's ongoing study of antiquity, he is also engaging in the act of recombination. He selected specific references perhaps in hopes of yielding a more harmonious compositional outcome. This recombination would later become even more central to Peruzzi's practice once his talents took him into the realm of scenographic design; the evidence that this is occurring at this earlier point, though, further underscores the like-mindedness of Peruzzi and Raphael at this stage in their respective careers. What these references also reinforce is that Peruzzi was able to pull elements of a visual language from earlier projects into his work at Chigi's villa and might suggest that Peruzzi helped to pave the way for Raphael's evolution through his projects at the villa alongside Raphael's direct confrontation with Sebastiano del Piombo.

Upon arrival, Sebastiano was tasked first with the execution of the frescoed lunettes that encircle the grand hall illustrating scenes from Ovid's *Metamorphoses*. Sebastiano had not previously attempted the medium of fresco, thus transforming the series into a challenge akin—albeit on a much smaller scale—to that presented to Michelangelo in the fresco commission for the Sistine Chapel ceiling. Whereas Sebastiano faltered in his first lunette frescoes—described in Hirst's monograph as "verging on sheer incompetence"—he accomplished more in the accompanying *Polyphemus* that filled one of the room's larger registers.[37] As such, they have worked against a sufficient analysis of Sebastiano's accompanying *Polyphemus*, which is more illustrative of the artist's skill (Fig. 11).

In Ovid's *Metamorphoses*, Polyphemus was the gigantic Cyclops who fell in love with the Nereid Galatea. His affection was left unrequited, as Galatea already loved Acis. Polyphemus grew jealous and, realizing his competition for Galatea was futile, killed Acis. As the story goes, Galatea was so distraught over the death of her love that she transformed his flowing blood into the waters of

37 Hirst, 35. Quinlan-McGrath echoed the troubles Sebastiano experienced with the lunettes: "he produced no memorable images here which would be copied by generations of later artists" (Quinlan-McGrath, "The Villa," 294–295). Frommel suggests that it was Sebastiano's struggles that encouraged Chigi to pull him off of work on the lunettes one segment shy of completion to instead focus on *Polyphemus*, leaving room for Peruzzi's monumental portrait head. So difficult was the technique of fresco for Sebastiano that the *Polyphemus* was his last effort in the medium (Frommel et al., "La Villa," 2: entry 141, 181).

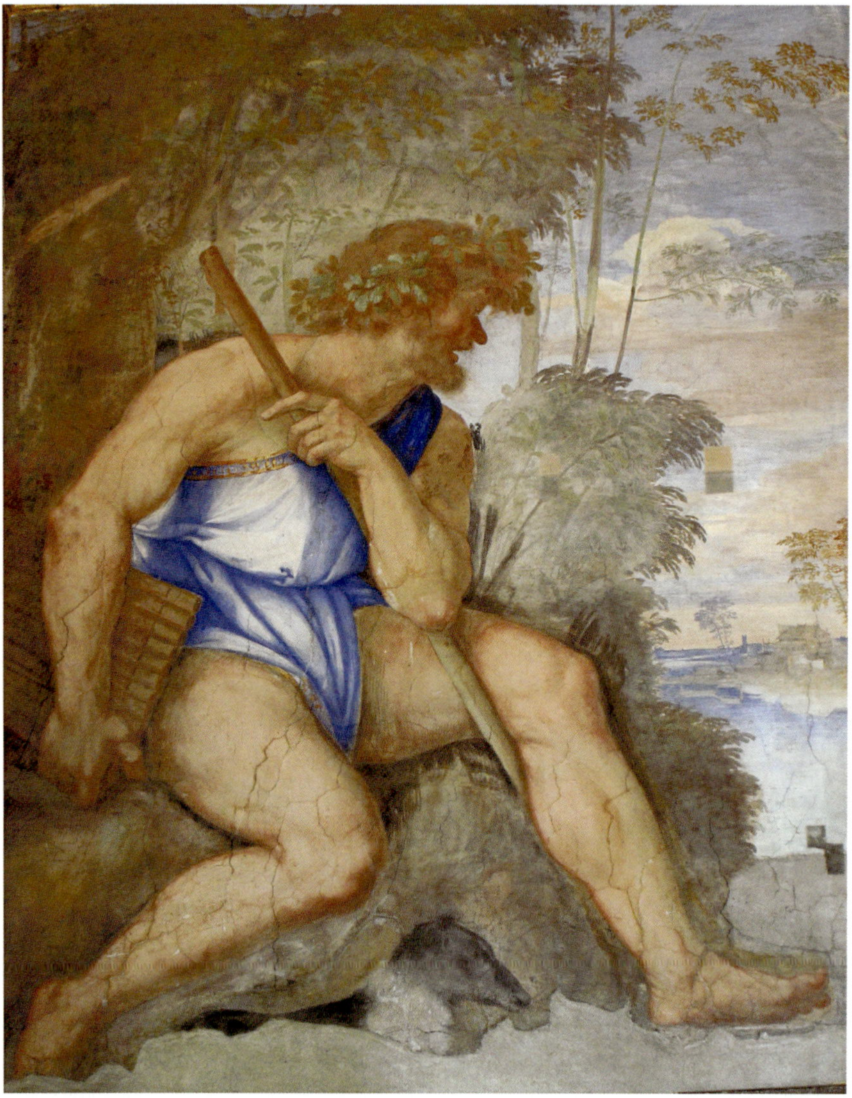

FIGURE 11 Sebastiano del Piombo, *Polyphemus*, 1512. Fresco
VILLA FARNESINA, ROME—AUTHOR'S IMAGE

the Acis River. Rivalry was the nexus of this story, so it was a fitting narrative through which a new rivalry would begin. Sebastiano's rendering of *Polyphemus* captures this foreboding sense in pose, yet he tempers this intensity with his coloristic abilities. Here Polyphemus sits astride a rock outcropping, his entire figure captured rotating to his left. His gaze, permanently fixed in the direction of the adjacent *Galatea*, created an indelible connection between the two panels while also assisting Sebastiano in overcoming the difficulties of rendering a Cyclops's distinctive facial features.[38] Even with the loss over time of Sebastiano's *a secco* additions, the figure of Polyphemus nevertheless projects from the wall. The striking depth of color in his blue robes combined with the terra cotta detailing of his musculature are accentuated against the soft, ethereal foliage that constructs his backdrop. In all, *Polyphemus* more than compensates for the pictorial struggles exhibited in Sebastiano's lunettes; indeed, in addition to its skill and its characteristic Venetian *colore*, Sebastiano's *Polyphemus* was the gauntlet thrown, so to speak, challenging Raphael to what would become an ongoing competition between artists that would reverberate through their future contributions to the villa.

In his monograph on Sebastiano, Hirst ruminates on the visual precedents of Sebastiano's *Polyphemus* as being drawn from the work of Michelangelo, who had, according to some accounts, already become a close associate of Sebastiano. As Hirst comments, "a hint of the Sistine *ignudi* may be suspected to lie behind Sebastiano's seated *Juno*; in the slightly later *Polyphemus*, the influence seems explicit and the figure a tribute to the *ignudo* above and to the right of Joel, carried out in Michelangelo's first campaign in the chapel."[39] If the accounts of the relationship between Sebastiano and Michelangelo are accurate—that is, that the two were veritable allies feeding off of each other, with Michelangelo seeking to harvest the power of Sebastiano's Venetian *colorito* while Sebastiano gleaned what he could of Michelangelo's mastery of Florentine *disegno*—it would be logical for Sebastiano to offer such quotations of Michelangelo's work here. The significance, though, of such references grows given the fact that Raphael, the artists tasked with creating *Polyphemus*' partner panel, was already considered one of Michelangelo's chief rivals. Recall, in the previous chapter, that visual evidence suggests that Raphael was borrowing from Michelangelo's Sistine cycle even before it was complete; that Sebastiano would invoke elements of this same cycle seems a particularly bold statement, not only of his allegiance with Michelangelo but of his desire to compete with Raphael, particularly in light of the fact that Michelangelo was never offered a commission within Chigi's villa.[40]

---

38 Theses struggles are revealed in the sketches uncovered on the *arriccio* below *Polyphemus*, wherein it appears Sebastiano attempted a frontal composition and soon realized the challenges of portraying a one-eyed visage. Additional adjacent sketches he soon after switched to a profile approach (Frommel et al., "La Villa," cat. nos. 125, 128–129).

39 Ibid.

40 Barbieri reiterates this surrogate status by highlighting Vasari's use of the term in the context of Sebastiano's relationship with Michelangelo (Barbieri, "The Competition," 145).

A visual comparison between Sebastiano's *Polyphemus* and Michelangelo's *ignudi* perched above the figure of Joel, however, undermines Hirst's argument. To begin, one can assume that, while Hirst references the *ignudo* "above and to the right of Joel," he instead is referring to the *ignudo* on Joel's right, which makes sense, as it is this figure that at least assumes the same directionality of Sebastiano's *Polyphemus*. If this assumption is correct, one can find only vague similarities between this figure and that of Sebastiano's Cyclops. Both figures are seated and exhibit vaguely similar postures, however the similarities end there. Instead of the figural torsion one finds in *Polyphemus*, Michelangelo's *ignudo* faces wholly to the left, with only his gaze turned slightly inward and downward. Furthermore, Sebastiano incorporated a more refined musculature than the undulating ripples used in the *ignudo*'s rendering, which further distances this connection with the *ignudo* as a visual precedent for Sebastiano's Cyclops. Finally, while it is generally agreed upon that Michelangelo and Sebastiano became fast friends following the Venetians arrival in Rome, it is not clear exactly how friendly they were when work on *Polyphemus* began. Had this friendship not yet taken root, then, to quote Michelangelo would require viewing of Michelangelo's emerging Sistine ceiling, which in 1511, was not only incomplete but also closed to the public.[41]

This is not to discount the potential influence of Michelangelo's work on Sebastiano; rather it is to propose that additional visual influences are at play, perhaps to the extent that Sebastiano himself was contemplating his own form of recombination using themes from Raphael.[42] Specifically, it can be argued that Sebastiano here quotes Raphael's figure of Apollo as rendered in the *Parnassus* in the Stanza della Segnatura. While it is more speculative to argue that Sebastiano had opportunity to view Michelangelo's Sistine series, it is more certain that Sebastiano was afforded the opportunity to view Raphael's completed Stanza della Segnatura. Such a visit was a turning point in Sebastiano's career: as Rona Goffen has commented, "it is impossible to exaggerate the impact of

41 According to Vasari, Raphael was able to view the Sistine program (Vasari, *Lives*, I: 723); again, though there is little else to substantiate this claim. Meanwhile, the only public viewing of the progress on the Sistine Chapel was on the Feast of the Assumption (the fourteenth and fifteenth of August), but Sebastiano reportedly did not arrive in the city until the very end of that month.

42 Goffen tries to ameliorate the connection between Sebastiano and Michelangelo by proposing former was not quoting a singular of the latter's *ignudo* but rather "combined several ... evoking all of them though not replicating any one of them exactly," (Goffen, *Renaissance Rivals*, 231) but even an amalgam of these figures still creates an inconclusive connection.

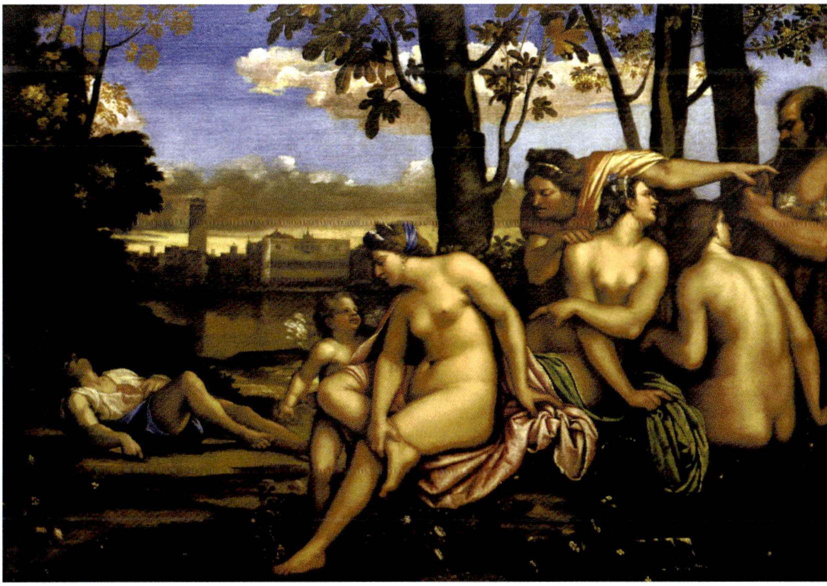

FIGURE 12 Sebastiano del Piombo, *Death of Adonis*, 1511–1512. Oil on canvas, 189 by 285 cm
GALLERIA DEGLI UFFIZI, FLORENCE/ALAMY

[the stanza's] two great cycles on Sebastiano."[43] Evidence of the impact of this viewing can be seen in Sebastiano's *Death of Adonis*, commissioned by Chigi at approximately the same time as Sebastiano's arrival at Chigi's villa (Fig. 12).[44]

It seems significant that Sebastiano would embark on his first recorded rendering of a fully mythological scene, a strong divergence from the religious narratives that played out in his prior works, shortly after having viewed Raphael's Vatican fresco cycle. Moreover, *Death of Adonis* arguably marks Sebastiano's first use of an ancient prototype in his paintings, that of either the *Spinario* or the *Nympha alla Spina* in his figure of Venus.[45] Here, the mythological scene plays out across the foreground of the composition, while in the dis-

43 Ibid., 229.

44 Frommel dates this work to being simultaneous to Sebastiano's work on the lunettes of the Loggia di Galatea, approximately 1511–1512 (Frommel, "La Villa," 91).

45 Sebastiano's Venus might also be quoting the ancient sculpture *Venus Binding Her Sandal*; For more on *Venus Binding Her Sandal*, see: Bober, *Renaissance Artists*, 64, no. 20. The *Nympha alla Spina*, so named by Bober, was part of the Caffarelli family collection by 1500 (Bober, *Renaissance Artists*, 97, no. 61 and 61a). If the ancient source referenced in this instance is indeed the *Nympha alla Spina*, Sebastiano's quotation of it could allude to his own antiquarian interests, as he patently restored this piece from its fragmentary state into a depiction of Venus.

tant background across a lake one sees the sun setting on Venice, the *campanile* of San Marco and the Palazzo Ducale identifiable along the skyline. The fact that the sun is setting on Venice, which one cannot help but consider as a questioning of abandoning his Venetian style of painting in favor of a Roman one, speaks to Sebastiano's contemplation and preparation to engage with the new artistic arena available to him in Rome, specifically the work of Raphael. Thus, if *Death of Adonis* reflect a general confrontation of early *cinquecento* Roman painting, Sebastiano's *Polyphemus* is a confrontation directed specifically at Raphael. Originally intended as one register within an all-encompassing mural,[46] Sebastiano's *Polyphemus*, completed at times side by side with Raphael,[47] arguably borrowed from Raphael's *Parnassus* and thus launched an unprecedented dialogue with Raphael that persisted throughout the remainder of Raphael's career.

Comparison, for example, between Raphael's figure of Apollo and Sebastiano's *Polyphemus* reveals striking parallels. Polyphemus appears almost as an unkempt Apollo, sporting a similar blue drapery and figural torsion as he turns to gaze upon his muse, Galatea. Furthermore, Polyphemus exhibits a bulkier physique than that of Apollo, a more Herculean stature that perhaps most clearly reflects the impact of Michelangelo's *ignudi*. He too rests upon a rock outcropping adjacent to a coursing stream, and is crowned similarly with a wreath of laurels, yet replacing Apollo's *lira da braccio* is the worn syrinx, or panpipe, in Polyphemus' grasp. Though their instruments differ, the design of each furthers a connection between *Polyphemus* and Raphael's scene of *Parnassus*. The *lira da braccio* stands in contrast to the other instruments depicted in Raphael's *Parnassus* as it was a contemporary invention, appearing for the first time in courtly performances around the end of the fifteenth century.[48]

46 After 1514, Chigi abandoned more ambitious plans for decorations in the Loggia di Galatea, for reasons unknown. There is some speculation that damage to his property following a swelling of the Tiber River in 1514 shifted his attentions and perhaps caused the reduction in scale.

47 As Goffen comments: "whether the two masters worked side by side on their adjacent frescoes is not documented but would seem to have been unavoidable at least during part of the two-year period when their murals were painted." (Goffen *Renaissance Rivals*, 230).

48 For more, please see: S.S. Brown, *The Lira Da Braccio* (Bloomington: Indiana University Press, 1995), 1; L. Freedman. "Apollo's Glance in Raphael's 'Parnassus'." *Source: Notes in the History of Art*, 16 (2) (1997): 20–25. Winternitz goes on to suggest that Raphael's inclusion of this contemporary deviation was in part to emphasize the allusions to the virtuosic solo player, as Apollo was to be interpreted, and also its role as the instrument of *cinquecento* poet-musicians ("Il Parnaso," 198–199). Rowland later noted that Raphael also

Further complicating Apollo's instrument is the fact that it bears nine strings, which was two more than a *lira da braccio*'s traditional number. Winternitz proposed this deviation was intentional, suggesting Raphael desired a visual, or numerical, allusion to the Nine Muses.[49]

One finds, though, a parallel number in Sebastiano's depiction of Polyphemus' instrument. A careful count reveals nine pipes of the syrinx appearing above the grip of the Cyclops' hand, one shy of the total number of 10 pipes that traditionally comprise a syrinx. This numerical connection not only reinforces the proposal that Sebastiano had carefully scrutinized Raphael's *Parnassus* but also that the Venetian was cognizant of Raphael's included numerical allusion and wished to invoke it in his rendering of *Polyphemus*. In doing so, Sebastiano further solidified both the link between *Polyphemus* and its cited source, *Parnassus*, and the desired connections between Chigi's villa and a new "Parnassus."

The panpipe was an instrument most often relegated to pastoral shepherds, thus symbolizing, as Luba Freedman argues, "that [*Polyphemus*'] efforts were crude and unsophisticated."[50] From another perspective, though, this parallel between the stringed instrument of Apollo and the panpipe of Polyphemus recalls the story of Apollo and Marsyas. In that narrative, the competition for supremacy—rigged by the fact that victory was declared by Apollo's adoring muses—resulted in the violent end of Marsyas. This creates a compositional space with dual meaning; on the one hand, if Sebastiano was quoting Raphael's work in the Stanza della Segnatura by drawing parallels to his Apollo, one could suggest that Sebastiano was paying homage to Raphael's abilities. On the other hand, though, if Sebastiano was in fact well-versed in Michelangelo's Sistine ceiling and, by association, aware that Raphael had borrowed several figures for his scene of *Parnassus*, Sebastiano's *Polyphemus* then becomes a biting critique of the manner in which Raphael was "rigging" the system of Roman painting.

---

updates Apollo's instrument from a Classical lyre to the Renaissance *lira da braccio* to boost his resonance with Julius' entourage. For more, see: Rowland, "The Vatican Stanze"; Rowland, *The Culture of the High Renaissance*.

49 Winternitz, "Il Parnaso," 198–199; also see: F. Gaffori, *Theorica musicae* (NY: Broude, 1967), I: 2.

50 Freedman, *Classical Myths*, 78–79. Winternitz commented that the syrinx becomes the conventional instrument represented in Polyphemus' possession ("Il Parnaso di Raffaello," *Gli strumenti musicali e il loro simbolismo nell'arte occidentale* (Turin, 1982), 191); since Sebastiano's rendering of the Cyclops is, by all accounts, the first since antiquity, one can safely credit his composition as inaugurating this trend.

These connections might also help to explain why, in his lines dedicated to Chigi's villa, Egidio Gallo likens the grounds, out of all possible allusions, to Parnassus: "Here within perpetually the suavest distinctions the voice of Phoebus and the nine Muses resonate among themselves. Here within is the gathering of the poets, wither/the poets come together to practice sacred poetry with varied verse."[51] The quotation of Raphael's *Parnassus*, however, goes beyond mere artistic emulation. Indeed, for as much as Sebastiano here plays on Raphael's composition, he is at the same time engaging in an important discourse with Raphael. On the one hand, Sebastiano's quotation of this monumental scene can be read as a commentary on Raphael's growing divine status. Indeed, as Barbieri comments, already by 1512 "Raphael was a central figure at the papal court, celebrated in countless poems and epigrams ... In fact, much before Michelangelo, it was Raphael who was celebrated as 'divine.'"[52] On the other hand, just as *Polyphemus* can be read as commentary on Raphael's status, so too does it bear resonance as a symbol of Sebastiano's growing acclaim.[53] Arriving in Rome as a relative unknown artist in 1511, Sebastiano was faced with the insurmountable "triumph" of Raphael, whose already-established success was a direct contrast to the young Venetian's position. Sebastiano was thus left to wallow in the quandary of how to surpass his rival, yet, just as Polyphemus eventually reaped his revenge on his love, so too was Sebastiano confident that his competition with Raphael was only just beginning.

Thus it seems pertinent that Vasari chose to open Sebastiano's biography, albeit many decades later, thus: "the first profession of Sebastiano, so many declare, was not painting, but music, since besides being a singer, he much delighted to play various kinds of instruments, and particularly the lute, because on that instrument all the parts can be played, without any accompani-

---

51 Quinlan-McGrath, "Aegidius Gallus, De Viridario Agustini Chigii Vera Libellus. Introduction, Latin Text and English Translation." *Humanistica Lovaniensia—Journal of Neo-Latin Studies*, Vol. 38 (1989), 5: 147–150, 91. Sixteenth-century writer Natalis Comes echoed the words of Gallo: "the spirit of Apollo forcefully moves these Muses; residing among them, he embraces the universe" (Natalis Comes, *Mythologiae sive explicationis fabularum libri decem, in quibus omnia prope Naturalis & Marlis Philosophiae dogmata contenta fuisse deomonstatur* (Padua, 1616), 583); the illustration of the Muses included in Comes' 1616 edition (7: 403) is closely modeled after Raphael's *Parnassus*.

52 Barbieri, "The Competition," 147.

53 As Goffen notes in her analysis of Polyphemus' inborn *pathos*: "[*he*] invites the beholder to sympathize with his plight ... and [*know*] that the story does not end there" (Goffen, *Renaissance Rivals*, 234).

ment."[54] Vasari's musical allusion, particularly its reference to Sebastiano's preference for performing "without any accompaniment," could allude to Sebastiano's potential challenge to Raphael's artistic supremacy while also perhaps intimating a position of painterly isolation—that is, that Sebastiano preferred to work alone. This individual approach, diametrically opposed to Raphael's collaborative *esprit* as illustrated through both his later Farnesina commissions and the management of his workshop, is nevertheless tempered by the inclusion of the rustic panpipes, a symbolic gesture of relative humility. Thus this navigation between modesty and hubris added arguably another valence of symbolism to the inclusion of Polyphemus' worn panpipes.

Furthermore, by choosing to portray Polyphemus as the blundering poet, Sebastiano draws direct reference to the Horatian aphorism *ut pictura poesis*, "just as in painting, so is poetry." This idiom bore particular resonance for Raphael, who featured himself as an intellectual associate of humanist circles in sixteenth-century Rome. Thus, he contemplated at great length the indelible rhetorical connections between painting and poetry, as evidenced in his work in the Vatican stanze and in the "fundamental sense of the unity of human creative force" that Rowland identified in Raphael's work.[55] Simultaneously, *ut pictura poesis* related to Sebastiano's painting as well, particularly with the poetic ties so often associated with sixteenth-century Venetian painting. The notion that paintings were *poesie*, literally a form of pastoral poetry themselves, would become central to the later career of Sebastiano's contemporary, Titian. Titian's eventual use of this term, to briefly recall Campbell's argument, was to reflect a grafting of artistic styles. That such a theme was already emerging in Titian's paintings in the first years of the sixteenth century, when Titian and Sebastiano were both in Venice, suggests that Sebastiano might have picked up a similar approach to painting and perhaps implemented it in *Polyphemus* as a declaration of a growing Venetian tradition as it was transplanted to Rome. Thus the poetical aspect of Sebastiano's *Polyphemus* can be seen as being both literal, in its rekindling the ancient prose, and methodological, contemplating the mechanics of poetry and its relation to painting.

With these connections in mind, Sebastiano's *Polyphemus* becomes its own sort of visual treatise, merging the ancient poetry of Rome with the contempo-

54 Vasari, *Lives*, I: 140. Interestingly, Bartalini makes note of the display of Sebastiano's *Death of Adonis* within the Farnesina's music room: "la 'tavola picta grande' 'con figure de più donne nude et belle' era allora, alla fine del 1520, in una camera del piano superiore, 'adpresso la Salotta', dove si era soliti fare della musica" (Bartalini, "Due episodi," 18).

55 Rowland, "Raphael, Angelo Colocci," 513.

raneous artistic poetry of Venice.[56] It at once gives credence to the supremacy of Raphael's visual style while also challenging it, proposing an alternative mode of representation in the battle for artistic superiority in Rome. One must consider momentarily what an impact such a visual exposition would have made for visitors to the villa, particularly Chigi's circle of humanist associates who frequented the grounds.[57] For those literati milling about a metaphorical Parnassus outside as they gazed into the Loggia unto Sebastiano's allusion to Parnassus, the bounds of poetry and painting would blur before their eyes.

If Sebastiano's Polyphemus was indeed a challenge presented to Raphael through the emulation of Raphael's earlier work—using, as it were, his own visual vocabulary—then Raphael's response to Sebastiano's visual provocation in *Galatea* (Fig. 13) is equally powerful. He could have responded to Sebastiano's image with an emulation of his own work in *Parnassus*; he could have also aimed to create a visual commentary on Venetian *colorito* akin to what he had accomplished when working alongside Lotto. Instead, Raphael enters into a new, advanced mode of antique revival. In *Galatea*, Raphael for the first time fully explores the pictorial potential of antiquity while also quoting contemporary sources to create his own sort of visual treatise. The included figures, all of whom could have been borrowed from an antique fragment, come together to create a rather monumental composition that exalts the power of *all'antica* painting in a *cinquecento* interior.

The fact that this dynamic composition was created in part in tandem with and also in response to Sebastiano's *Polyphemus* suggests that Raphael's engagement with Sebastiano arguably encouraged Raphael's launch into a new style of painting as witnessed in *Galatea*. On the other hand, while *Polyphemus* and *Galatea* stood in direct stylistic competition with one another, these compositions nevertheless worked together to create a visually dynamic interior, one that would undoubtedly elicit both intellectual discussions on contemporary artistic practice and the mythological allusions connecting the villa's interior to its equally lavish outdoor grounds. This subtle tempering of competition with a hint of collaboration to produce a more perfect product, *un*

---

56 This treatise-like quality to Sebastiano's work is echoed in his later career, as argued in: E. Calvillo, "Authoritative Copies and Divine Originals: Lucretian Metaphor, Painting on Stone, and the Problem of Originality in Michelangelo's Rome." *Renaissance Quarterly*, 66 (2) (Summer 2013), 453–508.

57 This coterie included Cornelio Benigno, Egidio Gallo, the storied Roman courtesan Imperia, Matteo Bandello, Pietro Aretino, Pietro Bembo, Cardinal Bernardo Dovizi Bibbiena, and Baldassarre Castiglione. For more, see: Quinlan-McGrath, "The Villa," 42.

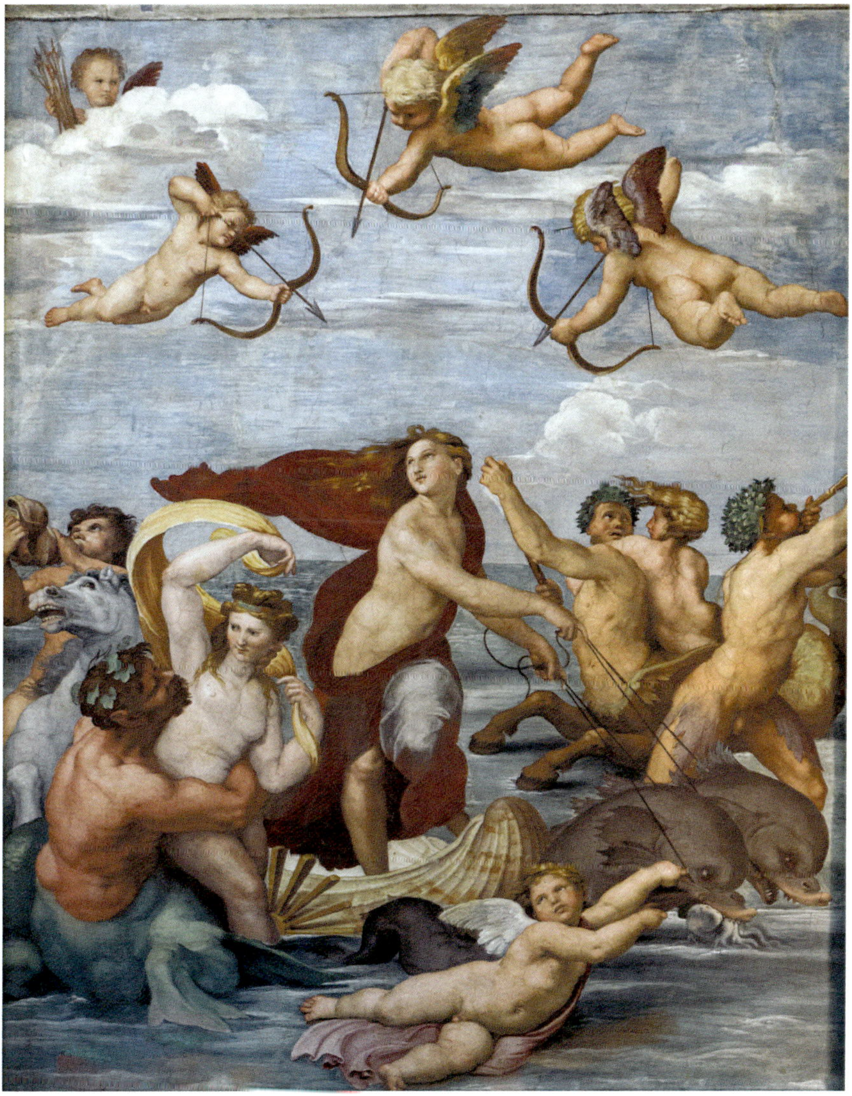

FIGURE 13 Raphael, *The Triumph of Galatea*, 1511. Fresco; 205 by 254 cm
VILLA FARNESINA, ROME/ALAMY

migliore perfectione, would become a central theme throughout Raphael's commitments at the Farnesina.

Raphael showcased Galatea at the center of his composition, dwarfed in size compared to the adjacent *Polyphemus* and gazing backward in his general direction. The red drapery in which she is enveloped whips behind her in the wind as she is pulled forward through the sea on a shell chariot led by two dolphins, one of which has just caught an octopus. Surrounding her are a gathering of sea gods, Tritons, and *putti* in various states, from one riding a sea horse at left to another circling overhead poised to shoot Galatea with Cupid's arrow.[58] In sum, *Galatea* is at once a composition that fits within its intended narrative while also indicating an important shift in Raphael's approach toward the *all'antica*.

Though scholarly consensus agrees that Raphael's intended subject was *Galatea*, it seems worthy of mention that Raphael, amid reinvention and the pursuit of *all'antica* themes, perhaps intended this fleeing female figure to also allude to Venus. Nineteenth-century scholars, such as J.J. Haus, identified this image as one of Venus, not Galatea, to establish visual continuity with the neighboring Loggia di Amore e Psiche.[59] This position was revived by Christoph Thoenes, who suggested that Raphael's depiction was an allegorical representation of both earthly and divine Venus.[60] While any attempt to explain her pairing with *Polyphemus* proves challenging, there are clear connections between visual and antique precedents for depictions of Venus. The fact, for example, that Raphael's composition echoes that of Sandro Botticelli's *Birth of Venus* (1486) seems significant, particularly in light of the fact that both were supposedly derived from the similar source of Angelo Poliziano's *Giostra*.[61] The possibility that Raphael alludes to Venus in his depiction of *Galatea* not only conflates imagery of Venus and Galatea but it also provides a unifying quality to the main visual programs of the villa. Referencing Venus here, the only such reference included in the Loggia di Galatea, not only established a connection with the later Loggia di Amore e Psiche next door, as Haus suggested; it also united this visual program with the Sala delle Prospettive upstairs, wherein Peruzzi, as will be discussed later, included his own version of *The Triumph of Venus*, while also further strengthening the connection with Chigi's outdoor splendors. On approach to the loggia, gazing through the trees into the open archways ahead, one could assume from a distance this monumental depiction

58 Vasari, *Lives*, I: 723.

59 J.J. Haus, *Riflessioni di un oltramontano sulla creduta Galatea di Raffael d'Urbino* (Palermo: n.p. 1816).

60 C. Thoenes, "Zu Raffaels Galatea," in Lucius Grisebach and Konrad Renger, eds., *Festschrift für Otto von Simson zum 65. Gerburtstag* (Vienna: Propyläen Verlag, 1977), 231–244.

61 Specifically, stanza 118, which reads: "duo formosi delfini un carro tirono: /sovresso è Galatea che 'l fren corregge, / e quei notando parimente spirono; ruotasi attorno più lasciva gregge: / qual le salse onde sputa, e quai s'aggirono, / qual par che per amor giuochi e vanegge; / la bella ninfa colle suore fide / di si rozo cantor vezzosa ride," as published in: S. Orlando, *Poesie Italiane* (Milan: Rizzoli, 1988), 26. Förster was the first to suggest this connection to Poliziano's writings (Förster, 57–60).

was indeed Venus, brought to life by the trembling branches as they moved with the breeze. Upon coming closer however, and becoming absorbed in the liquid music of the nearby fountains, a viewer could witness the transformation of Venus into Galatea.

Even without these potential allusions to Venus in mind, Raphael's *Galatea* nevertheless appears as a total opposite to Sebastiano's Cyclops. In some respects such division follows the narrative being retold—that is, the clear division of space and different vantage points employed reinforce that Galatea is forever out of Polyphemus' reach. Thus, Raphael did not merely respond to *Polyphemus* through an emulation of Sebastiano's technique; rather, he charted a new course for painting and, subsequently, for his career. With no extant representations of Galatea on which to base his rendition, Raphael was forced to, in the words of Rijser, craft an "assemblage of pictorial elements from different sources [*to*] reflect his 'divine creation' of the ideal picture, conforming to the procedure of Zeuxis, but now applied to fragmentary remains of sculpture rather than living maidens."[62] Sebastiano was faced with a similar challenge in his depiction of *Polyphemus*, yet it seems Raphael's *Galatea* goes further by incorporating visual references that cross chronology and media. Two intriguing inclusions, quite often overlooked by scholars, bear deliberate reference to the ancient world. One of Galatea's charging dolphins devours an octopus, an allegorical inclusion that recalls the ancient poet Oppian's *Halieutica* and his discussion of the demeanor of marine creatures.[63] Also noteworthy is the curious paddlewheel feature of Galatea's shell that, according to Millard Meiss, is remarkably novel.[64] Tracing the literary precedents in the writings of Philostratus[65] and Poliziano, from whom Raphael derived the basic concept of the *carro*, or chariot, on which Galatea rides, Meiss surmises, "he found them not quite what he wanted. Abandoning the chariot he gave the nymph a sort of super-shell … unprecedented in the arts and in iconographic tradition."[66] This feature, which became absorbed into the subsequent iconography of Galatea,[67] has never been further probed, however it merits reevaluation in light of Peruzzi's

62 D. Rijser, *Raphael's Poetics: Art and Poetry in High Renaissance Rome*. (Amsterdam: Amsterdam University Press, 2012), 382.

63 Oppian, *Halieutica* (Loeb Classical Library, 1928), 425–427.

64 M. Meiss, "Raphael's Mechanized Seashell: Notes on a Myth, Technology and Iconographic Tradition," *The Painter's Choice: Problems in the Interpretation of Renaissance Art* (New York: Harper and Row, 1976), 203–211.

65 Philostratus, *Immagines* II, 18, "Cyclopes," trans. by Arthur Fairbanks (London: W. Heinemann, 1931).

66 Meiss, 205–206.

67 Later versions by Marcantonio Raimondi, Pietro da Cortona, and the circle of Annibale

concurrent developing plans for a water wheel structure for Chigi's gardens. Frommel comments on a monumental waterwheel engineered by Peruzzi that debuted at the first of Chigi's lavish festivities 1518.[68] Its aim was to facilitate water movement from the Tiber to both irrigate the gardens and replenish the fountains and was, from contemporary reports, a feat of engineering that perhaps even included, according to Palladio's previously recounted description, a musical component.[69] The state of the water wheel's construction at the time Raphael was executing *Galatea* is unknown. It is, however, plausible that Raphael was aware of Peruzzi's designs, and thus chose to play upon this future engineering accomplishment before it had been executed.

This playful commentary on Peruzzi's waterworks was not the only reference Raphael included in *Galatea.* As Quinlan-McGrath comments, Raphael's positioning of a seahorse at left engages with the same beast included in Peruzzi's rendition of Pisces in the spandrel on the opposite side of the room.[70] This visual connection created between the two works was perhaps Raphael's response to Peruzzi's quotation of the *Three Graces* in his depiction of *Venus in Capricorn* that was positioned directly above *Galatea.* Thus Raphael uses his composition to draw (potentially lighthearted) connections with Peruzzi that applaud his associate's accomplishments, imply a collegial relationship already established between them, and also further tie this visual representation to the actual gardens outside.

Raphael's visual connections within *Galatea* continue. The central *putto* in the lower register, for example, quotes Michelangelo's contemporary sculpted

Carracci included this paddlewheel feature; also appears in the later visual programs developed by Raphael's workshop artists, such as the Villa Lante at Gianicolo.

68 Frommel, *Die Farnesina*, 8; Cremona, 528; L. von Pastor, *Geschichte der Päpste im Zeitalter der Renaissance und der Glaubensspaltung: von der Wahl Leos X. bis zum Tode Klemens' VII. (1513–1534), Vol. 1 Leo X* (Freiburg im Breisgau: Herder, 1907), 152. Finally, similar mention was made in the account of a member of Pope Leo X's coterie who accompanied him to the infamous festivities on 27 February 1518: "Il zardino bellissimo e grando, et havia consegnato una Fontana soto tera che toleva l'aqua d'il Tevere et con alcuni ingegni butavano l'aqua per il zardino; ch'è sta un bel veder" (L. von Pastor, *Geschichte der Päpste seit dem Ausgang des Mittelalters* (Freiburg, 1885–1933), vol. 28, 152).

69 A letter dated 27 January 1519 to Chigi from Antonio and Nicola Burchiella, presumably engineers themselves, talks of Chigi's desire for a fountain in the garden and the necessity to mechanize water movement, either from drilling into the ground or pulling it from the Tiber, to feed it. (O. Montenovesi, *Agostino Chigi banchiere e appaltatore dell'allume di Tolfa.* Archivio della Società Romana si Storia Patria, 60 (Rome: 1938), 121). Chapter Nine of Vitruvius' tenth book on architecture, as translated in: Rowland and Howe, 127–128.

70 Quinlan-McGrath, "The Villa," 315.

relief, the *Taddei Tondo* (1504–1506; Royal Academy of Arts, London).[71] In addition to this Michelangelesque reference, Raphael also arguably quotes the popular fragment *Torso Belvedere* in the figure of the Triton at lower left. This quotation has also been carried over into Raphael's depiction of Galatea herself, whose rendition has been critiqued over history as being overly muscular.[72] Indeed, a review of the *giornate* necessary to complete the *Galatea* reveals Raphael's division of her figure at upper thigh, the same axis upon which the lower extremities of the *Torso Belvedere* are truncated.[73] Finally, Raphael was careful also to reference Sebastiano by adopting his color-centric technique. As Barbieri points out, though Raphael conjured a Galatea seemingly otherworldly by comparison to that of Sebastiano's *Polyphemus*, he nevertheless expended careful observation on Sebastiano's glaze-like technique of pigment application to achieve a unique balance of color.[74]

It is worth noting that conspicuously missing from the loggia is the third protagonist of the narrative, Acis. His absence is not altogether remarkable aside from the fact that it draws attention to the unfinished state of the loggia. Though the exact plans have not survived, common consensus suggests Chigi envisioned the continuation of this monumental mural series around the room. Such a plan was most likely dashed with the massive flood of the Tiber River in 1514 that shifted Chigi's attention to the repair of damage to the villa property. As such, one is left only left to imagine the scope of competition that could have been achieved had Chigi's original plans materialized. Regardless, the fact that Sebastiano and Raphael stand alone in competition on the loggia's walls, accentuated by the white stucco panels that accompanied them, one is struck with the visual impact these works would have had on a viewer in Chigi's day.

Beyond the loggia, Raphael and Sebastiano engaged in career-spanning competition.[75] Later connections, for example, between Sebastiano's *Portrait of a Young Woman (Dorothea)* (1512–1513; Gemäldegalerie, Berlin) and both

71 Rijser, 383; Raphael had already cited this tondo in his *Virgin and Child* (*Bridgewater Madonna*) of 1507.

72 Ibid.

73 As illustrated in Tantillo, "Restauri," 46, no. 9. According to her analysis, both Sebastiano's *Polyphemus* and Raphael's *Galatea* required thirteen days of work.

74 Raphael's interest in the Venetian technique could have contributed to his close camaraderie with Giovanni da Udine, who had trained under Giorgione (M. Hochmann, *Venise et Rome 1500–1600: deux écoles de peinture et leurs échanges*. (Genève: Droz, 2004), 173).

75 Raphael's response to Sebastiano could arguably have contributed to the development of Raphael's pictorial "vernacular," an element of his later works gaining increasing schol-

Raphael's *La Donna Velata* (1512–1513; Palazzo Pitti, Florence) and *La Fornarina* (1520; Palazzo Barberini), have been cited by scholars,[76] as have relationships between Raphael's *Liberation of Saint Peter* in the Stanza di Eliodoro with his atmospheric treatment of Sebastiano's Viterbo *Lamentation* (1516–1517; Museo Civico, Viterbo).[77] The capstone of these quotations was that between Sebastiano's *The Raising of Lazarus* (1517–1519; The National Gallery, London) and Raphael's *Transfiguration* (begun 1516; Pinacoteca Vaticana), wherein the borrowing of ideas became so extreme that Raphael orchestrated that the two works never be in close enough proximity for charges of copying to be leveled.[78] What is fascinating to note, though, is that several of these works from which Raphael was to have borrowed were themselves collaborative productions. Since Michelangelo and Sebastiano had fostered their friendship following the Venetian's arrival in Rome, the two had formed their own quasi-collaborative relationship. Evidence that the two had become allies can be seen as early as 1514, when Sebastiano purportedly used a drawing by Michelangelo (now lost) for his *Lamentation* (1514; Museo Civico, Viterbo). Several such collaborative creations ensued between Sebastiano and Michelangelo in the years to come—including, ironically, the *Raising of Lazarus* (1517–1519; National Gallery, London) from which Sebastiano argued Raphael stole.

By this late point in Raphael's career, one must question the nature of this borrowing. Was it so extreme to have been the potential undoing of Raphael's reputation, as Sebastiano's writing implies? Or, was it perhaps that Sebastiano,

---

arly attention. For more, see: P. Reilly, "Raphael's *Fire in the Borgo* and the Italian Pictorial Vernacular." *The Art Bulletin*, 92 (4) (Dec. 2010), 308–325.

76 K. Vahland, "Sebastiano and Raphael," in G. Scandiani, ed., *Sebastiano del Piombo, 1485–1547*. (Milan: Motta, 2008), 29; Goffen, "Raphael's Designer Labels," 135.

77 This parallel with Sebastiano's Viterbo *Lamentation* becomes all the more striking here as this was a collaborative creation between Michelangelo and Sebastiano, as will be discussed briefly in a later chapter.

78 Interpretation of a letter from Domenico da Terranuova to Michelangelo in 1518 reveals Raphael aimed to have Sebastiano's painting framed in France to spite Sebastiano ("per fare dispecto a Bastiano." (G. Poggi, P. Barocchi, and R. Ristori, *Il Carteggio di Michelangelo* (Firenze: Sansoni, 1965–1983), Vol. 2, 38). As Sheryl Reiss posits: "Hirst and others believe, rightly, I think, that Raphael was "lobbying" to have Sebastiano's painting framed *in situ*, that is to say, in Narbonne, in order that the two works not be compared by a sophisticated Roman audience under the best possible circumstances. Sebastiano, who in retaliation seemingly planned to tell the Cardinal that Raphael robbed him of at least three ducats a day, won this round and his picture was framed and gilt in Rome" (S. Reiss, "Cardinal Giulio de' Medici as a Patron of Art, 1513–1523" (PhD Diss., 1992), 316; Golzio, 71–72; Hirst, 68–69); A. Henning, *Raffaels Transfiguration und der Wettstreit um die Farbe: koloritgeschichtliche Untersuchung zur römischen Hochrenaissance* (München: Deutscher Kunstverlag, 2005) 29; and Vahland, 35.

by these later years of the 1510s, felt so far outside of Raphael's orbit—despite the ever-growing network of workshop participants within it—and the visual language that they had come to share? Was it perhaps part of the larger narrative of Sebastiano's alliance with Michelangelo, a union that would also disintegrate in the years to come? One cannot be sure, but what seems clear is that, at the point of their initial meeting within the chambers of Chigi's villa, a unique spark was struck. Sebastiano's ingenious quotation of Raphael's *Parnassus* both defined the iconographic conventions for future renditions of Polyphemus and figuratively called for Raphael's response, which yielded Raphael's unprecedented revival of an *all'antica* theme.

For Sebastiano, it was this rivalry with Raphael that kept him at his best, at least according to biographer Giorgio Vasari, who went so far as to posit, "while the competition of art between [Sebastiano] and Raphael lasted, … he tired himself continuously, so as to not be held inferior."[79] Perhaps what Vasari alluded to here was that Sebastiano could only thrive on competition and the desire for superiority, a point again reinforced in later years following Raphael's death when he demeaned the members of Raphael's workshop by calling them simply Raphael's "garzoni" rather than recognizing their individual identities as artists and collaborators. To be fair, such terms were used when Sebastiano was competing once again—this time for control of Raphael's outstanding projects at the Vatican—but the phrasing nevertheless suggests that Sebastiano had lost the spark of inspiration that could have grown following his engagement with Raphael in Chigi's villa.

For Raphael, responding to Sebastiano's composition with his wholly antique treatment of *Galatea* reflected another landmark in his development. It would seem that Sebastiano's mode of competition worked counter to Raphael's preference for repetition and recombination of visual elements; this clash, in turn, might have provided the impetus for Raphael's alignment with Peruzzi and subsequent forays into the fields of archaeology and architecture; it might have also helped Raphael to formulate the foundations for his workshop that would become so invaluable to him in the years to follow. Thus, when *Galatea* is contextualized chronologically as a contemporaneous product to Raphael's first architectural projects, Sebastiano's challenge emerges as a potential catalyst to Raphael's multifarious interests, encouraging not only a rapid transformation of his painterly technique but also a merger of these ideas with his interests in architecture and archaeology that he would explore alongside his colleague Peruzzi in the years to come.

79 Vasari, *Lives*, 140; A.F. Tempesti, *Rafaello e Michelangelo*, exhibition catalogue. (Florence: Casa Buonarroti, 1984), 15.

CHAPTER 3

Collaborative Practice and Emerging Workshop Mentalities

1 Partnering with Peruzzi

It would be 1517 before Peruzzi would embark on another painterly project at Chigi's villa; when he did so, however, the product of his efforts, known as the Sala delle Prospettive, continued this practice of visual exchange. In the interim years since Raphael's *Galatea*, Peruzzi and Raphael appear to have found a kinship. Practically the same age, the two became close associates, such that Raphael served as guarantor for a property rented by Peruzzi in Rome in late 1511.[1] Thus, whereas Sebastiano was a rival to Raphael, it seems that Peruzzi was a closer colleague and friend with whom a sharing of visual ideas would ensue over the decade.

Emphasizing this connection between Raphael and Peruzzi is the fact that it was during this period that Raphael added to his list of specialties that of architect. Though little evidence of this phase of his production remains, Raphael was involved in several commissions from 1514 onward, including two projects on the grounds of Chigi's villa.[2] These comprised a porticoed loggia at the riverfront edge of Chigi's property as well as an elaborate stables, both so sumptuous to have served as locales for storied banquets.[3] All that remains today of these once ambitious structures, though, is a fragment of the lower story of the stables, and the absence of thorough preparatory drawings makes it

1 November 18–21, 1511; Golzio, 24. Cristiano Tessari suggests that Peruzzi and Raphael might have met as early as the turn of the century (Tessari, 20), a point reinforced in the earlier proposal of Peruzzi and Raphael's shared prototype in the Sienese *Three Graces*.

2 Ray reinforces this point: "Il nodo del problema sta nei documenti che, nell'insieme, sono troppo frammentari e lacunose, e lasciano pertanto in ombra ampie zone dell'opera. I disegni, in particolare, sono molto pochi, non soltanto in rapporto ai disegni di figura che conosciamo, ma anche in sé per sé." (S. Ray, "Il Volo di Icaro," in C.L. Frommel, S. Ray, and M. Tafuri, eds., *Raffaello Architetto* (Milan: Electra, 1984), 47); for more, see: J. Shearman, "Raphael as Architect," *Journal of the Royal Society of Arts*, 116 (5141) (April 1968), 388–409; Talvacchia, *Raphael*, 141.

3 The attribution of the riverfront casino to Raphael was first proposed by Gaspare Celio in 1638 (Celio, 128), and subsequently accepted by Geymüller (Enrico di Geymüller, *Raffaello Sanzio studiato come architetto con l'aiuto di nuovi documenti* (Milan: Hoepli, 1884), 38f.) and Frommel (Frommel, *Die Farnesina*, 32–33).

 | DOI:10.1163/9789004430488_005

nearly impossible to reconstruct these buildings without considerable conjecture. Assembling what is known about this riverfront structure, though, reveals a casino incorporating both an emulation of an ancient nymphaeum and an underground grotto that facilitated Peruzzi's previously-mentioned plans for elaborate garden features.[4] Comparisons made between a Raphael drawing at Lille linked to the casino project and a supposed sketch of the nymphaeum at Genazzano authored by Peruzzi (U529A*r*) reinforce the potential that there was a level of collaboration at play between the two men.[5] If this were indeed the case, then the casino serves to illustrate another key landmark wherein Raphael's collaborative exchange with Peruzzi resulted in a riverfront structure that not only incorporated one of the earliest nymphaea of Renaissance Rome—furthering the previously discussed allusions to Parnassus conjured elsewhere on Chigi's property—but also accomplished the functional task of accommodating Peruzzi's grand garden water features. Beyond these collaborative connections, though, there is little evidence to illuminate that a shared vocabulary of architectural phrases was being exchanged.

More solid evidence of such an exchange between Peruzzi and Raphael can be found in Peruzzi's Sala delle Prospettive (Fig. 14), a space that reflects both his incredible mastery of painterly perspective and *trompe-l'oeil* illusion while also bearing evidence of his borrowing of visual quotations from both Raphael and Sebastiano. Creating the illusion of an open-air *all'antica* structure, the Sala delle Prospettive appears as painted loggias on three of the four walls that reveal the expanse of Rome and the countryside beyond. As a testament to his status as "principe dei prospettici pratici," Peruzzi oriented the columns lining these walls such that a viewer facing north toward the monumental hearth would be treated to a *trompe-l'oeil* revelation of the city.[6] Multi-colored faux

4 For more on this reconstruction, see: A. Culotta, "A Novel Nymphaeum: Raphael's Inaugural Architectural Commission in Rome Reconsidered." *Rutgers Art Review*, 31 (Summer 2015), 4–19.

5 For more on the Lille drawing, see: S. Ray, "Il Volo di Icaro," in C.L. Frommel, S. Ray, and M. Tafuri, eds., *Raffaello Architetto* (Milan: Electra, 1984), 47. For more on the Genazzano sketch, see: P.D. Britton, "A Peruzzi Drawing and the Nymphaeum at Genazzano." *Notes In the History of Art*, 19 (4) (Summer 2000), 1–6; M. Licht, ed., *L'Edificio a pianta centrale: Lo sviluppo del disegno architettonico nel Rinascimento* (Florence, 1984) 93–94. For more on the nymphaeum form, see: F. Alvarez, "The Renaissance Nymphaeum: Its Origins and Its Development in Rome and Vicinity" (PhD diss., Columbia University, 1981) and E. McDougall, "The Sleeping Nymph: Origins of a Humanist Fountain Type," *The Art Bulletin*, 57 (3) (Sep., 1975), 357–365.

6 I. Danti, *Le due regole della prospettiva pratica* (Rome: Francesco Zannetti, 1583), 68; Quinlan-McGrath, "The Villa," 375; C. Cieri, "Sala delle Prospettive: via, storia, e funzione della sala," in S. Rossi and K. Cassanelli, eds., *Di luoghi di Raffaello a Roma* (Rome; Multigrafica Editrice, 1983), 70.

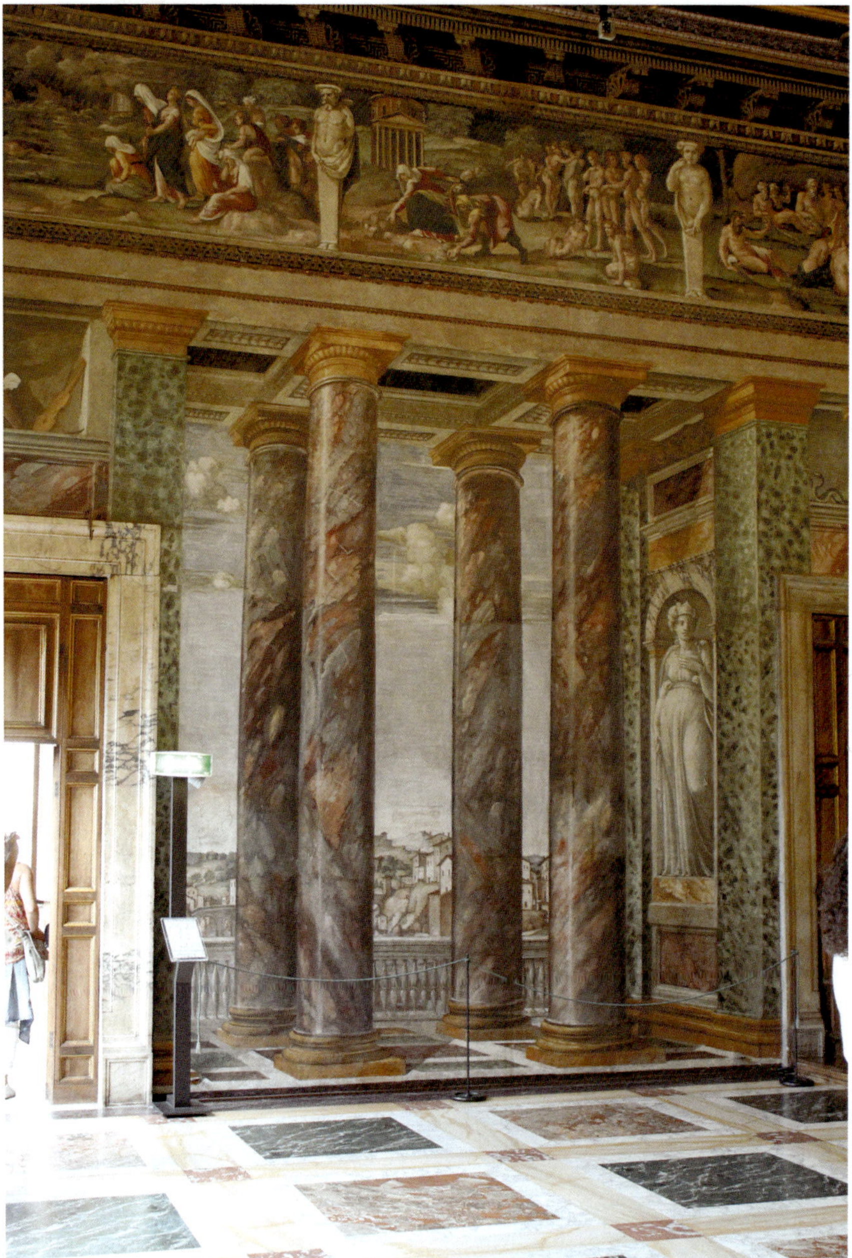

FIGURE 14 Baldassarre Peruzzi, Sala delle Prospettive, 1515–1517. Fresco
VILLA FARNESINA, ROME—AUTHOR'S IMAGE

marble revetments, an upper-register narrative frieze depicting stories from Ovid's *Metamorphoses* and demarcated by herms, only amplified the magnificence of the space. Sandwiched between this uppermost register and the cornices of the doorways below are paired fictive niches, each inhabited by an ancient Roman god or goddess, creating a layout that reinforced the distinctions between the celestial and terrestrial realms. With this in mind, Peruzzi's Sala delle Prospettive alludes to Chigi's dominion as the symbolic Parnassus on earth, a revered space wherein the gods and their consorts could dwell, wherein the seasons met in perfect harmony, and wherein the concordant theme of the cycle of life—love, death, and rebirth—could reign.

For as much as this room emphasized the extravagance of Chigi's domain, the classical references woven throughout served as a visual testament to Peruzzi's affinities for antiquity and for visual phrases from the work of both Sebastiano and Raphael.[7] From this perspective, Peruzzi's frieze in the Sala delle Prospettive becomes akin to Raphael's *Galatea* in that it presents a network of references to works both classical and contemporary and was perhaps an effort to stake his own claim in the emerging field of *all'antica* painting. Classical and contemporary connections can be seen throughout this upper register fresco cycle; however, only a few from the northern wall—that which would have served as the main focal point of viewing—will be highlighted here. Near the joinder between scenes of *Apollo and Daphne* and *Venus and Adonis* in the northwestern corner, for example, a reclining male nude figure appears as a direct quotation of the colossal ancient river god statue known as *Marforio*, which at the time would have been on view in the Roman Forum.[8] Perhaps thanks to this unfettered access—or his personal preference for the sculpture—the *Marforio* reappears in the background of the scene. This mirror replica that reveals the opposite side of the figure is reminiscent of contemporaneous sketches after the antique that capture the same sculpture from various vantage points. At the same time, this classical figure draws undeniable parallels to the reclining nude in Raphael's previously-mentioned depiction of *The Judgment of Paris*.[9] This reflexivity of quotations—in other words, that

7 For more on the modeling of figures after antiquity, see: N. Dacos, "Peruzzi. Dalla Farnesina alla Cancelleria. Qualche Proposta per la Bottega della Pittore." In M. Fagiolo and M.L. Madonna, *Baldassarre Peruzzi: Pittura, Scena, e Architettura nel Cinquecento* (Rome: Enciclopedia Italiana, 1987), 469–490.

8 Raphael's associate Andrea Fulvio was the first to clearly identify this sculpture as that of a river god, suggesting the name "Marforio" was derived from Nar Fluvius, a Tiber tributary (*Antiquitates Urbis*, 156f.). Bober comments that *Marforio* stood near the Arch of Septimius Severus until 1588, when it was moved to the Capitoline Museum (Bober, *Renaissance Artists*, 100, no. 64).

9 Raimondi's print dates to around 1510–1520, suggesting Raphael's drawing would have had

Peruzzi is quoting antiquity while concurrently citing Raphael, who arguably was also inspired by the same antique source—deepens upon consideration of Coffin's mention of the presence of a Tiber river god sculpture displayed within Chigi's complex.[10] One can imagine that this ancient river god would had been similarly posed as *Marforio*, suggesting that Peruzzi's inclusion of this quotation was also intended to implicate Chigi's holdings, as Chigi counted an ancient sculpture of a river god among his antiquities collection. This multidimensional citation implies dynamism in Peruzzi's artistic approach akin to, if not surpassing, that witnessed in the earlier Loggia di Galatea: here he collapsed a complex set of references into an otherwise straightforward visual narrative.

The same such multifaceted references can also be seen in *Venus and Adonis*, alternatively known as *Venus at Her Bath*.[11] Compositional comparison of this vignette, reveals that Peruzzi drew heavily from Sebastiano's *Death of Adonis*.[12] Peruzzi's dying Adonis at left assumes a nearly identical posture to that of Sebastiano's painting; his Venus does as well, however with one notable adjustment. Recall that Sebastiano's Venus exhibits a rigidly flexed right foot, giving her overall posture a wrenching quality as she tugs right leg over left similar to the ancient *Spinario* or *Nympha alla Spina*. Peruzzi's Venus instead crossed left over right in a pose that was more graceful but that also found its source in antiquity. Specifically, it recalls a fragmentary nymph statue that appears in another of Peruzzi's drawings (*Study of a Seated Woman*, Walker Art Gallery inv. 1995.244).[13]

---

to predate this time period (Grazia Bernini Pezzini, Stagnia Massari, Simonetta Prosperi Valenti Rodinò, *Raphael Invenit: stampe da Raffaello nelle collezioni dell'Istituto Nazionale per la Grafica* (Rome: Quasar, 1985), 242).

10 Coffin, *The Villa*, 87.

11 Gianfranco Malafarina, *La Villa Farnesina a Roma* (Modena: Franco Cosimo Panini Editore, 2003), 68; Dacos, "Peruzzi. Dalla Farnesina alla Cancelleria," 474.

12 In his book, *Sebastiano del Piombo* (Basel: Holbein-Verlag, 1942), Lultpold Dussier first suggested that Peruzzi used Sebastiano's version as a model, yet he made no note of Peruzzi's significant variations noted here. Bartalini suggests that this painting might have been displayed in a nearby music room: "la 'tavola picta grande' 'configure de più donne nude et belle' era allora, alla fina del 1520, in una camera del piano superiore, 'adpresso la Salotta', dove si era soliti fare della musica" (Bartalini, "Due episodi," 18).

13 Valeria Cafà identifies another drawing of this antique sculpture as the work of Peruzzi (as illustrated in "Divinità a pezzi: Prove di restauro di scultura antica nei disegni di Baldassarre Peruzzi." In M. Beltramini and C. Elam, eds., *Some Degree of Happiness: Studi di Storia dell'Architettura in Onore di Howard Burns* (Pisa: Edizione della Normale, 2010), 697, no. 88). This drawing is more finished that the one held by the Walker Art Gallery, however it is problematic from this author's perspective that the border bears the inscription

Similar parallels can be found as one progresses to the subsequent scene of *The Triumph of Bacchus*. This was a subject commissioned by Raphael from Duke Alfonso D'Este yet that was rendered only in sketch form between 1517 and 1519 (one version of which survives—*The Triumph of Bacchus in India*, Vienna, Graphische Sammlung Albertina, SR 533, inv. 444).[14] Even in such a preliminary state, however, Raphael's sketch and Peruzzi's composition of *The Triumph of Bacchus* share important quotations.[15] Beyond the shared echo of being modeled from an ancient Roman relief, one of the most notable parallels is the figure that appears at the center of Raphael's design, kneeling to the ground as he supports the weight of Bacchus. This man appears in Peruzzi's version as well, however transposed and shifted to the lower-right corner to take on the role of processional observer. Also shared are the pipe and cymbal players. In Raphael's sketch these paired figures appear in the lower left-hand corner, the torsion of the horn player having been contemplated in earlier Raphael studies of Michelangelo's *Battle at Cascina*.[16] In Peruzzi's vignette this pair appears again, yet again transposed, perhaps in an effort to avoid the complex anatomical twist that Raphael's arrangement required. With Raphael's sketch left undated, it is impossible to discern whose designs came first and thus who was imitating whom; nevertheless, these cross-compositional quotations suggest an important moment of artistic exchange.

Near the end of this wall is Peruzzi's envisioning of *Parnassus*, an allusion to Chigi's complex as much as it again invokes Raphael and his Vatican scene of the same subject. As discussed in the previous chapter, allusions to Parnassus

"A. Caracci." Cafà offers no explanation as to its presence, nor does she provide further reliable reference to support this attribution, so for the purposes of this examination it will be excluded from discussion as a relevant example of Peruzzi's work. The idea that Peruzzi deliberately quoted Sebastiano's painting in his designs for the Sala delle Prospettive is reinforced in the alteration of the figure's position from sketch to final fresco. The Walter sketch is imagined after a fragmentary *Statue of a Muse* (Dresden, Sculpturesammlung, Hm241) that is missing both arms and head. In the Walter image, Peruzzi rebuilds this figure as a contemplative, almost melancholic woman, her right elbow resting on her thigh as she lays her head on the back of her hand. In the Sala delle Prospettive fresco, the lower half of the figure stays true the organization seen in the drawing, yet the upper body has transformed into a near exact echo of Sebastiano's Venus in *Death of Adonis*.

14 K. Oberhuber, *Roma e lo Stile Classico di Raffaello* (Milan: Electa, 1999), 142; J.K.G. Shearman, "Alfonso D'Este's Camerino," in A. Chastel, ed. *"Il se Rendit en Italie": Études Offertes à André Chastel* (Paris: Elefante, 1987), 209–230. The version included in the Ashmolean collection (A97) and that attributed to Conrad Martin Metz (British, Museum, 1789) are two examples of such faithful copies.

15 As Cieri comments, preparatory sketches in the Louvre (Cabinet de Dessins, no. 592) confirm Peruzzi's hand in the design of this composition. (Cieri, 69).

16 Joannides, 171, no. 157*v*.

were often invoked as part of the humanist *vigna* for its ties with mythology and its prominence therein as both the home of the Muses and the sacred haven of Apollo, god of music and poetry.[17] By including a scene of Mount Helicon here, however, Peruzzi reinforced allusions to Parnassus while also carefully distinguishing his scene from it. Mount Helicon was considered in ancient sources the equivalent to Parnassus as the locale for poetic inspiration and divine dwelling as well as the site of the Hippocrene spring, born from the ground by Pegasus' stamping foot.[18] While equivalent in mythological connotations, representations of Mount Helicon had vanished since antiquity. Accordingly, Peruzzi's revival of the lost landmark is undoubtedly significant.

Added to this revival is another notable instance herein of an antique quotation, again in the form of two kneeling figures in the foreground. These male figures adopt a strikingly similar pose to that of the first century CE *L'Arrontino* that formed part of Chigi's antique collection. The kneeling figure to the left of the scene, next to the protrusion of the hearth and seemingly projecting from the wall with the careful extension of one knee beyond the implied picture plane, is perhaps the clearest copy of *L'Arrontino's* pose. The position of the legs and the outstretched arms both mimic the sculpture's organization exactly. The kneeling figure to the right of the composition also echoes *L'Arrontino*, albeit vaguely; however, the unusual placement of the figure immediately behind him serves a function similar to the mirrored river god seen in *Apollo and Daphne*. In other words, this pairing of figures presents two perspectives on this translation of the *L'Arrontino's* form, views one cannot overlook for here again the frontal figure's knee projects beyond the visual picture plane. This practice, in some regards, speaks to the act of reassembling and reanimating ancient sculpture, sixteenth-century practices indelibly linked to both archaeology and *all'antica* artistic expression. Peruzzi's imagery in *Parnassus* is important not only for its *all'antica* references but also for the parallels it drew with contemporary depictions through its blending of visual elements of both periods.

The final scene on the north wall is that of *The Triumph of Venus*, a vibrant maritime vignette that again simultaneously recalls both classical and contemporary sources. Most importantly, Peruzzi's design bears direct quotations of Raphael's *Galatea*, including the figure of the conch-blower at near center of the scene, the *cavallo marino*, at far right, and the flying putti overhead.[19] Thus, just as Raphael's *Galatea* serves as a unique intersection of elements both past

---

17 For more on this tradition, see: Stinger, 199; and Christian, *Empire*, 178–182.

18 Cieri, 70.

19 Cieri refers to only the conch-blower as "una chiara citazione dalla *Galatea* di Raffaello," (Ibid., 70), however these additional comparative elements are also clearly borrowed.

and present, Peruzzi's *Triumph of Venus* and arguably all his episodes on this north wall, if not the entire room, represent a similar anachronism. While borrowing across temporal zones, he is also a master pasticheur, piecing together iconographic symbolism with such finesse that he is able to convey not only the overarching propaganda for his patron but also an engagement with the other artists at work in the villa.

While Peruzzi expanded upon the visual references incorporated into this Sala delle Prospettive cycle in a seeming continuation of the practice seen in first years working for Chigi, the context of this exchange had changed decidedly. On the one hand, Peruzzi had grown in prestige since his early work at Chigi's villa. Vasari noted, for example, his commission from Pope Julius II to fresco his Vatican aviary in chiaroscuro scenes.[20] By the 1510s he also was involved with the charitable Confraternity of San Rocco and would eventually provide designs for their church renovations.[21] In addition, the success of his frescoes in the apse of Sant'Onofrio—executed with the assistance of Giovanni da Udine—had garnered him additional such projects, such as those for the nave San Pietro in Montorio.[22] Both Raphael and Peruzzi had also joined forces for the commission to complete the ceiling fresco at the Palazzo della Cancelleria. Known the *Volta Dorata* (1516–1518), for its quotations of the first-century CE Domus Aurea ceiling, the project exuded so seamless a merger of the two artist's styles that might be seen as the ultimate illustration of their like-mindedness.[23]

20 Vasari, *Lives*, I: 810.

21 For more on Peruzzi's connections with the Confraternity of San Rocco, see: V. Zanchettin, "Costruire nell'antico: Roma, Campo Marzio, 1508–1523: Peruzzi, al confraternità di San Rocco e i cantieri intorno al Mausoleo di Augusto." In C.L. Frommel, *Baldassarre Peruzzi, 1481–1536* (Venice: Marsilio, 2005), 123–153.

22 Huppert points out in the case of the Sant'Onofrio frescoes that "although debate continues about the roles that Peruzzi and Jacopo Ripanda played in the execution of these frescoes, a drawing by Peruzzi supports his involvement" (Ibid., 22). The drawing she mentions, depicting a group of sibyls, is discussed in: L. Testa, "Gli affreschi absidali della chiesa di Sant'Onofrio al Gianicolo: committenza, interpretazione ed attribuzione," *Storia dell'arte* 21 (1989), 171–186.

23 Achim Gnann has suggested that the project became a joint commission out of choice (A. Gnann, "Peruzzi oder Raphael? Zu den Entwürfen für die Fresken der *Volta Dorata* in der Cancelleria," in C.L. Frommel et al., eds., *Baldassarre Peruzzi 1481–1536* (Venice: Marsilio, 2005), 199–212). Gnann identified several sketches by Raphael's hand as pertaining to the designs for the *Volta Dorata*. Huppert reiterates this point: "while Raphael may have received the commission and initially conceived of the overall design, it was Peruzzi who carried out the work, instituting changes to Raphael's proposal as he went" (Huppert, "Peruzzi and Rome," 23).

Perhaps most importantly, though, by the time Peruzzi returned to Chigi's villa, he was also managing his own flourishing workshop, which has been considered by modern scholars as second only to that composed by Raphael.[24] No comprehensive documentation of the scope or members of Peruzzi's circle exists. It seems, though, that by 1517 this network was so well established that Peruzzi, while crucial to the inception of the Sala delle Prospettive, delegated most of its execution to his workshop.[25]

2 Raphael's Workshop Takes Form

Raphael, meanwhile, had been busy cultivating his workshop since the early years of the decade. For example, by the time he had completed work in the Stanza della Segnatura and turned his attentions to *Galatea*, he had also developed a collaborative relationship with engraver Marcantonio Raimondi as early as 1510.[26] As if he needed to expand his presence into the realm of printmaking, Raphael went so far as to create drawings, such as *The Judgment of Paris* (Fig. 15) and *Massacre of the Innocents* (1511–1512; Szépmûvészeti Múzeum, Budapest), that were destined for the express purpose of translation into print.[27]

---

24 K. Oberhuber, "Lo stile classico di Raffaello e la sua evoluzione a Roma fino al 1527," in K. Oberhuber, ed., *Roma e lo stile classico di Raffaello* (Milan: Electa, 1999), 20.

25 N. Dacos, "Ni Polidoro, ni Peruzzi: Maturino," *Revue de l'Art*, 57 (1982), 17; Cieri, "Sala delle Prospettive," 67; Peruzzi's authorship of the frieze was first suggested in by Förster (*Farnesina Studien*, 88) and subsequently reinforced by Crowe and Cavalcaselle (J.A. Crowe and G.B. Cavalcaselle, A *History of Painting in Italy, Umbria, Florence and Siena from the Second to the Sixteenth Century* (London: J. Murray, 1903–1914), 6: 19–20).

26 It was not long after that Raphael selected one of his entourage, Baviero de' Carocci (also known as Il Baviera) to oversee the replication and distribution of prints after Raphael's works, including the control of the plates made after his work. For more on Il Baviera, see: D. Landau and P.W. Parshall, *The Renaissance Print* (New Haven: Yale University Press, 1994), 121–122; Wolk-Simon, "Competition, Collaboration, and Specialization," 3.

27 No full preparatory drawing by Raphael of *The Judgment of Paris* has been discovered. Lisa Pon argued that Raphael employed printmaker's techniques in the use of counterproofs in some of his drawings, suggesting yet another means through which he was able to adopt the practices of another discipline into his own practice; for more, see: L. Pon, "Marcantonio and Raphael," *Print Quarterly*, 16 (4) (December 1999), 368–370. She also notes that Raphael would have had access to Raimondi's press installed in his home, however it seems equally plausible that Chigi might have also granted Raphael access to the press he had funded for Kallierges in Rome. For more on this press, see: S. Fogelmark, "The Anonymous Rome 1522 Chrysoloras: A Newly Discovered Greek Press." *The Papers of the Bibliographic Society of America*, 97 (1) (March 2003), 5–42.

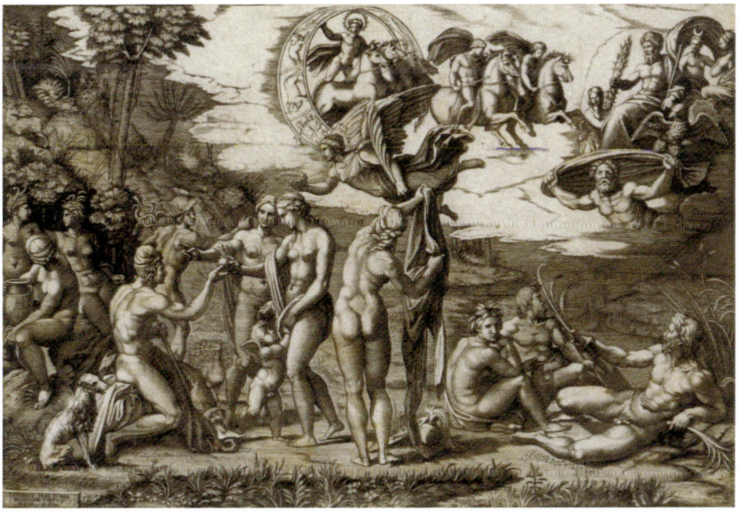

FIGURE 15 Marcantonio Raimondi (after Raphael), *The Judgment of Paris*, circa 1510–1520. Engraving; 29.1 by 43.7 cm
METROPOLITAN MUSEUM OF ART (PD)

Beyond such collaborative endeavors, Raphael was also building his workshop circle. Vasari shared that Giulio Pippi—later dubbed Giulio Romano for his Roman origins—was an early addition to Raphael's cohort and purportedly transformed rapidly into his closest associate.[28] Despite his young age—born in 1499, he was 16 years Raphael's junior—Romano was nevertheless most likely enlisted as Raphael's apprentice around 1510–1511 at a moment that Frommel romanticized thus: "when Pietro Pippi accompanied his young son to visit Raphael, the artist had just completed the *School of Athens*, which aroused great admiration if not without a certain fuss—nor would it be the last time for this precocious adolescent."[29] While this arrival in Raphael's orbit relies on some supposition, it is supported by the documentation of Romano's presence as working with Raphael in both the Vatican stanze and the frescoes of Chigi's villa not long after.[30]

---

28 "Among his many, or rather innumerable, disciples, the greater number of whom became able masters, Raffaello da Urbino had not one who imitated him more closely in manner, invention, design, and colouring, than did Giulio Romano" (Vasari, *Lives*, II: 118). Also see: E.H. Gombrich, "'Anticamente moderni e modernamente antichi'. Notes on the critical fortune of Giulio Romano, painter." In C. Frommel and R. Schofield, eds., *Giulio Romano* (UK: Cambridge University Press, 1998), 7.

29 C.L. Frommel, "The Roman works of Giulio," In C. Frommel and R. Schofield, eds., *Giulio Romano* (UK: Cambridge University Press, 1998), 56–57 (56–89).

30 His first documented work appeared in the dados scenes of the Stanza dell'Incendio in

Nearly simultaneous with Romano's arrival would have been both da Udine and Gianfrancesco Penni. Born in Friuli in the later 1480s or 1490s, Giovanni Nanni, later Giovanni da Udine, unfortunately, is not well preserved in biographic form. Though the details of da Udine's early life are vague, it is believed that he trained in Venice, perhaps in the studio of the elusive Giorgione, and arrived in Rome around 1510.[31] He was a strong addition to Raphael's workshop: only slightly younger than Raphael, da Udine was not only a master depicter of flora and fauna but also brought an expert understanding of the ancient art of stucco. Thus, he became an essential member of Raphael's entourage not only for his connections with the Venetian tradition but also for his eventual specialization in the art of grotteschi, a talent that Raphael could not surpass. Da Udine's first documented work in Rome, though, was the previously mentioned work with Peruzzi with the apse of Sant'Onofrio; he collaborated again with Peruzzi in the renovation of the chapel of Saint Helena in Santa Croce in Gerusalemme (1513). It was perhaps, as argued by Riccardo Averini, in theses spaces, and in collaboration with Peruzzi, that da Udine set himself on course to become a specialist in stucco.[32]

Penni, meanwhile, hailed from Florentine origins but fell into Raphael's orbit at a similarly young age as his colleague Romano.[33] Whereas Romano espoused a more passionate and dynamic compositional style, Penni absorbed an ordered refinement and, according to Vasari, "imitated in his drawings the manner of Raffaello, and never ceased to follow it."[34] While his first work for Raphael is not as clearly documented, Vasari notes that Penni helped with the development of the cartoons for Raphael's planned works at the Villa Farnesina, presumably for the Loggia Cupid and Psyche, later in the decade. Romano and Penni would become the backbone of Raphael's consort of artists, particularly in his capstone Loggia di Amore e Psiche at Chigi's villa, but they only begin the story of this cast of characters whose individual abilities

---

1514. A. Gnann, "Raphael's Workshop in Rome," 19; Hartt earlier identified Giulio Romano's earliest work—that for preparatory drawings for Raphael's tapestries—around 1515 (F. Hartt, *Giulio Romano* (NY: Hacker Art Books, 1981), I: 13), however Gérard-Julien Salvy has noted Giulio's presence in in Raphael's workshop as early as 1510–1511 (*Giulio Romano* (Paris: Éditions de la Lagune, 1994), 18).

31 Averini notes da Udine's notes that da Udine's departure from Venice was owed in part to the death of Giorgione (R. Averini, "Giovanni da Udine, inventore di grotteschi e Stucchi." *Studi Romani*, Anno V (1957), 37).

32 Averini, 38.

33 Gnann suggests that he might have joined Raphael in Rome as early as 1508. (Gnann, "Raphael's Workshop", 20).

34 Vasari, *Lives*, I: 819.

combined with a shared visual language of forms to dominate artistic expression in Rome in the years to come.

This workshop, which between 1510 and 1517 had blossomed into a powerhouse team of talents housed in Bramante's Palazzo Caprini, was, as previously mentioned, a place of equals wherein artists, though individually seeking acclaim, nevertheless shared ideas and techniques that were then infused into Raphael's commissions.[35] As Ray comments, with the advent of Raphael's radical workshop managerial style, "[Raphael] was no longer 'the master,' and students were not there simply 'to help'."[36] As time progressed and as Raphael became increasingly committed to projects, his workshop of artists assumed an increasingly larger role in his commissions. The aim of the remainder of this chapter, then, is to explore the projects of the final years of the 1510s where these workshop associates began to contribute more substantially to the brand that was Raphael. The goal here is not an exhaustive analysis of each space, but rather to highlight the hints throughout these projects of both the novelty in Raphael's oversight of this network and the ways in which these artists began to adopt the practice of a shared visual language. In other words, as Raphael granted these associates increasing levels of authority in commissions, it can be seen that each artist's works communicated with one another in a more seamless blend of references and narrative to convey the various elements of each elaborate visual program.

3 The Capstone of Chigi's Villa

Such an assessment of the workshop mentalities in these final years of Raphael's care might begin with a look to the final projects with which Raphael and Peruzzi were tasked at Chigi's villa that involved the planned pairing of an *all'antica* frescoed façade with the elaborately rendered Loggia di Amore e Psiche inside the entryway.[37] This juncture was a crucial one, as it marked

35 Shearman, "The Organization of Raphael's Workshop," 40.

36 Ray, "Il Volo di Icaro," 54. Talvacchia echoes a similar sentiment, stressing that this collaboration was a key factor in Raphael's artistic innovation (Talvacchia, *Raphael*, 186).

37 As Quinlan-McGrath comments: "in considering Chigi's motivations [for such banquets], it would seem that the main problem in portraying him as a social climber is that he had nowhere to climb. His only competition was the Vatican, and Leo X bankrupted it in three years, while Agostino was still going stronger than ever in 1519. The noble Roman families like the Colonna and Orsini were hard pressed to match his political power and wealth, and if he was in competition, it was probably only to outdo his own last extravaganza" (Quinlan-McGrath, "The Villa," 176).

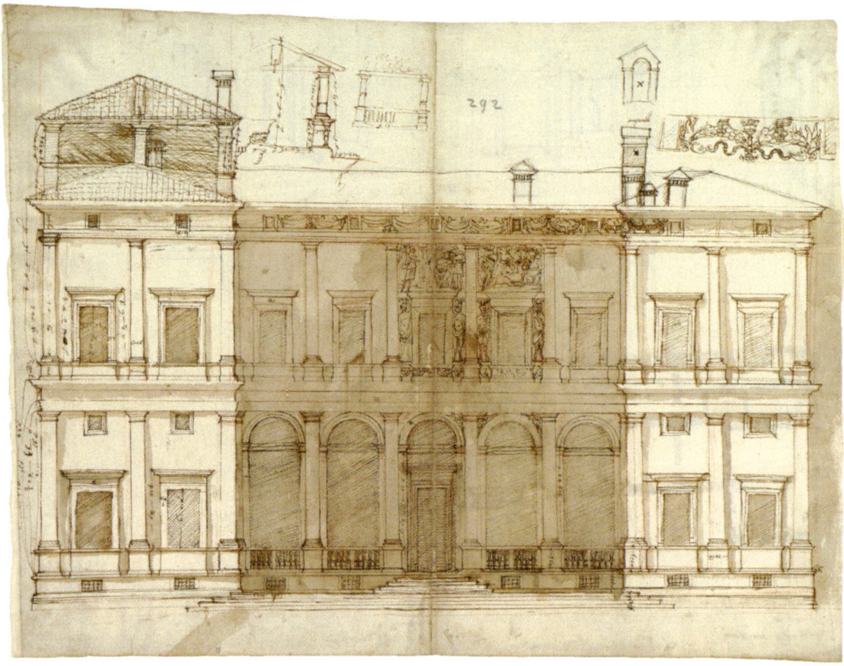

FIGURE 16 Anonymous (French), *Villa of Agostino Chigi*, early to mid-16th century. Dark brown ink, black chalk, and incised lines; 43.5 by 57 cm
METROPOLITAN MUSEUM OF ART (PD)

the capstone of work for Chigi for both Peruzzi—whose concepts for the façade decoration would have completed the illusion of his landmark *scaenae frons*—and Raphael, whose presence in the Loggia di Amore e Psiche was delegated primarily to the hands of Romano, Penni, and da Udine.[38] Given the rumored development of Peruzzi's workshop at this point, and also given that much of his Sala delle Prospettive, recall, had been completed by his workshop, it seems reasonable to propose that Peruzzi's workshop would have played a prominent role in the façade visual program, portions of which are intimated in an anony-

38 As Varoli-Piazza comments, "anche se affidata in gran parte ai suoi collaboratori, e seguendo i lavori molto da vicino" (R. Varoli-Piazza, "Un Esempio di Concinnitas," in Rosalia Varoli-Piazza, *Raffaello: La Loggia di Amore e Psiche all Farnesina* (Cinisello Balsamo, Milan: Silvana, 2002), 58). For a thorough examination of the flora and vegetation depicted in Giovanni da Udine's fictive pergola motifs, see: G. Caneva, *Il Mondo di Cerere nella Loggia di Psiche: Villa Farnesina, Sede dell'Accademia Nazionale dei Lincei* (Rome: Fratelli Palombi, 1992).

mous French sketch of Chigi's villa façade wherein two of the upper level bays have been adorned with quick narrative sketches (Fig. 16). At the very least, one could propose that both Polidoro di Caravaggio and Maturino aided Peruzzi, as the trio made a reputation around Rome for their frescoed façades. If this was indeed the case, these capstone projects might have served as the singular space in which this entire network was working together at the same time.[39]

While an extensive discussion of these planned programs is unnecessary as both were left incomplete, a brief mention of what was planned is merited as it illustrates how these teams of artists could so fluidly develop a visual program that united both interior and exterior spaces. The Loggia di Amore e Psiche (Fig. 17), loosely based on the story recounted in second century CE writer Apulieus' *The Golden Ass*, recounts in episodic form the trials and tribulations of the love affair between the mortal and the god. Originally envisioned as an all-encompassing visual program, what is seen today represents only the first stage of this program as executed primarily by Romano and da Udine. In sum, it consists of two central planes composed in *quadro riportato* that are surrounded by ten narrative spandrels and fourteen accompanying severies. Each of these spandrel scenes is divided by both floriated festoons and garlands that outline the architectural framework of the loggia and severies that depict various *putti* aloft with the attributes of various deities. Both of the two central ceiling panels are depicted as fictive tapestries shielding the viewer from an imagined sun, suggested only by the bits of blue sky that seep through at its seams. Together, these components retell the tale of Psyche, a maiden considered more striking than Venus herself. Throughout the cycle, Psyche experiences jealousy, deceit, and love on a prolonged quest to placate Venus and reunite with Cupid that culminates in a visit to Mount Olympus for a council in front of Jupiter and, in finale, her wedding to Cupid.

Though Leonardo Sellaio, associate of Michelangelo, belittled the room as a "shameful thing for a grand master," the Loggia di Amore e Psiche as produced by Romano and Penni was nevertheless remarkable for its *all'antica* revival of an antique narrative.[40] From its call upon classical models—*Psyche Borne to Olympus* (*Mercury and Psyche*), for example, has been noted by scholars for

39 Missing would be Perino del Vaga, however it is possible that he too was present as *Loves of the Gods* would appear in a print series he prepared under the patronage of Il Baviera in 1527. For more on this set of engravings, see: C.M. Burlingham, *Perino del Vaga's Designs for the Loves of the Gods* (M.A. Thesis, Oberlin College, 1980).

40 In a letter to Michelangelo dated 1 January 1518, Leonardo Sellaio quips that the loggia is a "chose vituperosa ad un gran maestro, peggio che l'ultima stanza del Palazzo assai." For more, see: P. D'Ancona, *Gli Affreschi della Farnesina in Roma* (Milan: Edizione del Milione, 1955).

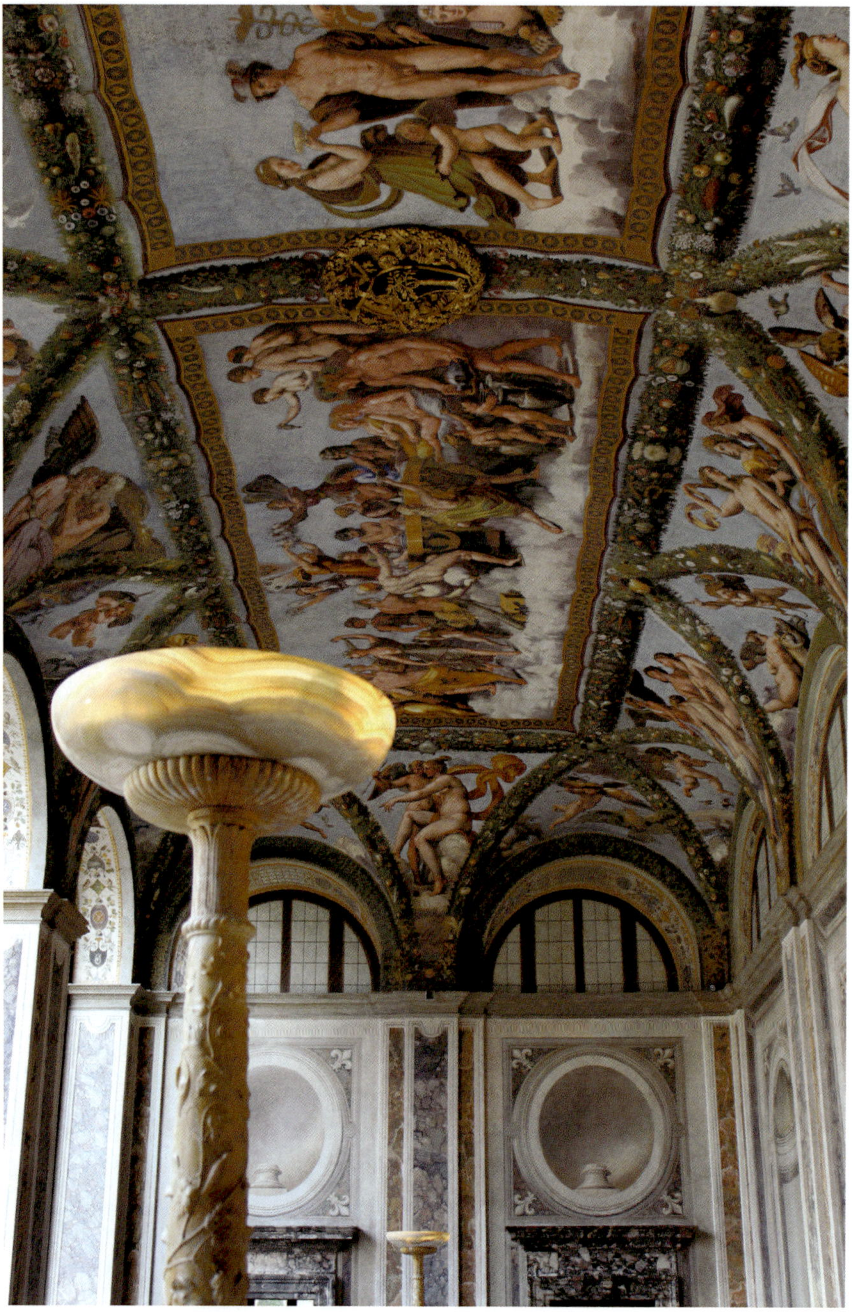

FIGURE 17 Loggia di Amore e Psiche
VILLA CHIGI (VILLA FARNESINA), ROME/ALAMY

its borrowing from wall paintings at the Domus Aurea and at Pompeii—to its compelling fictive pergola designed to appear as ethereal as the walls of a garden pergola adorned with variegated floriated festoons (and perhaps not that unlike the pergolated walkways of Chigi's gardens just outside), the imagery conjured by Romano and Penni revealed how carefully they had digested the forms and themes of antiquity.[41]

Though never completed, there is evidence to suggest that another narrative cycle was planned for the lower scenes as well. Had this lower portion been completed, one can imagine how it might have heightened the theatrical sensation of the space, as these lower registers would have been visible from the *scaenae frons* forecourt through the open archways of the loggia. From this perspective, they could be seen as another instance of recombination, not in that they borrowed visual elements from each other but rather because they would have required a blending of visual phrases from past and present into a harmonious whole that would function both from the vantage of the *scaenae frons* forecourt as well as inside the loggia.[42] With Raphael's mortal story of Psyche being revealed through the open archways of the entryway, the *scaenae frons* would ascend with Peruzzi's carefully curated imagery of the gods,

41 For more on the loggia's visual program, including some of the lunettes destroyed during Maratta's 1693 restoration, see: P. Letarouilly, "Vedute Prospettica dell'interno della loggia" *Édifices de Rome Moderne* (Paris, 1840–1857), tav. 102; Cherubino Alberti, "Loggia di Psiche," 1583, in S. Prosperi Valenti Rodinò, in *Raphael Invenit: Stampe da Raffaello nelle Collezione dell'Istituto Nazionale per a Grafica* (Rome: Edizione Quasar, 1985); F. Cappellati, "La storia di Psiche, il mito di Raffaello. In margine alla storia dei restauri antichi," in R. Varoli-Piazza, ed., *Raffaello La Loggia di Amore e Psiche alla Farnesina* (Milan: Silvana Editoriale, 2002), 45; N. Dorigny's *Favola di Amore e Psiche* (Rome: Istituto Nazionale per la Grafica, 1693). For more on connections to antique examples, see: Dussler, 98.

42 Nineteenth-century theorist Antoine Quatremère de Quincy who first noted the incomplete state of the loggia's decoration (A. Quatremère de Quincy, *History of the Life and Works of Raffaello*, trans. by W. Hazlitt from third Parisian edition (London: Bell and Daldy, 1869), 352). For more, see: Shearman, "Die Loggia der Psyche," 64–66; and Schwarzenberg, "Psychen-Statue," 110, 115, 118–119. J.K.G. Shearman, "Raphael's Unexecuted Projects," 158–180; Shearman, "Die Loggia der Psyche"; K. Oberhuber, *Raphaels Zeichnungen* (Berlin: Gebr. Mann Verlag, 1972); E. Steinman, "Amor und Psyche, ein Freskenzyklus aus der Schule Raffael's in der Engelsburg zu Rom," *Zeitschrift für Bildended Kunst* 13 (1902), 86–93; Hoogewoorf, 15; A. von Salis, *Antike und Renaissance: Über Nachleben und Weiterwirken der alten in der neueren Kunst* (Erlenbach-Zürich: E. Rentsch, 1947), 198–199; Quinlan-McGrath, "The Villa," 497–505. For a full discussion of proposed imagery for these lower registers of the loggia and how they related to the reconstructed plan for the façade frescoes, please see: A. Culotta, "The Dramatic Side of Breaking Bad: Raphael, Peruzzi, and a Remarkable Revival of Vitruvius' *Scaenae Frons*." In J.C. Fischer, ed., *Breaking with Convention in Italian Art* (UK: Cambridge Scholars Publishing, 2017), 48–71.

designed, as the astrological ceiling had been, to convey a complex visual message all conjured in visual harmony. What makes this continuity even more noteworthy is that it now included the voices of Raphael's burgeoning workshop members. Raphael need not worry that the integrity of works ascribed to him would suffer from his lessened presence; these associates were well-equipped to build on the visual language that Raphael provided, riffing on his motifs and using the same visual elements as had their mentor to create in exchange with Peruzzi one of the most revolutionary spaces of early sixteenth-century Rome.

The practice of borrowing form and recombining visual phrases became increasingly prevalent in the other projects at which Raphael's team was at work simultaneously. A look to the Stanza dell'Incendio (1514–1517); the Sala di Costantino (1514–1520); the Loggetta and Stuffetta of Cardinal Bernardo Dovizi Bibbiena (1516); the Sala dei Palafrenieri (1517); and the Vatican Loggie (1516–1519) can illustrate how this team consistently employed a similar means of compositional development that echoed Raphael's earlier instances of visual recombination. Just as at Chigi's villa, it is across these spaces that one can trace a slow transition of control: with Raphael taking on a growing number of commissions, he began to rely increasingly on his workshop artists. Given this, these spaces reveal how Raphael continued to imbue upon his workshop circle the importance of a shared artistic language as a sourcebook for compositional novelty.

4 The Stanza dell'Incendio

As approximate bookends to Raphael's work in the Vatican stanze, the Stanza della Segnatura and the Stanza dell'Incendio have received distinct scholarly receptions. Whereas the former chamber was hailed as a peak moment of Renaissance production, as noted earlier on, the latter, wherein workshop members played an increasingly important role, has been characterized as exhibiting a progressive degradation in skill in inverse relation to Raphael's presence.[43] Recent scholars have worked to re-exalt this later room as an impor-

43 As many scholars have pointed to, this language is perhaps at its most harsh in the analysis by Frederick Hartt, who uses terms such as "disharmony" and "disturbing dualism" to describe the titular frame, *Fire in the Borgo*, ultimately concluding "that Raphael himself could have been responsible for it is unthinkable." F. Hartt, "Raphael and Giulio Romano: With Notes on the Raphael School." *The Art Bulletin* 26, no. 2 (1944), 70. This discounting

tant space of artistic exchange, a status to be expanded upon here by situating this chamber's imagery within the context of Raphael's workshop. By reexamining the way in which these decorated chambers can be seen as spaces to both inform and collaborate, one can trace the enduring nature of Raphaelesque language among his workshop participants, not solely as a symbol of their indebtedness to the artist, but rather as a suggestion of their innate abilities to extend Raphael's vision through collaboration, recombination, and innovation.

Though work commenced within the Stanza del'Incendio only a few years following the Stanza della Segnatura's completion, the dynamics of both the papacy and those of Raphael's working relationships had changed. Recall that Pope Julius II, the original patron of Raphael's Vatican projects, died in February of 1513 and left final design decisions for this space to be determined by his successor, Pope Leo X. While much of Pope Julius' legacy remained—Nesselrath's report on late twentieth-century restorations of the chamber, for example, noted the enduring presence of Julius' *imprese* (the acorn) flanking *Fire in the Borgo* (Fig. 18)—it is clear that Leo played a substantial role in these selected images, as all four commemorate Leos of the past alongside members of the Medici family to further exalt his own papacy.[44] From *Fire in the Borgo*, which commemorates Pope Leo IV's miraculous cessation of a fire raging in the Borgo neighborhood in the ninth century, the following scene depicts the *Coronation of Charlemagne*, when Pope Leo III officially dubbed Charlemagne the Holy Roman Emperor in 800. Adjacent is the *Oath of Leo III*, which depicts the purification of Pope Leo III at Saint Peter's altar; and finally, the *Battle at Ostia* appears, showcasing Pope Leo IV's naval victory over the Saracens in 849 CE.

Acts of recombination are immediately visible in *Fire in the Borgo*. In her 2010 article, for example, Patricia Reilly reinterpreted the pastiche of references therein—all of which she attributed to Raphael—as a sort of visual treatise that proclaimed Raphael's critique of Michelangelo through a somewhat exag-

of these works remained the standard for many years and perhaps has hampered deeper analysis of this imagery. Hartt's analysis ascribed much of the authorship to Raphael's lead disciple, Giulio Romano, though later analysis by Joannides suggests Gianfrancesco Penni played a role at least in *The Coronation of Charlemagne*; regardless, we can be certain that, though he may have been the chief designer, Raphael was not alone in the creation of these four frescoes.

44 A. Nesselrath, "Art-Historical Findings during the Restoration of the Stanza Dell'Incendio." *Master Drawings*, 30 (1) (1992), 33. Frommel notes that the remaining images by Perugino recall the room's past legacy (C.L. Frommel, *Raffaello: Le Stanze*, 55).

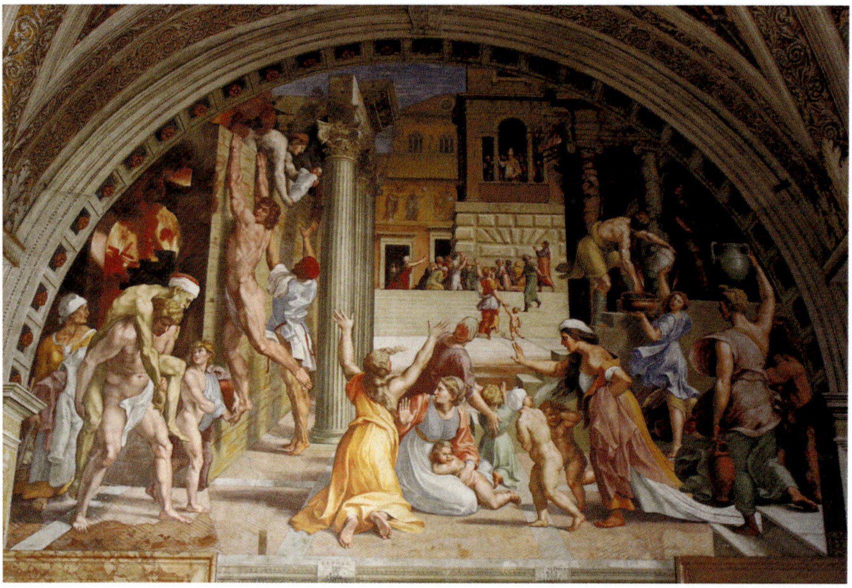

FIGURE 18 Raphael, Giulio Romano, and Gianfrancesco Penni, *Fire in the Borgo*, 1514–1517; Fresco; 670 cm
STANZA DELL'INCENDIO, VATICAN PALACE (PD)

gerated contrast of excess versus decorum. The tension, as Reilly noted, seems to align in direct parallel to the writings of Pietro Bembo: "when considered in light of Bembo's dictate that poets should be judged on 'how much *piacevolezza* and how much *gravità* they have created and distributed throughout their compositions,' Raphael's *Fire in the Borgo* can be seen as a demonstration of his ability to do just that in pictorial form."[45] This interpretation allows for a powerful update to the messaging of this space, which, like the Stanza della Segnatura, was targeting the delight of the patron and his consort.[46]

At the same time, however, this means of compositional development can be seen as an extension or continuation of what Raphael had accomplished several years prior in the Stanza della Segnatura. There, recall, Raphael selected several figures from Michelangelo's emerging imagery for the Sistine ceiling and repurposed them into his scene of *Parnassus*, perhaps in critique but

45 Reilly, "Raphael's 'Fire in the Borgo,'" 317.

46 As Reilly concludes, "such a send-up as this would have been wholeheartedly appreciated by the elite group of courtiers that regularly dined with Leo in front of this work" ("Raphael's 'Fire in the Borgo,'" 318). This point has been furthered in Christoph Frommel's most recent analysis of the space, which highlights the celebration of the Medici family alongside "desired piety" that occurs across the room's compositions (Frommel, "La Stanza dell'Incendio di Borgo," 66).

also perhaps as part of his growth in his visual lexicon. At the same time he borrowed from rival Michelangelo, he also collaborated through close consultations with Inghirami to conjure the essential narratives and with Lotto for the creation of *Jurisprudence*. Regardless of the exact nature of ideological exchange, what this connection showcases is that even at the outset of his various Vatican projects, Raphael embraced a strikingly collaborative mode for compositional development.

Returning to *Fire in the Borgo*, it would seem that Raphael had further grown this visual language into a decidedly more comprehensive riff, one that involves a direct assembly of visual reference that can, as Reilly argued, be seen as a critic on Michelangelo. Simultaneous, though, might also have been a bold statement on working practice. In other words, Raphael might have been encapsulating his style here not only as means to delight Pope Leo and his humanist colleagues, but also as symbol of the similar, collaborative blend of references that Raphael encouraged in the working relationships with his students. Thus, whereas his work in the Segnatura could be positioned in part as celebrating his own accomplishments, perhaps the Stanza dell'Incendio was envisioned as a testament to the spirit of collaborative engagement, the recombination of multiple sources, and transition of control from Raphael to his workshop participants, namely Romano and Penni, both of whom have been credited with a substantial amount of work in the chamber.

Scholarly consensus suggests that Raphael's major physical contributions to this chamber ended after *Fire in the Borgo*. Since he still proved important in the design of both *Battle at Ostia* and *The Coronation of Charlemagne* but left most of the work to his colleagues (little evidence links Raphael's designs to the final version of *The Oath of Leo III*), one can look more closely at these two compositions and consider whether they echo a set of complicated visual messages similar to those presented in *Fire in the Borgo*.

One can examine first how this might occur in *The Coronation of Charlemagne* (Fig. 19), where evidence suggests that Raphael worked more closely with his workshop colleagues in the compositional development. Positioned immediately adjacent to *Fire in the Borgo*, here rows of bishops and cardinals dutifully watch as Charlemagne is crowned the First Holy Roman Emperor by Pope Leo III in the year 800. One can note, however, the conspicuous bishop who, seated in the crowd attending the coronation, looks not at the proceedings but rather across the room at *Fire in the Borgo*. Raphael's preparatory sketches tell us that he was the inventor of this distracted bishop, which suggests that he wanted a visual device to pull the eye back to the *Borgo*.

This fits within the previously mentioned messaging of the room in terms of the admiration of the pope's accomplishments—in other words, if the viewer's

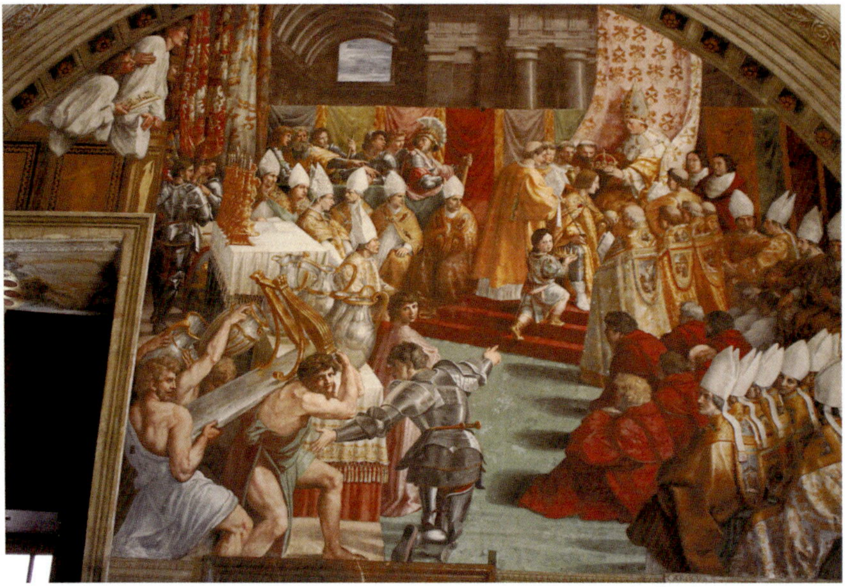

FIGURE 19 Detail, Giulio Romano, Gianfrancesco Penni, and Polidoro da Caravaggio, *Coronation of Charlemagne*, 1516–1517. Fresco; 670 cm
VATICAN PALACE—AUTHOR'S IMAGE

eye is somehow pulled away from the *Fire in the Borgo* this returns them to it—but it can also be seen as means of connecting the two compositions and perhaps suggesting that the same recombination or pastiche of elements seen in *Fire in the Borgo* are also happening there. While arguably not as dynamic an assembly of motifs as *Fire in the Borgo, The Coronation* nevertheless offers a physical pastiche of styles as it reflects the work of Raphael alongside Romano and Penni. One can also see a small play with compositional space: the scene's *modello* (circa 1516–1517; held by the Querini Stampalia, Venice), most often attributed to Penni, reveals a more dedicated study of architecture, perhaps to suggest the interior of Saint Peter's Basilica as would be typical of the narrative. In the final version, however, this classical architecture is obscured by an extended drapery that visually bisects the space to play with midground and background while also affording the opportunity to pack additional figures into the distant reaches. This play of space is reinforced by the foreground figure in armor who gestures boldly through the central void of the composition to nearly touch the foot of the young crown bearer (commonly identified as Ippolito de Medici).

A similarly inventive exchange occurs in *The Battle at Ostia* (Fig. 20), wherein the impetus of creation fell more directly on these workshop members and thus reflects an even more dynamic assembly of references. Carmen Bambach, for

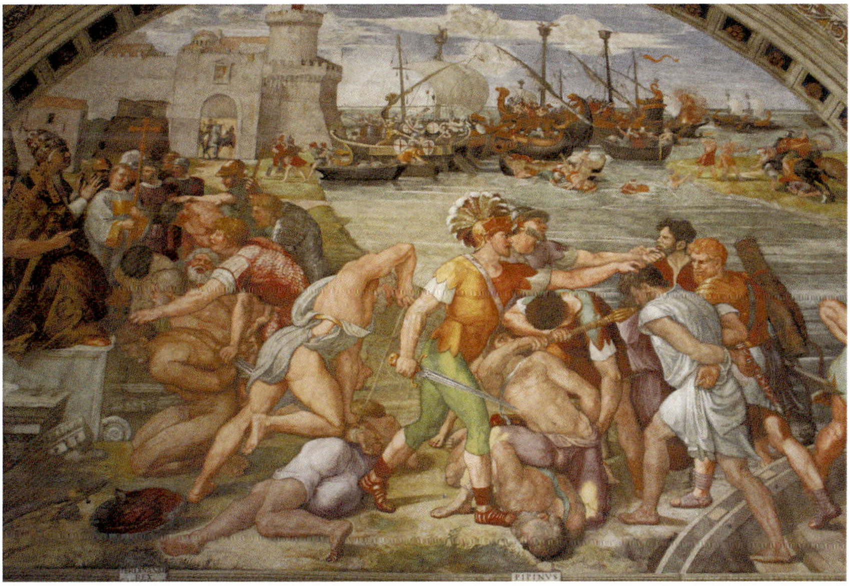

FIGURE 20 Giulio Romano, Gianfrancesco Penni, and Polidoro da Caravaggio, *Battle of Ostia*, 1516–1517. Fresco; 670 cm
VATICAN PALACE—AUTHOR'S IMAGE

example, has noted the indebtedness to Leonardo in this composition's design, suggesting specific parallels to the preparatory drawings for the Florentine *Battle of Anghiari* (1505–1508).[47] Leonardo had proven to be one of Raphael's key sources during the early days of his developing visual language, so the incorporation of such quotations here could be for several reasons. One that seems particularly likely, given the fact that this work was mostly the creation of his workshop members, is that they too were returning to the sources from which Raphael had drawn his earlier inspiration. Whether this study occurred organically or was prompted by Raphael's suggestion, it can be seen as illustrating how this practice of borrowing visual elements and recombining them was passed between artists.

Expanding from Bambach's observations, it seems that these workshop artists also continued in *The Battle at Ostia* (Fig. 20) the play on Michelangelo's work that Raphael had commenced in *Fire in the Borgo*. Beyond Shearman's observation that the layout of the composition draws direct parallels to Michelangelo's scene of *The Flood* from the Sistine ceiling, one can also note that many of these figures are inspired by Michelangelo's designs. To return to

47 C. Bambach, "Leonardo and Raphael in Rome in 1513–1516." *Late Raphael*, 30.

Reilly's analysis momentarily, she notes that the elongated and overextended male nude that dangles in *Fire in the Borgo* bears potential compositional connections with Michelangelo's rendition of Haman. If one looks to the additional pendentive motifs depicted in Michelangelo's ceiling, namely the adjacent *The Brazen Serpent* and the directly opposite *David and Goliath*, one can note parallels with several figures that appear in this Ostia scene. What this suggests is that perhaps, freed from a more formal management in the development of *The Coronation of Charlemagne*, these workshop artists relied on the recombinative inventiveness that Raphael had used in the same space for *Fire in the Borgo*.

It is important to note that *The Battle at Ostia* also incorporated references to Raphael. Such connections can be gleaned particularly in comparison with Raphael's earlier sketches by the artist of teams of battling figures. Drawings such as *Battle Scene with Prisoners* (circa 1507–1508; Ashmolean 538), *Two Nude Men* (circa 1507–1508; British Museum); and *Battle of Nude Youths* (circa 1513; Fitzwilliam Museum), all of which are tied to Raphael (save for *Battle of Nude Youths*, which has been alternately attributed to Giulio), reveal an array of characters that seem to align with the mass of humanity that dominates the conflict in *The Battle at Ostia*. What is interesting to note, though, in comparing these drawings to the finished fresco, is that while some figures are replicated rather identically, others give the impression or bear echoes of those in drawn form. What this underscores—perhaps one of the most important takeaways here—is that workshop members Romano and Penni were clearly not just copying Raphael's drawings. As the surviving visual evidence suggests, they had already by this point developed the ability to pick and choose points of visual reference, riffing as they pleased on the styles of their predecessors, their contemporaries, and their own mentor.

Raphael might not have known that his physical presence in the Vatican stanze was coming to an end—even a genius could not foresee his own death—but he was nevertheless perhaps already planning to entrust the remaining frescoes into the hands of his workshop so that he could turn his attention to the multitude of commissions still awaiting his attention. If this were true, it seems plausible that he is in some ways tailoring *The Fire in the Borgo* as a reminder for the need of inventiveness on the part of his workshop. Following this line of thought, it would seem that *The Coronation of Charlemagne* and *The Battle at Ostia* could be positioned as equal statements on the part of Raphael's workshop associates as to the reception and mastery of the exact practice Raphael had perfect during his Roman career and that would continue through his workshop members for years to come.

5 The Vatican Loggie

Part of the reason for Raphael's delegation of duties in the Stanza dell'Incendio was that he was also working on other spaces in nearby chambers. Such was the nature of Raphael's demands that, as Paul Joannides noted in his account of the relationship between Raphael and da Udine in the latter years of the former's life: "in the years 1516–19, Raphael also practiced another form of collaboration, that of partial subcontracting."[48] What is intriguing is that in a space like the loggie one can note that Raphael gives da Udine an incredible amount of authority. It is possible that Raphael recognized Giovanni's abilities in the art of stucco surpassed his own talents or artistic bandwidth; regardless, da Udine's study of ancient stucco work made him a master of his generation. He had put these skills to use for his earlier contributions to Vatican projects: Raphael had tasked him with elements of the Loggetta and Stuffetta of Cardinal Bibbiena (1516–1517) as well as work alongside Perino del Vaga in the Sala dei Pontifici and a large frieze in the Sala dei Palafrenieri (1517), but what seems noteworthy in the Vatican Loggie project is that Raphael and da Udine seemingly collaborated so closely with one another.[49]

Originally designed by Donato Bramante as the linkage between the pontifical palace and the Belvedere, the tri-level portico became a crowning glory of the already elaborate Vatican visual program. The first two levels bore decorations, and each scheme was scaled to each space's importance and use: while the ground level, accessible to many, included more simple decorations, the second loggia, that reserved for the more private navigations of the pope himself and alternately known as "Raphael's Loggia," was described by Baldassarre Castiglione in summer of 1519 as being "as beautiful as possible."[50] Adorned with more than 50 narrative vignettes stretched across 13 vaults, the innovative visual program would have been accompanied by examples of Classical sculpture. This collection of antiquities included a representation of Mercury and of Diana of Ephesus, who bore connotations in the day as a symbolic rep-

48 Joannides, *The Drawings of Raphael*, 25.

49 Both Perino and Giovanni had assumed control of the work in the Sala dei Pontifici following Raphael's death. For more on this transfer, see. N. Dacos and C. Furlan, *Giovanni da Udine 1487–1561* (Friuli-Venezia Giulia: Cassamassima 1987), 101.

50 Golzio, 100; Shearman, *Raphael in Early Modern Sources*, I: 459–460. The fact that the two upper levels of this triple-tier portico were reserved for the pope is recorded by Marcantonio Michiel, whose visited the space in December 1519 and noted the completion of the ground level decorated primarily by Giovanni da Udine's stucchi. For more, see: Golzio, 104; Both Perino and da Udine had assumed control of the work in the Sala dei Pontifici following Raphael's death.

resentation of Nature.[51] Adding to this elegant interior was a floor originally also lavishly laid with vibrant tiles from the workshops of Luca della Robbia. These have since been replaced, as exposure to the elements erased some portions of the loggia's decorations, but the space nevertheless still tells the story of Raphael's working process and the authority of his associates like Giovanni da Udine in that process.

Given that Bramante's inspiration in the loggia's architecture derived from ancient structures like the Tabularium and the Septizonium, Raphael followed suit by designing a space that recalled antiquity in its design. As Dacos has noted, Raphael punctuated the loggia's interior with the articulated engaged arches that served to subdivide the space into a series of bays capped with vaults recalling ancient ideals yet also filled with Biblical imagery.[52] Just as he had done at Chigi's villa, however, Raphael also makes reference to Peruzzi in the manner in which he subdivided these loggia vaults, which recalled the visual scaffolding of the ceiling in the Loggia di Galatea.[53] A look to Vault XI, however, which depicts scenes from the life of Moses, also seems to imply a play of perspective and a hint of trompe-l'oeil elevation that Peruzzi had so spectacularly incorporated into his Sala delle Prospettive.

Joannides notes only two preparatory drawing by Raphael's hand that survive. The first of these is a *modello* depicting *Moses Receiving the Tablets of the Law* (Paris, Louvre, 3849; Joannides, no. 389). Such a clear preparation for a work to be executed by a student would be customary in a conventional workshop space, however it is clear, looking to the additional surviving drawing, that Raphael was here allowing substantial artistic license. The second work is a small black chalk drawing depicting *David and Goliath* (Albertina, Bd. VII, 178; Joannides, no. 390). A look to this work reveals substantial reworking overtime, and it is also noteworthy as it lays out the figures but little else in the scene. Joannides suggests that this was owed to the fact that "Raphael, who, Vasari says, prepared all the histories for the Loggia, designed only the key figures in the scenes, and left his pupils to complete the compositions more or less

51 The sculpture of Mercury is noted in by Paolo Giovio (Golzio, 194; Shearman, *Raphael in Early Modern Sources*, I: 884–886). It was Marcantonio Michiel who noted the second figure as "una idea della Natura quale è la statua della loggia, con duoi cani appresso" (Shearman, *Raphael in Early Modern Sources*, I 1519/41, 450–460). For more, see: J. Fletcher, "Marcantonio Michiel: His Friends and Collection." *The Burlington Magazine*, 123 (1981), 453–467. Diana of Ephesus also features prominently in the frescoed decorations of the room.

52 N. Dacos, *The Loggia of Raphael: A Vatican Art Treasure*, trans. Josephine Bacon (New York: Abbeville Press Publishers, 2008), 20; For more, see: J. Daley, "The Vault Decoration of Raphael's Loggie" (PhD diss., New York University, 1962).

53 For more, see: Dacos, *The Loggia of Raphael*, 20.

independently."[54] In other words, this drawing serves as visual evidence that Raphael was entrusting his workshop members to employ their own abilities as artists to blend and combine the various elements of each frame.

Most assuredly, Raphael tasked the various stucco reliefs of the Loggia to da Udine, who was allowed relative freedom to choose his subjects. These additions, which serve to frame the room along the intrados and within the severies, also play with the illusion of surface throughout the loggia's bays, as occasional stucco panels appear inset within the painted grotesques. For many of these scenes, it would seem that da Udine looked to the stories of Bacchus, as Dacos has noted that several of his figures are borrowed from the *Indian Triumph of Bacchus* sarcophagus relief (second century CE; Palazzo Rospligiosi, Rome) and the *Triumph of Bacchus and Ariadne* alongside representations of other various divinities.[55] Beyond Classical references, quotations of more contemporary narrative and figures abound. A roundel relief, for example, near one of the loggia's central pilasters retells a scene from the story of sixth-century Roman king Mucius Scaevola, which was based on a contemporary plaquette attributed to Melioli.[56] Nearby is a panel depicting the elephant Hanno, who had come to Rome in 1514 in celebration of Pope Leo X's ascendance to the papacy but whose death soon after resulted in a monument erected to the animal in the Vatican gardens.

Though most of the preliminary designs for the room were penned by Raphael, da Udine was given exclusive control in the space, and it would seem that recombination of various elements—alluding to developing conversations between styles both past and present—was crucial to his contributions to the Stuffetta and the Loggetta.[57] Building on the concept of emulating an ancient Roman calidarium, da Udine garnered inspiration for this set of rooms from antiquity: in addition to sourcing motifs from a previous visit to newly unearthed ancient painted rooms near San Pietro in Vincoli,[58] he also

---

54 Joannides, *The Drawing of Raphael*, 112.

55 N. Dacos, *Le Logge di Raffaello, Maestro e bottega di fronte all'antico* (Rome: Istituto poligrafico e zecco del Stato, Libraria dello Stato, 1986), 238; the sarcophagus relief is documented in P.P. Bober and Rubenstein, 1986, no. 77. It is important to note that Giovanni da Udine most likely contracted the assistance of Lorenzetto and Giorgio di Giovanni to create the breadth of these stucco scenes. For more on the attributions of individual panels, see: Dacos, *The Loggia of Raphael*.

56 For more on this bronze plaquette, see: Dacos, *Le Logge di Raffaello*.

57 R. de Campos, "La Stufetta del Cardinal Bibbiena in Vaticano e il suo restauro." *Römisches Jahrbuch für Kunstgeschichte*, 20 (1983), 221–240; Dacos and Furlan.

58 Vasari mentions their visit to these well-preserved rooms as highly inspirational, yet the date of this visit is uncertain. Dating of this work is confirmed by a letter sent to Bembo

incorporated classisizing elements from the submerged Volta Dorata of Nero's famed palace. The result was, according to Jones and Penny, immediately reminiscent of an ancient Roman interior.[59] In other words, Udine recalled these ancient phrases with such affinity, and interspersed them with what Natsumi Nonaka described as "a painted menagerie with a classicizing twist,"[60] that this stuffetta project can be seen as showcasing Udine's parallel alignment with Raphael's approach to compositional innovation.

The same level of oversight was granted Giovanni in the nearby Loggetta, which again reveals a careful study of ancient spaces but also bears signifiers of invention. Dacos described it as "a total reinvention of Roman ornamentation, modernized in the blink of an eye," which reinforces the extent to which Raphael and his workshop artists had studied and digested the ideals of antiquity.[61] It also indicates that as these workshop artists like Giovanni da Udine began to assume greater control over projects, they nevertheless continued to embody a shared vision that involved the artful recombination of motifs. Here ancient meets modern in a captivating manner made possible by Giovanni da Udine: while embodying the ancient style of fresco embellishments known as *compendiaria*, which involved direct drawing unto plaster (rather than by careful preparation through cartoons, pouncing, and underdrawing), he served as the central catalyst of this modernization of which Dacos speaks.

6 Sala di Costantino

While Raphael played a documented role in the creation of the imagery in the Sala dell'Incendio, the extent to which he contributed to the final "room," the Sala di Costantino, is even more debatable. This room was situated at the nexus of several of the spaces with which Raphael had been tasked within the Vatican apartment—one could enter the Stanza d'Eliodoro to the west; to the north, one had access to the Vatican Loggie—and it was designed to

---

from Raphael on 19 April 1516 that suggests the work was only in its design phases; another letter, this time sent form Bembo to the Cardinal, notes the completion of the stuffetta in June of that year. For both see: Golzio, 43–44 and 48; Shearman, *Raphael in Early Modern Sources*, 1516/8, 240–243 and 1516/16, 252.

59 According to Jones and Penny, these chambers for Cardinal Bibbiena were "the earliest surviving rooms to be created in modern Europe which can be mistaken, even by expert eyes, for decorations of the early Roman Empire" (Jones and Penny, 192).

60 N. Nonaka, *Renaissance Porticoes and Painted Pergolas: Nature and Culture in Early Modern Italy* (NY: Routledge, 2017), 55.

61 Dacos, *The Loggia of Raphael*, 33.

showcase key moments from the life of Constantine: *The Battle of Milvian Bridge* on the southern wall; *The Adlocutio of Constantine* (*The Vision of the True Cross*) to the east; *The Donation of Constantine* and *The Baptism of Constantine*.[62]

Though the commission for this space was awarded in 1514, early work lagged, such that by the time of Raphael's death the room existed primarily in sketch form with only a few portions frescoed. Most scholars agree that, while Raphael developed the concepts for the room's overall visual program, Romano and Penni played a very large role in the room's actual creation, although it is not certain that this was the case.[63] Some have noted the letter authored by Sebastiano del Piombo that criticized the fact that his workshop members had in their possession drawings from Raphael from which they were to conjure their own designs.[64]

Perhaps as reinforcement to Sebastiano's charges, the examination of the surviving preparatory sketches for these compositions reveals evidence of this invention on the part of these workshop members. Joannides' analysis identifies two surviving drawings relating to *The Adlocutio of Constantine*—a sheet depicting an *Advancing Soldier* (Uffizi 542E; Joannides, no. 444*r*) by Raphael and an *Adlocutio* compositional study assigned to Penni (Chatsworth 175; Joannides, no. 445). In the case of this first drawing, one can note the same strategy as seen in examples such as the previously mentioned *David and Goliath*: though the details of the figure are clearly delineated, Raphael leaves the setting and context in the hand of Penni. In the case of the second compositional study, arguably authored by Penni, one finds a complete scene, but it is one that differs from the final wall design.

As Joannides notes: "in the fresco the right-hand group was placed in the background, and many other changes and insertions were made which clearly demonstrate how quickly Raphael's school diverged from his conception after his death."[65] It is true that numerous deviations from this sketch occur, including the addition of armor or other adjustments to the dress of some of the figures; the addition of the elaborate row of tents that appear behind the figure of Constantine and extend backward into the scene; and the prominent golden eagle aloft among the other Roman standards that dot the crowd. Rather

62 As Rolf Quednau notes, under Pope Leo X these spaces were to be redesigned and redecorated to reflect their locus as the "aulae pontificum" (Quednau, 26). For more, see: R. Quednau, *Die Sala di Costantino im Vatikanischen Palast* (NY: Georg Olms Verlag, 1979).

63 Joannides, *The Drawings of Raphael*, 26.

64 Letter documented in: Golzio, 132.

65 Joannides, *The Drawings of Raphael*, 244.

than seeing this as an abandonment of Raphael's ideas, as Joannides' phrasing implies, it would seem instead to be exactly the sort of inventiveness that Raphael encouraged among his workshop artists. A similar argument can be made in light of Laura Giles' recent connection between a sketch of an upraised hand in the collection of the Art Institute of Chicago.[66] She proposes that this hand was rendered by Raphael in preparation for the depiction of Saint Peter in the Sala di Costantino, yet it leaves ample room for Giulio Romano, the artist who completed this figure, to proceed as he wished.

7 Beyond the Vatican

Raphael's sudden death on 6 April 1520 was a shock to all and in many ways foreshadowed the impending demise of artistic *largesse* that defined the first decades of the *cinquecento*. In addition to the large number of unfinished and unrealized projects that remained following his sudden passing, though, Raphael also left behind a circle of artists who, as has been shown in these previous pages, had developed their own ability to select motifs or phrases from masters past and recombine them into dynamic new works. In short, he had passed on to this circle his visual lexicon and the ability to quote, to riff, to repeat in a manner that still bore a sense of originality, and they had absorbed these skills just as he had done in earlier years.

While the examples noted here showcase this inheritance among the workshop artists, the use of this visual language can be traced well beyond Raphael's lifetime. In addition to the conclusion of these Vatican commissions, the team of artists that once comprised Raphael's workshop embarked on even more projects in which they demonstrated this working process. Upon Raphael's death, Romano stepped up, as did Penni, as the guiding forces for remaining workshop members.[67] In addition to teaming up with Giovanni da Udine for the plans for the Villa Madama, Romano also stepped in as Raphael's replacement for several projects, realizing, for example, the Palazzo Missini Ossoli (1519–1520) and seeing the Palazzo Alberini to completion in 1521.[68]

66 For more on this drawing, see: L.M. Giles, "A Drawing by Raphael for the Sala di Costantino." *Master Drawings*, 37 (2) (Summer, 1999), 156–164.

67 Hartt presumed that Penni played a minor role: "given the apparent weakness of Penni's personality, it can be assumed that the controlling voice was exercised by Giulio" (Hartt, *Giulio Romano*, I: 37).

68 For more on the designs for the Palazzo Missini Ossoli, see: C. Frommel, *Der römische Palastbau*, I: 137 ff. and 164; II: 251 ff.; III: 105 ff.

He also worked very closely with Penni. For example, the duo orchestrated the purchase of the Ciampolini collection of antiquities in September 1520 to further their joint study of antiquity, a practice that had been encouraged during Raphael's lifetime.[69] Their completion of the work in the Sala di Costantino between 1520 and 1524 followed the preliminary plans of Raphael.[70] Completion of this commission was a landmark, as the duo had been forced to wrest the project away from potential theft by Michelangelo and Sebastiano del Piombo.[71]

At the same time they completed Raphael's outstanding commissions for the Massimi Chapel at Santa Trinità ai Monti, Penni and Romano also collaborated on *The Coronation of the Virgin* (*Madonna of Monteluce*) (c. 1523; Pinacoteca Vaticana) (Fig. 21), a commission originally requested from Raphael by the nuns of the Monteluce convent in 1503.[72] This collaborative endeavor represented quite literally the joining of two artists' works: the Assumption (depicted in the lower half) and the Coronation (envisioned above), which were painted by Romano and Penni, respectively, and then merged together.[73] Taken in sum, Romano and Penni's creation becomes strikingly similar to Raphael's *Oddi Altarpiece* (*The Coronation of the Virgin*), between 1502–1504. This autograph work, commissioned by the Oddi family for the Church of San Francesco al Prato in Perugia, was perhaps the source of inspiration for the Monteluce nuns' commission.[74] This is noteworthy because, in addition to scholarship suggesting

69 R. Lanciani, "La Raccolta antiquaria di Giovanni Ciampolini," *Bolletino della Commissione archaeologica communale di Roma*, 27 (1899), 101–115.

70 After being tasked with the completion of this cycle, Giulio and Penni continued work through 1524, pausing briefly during the reign of Pope Hadrian VI (1522–1523); payments for this work were recorded between February 1524 and July 1525 (as noted in the brief chronology included in C. Frommel and R. Schofield, *Giulio Romano* (UK: Cambridge University Press, 1998), 329).

71 Gnann, "Raphael's Workshop," 20.

72 For more, see: F. Mancinelli, "Restauri in Vaticano in occasione del centenario raffaellesco." In M.S. Hamoud and M.L. Strocchi, *Studi su Raffaello* (Urbino: QuattroVenti, 1987), 481. The contract for this painting's completion is dated June 1523 (as noted in the brief chronology included in C. Frommel and R. Schofield, *Giulio Romano*, 328). For more on the Massimi Chapel, see: J.A. Gere, "Two Fresco Cycles by Perino del Vaga: The Massimi Chapel and the Saola Paolina." *The Burlington Magazine* 102 (682) (Jan., 1960), 8–17 and 19; C.L.C.E. Whitcombe, "The Chapel of the Courtesan and the Quarrel of the Magdalens." *The Art Bulletin*, 84 (2) (Jun., 2002), 273–292.

73 Mancinelli, "Restauri," 482–483.

74 Fabrizio Mancinelli notes that the nuns of Monteluce had indeed commissioned two versions of the *Coronation of the Virgin* from Raphael, however there is no document to confirm that Raphael was supposed to execute both with such similarities in design. For more on the *Oddi Altarpiece*, see: F. Mancinelli, "The *Coronation of the Virgin* by Raphael." *Studies in the History of Art* 17: Symposium Papers V: Raphael Before Rome (1986), 127–136.

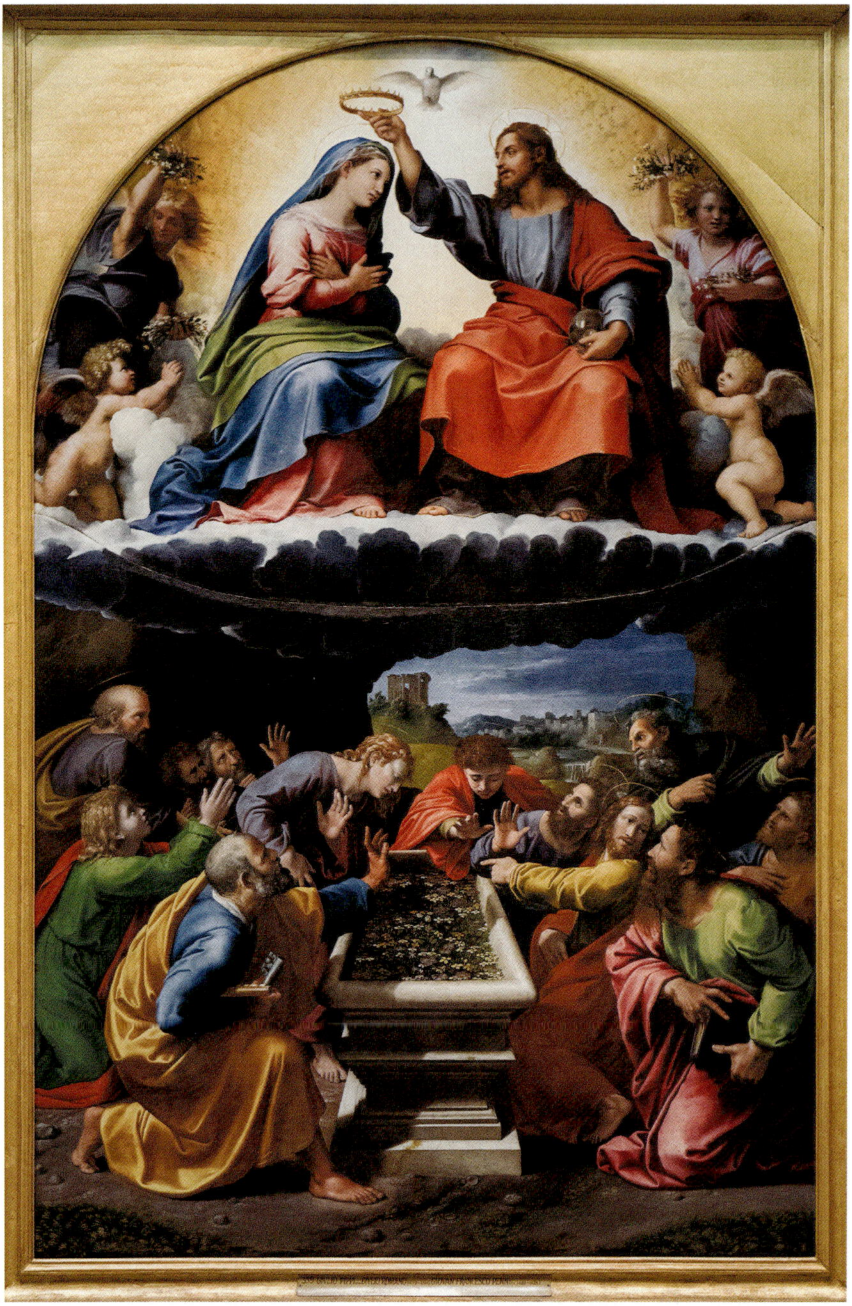

FIGURE 21 Giulio Romano and Gianfrancesco Penni, *The Coronation of the Virgin* (*Madonna of Monteluce*), c. 1523. Oil on panel; 354 by 232 cm; PINACOTECA VATICANA/ALAMY

that both Romano and Penni looked to Raphael's drawings for their respective creations, they resultingly conjure a composition that is highly similar—yet sufficiently different—to distinguish the artistic hands at work.

The upper panel, most likely executed by Romano and relatively faithful to a documented sketch by Raphael, maintains substantial allegiance to Raphael's same scene in the *Oddi Altarpiece*, however it seems that Penni, who is often assigned to the lower panel portion, took more license in his rendering of the vacant tomb and the surprised apostles who surround it. Rather than positioning the central tomb so that it runs at a diagonal across the composition, Penni placed it at exact center, as if it is the guiding orthogonal leading the eye to the far reaches of the painting. Such positioning expands the view of the interior of the sarcophagus that, though filled with flowers, is undeniably vacant. Those who surround this opened vessel amplify the shock of this discovery and display much more animated postures and expressions than those seen in Raphael's earlier work. These modifications are noteworthy because they echo a similar visual exchange from Raphael's early days. Just as Raphael borrowed from Perugino's *Marriage of the Virgin* (1500–1502) for his own composition (*Marriage of the Virgin*, or *La Spozalizio*, 1054), so too were Penni and Romano emulating Raphael's original composition. What differentiates this composition, however, is that in place of mere emulation there is also a desire to innovate.

This can be seen in the dramatic repositioning of the sarcophagus. As Fabrizio Mancinelli noted in his analysis of Raphael's *Oddi Altarpiece*, the fact that Raphael placed the tomb in so prominent a place contributed to the overall triumph of the image: "The central position and hence the importance of the sarcophagus were certainly Raphael's own invention," Mancinelli comments, "emphasizing the essentially funerary function of the chapel for which the painting was destined."[75] Given this symbolic importance of the sarcophagus, it seems noteworthy that Penni's painting pulls this vessel even more prominently into the foreground of the scene. This prominence is perhaps owed to the original destination of this scene—source suggest that Penni began work on this portion for an altarpiece destined for Agostino Chigi's chapel in the Roman Church of Santa Maria del Popolo—but what it suggests compositionally is that these artists, particularly Penni, were interested in a continuing conversation in the style of Raphael when developing innovative compositions.[76]

75 Mancinelli, "The *Coronation of the Virgin* by Raphael," 128.

76 Perhaps the most pronounced engagement between Penni and Raphael's work was his efforts to envision scenes from the life of Christ for a series of tapestries commissioned by Pope Clement VII in 1524. For more on these tapestries, see: C. Hope, "The Tapestries of the

What these examples showcase is that Raphael between 1514 and 1520 had developed a seemingly ideal working process, having assembled a team of talented artists who understood and implemented this essential practice of a visual vocabulary on which they could build, or riff, to innovate. This gave Raphael the confidence to keep accepting new commissions while allowing these workshop figures to become steeped in the language of these figures and forms and consider the ways in which they could use them for their own invention. Raphael could not have known his death was imminent; had he lived, one can only imagine how prolific his "brand" would have become. Yet, despite his demise, this novel approach lived on in the artistic processes of his workshop members as well as in the work of Peruzzi, as will be showcased in the following chapters.

Scuola Nuova in the Vatican Museum" (MA thesis, Courtauld Institute, 1968). This project is not discussed here, however, in the sake of maintaining focus primarily on collaborative efforts between these figures after Raphael's death.

CHAPTER 4

Giovanni da Udine, Perino, and Polidoro da Caravaggio at the Palazzo Baldassini

Though it was designed and partially decorated even before Raphael died, the Palazzo Baldassini (Fig. 22) offers a marvelous example to illustrate how the artists of Raphael's circle transferred a similar working style to projects outside of his shadow. Designed by Antonio da Sangallo the Younger, an associate of Raphael's circle, the palace was commissioned by Melchiorre Baldassini. Inside, it embodied a dynamic array of compositional references wherein the work of Giovanni da Udine, Perino del Vaga, Polidoro da Caravaggio, and Maturino da Firenze incorporated some of the same visual vocabulary employed in their other projects. Though these artists were embarking on one of their first major projects beyond Raphael's reach, one can note that the same artistic recombination is at play. While many portions of this interior suite are left in a ruinous state after the building's tumultuous history, enough visual evidence can nevertheless be noted from the remaining imagery to suggest that the recombination of visual phrases inspired by Raphael's working style was a practice still alive and well among these artists.

1 Melchiorre Baldassini (1470–1522)

Melchiorre Baldassini was a Neapolitan jurist who arrived in Rome in the 1510s and rose quickly in importance in the Papal court.[1] His first documented work in Rome dates to 1512, when he reportedly assisted Pope Julius II with the fourth session of the Lateran Council. The following year, Baldassini not only received the ceremonial title of "The Count of Palatine," but he was also nominated to

1 For more on the Baldassini family, see: E. Bentivoglio, "I Baldassini e le loro case: Il palazzo delle "2 Torre," il palazzo del magone; il palazzo del Card. Enkenvort." *Brevi Note per la storia, la topgrafia, l'architettura di Roma nel XVI secolo* (Rome, 1986); D. van Amayden, *La storia delle famiglie romane* (Rome: A. Bertini, 1941), 205. A complete biography of Baldassini can be found in: P. Craveri, "Baldassini Melchiorre." *Dizionario biografico degli Italiani* 5 (1963), 452.

 | DOI:10.1163/9789004430488_006

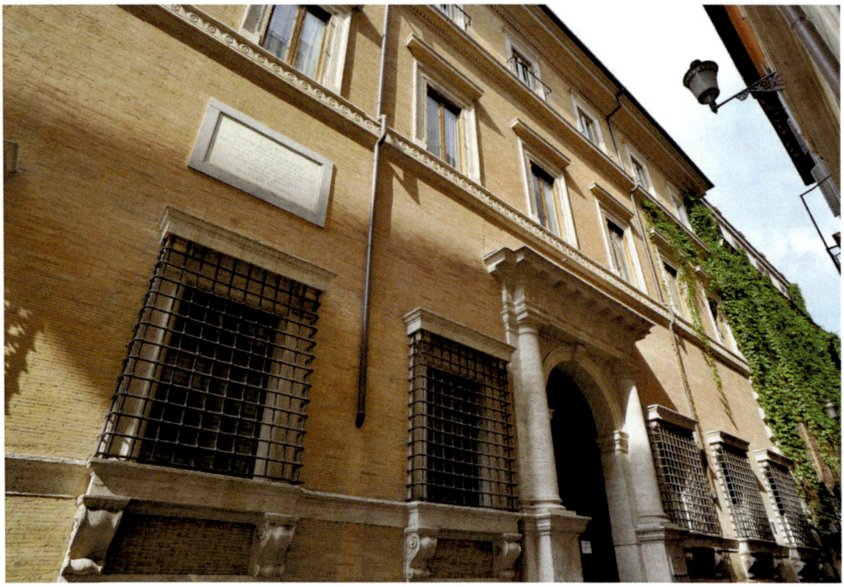

FIGURE 22 Antonio da Sangallo the Younger, Palazzo Baldassin, begun 1515–1516
ROME/ALAMY

become a lecturer of civil law at Archiginnasio, La Sapienza.[2] Accolades only continued to follow Baldassini over the subsequent years.[3]

Aside from professional accomplishments, Baldassini is forever tied to his commission of a palazzo along the via di Copelle that Laura Gigli described as a "splendid testimony to a wonderous cultural moment."[4] Rather than enjoying the swift breezes and sweeping views that a location along the Tiber River

---

2 This nomination is recorded in the papal bull, *Dum suvaissimae atque uberes fructus*, date 5 November 1513 (L. Gigli, "Melchiorre Baldassini *inisgnis Sacri Consistorii Advocatus*," in M. Cogotti and L. Gigli, *Palazzo Baldassini* (Rome: L'erma di Bretschneider, 1995), 8); for more on Baldassini's role at the university, see: G. Marini, *Lettera al chiarissimo Monsignor Giuseppe Muti Papazzurri già Casali, nella quale s'illustrati il ruolo de' professori dell'archiginnasio romano per l'anno* MDXIV (Rome, 1797), 22–23; M. Renassi, *Storia dell'Università degli studi di Roma …* II (Rome, 1804), 52.

3 For more, see: R.U. Montini, *Palazzo Baldassini e L'Arte di Giovanni da Udine* (Rome: Istituto di Studi Romani Editore, 1957), 11. G.D. Mansi, *Sacrorum Conciliorum … collection*, XXXII (Paris, 1902), col. 750; C. Cartari, *Advocatorum S. Consistorii syllabum* (Rome, 1656), CI–CIV; L. von Pastor, *Storia del Papi* IV, 2 (Rome, 1912), 39 (note 3); also P. Caveri, "Baldassini Melchiorre," in *Dizionario Biografico degli Italiani* 5 (1063), 452; Bentivoglio, "I Baldassini," 1; P. Giovio, *Le vite di Leon decimo et d'Adriano sesto* … trad. M.L. Domenichi (Venice, 1557), c. 118v.

4 L. Gigli, "Melchiorre Baldassini *insignis Sacri Consistorii Advocatus*," in L. Gigli and M. Cogotti, *Palazzo Baldassini* (Rome: L'Erma di Bretschneider, 1995), 7.

might have offered, Baldassini instead sited his dwelling at the crux of Roman civic life. Baldassini's selection of a location on the via delle Coppelle, as Enzo Bentivoglio noted, situated his dwelling in the heart of the five main rioni of the sixteenth century as well as the footprint of the ancient via Recta. This Roman road once stretched from the via Lata in the east to the Tiber River in the west and served as a key route for pilgrims on their way to the Vatican after fifteenth-century renovations cleared the thoroughfare from various medieval-era impediments.[5] Accordingly, this made the neighborhood by Baldassini's time a "pulsing center of social activity along a central city axis."[6] Joined by popular churches, such as that of San Salvatore il Lauro and Sant'Agostino, as well as notable residences, such as the palazzo of former Papal military commander Girolamo Riario (1443–1488), Baldassini's selected locale was also close to the Archiginnasio, where Baldassini held his professorial appointment.[7] The resulting abode was one of the most lavish to be built in the day to exemplify both the principles of grand palazzo architecture, thanks to Sangallo's designs, and the dynamism possible through its intriguing interior fresco cycles.

The timing for the palazzo's construction is debated. Renzo Montini points out that building would have probably waited until after Baldassini's official appointment with the Archiginnasio in 1513; there is also the appearance of an elephant in the decorative Doric frieze that most likely referenced the ill-fated Hanno, who, recall, had been imported to Rome for the celebration of Leo X's *posesso* in 1514.[8] Thus, Baldassini's chosen architect, Antonio da Sangallo the Younger (1484–1546), most likely commenced construction at some point between 1515 and 1516.[9] The focus of this examination is not upon the architectural composition of Baldassini's residence, yet a brief overview of Sangallo's

5 For more on the importance of this street, see: M. Cogotti, "Palazzo Baldassini," in L. Gigli and M. Cogotti, *Palazzo Baldassini* (Rome: L'Erma di Bretschneider, 1995), 17. For more on these early Roman streets, see: S. Bonamico, G. Molfetta, T. Porn, "Studio metodologico propedeutico ad un restauro conservative nel centro storico." *Capitolium* 9/10 (1966), 5–27.

6 Bentivoglio, "I Baldassini," 5; a similar point is made in: L. Gigli, "Il salone di Perin del Vaga in palazzo Baldassini fra rigore del disegno e immaginazione creativa," *Strenna dei Romanisti: Natale di Roma* (Fondazione Roma Arte-Musei, 2015), 259–284.

7 R.U. Montini, "Palazzo Baldassini Restaurato," *Studi Romani*, Anno V (1957), 42.

8 Montini, "Palazzo Baldassini Restaurato," 42. Redig de Campos suggests a starting date closer to 1520. For more, see: D. Redig de Campos, "Notizia su palazzo Baldassini," *Bolletino del Centro di Studi per la Storia dell'Architettura*, 10 (Rome: Casa dei Crescenzi, 1956), 10; A. Venturi, *Storia dell'arte italiana*, XI (1) (Milan, 1938), 551.

9 It is noted in a 1517–1518 census that Baldassini was living on the via di Copelle. For more, see: M. Armellini, "Un censimento della città di Roma sotto il pontificato di Leone X tratto da un codice inedito dell'Archivio Vaticano." *Gli Studi in Italia* (1882), 13; M. Cogotti, "Palazzo Baldassini," 20.

design seems essential for an overall understanding of the culture of palatial architecture in this historical moment and also to foreshadow Sangallo's enduring relationship with the work and workshop of Raphael.[10]

2 Sangallo's Designs

Like many of his contemporaries, Sangallo was guided in his designs (partially recorded in Uffizi drawings UA 1298 and UA 995) by Vitruvian principles for a palatial *domus*: a bold Doric order portal broke the clean geometry of the palazzo's 26-meter façade that runs a course of seven architraved windows across the upper floor. Six match below and are paired with "le finestre inginocchiate," so called for their lower, knee-level height and appearing in the designs of both Sangallo's Palazzo Farnese and the Palazzo Sacchetti.[11] These windows seemingly project outward from the façade to reinforce the bold crenellations of the rusticated corner of the first level of the structure, a feature that both Christoph Frommel and Joseph Connors have noted as a means to accentuate the powerful presence of the structure.[12] Along with domination was rational order: all of this was designed within the precise ratio of the façade's width to height as that of 1: $\sqrt{2}$.[13] The central axis that ran through the center of Sangallo's design allowed for an ample entry way that opened into a central courtyard styled in the Doric order to match the palazzo's exterior. This same axis continued through the rear loggia of the building and into the gardens beyond to cement the significant symmetry and order of Sangallo's design.[14]

10 Linda Wolk-Simon proposes construction dates as between 1516 and 1519 (L. Wolk-Simon, "Two early fresco cycles by Perino del Vaga: The Palazzo Baldassini and the Pucci Chapel," *Apollo*, CLV (481) (March 2002), 11–21). This means that the construction of the Palazzo Baldassini would have predated that for the Villa Lante by several years and would have also begun within Raphael's lifetime. This is important because it suggests that the architecture of Sangallo, though steeped in the classical moment, would perhaps not be as influenced by the ideologies of Raphael, whose architectural designs Sangallo would later be tasked with remedying (Vasari, II: 105).

11 Montini, "Palazzo Baldassini Restauro," 43. For reference, Sangallo developed designs for the Palazzo Farnese as early as 1517; he commenced work on the Palazzo Sacchetti in the early 1540s.

12 For more, see: J. Connors, "Borromini and Roman Urbanism," *AA Files* 2 (July 1982), 17; C. Frommel, *Der Römische Palastbau*, I: 11–24.

13 Gigli, "Il salone," 263.

14 For more on these elements, see: U. Novelli, "Rome: Palazzo Baldassini," in Tancredi Carunchio, ed., *Ricercha di Storia dell'arte: Propedeutica al restsauro; Techniche di Ricerca, richerche sulla technica*, 31 (La Nuova Italia Scientifica, 1987), 85–87.

Similar to architects like Peruzzi, Sangallo also followed Vitruvian precepts for the palazzo's footprint, setting a rectangular space deeper than it was wide upon the street. This required the annexation of an adjacent medieval tower along the via della Vacarella, which also allowed for a traditional cortile to open up the central core of the building.[15] Running a central axis through the structure, Sangallo used the main portal as an entrance hall that opened into a well-lit courtyard, echoing, albeit on a much more luxurious scale, the ancient Roman insula. This interior, airy courtyard became a space for ornament, from antiquities on display to a Doric frieze that offered a varied array of motifs across each metope. These Classical elements would have echoed well the original chiaroscuro decorations that Polidoro and Maturino had added to the building's exterior, a contribution that today has unfortunately disappeared.

Sangallo's artful revival of Vitruvian perfection was complemented inside with a remarkable array of imagery so striking that famed sixteenth-century humanist Pietro Bembo lauded it as "the most beautiful and well-made in Rome."[16] This splendor, though, is much subdued today. Following Baldassini's death on 10 September 1525, his wife Elisabetta remained at the palazzo for a handful of years, after which it was passed through an array of illustrious residents. Florentine poet Giovanni della Casa (1503–1556) rented the palazzo from 1533 to 1544; Cardinal Pietro Bembo (1470–1547) then moved in and stayed until his death in early 1547. By the end of the sixteenth century, the space of the palazzo was further subdivided, and residents turned over more rapidly. One such lodger was humanist writer Sperone Speroni (1500–1588), who lived in the palazzo during his time in Rome from 1574 to 1587.

The property finally returned to the hands of a (distant) Baldassini heir near the turn of the nineteenth century when it was acquired by Paolo Palma Baldassini and his wife Maria Raffaella Pane. By that point, though, the luster of the Renaissance palazzo had begun to wear away. Damage had been wrought on the *piano nobile* when a print shop was installed in the late 1780s, however the real destruction occurred following the sale of the palazzo to Andrea Nizzica in

---

15 Gigli, "Il salone," 262.

16 Letter from Bembo, originally dated 3 August 1544, as quoted in C.L. Frommel, *Der römisches Palastbau*, II: 23. Modifications of the space continued until acquisition of the palazzo on 28 February 1951 by the Società Immobilarie S. Gordiano Coppelle for the Istituto Luigi Sturzo, who began the restoration process. For more on this history, see: M. Cogotti, "Palazzo Baldassini," 44–60; for more on the Istituto Luigi Sturzo, please see: G. de Rosa, "L'Istituto Luigi Sturzo," in M. Cogotti and L. Gigli, *Palazzo Baldassini* (Rome: L'erma di Bretschneider, 1995), 71–75.

1831. Nizzica was a prominent fish wholesaler who placed profits over preservation of the historic structure, a testament to which was his division of the palazzo into independent chambers and apartments. Trampling the original footprint and disregarding the conservation of the interior frescoes, Nizzica also authorized the removal of several of the fresco panels conjured by Perino del Vaga in the second-level grand *salone*.[17]

Despite these drastic modifications, what is clear even in what remains is that Baldassini, like his fellow noblemen of his day, used this interior cycle to both encourage a celebration of the city's ancient roots while also lauding his own place within it. Baldassini himself held an affinity for ancient Roman culture: in addition to selecting a location for his home along one of the ancient city's main routes, Baldassini also amassed a handsome collection of antiquities that he displayed in the lavish gardens that extended beyond palazzo's courtyard.[18] Though only fragments of this collection remain, a visit to the modern villa, now owned by the Istituto Luigi Sturzo, revives an *all'antica* air.

3 Giovanni da Udine and the Quotation of Antiquity

Of all the decorated spaces in the Palazzo Baldassini, the chamber that reflects the most explicit study of ancient Roman wall painting is a small room nestled within the *piano terreno* that, in the words of Anna Cavallaro, is "little noted but is of unusual refinement" in its *all'antica* motifs (Fig. 23).[19] The theme of this room's imagery is decidedly Classical, derived most likely from da Udine's study of ancient Roman examples and in all respects showcasing the extent to which the artist had absorbed the imagery of including the famed cryptoporticus of the Domus Aurea.[20]

---

17 For more, see: M. Cogotti, "Palazzo Baldassini," 44–60; for more on the Istituto Luigi Sturzo, see: G. de Rosa, "L'Istituto Luigi Sturzo," in M. Cogotti and L. Gigli, *Palazzo Baldassini* (Rome: L'erma di Bretschneider, 1995), 71–75.

18 Gigli, "Melchiore Baldassini *insignis*," 9. There is no inventory of these sculptures, though, and their dissemination in the centuries following make it nearly impossible to reconstruct the holdings that Baldassini once boasted. The gardens are also gone, as the expansion of the Istituto Culturale Luigi Sturzo required the building of an auxiliary structure that expands upon the footprint that these gardens would have originally consumed.

19 A. Cavallaro, "Bottega di Giovanni da Udine" in L. Cassanelli and S. Rossi, *Oltre Raffaello: aspetti della cultura figurativa del cinquecento romano* (Rome: Multigrafica Editrice, 1984), 45.

20 We know of da Udine's presence within the remnants of the Domus Aurea as he left an inscription: "Zuan da Udene firlano" on the interior wall (no. 137, as illustrated in: N. Dacos, "Per la storia della grottesche: la riscoperta della Domus Aurea." *Bolletino d'Arte* 1–2 (V)

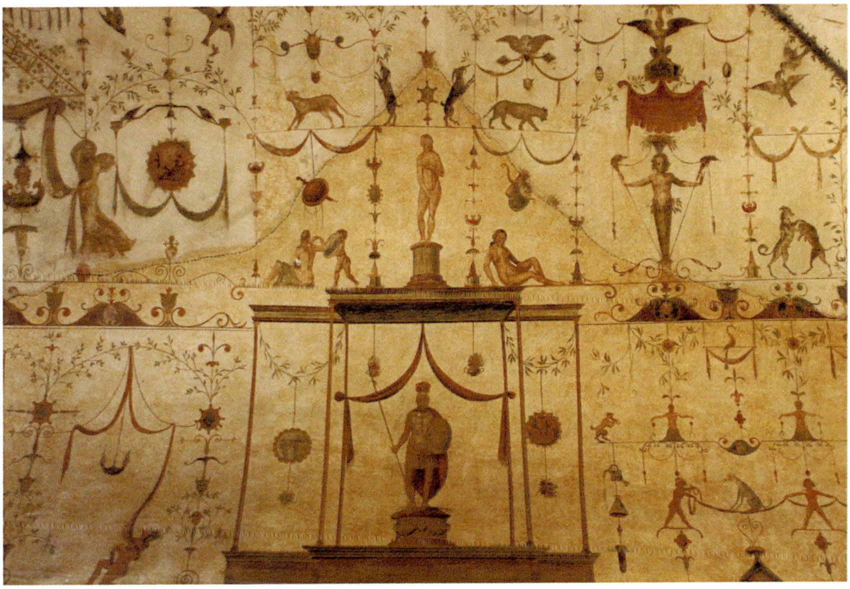

FIGURE 23 Detail of Giovanni da Udine's *grotteschi* (with restorations)
PALAZZO BALDASSINI, ROME—AUTHOR'S IMAGE

Organized around a delicate pergola framework, da Udine's ceiling offers a central panel that features an array of sixteen creatures ranging from the exotic—including a monkey and a rhinoceros—to the fantastical, such as the chimera that appears in the delicately outlined network. These animals flank a central symbol of the Baldassini family *stemma*, and serve as the foundation for the array of motifs that progress down the arced sides of the ceiling. Garlands, trophies, and candelabra subtly yet visually connect smaller fictive constructions that progress around the perimeter of the room and house representations of various deities, including Ceres and Mars, Neptune and Jupiter, Venus, Bacchus, and Opis, all set against a white field with accents of Pompeii red.

This room is not the first space in which one finds da Udine's mastery of the *all'antica* style at play; his earlier work in the Vatican's Sala dei Palifrenieri and Sala dei Pontifici, wherein da Udine worked with Perino del Vaga to render a cycle of astrological personifications in fresco form, revealed compositional

(1966), 43–49). Gigli also highlights the design parallels with those of the stuffetta of Cardinal Bibbiena and the Loggia of Leo X (Gigli, "La decorazione di palazzo Baldassini," in M. Cogotti and L. Gigli, *Palazzo Baldassini* (Rome: L'erma di Bretschneider, 1995), 64).

elements that also borrowed from his study of motifs in the Domus Aurea.[21] Akin to this work at the Vatican Loggia, yet introducing his full mastery of the *grotteschi* technique in the domestic realm, this small chamber reimagines the motifs discovered in the cryptoporticus of Nero's once lavish estate.

This space also exhibits da Udine's reuse of references in a recombination of motifs as an indication that he too was still employing the visual language espoused in Raphael's workshop. In addition to the fact that the forms in this diminutive room generally recall those created alongside Raphael for the Stuffetta and Loggetta of Cardinal Bibbiena (1516–1517), one can also note that da Udine actually recycles some specific elements. Riccardo Averini, in his analysis of the space in the midst of these restoration efforts, noted that the motifs of the vault frescoes in the Palazzo Baldassini are near duplicates to those seen in the Ucelleria of Pope Leo X's loggia.[22] They also bear parallels to Bibbiena's Loggetta, wherein a similar array of architectural and vegetal motifs gracefully line the walls in a visual decorum one would expect from a Roman villa. What these connections imply is that da Udine is calling upon these earlier examples as visual phrases he can extract and repurpose, using a means of recombination that brings earlier-used forms in a novel composition.

Moreover, given these parallels, it is interesting to assess the potential significance of the characters put on display. In Bibbiena's Loggetta, for example, one would have originally seen three central painted panels—a scene of *Apollo and Marsyas*, *Olympus Praying to Apollo*, and *Apollo and Marsyas* (now lost)—nestled among the various decorative elements of flora and fauna. The inclusion of this cycle could perhaps be Bibbiena's clever way of visually connecting this loggetta with the imagery elsewhere in the Vatican—as noted earlier, Apollo looms large in Raphael's encapsulation of *Parnassus*—and while it is pure supposition, it is enticing to consider that Raphael might have deliberately conjured such a parallel for his patron. The image of Apollo also takes on ecclesiastical significance as he is a Pagan deity who also alludes to Christian divinity: not only does Constantine witness the solar god Apollo before his auspicious defeat of Maxentius at the Milvian Bridge in 312 CE, but, as Diskin Clay points out, Apollo was also seen through the vantage of humanist writers

21 N. Dacos and C. Furlan, *Giovanni da Udine 1487–1561* (Friuli-Venezia Giulia: Cassamassima 1987), 109.

22 Averini, 29–38. Averini uses this observation to confirm past speculation that the vault frescoes in Leo's loggia were indeed by Udine, not Raphael (Averini, 29–30). More evidence of Giovanni's involvement was noted in the stuffetta as the designs parallel the master's work in the Palazzo Grimani as well as frieze designs in the Villa Madama.

like Dante Alighieri as a parallel to God himself.[23] From Dante's perspective, the narrative of Apollo and Marsyas was particularly relevant to this symbolic allusion, as "in this invocation *good* Apollo is also divine power (*divina virtù*) and father (*padre*)."[24] To find such potential symbolism in a space dedicated to Cardinal Bibbiena, who himself was a writer of comedies and also connected to Florentine and Roman humanist circles, would be plausible, given the impressive array of allusions cast in these various Vatican chambers. Just as Raphael had created the allusion-packed scenes of the Stanza della Segnatura for Julius II, so too could have da Udine constructed a similar network of references for Bibbiena and perhaps, as an extension, for Baldassini as well in this *piano terreno* chamber.

One must wonder, for instance, if the deities included in their well-defined architectural spaces were intended to combine into some larger mythological or astrological network. Do Mars and Jupiter align in this space to assume the parameters of an astrological chart? Are the pairing of gods somehow the more diminutive parallel to the grand prophets that line the *salone* on the second level? Were they merely pairings to reflect the key figures of a Roman pantheon? Setting aside a definitive reading of the space, it is clear that da Udine is executing a remarkable manifestation of *all'antica* form built upon the elements of a visual lexicon developed in the years prior.

This can be seen, once again, as a study of the past and present. On the one hand, da Udine's pergola design can be seen as an echo of that created under Raphael's supervision in Chigi's Loggia di Amore e Psiche (and nearly simultaneous with the creation of the Baldassini *all'antica* chamber). It also echoes the trompe-l'oeil trellises that da Udine incorporated into later loggie designs. Da Udine would indeed carry this novelty forward in his career. Shortly after his work at the Palazzo Baldassini, he collaborate with Baldassarre Peruzzi in late 1520 to develop the visual program for the stuffetta of Cardinal Riario at the Palazzo della Cancelleria. Here da Udine would carry his *all'antica* revival to new heights by transforming the room into the form of a fictive pergola supported at its corners by elaborate foliage that, in the words of Dacos, bears a unique "freshness" as if capturing live nature.[25] This suggests that this novelty and experimentation—both with antique forms and with spatial illusions—had become part of da Udine's own visual language. Accordingly, this space

23 D. Clay, "Dante's Parnassus: Raphael's Parnaso." *Arion: A Journal of Humanities and the Classics*, 22 (2) (Fall 2014), 9 (3–32).

24 Clay, "Dante's Parnassus," 8.

25 Dacos and Furlan, *Giovanni da Udine*, 101.

at the Palazzo Baldassini becomes part of this larger conceptual conversation that endured over the course of his career.

Da Udine would carry this same novelty with him to his work at the left-to-languish Villa Madama as well as later at Castel Sant'Angelo, wherein he created a stuffetta for Pope Clement VII between 1527 and 1530 following the Sack of Rome.[26] This space featured an array of empty thrones scattered with rumpled garments, the implication being that the gods who normally would be alighting there have instead gone off to bathe. Fitting for a bathing chamber, these scenes also reflect da Udine's ongoing relationships with Raphael's former workshop group: in addition to Giulio Romano's assistance in drafting the visual scheme for the stuffetta, da Udine also teamed up with Polidoro da Caravaggio, a colleague with whom he had undoubtedly brushed shoulders at the Palazzo Baldassini.

4 Perino del Vaga, Polidoro da Caravaggio, and the *Piano Nobile*

Shortly after Giovanni conjured his *all'antica* suite on the *piano terreno*, work began upstairs on a series of images that decorated several of the main chambers of Baldassini's residence.[27] These included a large grand *salone* decorated primarily by Perino del Vaga that ran along the northern exposure of the palazzo. This larger chamber opened at its western end into a smaller room, most likely Baldassini's private study, that was adorned around its upper register with a series of vignettes framed by Polidoro da Caravaggio. Just adjacent to this study was a small stuffetta, featuring additional scenes conjured by Polidoro and his close associate, Maturino da Firenze. This series of chambers and the various narratives that they relay share further insights into how these artists continued to manage their commissions just as they had done during Raphael's time through both references to Raphael's work and in their overall approach to compositional development and complexity.

---

26 Ibid., 121. Dacos and Furlan propose dates between 1525 and 1534.

27 Gigli does not offer a set date for del Vaga's work, stating instead that it "condotta a termine probabilmente negli anni '20." (Cogotti and Gigli, "La decorazione," 65), an approximate date supported by other scholars as well: E. Parma Armanti, *Perin del Vaga: l'anello mancante* (Genoa, 1986), 34–50; 254–257; L. Wolk-Simon, "Studies in Perino del Vaga's Early Career" (PhD diss, Ann Arbor, 1987), 162–235; A. Gnann, in K. Oberhuber (ed.), *Roma e lo stile classico di Raffaello*, exh. cat. (Palazzo Te, Mantua, 1999), 186–187; and E. Parma in idem (ed.), *Perino del Vaga tra Raffaello e Michelangelo*, exh. cat. (Palazzo Te, Mantua, 2001), 108–110.

Admittedly, this larger room that was decorated primarily by Perino del Vaga presents numerous problems due to the relatively poor preservation and modification of these rooms over time. For example, Baldassini's assuredly impressive stuffetta has now been reduced to a small corridor that connects the study to the main annex of the palazzo; what has not been lost of Perino del Vaga's frescoes has been diminished due to the ongoing exposure of sunlight within the large and window-filled *salone*. Polidoro's frescoes in the study are perhaps the easiest to read, though this is because of monumental restorations in the space over the years. Furthermore, while both Perino's and Polidoro's suites of images are enigmatic, it is perhaps Polidoro's cycle that, though best preserved, is most difficult to decipher. Nevertheless, it seems valuable to look once more at these spaces to tease out hints of this ongoing visual language shared between these artistic colleagues.

Though painfully fragmentary, Perino's fresco cycle in the palazzo's grand *salone* has been hailed in recent times by Wolk-Simon as ranking "among the most important artistic campaigns undertaken in Rome in the years bracketed by Raphael's death and the Sack."[28] This cycle was most assuredly a crucial one, as it would have been his first completed in the wake of Raphael's death. Perhaps the most successful painter to emerge from Raphael's circle, and yet also debatably attached to said circle, Perino was born in 1501 outside of Florence.[29] Left in his early years to grow up with relatives following his mother's death and his father's departure for France, Perino began his dedicated artistic training under the guidance of Ridolfo Ghirlandaio. Some of his earliest documented drawings were derived from his study after Michelangelo's *Battle at Cascina* in Florence's Sala dei Cinquecento, and as those knowledgeable of Perino's career will be aware, the influence of Michelangelo on Perino's style would only grow in the years to come.[30] Nevertheless, it was

28 Wolk-Simon, "Two early fresco cycles," 18. Gnann also notes it as being rival only to Baldassarre Peruzzi's Sala delle Prospettive at the Villa Farnesina in terms of its illusionistic elements (A. Gnann, in K. Oberhuber, ed., *Roma e lo stile classic di Raffaello*, exh. cat., Palazzo Te (Mantua, 1999), 187–188).

29 Oberhuber reiterates: "Perino non fu un vero allievo di Raffaello, né uno dei suoi intimi; piuttosto, ricevette le sue commissioni come giovane e dotato maestro fiorentino, altamente apprezzato per la sua finezza e il suo talento, e imparò quanto più poté dall'esempio del grande artista" (K. Oberhuber, "Perino del Vaga e Raffaello," 51). Also see: K. Oberhuber, "Die Werkstatt Raffaels" (*Künstlerwerkstätten Der Renaissance / Sylvie Béguin … Hrsg. Von Roberto Cassanelli*, 1988), 257–274.

30 B.F. Davidson, ed., *Mostra di disegni di Perino del Vaga e la sua cerchia* (Firenze: Leo S. Olschki Editore, 1966), 4. Gnann also suggests that Perino worked on decorations for triumphal arches for Pope Leo X in 1515 (Gnann, "Raphael's Workshop," 21).

Perino's connections with Ghirlandaio that helped to facilitate his move to Rome as a young man around 1516, and it was there that Perino found initial work for Raphael's Vatican projects and soon after connected with this network of artists. Noteworthy though is the fact that, unlike these colleagues, Perino joined in this group as an already-developed artist. He aided in da Udine's work in the Vatican Loggia, for example, and also executed works in the Borgia apartments.

Perino also built a strong bond with Penni, whom Paul Joannides has suggested was Perino's mentor of sorts within this larger circle.[31] He showcased this connection with a reinterpretation of a drawing, *Study of Three Figures* for the base of Pilaster x of Raphael's Loggia (1518; National Gallery of Scotland, Edinburgh), wherein he traced the connections between both artists in the page. This blended exchange also took place with Raphael as well. Joannides notes, for instance, the previously mentioned surviving drawing of the *Triumph of Bacchus*, which has been attributed to all three artists: Penni (by Oberhuber); Perino (by Pouncy and Gere); and Raphael.[32]

Perino's compositions were also exalted by the writers of his era, with descriptions of this space included in the accounts both Vasari and Giovanni Battista Armenini (1587).[33] It is through these writings that one can gain a sense of how this space would have originally appeared, its grandeur unfortunately long-since diminished thanks to the substantial modifications that the room underwent.

Vasari's description recalls the subdivision of the walls into fictive niches. "In the larger niches," he continues:

> … are various figures of philosophers, two in each niche, and in some one only, and in the smaller niches are cherubs, partly nude and partly veiled, while above those small niches are some heads of women painted to appear as marble. Above the cornice that crowns the pilasters there fol-

31 P. Joannides, "Some New Drawings by Perino del Vaga." In E. Parma, ed., *Perino del Vaga: Prima, Durante, Dopo*. Atti delle Giornate Internazionale di Studio, Genova 26–27 maggio 2001, Palazzo Doria 'del Prinicpe (Genova: De Ferrari, 2004), 14.

32 As cited in Achim Gnann's *Roma e lo Stilo Classico di Raffaello, 1515–1527*, (Milan 1999), no. 82.

33 G.B. Armenini, *De veri precetti della pittura* (Ravenna, 1587; reprinted NY, 1971); 177–178; Vasari, *Lives*. A brief note of Perino del Vaga's work at the palazzo was also noted in Fillippo Titi's seventeenth-century guidebook of Rome: "Perino del Vaga dipinse alcuni filosofi, e puttini; e negli spazi più ampli, storie romane, e sopra un bel cammino la Pace, che brucia varie sorte d'armi" (F. Titi, *Descrizione delle Pitture, Sculture e Architetture esposte in Roma*, published 1674 and revised by G. Bottari, 1763), 404.

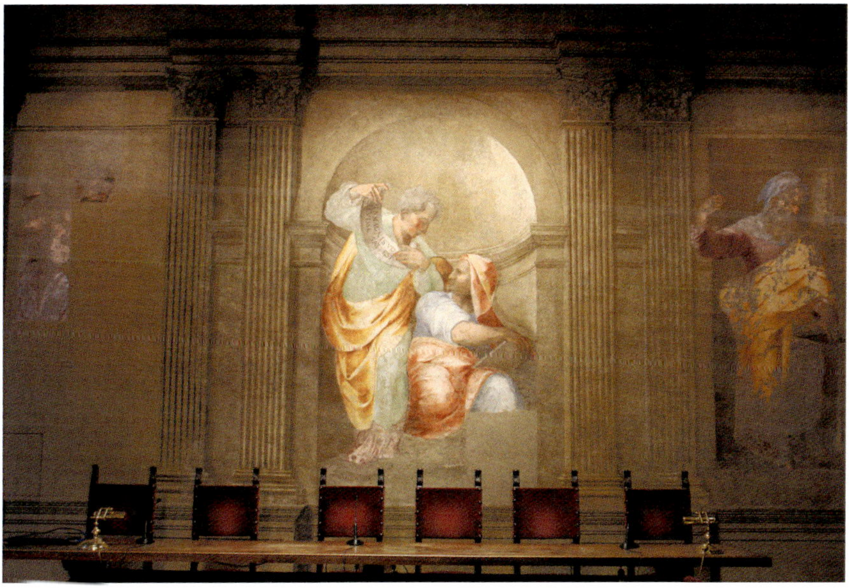

FIGURE 24 Perino del Vaga, Partial view of surviving *salone* frescoes
PALAZZO BALDASSINI, ROME—AUTHOR'S IMAGE

> lows a second series of pictures, separated from the first series below, with scenes in figures of no great size from the history of the Romans, beginning with Romulus and ending with Numa Pompilius. There are likewise various ornaments in imitation of different kinds of marble, and over the beautiful chimney of stone is a figure of Peace burning arms and trophies, which is very lifelike.[34]

Dissecting Vasari's description of the chamber, much of which was corroborated by Armenini's 1587 recounting, one can note that he alludes to two zones of decoration. In the lower register, fictive Corinthian pilasters punctuate a series of niches that vary in dimension and that would have originally depicted various figural groups that Vasari groups simply as philosophers (two of these niche groupings survive) (Fig. 24).[35] In the upper register, a series of narrative vignettes wrap around the room, broken by cary-

34 Vasari, "Life of Perino del Vaga," *Lives* II; 160.

35 Gigli notes a connection with these niche figure and those that appear at Palazzo of Cardinal Domenico Della Rovere in the Borgo, those in the Palafrenieri of the Vatican palace, and the Chigi Chapel of Santa Maria del Popolo in their celebration of the virtue, intellectualism, and status of the patron (Gigli, "La decorazione," 67).

atid figures and yet connected by a continuous decorative frieze overhead. Though once undoubtedly captivating, this lower register of images is today only fragmentary. The southern wall particularly is virtually empty of surviving decorations. Appearing on the eastern wall in one of the remaining fictive niches is a kneeling male figure who gestures towards a tablet and turns upward to gaze upon another male figure who is seemingly rushing into the scene. The space of the upper register is also now mostly obscured due to the dropped ceiling installed in the chamber, but parts of this upper cycle, having been extracted years ago, can nevertheless shed insights on the chamber's design.

While many sources connect the majority of the imagery in this room to the hand of Perino del Vaga, authorship of these respective portions is still debated. In discussing this *salone*, Vasari assigns authorship to Perino alone.[36] Since Vasari's summary, scholars have tended to agree that the lower philosopher niches are creations by Perino, as surviving drawings by Perino—particularly *Two Philosophers Standing Inside a Niche* (Uffizi n. 13561F)—so closely parallel the final niche designs in the manner that the figures are rendered. It is in these preparatory drawings that one can see the lasting influence of Raphael on Perino's development. As was mentioned earlier, Perino was somewhat unique among Raphael's workshop cohort in part because he so easily absorbed Raphael's technique while infusing it with the style of colleagues. It is perhaps this quality in his work that contributed to his professional alignment with Raphael, as it would seem he was equally capable of the translations of the visual vernacular used within this artistic circle.

Above, the singular panels depict the story of the making of Rome, overseen on the western wall by the reclining figures of Egeria and Numa Pompilius as they prepare to slaughter a calf. These are some of the few decorative panels to survive. The scene that Vasari notes above the hearth depicting *Peace Burning Arms and Trophies*, for example, is completely obliterated. Fragmentary elements of a scene of *Romulus* as well as a scene of *Numa and Egeria* still appear on the walls of the chamber, but little else is visible.[37] The best-preserved panels from this upper series are those depicting *The Judgment of Zaleucus* and *Tarquinius Priscus Founding the Temple of Jupiter on the Capitoline*, which were

36 Vasari, II: 160.

37 Interestingly, as Linda Wolk-Simon has noted, the remaining portion of the *Romulus* fresco visible in the Palazzo Baldassini chamber bears compositional parallels to another panel of *Romulus* created by Perino del Vaga for the Palazzo Massimo al Colonne, designed and built by Baldassarre Peruzzi between 1532 and 1536 (Wolk-Simon, "Two early fresco cycles," 12).

artfully removed in the nineteenth century and transferred to canvas to eventually become part of the Galleria degli Uffizi's collection.[38]

Taken in sum, this fresco cycle has been seen as a metaphorical exaltation of ancient prestige of both profession and personality of the patron Baldassini. Gigli suggested, for example, that the theme of divine illumination—echoed in both the scene of *The Judgment of Zaleucus* and the depiction of Numa Pompilius—played into the narrative construction of a theme.[39] Wolk-Simon offered a similar interpretation: that this space celebrates the ancient installations of the tenets of law, wherein "the exalted, ancient and sacral origins of his profession … were proclaimed."[40] Taken independently, though, these narratives tie to important figures of ancient Rome. For example, Romulus, whose lineage traced to Aeneas and his arrival on the shores of Latium, harkened back to the very origins of Rome.[41] Lucius Tarquinius Priscus shared in the ancient legacy of Rome as well as he ruled as the fifth king of Rome in the late seventh and early sixth centuries BCE. The narrative of Zaleucus, though not tied as directly to Rome's origins, nevertheless also carried substantial ancient lore as Zaleucus was rumored to have resurrected the massive empire of Alexander the Great and to have subsequently established his own enduring dynasty. When considered on both the individual and universal levels, then, one can see how this suite of imagery that wrapped around the upper register of the room would have offered a survey of ancient history, grounding the new palazzo in antiquity just as these themes of military and regal triumph were balanced by the cerebral philosophers depicted below.

Amid these historical connotations, Perino was also careful to tie in references to the contemporary. Pierluigi de Castris, for example, noted the Michelangesque references in these panels, particularly the echoes of the unfinished *Battle at Cascina* that Perino studied as a student.[42] There are also questions of

38 These panels were removed in 1830 by painter Pellegrino Succi and transferred to canvas at the request of Vincecos Camuccini; they were also partially restored at that time by Succi's brother, Pietro. They were then purchased in 1880 by the Ministero della Pubblica Istruzione and added to the Uffizi's collection. For more, see: Golzio, 160–162; E. Parma Armani, in *Perino del Vaga tra Raffaello e Michelangelo*, exh. cat., Palazzo Te (Mantua, 2001), 108; Poggi 1909, 270; Redig de Campos 1956, 11; Wolk-Simon 1992, 61–62; Gigli, in Cogotti-Gilgi 1995, 66; Gnann, in Oberhuber-Gnann 1999, 186.

39 Gigli, "Il salone," 278.

40 Wolk-Simon, "Two early fresco cycles," 15.

41 For a discussion of the legacy of Romulus and the construction of Roman history, please see: A. Rodríguez Mayorgas, "Romulus, Aeneas and the Cultural Memory of the Roman Republic." *Atheneum*, 98 (1) (2010) 89–109.

42 P. Leone De Castris, *Polidoro da Caravaggio* (UK: Matthieson Fine Art, 2004), 75.

authorship that have been levied upon the program in this chamber: while it is generally agreed that Perino completed the lower series of philosophers, there is some debate as to the hands at work in the upper registers and accompanying monochrome scenes that appeared in the lower dado, or socle, zone. Deoclelio Redig de Campos, for example, suggested that da Udine was present in some of the panels; Montini goes so far as to suggest that Peruzzi was involved as well, proposing that elements of these scenes seem to recall Peruzzi's treatments at both Chigi's villa and within the Ponzetti Chapel of Santa Maria della Pace (1516).[43] Building on Montini's connection, one can note that the fictive architectural framework that Perino del Vaga constructed for this space—its neat division of zones defined by illusionistic pilasters and his play with perspectival illusions—in some respects parallels the framework Peruzzi developed for Chigi's Loggia di Galatea.

This proposed overlap of authorship—that is, that all of these artists were at work in this space—is plausible, as it was a typical means by which they worked together. What it also recalls, though, is the perennial attribution issues that plagued this consort of artists, namely, that it is nearly impossible in so many instances to delineate between artists' hands. This harmony of styles was what contributed to the earlier "brand" that was Raphael, but in instances like the Palazzo Baldassini one can propose that a similar harmony was being struck: a reuse of a visual language that at once recalls a larger web of artists but is, potentially, the work of only one individual.

That individuality, though, would nevertheless be again subsumed in the collective harmony of the overall decorative program of the Palazzo Baldassini and the messaging the patron wished to convey. This is perhaps illustrated best in the reuse of *all'antica* themes throughout, from da Udine's *grotteschi* designs in the *piano terreno* to the now-lost façade *sgraffitto* scenes by Polidoro and Maturino that were complemented by frescoed festoons adorning fictive imperial portraits above the main windows of the interior courtyard.[44] Such scenes, designed to cast illusions of relief sculpture, would have helped to transform the space into one of *all'antica* novelty.

One can imagine that Perino also wanted to share in this novelty, particularly given his own fascination with *grotteschi*. This is perhaps owed to the fact that Raphael often paired Perino with da Udine in workshop projects—at

43 Montini, 25; D. Redig de Campos, "Palazzo Baldassini," in *Osservatore Romano* (26 February 1956), 20. De Campos notes particularly the "animato dallo spirito di Raffaello" (de Campos, 20) in the space, which seems to further the argument that a lingering impact of the deceased artist was still impacting these new masters' design process.

44 de Castris, *Polidoro da Caravaggio: l'opera completa* (Naples: Electa, 2001), 69.

least, according to Vasari—and it is documented in the array of studies executed by Perino of such forms.[45] One fitting example is a drawing attributed to Perino that displays *A Panel of Grotesque Decoration* (circa 1545; British Museum 1918,0615.1). Assuming this attribution is correct, one can see here that Perino conjured a strikingly accurate *all'antica* wallscape, complete with a lower register of fictive relief panels topped with faux architectural recesses, in which figures flank elevated representations of deities. Additional sculptures surmount these two architectural interiors and are flanked by winged horses that seem to emerge from paired trellis structures and visually connect with the delicate garlands and additional vignettes that extend to the top of the sheet. When one considers this overall framework developed in this panel, it is not a far leap to suggest that it bears parallels to the way in which Perino structured the visual program in the Palazzo Baldassini chamber. There too a lower series of monochrome scenes encircled the room and were topped with fictive architectural niches. In addition, the separate historical scenes that appeared above these niches—so nicely enclosed by the caryatid figures that once framed each respective scene—seem to follow the same pattern as expressed in this *grotteschi* sheet.

This is not to suggest that this drawing was done in preparation for the Palazzo Baldassini's series, but rather to illustrate yet another source for the visual language that Perino employed in this room. Aware that his colleagues were bringing a similar energy to their various projects through the palazzo, Perino was perhaps invoking subtle reference to these ancient styles to ensure that this suite of images aligned with the visual themes seen elsewhere throughout the palazzo. To be certain of such a connection would require the ability to witness the room as it originally appeared. What remains, however, gives credence to the notion that Perino here was joining in this conversation of recombination. In addition to borrowing potentially from Raphael, from Michelangelo, from Peruzzi, and even potentially from his workshop contemporaries, Perino invested his cycle with a contemplation of the language of the *all'antica* style, seeking themes relevant to the patron and the city yet presenting them in such a manner as to create their own unique dialogue with the other spaces of the palazzo.

Though often overlooked, adjacent to Perino's grand *salone* series was a connected chamber encircled by a frescoed frieze conjured by Polidoro da Caravaggio (Figs. 25 and 26). This series includes ten panels that wrap around the upper reaches of the room and, though it is much better preserved, still

45 Vasari, *Lives*, II: 157–158.

lacks a full interpretation. Three scenes each appear on the two longer sides of the room, each scene broken by a carved wooden corbel extending from the ceiling's crossbeams. Only two appear on the shorter stretches of the wall and are subdivided not by corbels but rather by paired putti who support the Baldassini coat of arms. These putti are presented in a noteworthy manner, as it would seem that Polidoro wished them to be not simply adornment but rather visual devices to engage the viewer. On the southern wall, one notes that the right-hand cherub offers a rather fiendish glance, while his compatriot looks away and out of the room. This gaze, when tracked, leads through the doorway to the adjacent chamber decorated by Perino, so it is as if this curious little cherub is acting in a way to connect these two spaces visually.[46]

Opposite this duo on the northern wall, one finds a similar pair of putti, the one the left looking outward and across the room toward the doorway that would have once led to Baldassini's stuffetta. This cherub bears a less fiendish but decidedly mischievous expression as he turns away from his duties to uphold the Baldassini crest, perhaps, though not assuredly, as an allusion to the more fantastical mythologies that played out on the stuffetta's walls as compared to the soberer scenes of the study space. His associated putto grips firmly on the crest and leans into it to turn his upper body such that he can gaze not beyond the chamber, as his cross-chamber colleague does, but rather into the adjoining scene. This distinction in pose seems to suggest that this cherub is indicating the beginning of this ten-image cycle.

Few have attempted to interpret this series, but those who have noted a central theme of the history of Roman law, fitting in this application given Baldassini's professional role as a consistorial advocate and law professor. Wolk-Simon identified, for example, a scene of *Bringing the Law of The Twelve Tables*, a symbolic foundation to Roman law, with an accompanying panel showcasing the *Distribution of the Twelve Tables Among Ancient Jurists*. In addition, the sixth image of the series depicts a deathbed scene, which has been interpreted as either a variation on *The Death of Socrates* or, as Wolk-Simon has suggested, *The Last Testament of King Eudamidas*. This latter work is the only to be paired with a preparatory drawing (*A Deathbed Scene*, 1521–1522; National Gallery of Art). The final scene has been interpreted by Maria Celeste Cola as *Cybele Being Transported to Rome from Pergamum*, as it depicts a mass of figures attempting

46 This is not that unlike the same visual device used by Peruzzi in his creation of the large monochrome head in the Loggia di Galatea at the Villa Farnesina. For more, see: A.R. Culotta, "Baldassarre Peruzzi and the Architecture of Painting," *Sixteenth Century Journal*, 51 (1) (Spring 2020).

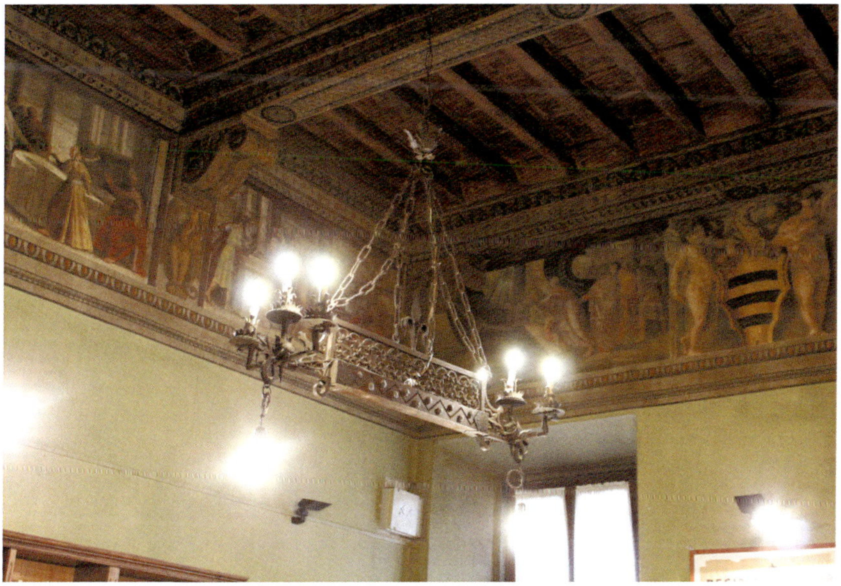

FIGURE 25 Portions of Polidoro's fresco cycle in Baldassini's study
PALAZZO BALDASSINI, ROME—AUTHOR'S IMAGE

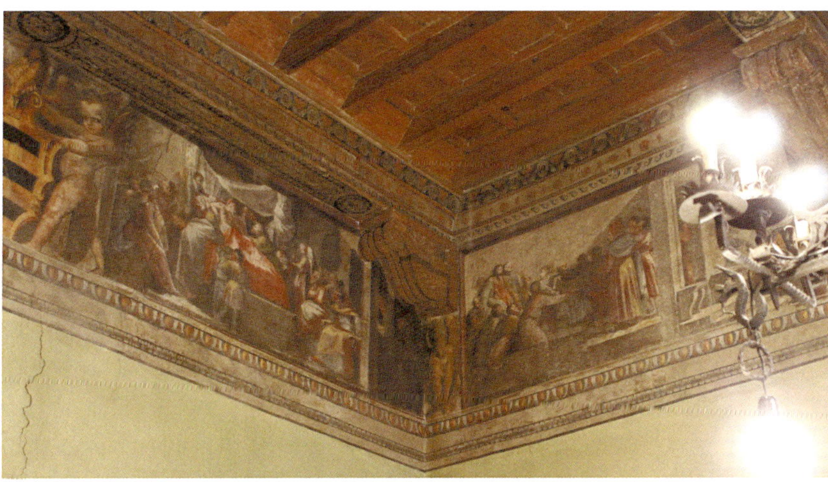

FIGURE 26 Portions of Polidoro's fresco cycle in Baldassini's study
PALAZZO BALDASSINI, ROME—AUTHOR'S IMAGE

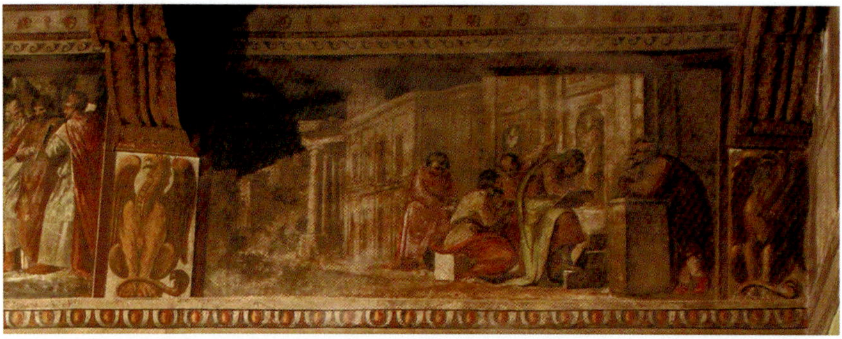

FIGURE 27 Polidoro, *Students at Work*
PALAZZO BALDASSINI, ROME—AUTHOR'S IMAGE

to load a votive statue unto a ship.[47] Beyond these four scenes scattered throughout the cycle, however, there is much left to be interpreted.

Beyond what has already been noted regarding these curious compositions, it seems important to note that Polidoro's use of elements from a shared visual language is perhaps not as transparent. For example, though Polidoro's surviving body of drawings reveals his penchant for studying antiquity (many of which would become his own sourcebook for frescoed façade decorations), few clear quotations from antiquity emerge in these scenes. One quotation does indeed stand out, though, and it is the scene in which it appears—so far unexplored satisfactorily in scholarship—that can be seen as illustrating so nicely the ways in which Polidoro, like his colleagues, put this visual language from past and present together. This is the vignette, called here *Students at Work*, in which one finds a team of students at work under the not-so-watchful supervision of a daydreaming master (Fig. 27).

"Daydreaming" is perhaps not the correct word, as it is apparent that this figure, hunched over an elevated marble plinth, refers to the traditional ancient depiction of Melpomene, the muse of tragedy. In such likenesses, Melpomene is draped over her plinth and consumed by folds of fabric, save for her right leg, which she crossed over her left to emerge from beneath this drapery. This at least is the way she appeared on the *Sarcophagus of the Muses*, an artifact from antiquity that also served as an earlier source of study for Raphael and others. Polidoro, though adjusting gender, nevertheless creates a relatively faithful

47 For more see: M.C. Cola, "Palazzo Baldassini," in F. Cappelletti and C. Cieri, eds., *La cultura artistica nelle dimore romane fra Quattrocento e Cinquecento: funzione e decorazione* (Università Degli Studi Di Roma "La Sapienza", Facoltà Di Lettere E Filosofia, Istituto Di Sotria Dell'Arte, 1991), 55–63. Cola's work is also cited in: M. Cogotti and L. Gigli, *Palazzo Baldassini* (Rome: L'erma di Bretschneider, 1995), 69–70.

copy, even muddling the foreshortening of the feet to ensure that this male figure's right foot appears in the very lowest portion of the scene. A figure in this posture—also unidentified—appears in the far-right background of the *School of Athens*, just above and to the left of Raphael and his colleagues in various guises, as he leans upon the base of the pilaster that ascends to the upper reaches of the fresco. This *School* figure hunches over a younger man crouched in the act of drawing, his tablet and stylus pulled up close to his face with the aid of an elevated and bent knee. Given these parallels, it would seem that Polidoro here selected as the anchor of this panel a figure that would recall both antiquity and Raphael. It is a small element in the overall visual scheme, however, it is significant in that it showcases the same mode of recombination of visual phrases to amplify the reading of the scene.

Could this be a clue to the overall narrative depicted in this vignette? Was Polidoro particularly clever here, referencing Raphael's *School* while also conjuring a version of his own? The references to Raphael do not end here. The four male figures grouped to the left of this male "Melpomene" seem in the midst of deep study, making the interpretation of this scene as one of schooling likely. Such a narrative would again align with the overall emphasis on this chamber on the learned law intellect of patron Baldassini, however it does not look as if these young men are studying legal edicts. Rather, their study is of the sweep of architecture that pulls across the scene in dramatic recession that serves as the background to the men who attend diligently to their drawing boards. The central figure in this four-man grouping gestures upward—not dissimilar in pose to the apostle that points in astonishment behind Saint Matthew in Raphael's *Transfiguration*—as if to stress the importance of the facades behind them. This emphasis on architecture, which bears echoes of the sweeping Bramantesque corridor that Raphael included in *School of Athens* as well as the architectural background of facades that appear in Raphael's cartoon for *The Sacrifice at Lystra* (1515–1516; Victoria & Albert Museum, London), combines with raking perspective to result in a rapid recession of these façades back into space.[48]

At the same time, this visual pull potentially implies a parallel to Perino's pull of perspective as seen in the neighboring grand *salone*; it could also be interpreted as a reference to Peruzzi as well. By this point, recall, Peruzzi and Polidoro had become close collaborators on frescoed facades across Rome; Peruzzi also had advanced the field of scenographic design. This sweep of architecture,

48 In comparing Polidoro's small fresco to this cartoon design, one could even surmise that the relief-carved plinth that appears at lower left could have proved the inspiration for the same element that appears in Polidoro's image.

which takes on a decidedly theatrical quality, thus might add to Polidoro's various references here to his close Sienese colleague. Carrying this observation to the larger cycle, one can note that Polidoro's scenes play with the viewer's perspective throughout. In the fourth scene, for example, in which an orator presents a tablet to an energetic crowd, Polidoro allows his cast of characters to weave between the architectural elements and goes so far as to plant a column at near center that obscures our reading of the scene. In the *Deathbed* scene, Polidoro conjures a rather archaic elevated perspective to offer the viewer a full pan of the space yet also endeavors to show us the space beyond the doorway at right. As the cycle progresses, this desire to showcase these different spaces becomes so pronounced that it is as if Polidoro is drawing inspiration from Michelangelo's Sistine pendentive depicting *The Punishment of Haman*. There, Michelangelo triumphed in a difficult compositional space to conjure the illusion of both an interior and exterior view; in Polidoro's scene of a heated council meeting, he uses a similar compositional device yet at the same time draws attention to its artifice (seen to the right of center in Fig. 26).

In this particular panel, a group of men are seated around two elevated figures. An air of suspense fills the composition, particularly as one can see the chariot—borrowed in design from the chariot in the scenes from the life of David in the Loggia for Leo x—poised for a quick departure outside. That illusion is disrupted, though, by the fact that Polidoro reveals that the wall enclosing this space ends just beyond the picture plane such that one can spy illuminating light overhead. By breaking this illusion, it is as if Polidoro is hoping to clue the viewer into the artifice of the image's scenography, to remind the viewer that this is indeed a constructed space that alludes to the work of his colleagues like Peruzzi. Such a nod to the education of the artist or the image of the workshop was, for this circle of artists, a relative rarity. One can note the prominent example of the artist's studio as documented in da Udine's *stuccheto* of the studio at work (Fig. 2) in the Vatican Loggia, however it would seem that Polidoro's image at the Palazzo Baldassini was more direct in its efforts to weave together various references that would have both pleased his patron while recalling the visual language of past and present.

In examining these contributions to the Palazzo Baldassini, one is treated to a fascinating array of motifs that expand understanding of one of the most marvelously decorated palazzi of early cinquecento Rome. Within these narratives, one can observe artists hard at work to conjure themes undoubtedly desired by their patron Baldassini but also infused with the novelty and multivalenced representations that were seen in the early days of Raphael's work in the Vatican stanza. This suggests that these artists had fully absorbed and mastered Raphael's recombinative use of a shared visual language by repeating and recombining elements from a variety of sources. That they were using it at the Palazzo Baldassini, outside of Raphael's purview and at a moment when they were defining their abilities beyond his shadow, indicates how effective they believed this approach to be. This is further reinforced by their subsequent work at the Villa Lante al Gianicolo.

CHAPTER 5

Romano, Penni, and Polidoro at the Villa Lante al Gianicolo

The Villa Lante was one of the first independent projects that the team pursued after Raphael's demise, and was built for Baldassarre Turini (1486–1543), a close associate of the Medici family who aspired to be part of the sixteenth-century generation of Roman elites.[1] Here, Giulio Romano, the de facto director of the workshop network following Raphael's death, worked alongside da Giovanni da Udine, Gianfrancesco Penni, and Polidoro da Caravaggio, and would build upon the same visual language explored during Raphael's lifetime. Just as at the Palazzo Baldassini, this recombination takes different forms, yet despite these differences it seems clear that these artists understood the potential that such recombination bore and upheld its continuity as a means of pursuing compositional novelty.

Diving into the details of this equally spectacular Roman residence, though, requires first a brief consideration of the context of the artistic atmosphere—particularly the ongoing prevalence of competition—in the wake of Raphael's death. Between 1520 and 1521, when Romano began work on the Villa Lante, Giulio and the other remaining members of Raphael's circle were still feeling the lingering pressures of Raphael's rivals, namely, Sebastiano and Michelangelo, who, recall, had joined forces in the previous decade and seemed to thrive in their partnership fueled on a shared dislike of Raphael. This acrimony did not dissipate following his death; rather, the members of Raphael's workshop took the brunt of this malice, as reflected in the previously noted exchange between Sebastiano and Michelangelo in September 1520 wherein Sebastiano bemoaned the fact that Romano and Penni had beat him out to complete the Vatican's Sala di Costantino and labels them as inferior.[2] Meanwhile, relations

1 Frommel parallels Turini's plans with those of the Palazzo Baldassini, suggesting that his original inspiration was a grand palace in the city but later changed his focus (C.L. Frommel, "Giulio Romano e la Progettazione di Villa Lante," in E.M. Steinby, *Ianiculum—Gianicolo: Storia, topografia, monumenti, leggende dall'antichità al rinascimento* (Rome, 1996), 119).

2 "… el Papa me ha hordinato che vi deba offerir la salla de' Pontifici da basso. […] E li dissi […] io non la farei, perché a me pare non esser inferior a li garzoni de Raffaello da Urbino …" (Golzio, 131; Shearman, *Raphael in Early Modern Sources*, I: 615). This proposed division of the project into two—the Sala di Costantino and the Sala dei Pontifici—indeed never occurred, as Perino and da Udine completed the latter. Wolk-Simon suggests that this continued patronage of Raphael's workshop members was in part owed to their artistic heritage:

 | DOI:10.1163/9789004430488_007

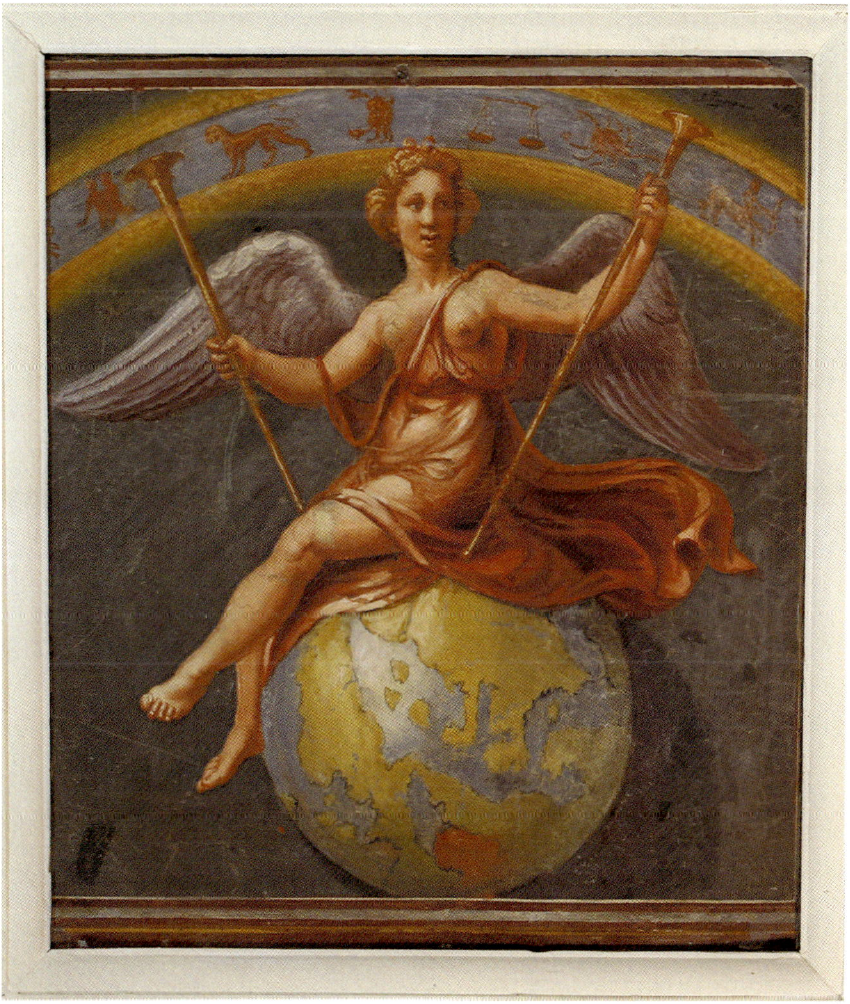

FIGURE 28 *Fame, Salone* ceiling fresco
ORIGINALLY FROM THE VILLA LANTE AL GIANICOLO—AUTHOR'S IMAGE

between these workshop members also experienced stressors. Letters sent between Cardinal Giulio de' Medici and associate Mario Maffei noted discord between Giulio and da Udine in the midst of their work at the Villa Ma-

"ties to Raphael, and an established and nearly incestuous patronage network, created a barricade around the still undecorated rooms of the Vatican palace that Sebastiano could not penetrate" (Wolk-Simon, "Competition, Collaboration," 7). A subsequent letter from Sebastiano to Michelangelo dated 7 September 1520 attempts to woo Michelangelo into becoming Sebastiano's collaborator for the room (Shearman, *Raphael in Early Modern Soures*, 1: 616); it would seem that his pleas in this instance went unanswered.

dama.[3] While the source and depth of their disagreement is unknown, this squabble is valuable to note here because it suggests critical junctures that, among other artistic relationships, might have resulted in a parting of paths. For Michelangelo and Sebastiano, anyway, this would be the case, as in the subsequent decade the working relationship between the two fractured irreparably. This was not, though, the outcome for Raphael's workshop associates. Despite such conflicts—more of which undoubtedly arose but were never documented—they continued to return to each other's company and call upon the same shared visual language for novelty.

1 Baldassarre Turini (1486–1543)

Turini was a bishop who arrived in Rome from Pescia in 1509 in order to serve as chamberlain to Cardinal Giovanni de' Medici (the future Pope Leo X).[4] Accordingly, Turini's status in Rome was an esteemed one that afforded him a more-than-comfortable lifestyle thanks to the substantial fortune he had amassed. Part of this fortune was poured into the building and decoration of his villa atop the Janiculum Hill.[5] This space was intended to broadcast Turini's status in Rome, to cement his connections within the city's ancient roots, and also to convey to visitors his intellect as well as his knowledge of art and history in the city. As Claudia Conforti has noted, Turini was an active patron of the arts whose name appears repeatedly among Vasari's chronicles.[6] He was of course also a learned individual, and the fact that he was so closely allied with the Medici family suggests that he would have understood the vast potential for architecture and interior decoration to serve as an aesthetic encapsulation of these aspects and thus would have carefully cultivated the styles and stories

3 For full text of the letters, see: R. LeFevre, "Un prelate del'500: Mario Maffei e la costruzione di Villa Madama." *L'Urbe*, 32 (1969), 1–11.

4 O. Merisalo, "Baldassarre Turini e la corte unmanistica medicea a Roma." In Tancredi Carunchio e Simo Örmä, *Villa Lante al Gianicolo: Storia della fabbrica e cronaca degli abitatori* (Rome: Palombi Editore, 2005), 151. For more, see: Cfr. ASRoma, Coll. Not. Capit. Fabianus de Cesis, vol. 519, f. 3, a ASRoman, Acrhivio Capitolino, sez. 66, Mandati, vol. 5, f. 13 citati in G. Stenius, 'Baldassarre Turini e le sue case romane sulla base dei documenti'. *OpIRF*, 1 (1981, 71, nn. 1,3); C. Conforti, "Baldassarre Turini: Funzionario Mediceo e Committente di Architettura," in E.M. Steinby, *Ianiculum—Gianicolo: Storia, topografia, monumenti, leggende dall'antichità al rinascimento* (Rome, 1996), 189–198.

5 O. Merisalo, "Baldassarre Turini, funzionario e mecenate." In F. Cantatore et al., eds., *Leone X: Finanza, mecenatismo, cultura*. Atti del Convegno Internazionale (Rome, 2015), 237–245.

6 For more on these connections, see: C. Conforti, "Baldassarre Turini."

therein. With this in mind, if one looks closer to the visual program that once adorned the interior—a task that requires a fair bit of reconstruction and imagination given the substantial changes in the space since Turini's tenure—one can argue that it too became a space primed for the shared visual language that its architect and associated team of artists would put into play.

2 A Challenge of Attribution and Dating

A relatively small-scale residence that nevertheless exuded impeccable luxury, the Villa Lante has thus far evaded the in-depth scholarly study afforded other sixteenth-century Roman villas. Its relatively small body of literature is owed in part to the fact that little information records its creation. Its foundation date, for example, eludes historical record, with one of the only concrete time stamps being the small graffito etched into the *salone*'s faux marble frescoes that notes the year 1527, which tells us only that at that point the villa and its interior program would have had to have been completed.[7] Even the authorship has been challenged: while most of the scholars who have worked on the villa have credited the design to the young Romano, the dearth of documentation surrounding the villa's construction has led some to suggest that perhaps it was the late design work of Raphael, a point extended through parallels drawn between the designs of this space and those for the partially-realized Villa Madama.[8]

The same issues of authorship plague the interior visual program, with debate still inconclusive over the artists who worked in the interior. While the stucco work of the loggia can be most clearly connected to da Udine, scholars have implicated nearly the entire gamut of the remaining artists from Raphael's workshop as having taken part in the villa's frescoed program.[9] Scholars such as

7 This graffito reads: "a dì de magio 1527 fo la presa di Roma." As recorded in Lilius; also see: Tancredi Carunchio, "La Villa Lante al Gianicolo: L'architettura e i suoi restauri." In T. Carunchio and S. Örmä, *Villa Lante al Gianicolo*, 23–76.

8 Prandi also noted the inherent language of Baldassarre Peruzzi's designs in Giulio's designs for Turini alongside the legacy of Raphael's architectural designs (A. Prandi, *Villa Lante al Gianicolo*, with a preface and introduction by T. Steinby (Rome: Edizioni dell'Ateneo, 1954), 95). For related comments, see: J.F. O'Gorman, "The Villa Lante in Rome: Some Drawings and Some Observations." *The Burlington Magazine*, 113 (816) (Mar., 1971), 132–138.

9 H. Lilius, *Villa Lante al Gianicolo: L'architettura e la decorazione pittorica*. 2 vols. (Roma: Acta Instituti Romani Finlandiae, 1981); also see: F. Sricchia Santoro, "Villa Lante, La decorazione del salone. Problemi di attribuzione." In E.M. Steinby, ed., *Ianiculum—Gianicolo: storia, topografia, monumenti, leggende dall'antichità al Rinascimento*, 225–236; and A. Gnann,

Fiorella Sricchia Santoro have noted the existence of at least one preparatory drawing by Polidoro da Caravaggio for *The Meeting of Janus and Saturn* (Musée du Louvre, inv. 6078*r*); Achim Gnann also proposed a connection between the group of women on the far bank in the scene of *The Escape of Clelia* as being associated with a *Study of Figures* (Albertina, inv. no. 399) attributed to Polidoro as well.[10] These visual connections seem to confirm his involvement in, at the very least, the design of the suite of imagery; Santoro also notes two additional sketches that seem to relate to the identified *Liberation of Clelia* (Bibliotheca Hertziana) and *The Escape of Clelia* (Gabinetto Disgeni e Stampe, Florence, St. Sc.692), the first of which she links to Romano.[11] Without clear authorship or dating for these two drawings, though, one must continue to speculate as to who was responsible for which components.

Later replicas of these four main compositions emerge predominantly through prints, yet they do little to help clarify. One example is a chiaroscuro woodcut purportedly Niccolò Vicentino that depicts a version of *Clelia Crossing the Tiber* (Philadelphia Museum of Art, 1985.52.317). This woodcut clearly echoes the similarly titled composition seen in the Villa Lante *salone*, however it is also clear that this print was executed after the days of Polidoro (this particular print proves problematic as it is clearly dated 1608 at the lower-left corner, which would make it nearly impossible to have been the work of Vicentino), which means that it cannot help to inform about the development of this *salone* scene nor the author of the same, nor can it reaffirm the narrative that it relays. Adding a layer of complication to the analysis of this work is the fact that a substantial portion of the frescoed ceiling of the villa's *salone*—outside of the stuccoed portico, perhaps the most splendid visual program of the *piano nobile*—was extricated in the nineteenth century, separating story and perhaps forever eliminating the possibility of a clear reading of the room and the artists at work.

These challenges of attribution recall a similar conundrum that faces Interpretation of the grand *salone* of the Palazzo Baldassini and thus perhaps serves as another illustration of the ways in which the hands of these artists could so easily combine in the creation of these visual programs such that it becomes

---

"Zur Beteililung des Polidoro da Caravaggio an der Ausmallung des Salone der Villa Lante." In E.M. Steinby, ed., *Ianiculum—Gianicolo: storia, topografia, monumenti, leggende dall'antichità al Rinascimento*, 237–259.

10 For more, see: A. Gnann, "Zur Beteiligung," 225–236.

11 For more, see: F.S. Santoro, "Villa Lante: La decorazione de salone. Problemi di attribuzione," in E.M. Steinby, ed., *Ianiculum—Gianicolo: storia topografia, monumenti, leggende dall'antichità al rinascimento* (Rome, 1996), 225–236.

difficult to tease apart their unique contributions. Had this team abandoned the approach of their former days, such uniformity would not be seen, and so its presence here reinforced that the artistic recombination using a shared visual language must have continued. Therefore, one can reconsider the architecture of the villa briefly and then investigate more fully the visual program within the context of the villa to make new arguments as to its meaning and the shared artistic mindset it might convey.

3 Romano's Designs

In employing Romano to design the villa (Fig. 29), Turini was undoubtedly calling upon the architect's connections with Raphael but at the same time was giving the young twenty-something innovator the opportunity to debut his own architectural voice. The result was, as Christoph Frommel has noted in his analysis of the structure, a space unique to its generation: "In no other Renaissance villa are a pleasurable setting, an architecture inspired by the beauty of living, classicizing frescoes, scintillating decorations and even small stucco sculptures integrated with comparable unity."[12] This unity and overwhelming lightness of design began in the very foundations of the structure. Turini's villa was not only sited on a historic hill of Rome—though not one of the original seven, the Janiculum was added to the litany of famous hills by the sixteenth century thanks to legacies of both Martial and Numa Pompilius—but recent analysis reveals that the villa itself used as its foundation a portion of Roman *opus concretum*. The fact that this brickwork is quite literally the basis of the structure suggests that either patron or architect (or both) wished to stress these historic ties.[13] Thus, Romano's design for the space was inherently Classical in its origins, recalling not only the legacy of Martial but also staying on trend, as it were, with the other villa complexes in the area (Chigi's villa, as one example, is within the line of sight of the Villa Lante).[14] Neat symmetry along with a combination of

---

12 Christoph Frommel, "The Roman Works of Giulio," 56. Echoed in: Hartt, *Giulio Romano*, I: 63.

13 Archaeological studies have discovered that Chigi's villa was also built on top of a lavish villa connected with Marcus Agrippa, however little suggests that Chigi or Peruzzi knew it was there.

14 For more, see: Martial, Epigrams, Book 4: 64, trans. translated in C. Vout, *The Hills of Rome: Signature of an Eternal City* (UK: Cambridge University Press, 2012), 200–203 (further analysis recounted in: C. Vout, "Sizing up Rome or theorising the overview," in S. Larmour and D. Spencer, eds., *The Sites of Rome: Time, Space, Memory* (Oxford), 295–322).

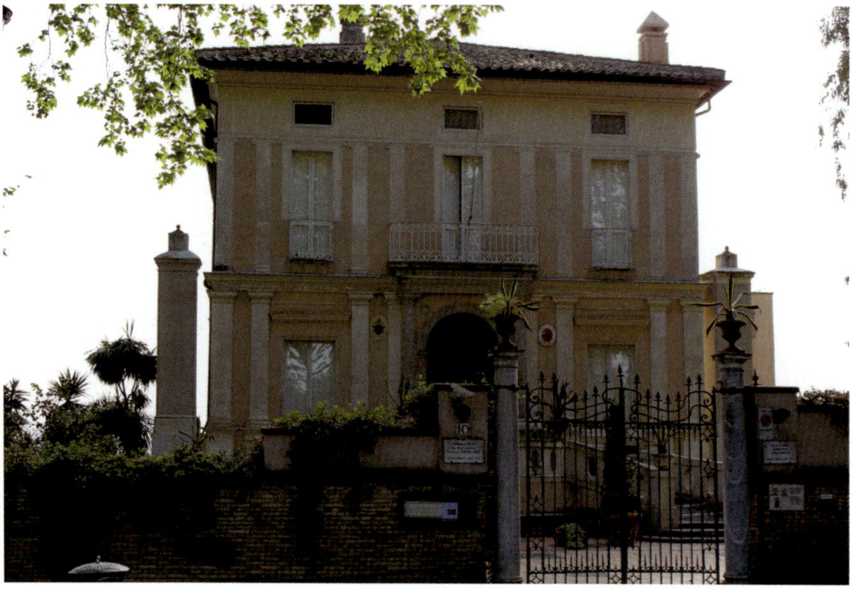

FIGURE 29 Giulio Romano
VILLA LANTE AL GIANICOLO, ROME—AUTHOR'S IMAGE

Doric and Ionic order pilasters define the hallmarks of Classical form as they were understood by early sixteenth-century architects.

This use of the Classical language of architecture would have undoubtedly stemmed from Romano's study of the architecture of Raphael as well as the designs of both Peruzzi and Bramante. Frommel makes note, for example, that it borrows an "analogue modesty" with the use of the colonnaded loggia that Peruzzi had employed at Chigi's villa only a handful of years earlier.[15] Moreover, Bramante's Tempietto, completed in 1515, rests on the same hill and thus could have served as immediate inspiration for him, if for nothing else than to further bolster the Classical allusions of the villa. Furthering this connection is the argument made by Christer Bruun in relation to a fragmentary panel recovered on the villa's grounds. Resembling a Doric frieze metope, Bruun concluded that Romano might have contemplated the addition of a Doric frieze for Turini's villa not unlike the frieze that Bramante incorporated in his diminutive monument for the Spanish king and queen.[16] Such an observation is furthered by the

15 Frommel, "Giulio Romano e la Progettazione," 121. Frommel also notes the parallels in room dimensions between Giulio's plan for the Villa Lante and those palazzi designed by Raphael and Bramante. For more, see: Frommel, "Giulio Romano e la Progettazione."

16 For more, see: C. Bruun, "Il fregio dorico di Villa Lante al Gianicolo. Un progetto sconosci-

connection of this reference to a similar Doric frieze that appears in Romano's later scenes of the Palazzo Tè, a quotation that Frederick Hartt suggested was owed to Giuliano da Sangallo's drawings of the extant Basilica Aemilia in Rome (Vat. Barb. La. 4424, fol. 26 ro.).[17] At the same time, one could also compare such a proposed frieze at Turini's villa to the similar Doric frieze that encircled Sangallo's interior courtyard for the Palazzo Baldassini, where, among other motifs, the previously-mentioned relief rendering of Hanno the elephant appeared.

The fact that Romano would call on such sources like Bramante or Sangallo is logical, as this was the legacy of study from which he was emerging. Giulio's exposure to architecture occurred during his mentorship with Raphael: his first documented architectural endeavor was that for the renovations of the Palazzo Branconio dell'Aquila (circa 1520), and, as Frommel as noted, there is evidence even earlier of Giulio's study of architecture alongside Raphael in graphic and painting form. Designs for *The Liberation of Saint Peter* and *Fire in the Borgo* (both 1514) reflect the shared interests in architectural design between Raphael and Romano. The symmetry between their respective architectural approaches can be seen in the designs for spaces like the Villa Madama, wherein the extent of Romano's contributions to the original plans are still debated.

As scholarship has shown, though, Romano executed monumental changes to that architectural plan, and some have pointed to similar deviations in his designs for the Villa Lante.[18] Perhaps this was to be expected, though, as it was, from most accounts, the first project on which Romano worked independently. Antonio Prandi, for example, reinforces the notion that Romano's design is not one that copies but rather one that navigates both Peruzzi's and Raphael's design sensibilities.[19] Thus, Prandi encapsulates the space as "an 'improvisa-

uto di Giulio Romano?" in E.M. Steinby, ed., *Ianiculum—Gianicolo: storia topografia, monumenti, leggende dall'antichità al rinascimento* (Rome, 1996), 141–162. Beyond Bruun's analysis, there is no additional evidence or documentation attests to such a frieze addition to Turini's villa, however Trygge Gestrin's article highlights the visual elements of a Turini crest relief panel that perhaps was associated with such a project. For more, see: T. Gestrin, "The *Stemma* of Baldassarre Turini: Remarks on the heraldry and architecture of Villa Lante al Gianicolo." In O. Merisalo and R. Vainio, eds., *Ad itum liberum: Essays in Honor of Anne Helttula* (Jyväskylä, 2007), 7–12.

17 Hartt, *Giulio Romano*, I: 8.

18 Frommel notes parallels between the façade design of the Villa Lante and the Villa Madama, noting that "not only the frieze of the architrave and the cornice with two S-curve mouldings, but above all the frieze—in the form of an elongated Ionic capital—speak the unmistakable language of the windows and doors of the Villa Lante" (Frommel, "The Roman work of Giulio," 61).

19 "… vale a dire là dove s'incontravano lo stile del Peruzzi e quello di Raffaello" (Prandi, 96–97).

tion,' exploding from the architect's mind and realized with furious immediacy: novelty at its most genuine state; and thus it becomes the most pure illumination of the architectural vision of Romano at his debut, and so is the most truthful sign of his personality: raw as much as it is vulgar, but authentic and frank."[20] This innovative improvisation, according to Tancredi Carunchio, must have occurred between 1518 and 1527, meaning that the early phases of construction very well could have overlapped with the final days of Raphael's lifetime. At the very least, it reminds us that work on this space potentially began concurrently to those final days of work in the Vatican stanze.

Perhaps while Romano was diligently implementing his architectural vision, a team of artists descended upon the interior to conjure several spectacular spaces. An open-air loggia spanned almost the entire eastern façade of the *piano nobile* and was replete with striking white stucco designs. These *stucchetti* were met with frescoes in every room on the first floor, totaling four chambers that consisted of a lavish *salone* and three similarly-scaled *sale* as they will be referred to here.[21] Designed in conjunction to create a harmonious interior visual program, these spaces each merit their own discussion as they illustrate individual instances where one can find the elements of this shared visual language being combined.

4 The Adjacent *Sale*

Upon entrance into the Villa Lante, visitors were greeted by an extended corridor that culminated in the grand *salone*; along this route, however, one could also detour into one of the three adjacent chambers, each of which is of similar dimension and which bear parallel decorative programs: each pane of the vaulted ceiling features a roundel portrait of a figure ensconced in a field of *all'antica* grotesque motifs. These panes encircle a central zone, which might have originally held the Turini *stemma* but has been restored to feature that of the later owners, the Lante family (Fig. 30).

The first *sala*, or the so-called cancelleria, includes male roundel portraits at the center of each pane of the vaulted ceiling. These likenesses have been most extensively discussed by Henrik Lilius, who proposes they reflect "likenesses

20 Prandi, 103.

21 These three chambers have alternately been titled by Henrik Lilius a study, an office, and a "cancelleria," respectively, but for the sake and simplicity of this analysis these three rooms will simple be noted to as the lateral rooms (*sale*) and numbered according to their location within the ground plan of the villa.

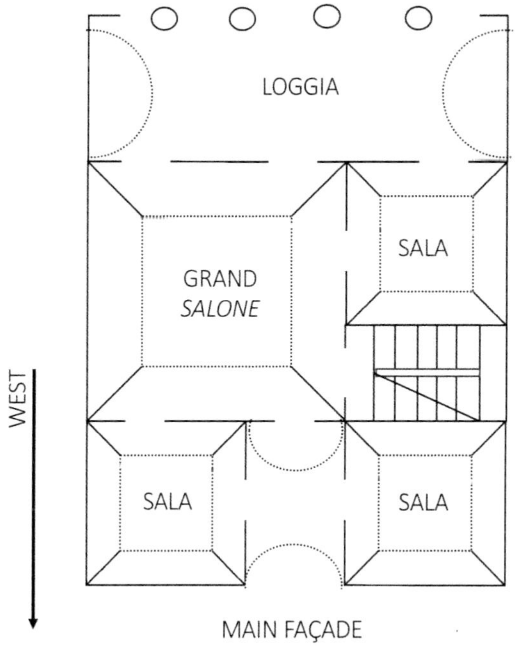

FIGURE 30 Plan of the *piano terreno*
VILLA LANTE AL GIANICOLO, ROME—
AUTHOR'S DIAGRAM

easily recognized and desired to be recognized."[22] He notes, for example, the pairing of a portrait of Raphael—again, the clearest of his identifications as it parallels his likeness as it appears in *Self-Portrait with a Friend* (1518; Louvre Museum)—alongside portraits of Petrarch and Dante, recognizable for their laurel crowns. Lilius identifies the final figure as Angelo Poliziano, based undoubtedly on the similarities between this roundel's depiction and the portrait of Poliziano included in Ridolfo Ghirlandaio's fresco cycle of the Capella Tornabuoni (1485–1490) in Florence's Santa Maria Novella.[23] These male portrait roundels are supported by a Classical amphora below and a festooned figure above that are linked by scrolling acanthus motifs. These central zones are flanked on either side by rectangular cartouches rendered in the *all'antica fondo nero* (black ground) style and retelling, in Lilius' interpretation, the mythological narratives of Jason and the Argonauts along with that of Marcus Curtius.[24]

22 Lilius, "Gli Affreschi," 123.
23 Ibid., 124.
24 Ibid., 128.

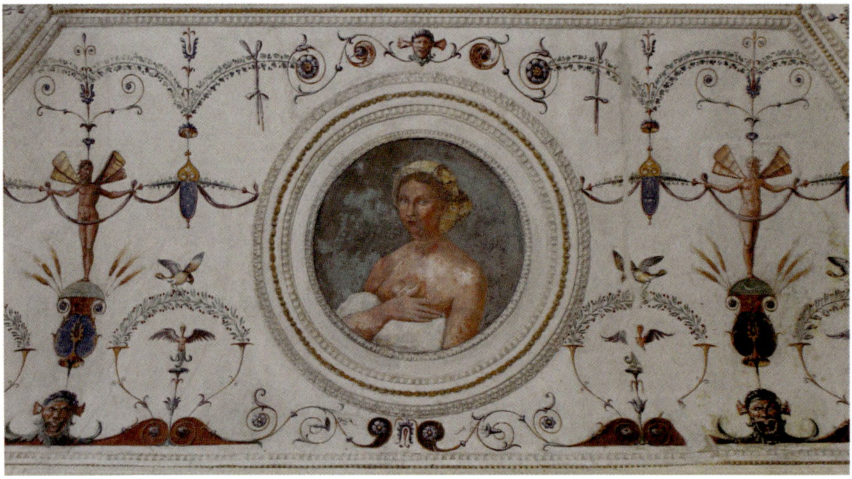

FIGURE 31 Detail of sala ceiling with portrait resembling Raphael's *La Fornarina*
VILLA LANTE AL GIANICOLO, ROME—AUTHOR'S IMAGE

These cartouches are supported below by prancing satyrs who hold up festooned garlands that dangle from the cartouche's frames. Unfurled ribbons and additional acanthus, whimsical dolphins, and leaping goats come together to complete scenes that clearly channel ancient Roman wall painting yet bring those concepts into the modern age with portrait roundels set in the center of each ceiling face.

As a compliment to this chamber of men, both across the hall and adjacent to the grand *salone* one finds two additional chambers that depict portraits of women in a similar format. It is in these female portraits that one can see the persistence of the workshop visual language of recombination most prominently at play. A review of the portraits of the women featured in these two rooms reveal a series of likenesses all of similar comportment. This is a point that has already been noted in Henrik Lilius' comprehensive analysis of the Villa, wherein he worked to link seven of these eight portraits to prior works by Raphael. In the first, northwestern *sala*, Lilius proposes that the women all echo some of Raphael's most iconic protagonists: beginning from the northern wall and moving clockwise, he notes parallels to *La Donna Velata* (1514–1515; Palazzo Pitti, Florence); *La Fornarina* (1518–1519; Galleria Nazionale d'Art Antica, Palazzo Barberini Rome) (Fig. 31); *La Donna Gravida* (1505–1506; Palazzo Pitti, Florence), and, finally, the muse Melpomene from Raphael's *Parnassus* (1509–1511) borrowed from within the Vatican stanze.

A visual comparison between these works supports Lilius' observations, although one must question the outlier of the muse among such identifiable portraits. Despite this distinction, if one accepts Lilius' interpretations, in this *sala* one can see a very literal revival of Raphael's approach, as if the artists at work in this room wanted to very clearly express a connection with his legacy. Lilius' interpretation of the several figures, like that which he likens to *La Donna Velata* and *La Fornarina*, seem without challenge; it does, however, seem important to note that the subjects seen in some of these portraits also appeared in collaborative compositions and works authored solely by workshop members. Giulio, for example, completed *Portrait of a Young Woman* (1518; Museum of Fine Arts Strasbourg), which bears striking similarity to Raphael's *La Donna Velata* and thus could have informed this reference's selection. Giulio also created *Woman at a Mirror* (circa 1520; Pushkin Museum, Moscow) at approximately the same time he worked at the Villa Lante, which might have further influenced the selection of this reference to Raphael's *La Fornarina*. These observations are made not to challenge Lilius' identifications, but rather to point out that perhaps what was occurring in this space was not just an emulation of Raphael's former work but also potentially a nod to this workshop and their ability to transform these types in new contexts.

The second *sala* features a more elaborate set of imagery that nevertheless revolves around a similar theme. Here, just as is seen in the *sala* featuring the male portraits, the roundels are framed by paired narrative cartouches embedded in similar webs of *all'antica* motifs. Lilius works to make similar connections between these portraits and other works from a larger circle of artists, this time proposing connections beyond Raphael. He notes, for example, that the portrait on the northern wall of the room bears similarities to Domenico Ghirlandaio's portrait of Lucrezia Tornabuoni (1427–1482) from *The Birth of the Baptist* in the Capella Tornabuoni; he also suggests that the adjacent portrait seems akin to the muse Thalia as rendered by Raphael after his study of the Sarcophagus of the Muses that once inhabited Chigi's collection of antiquities. For the final two images, Lilius suggests tentative links to a "speculative image of the Magdalene" from Raphael's *Santa Cecilia* (1514; Pinacoteca Nazionale, Bologna) and finally another muse, Euterpe, taken once again from Raphael's *Parnassus*. In general, Lilius' connections in this room are more speculative overall but tie to his theory that they are included as representations of famous women who were "personaggi storici."[25] His interpretation challenged the earlier reading of these portraits, made by J.G. Gutensohn and J. Thürmer in the nineteenth century, that proposed these likenesses represented the Classical poets, an interpretation furthered by Ludovico Gruner who named these poets'

25 Lilius, "Gli affreschi," 123.

loves in the nearby *sala* and suggested that the additional chamber's visage reflects personifications of the seasons.[26] Though Lilius challenged these past interpretations he nevertheless concluded that he too believes these chambers bear poetic symbolism, though he was careful to highlight that these more "modern" figures stand in contrast to the ancient characters that appear elsewhere in the villa.[27]

Revisiting this second *sala* of female portraits, however, particularly in light of the observations made in previous chapters, might help to bolster or expand Lilius' in-depth analysis of the visual program in these chambers. One perspective from which to advance is the reading that these women are allusions to muses. Some, as noted, bear direct references to the muses of Raphael's *Parnassus*: Thalia, as modeled from the previously-discussed *Sarcophagus of the Muses*, and Euterpe, who, as examined earlier, served as a vehicle through which Raphael was able to embody the visual language of Michelangelo in his early Vatican fresco. This is a small quotation extracted from a much larger work, but its implications are significant. By quoting Raphael's figure that in turn was also borrowed from his own study of Michelangelo—and that, coincidentally, fueled the rivalry between the two artists—the incorporation of this quotation became a larger reflection on the use of this visual language. On the one hand, it served as a visual reminder of the legacy of Raphael and the ways in which he worked to further develop his visual lexicon once arrived in Rome. On the other hand, it perhaps alludes to the very concept of a muse as a source of inspiration. So, just as this roundel portrait recalls an earlier work by Raphael, it also defines a new role, that within the larger program planned for Turini's villa.

One can sense, for example, how such parallels to *Parnassus* would have been fitting within the elegant and *all'antica* styling of Turini's villa as it could have drawn parallels to both the image that appeared in the Pope's chambers as well as to the overall siting of the villa. From this perspective, one can speculate that the desire here was to indeed juxtapose Turini's villa with that of Chigi's, situated just below the Janiculum as a potential statement of status. One hint that this connection was desired can be found in the elephant that appears in the small narrative panel to the left of the roundel portrait of Lucrezia (as identified by Lilius). Though not a common inclusion in the imagery of this story, this elephant was perhaps noted here as an homage to the previously mentioned elephant Hanno, whose journey to Rome in 1514 for the celebra-

26 For more on these portrait interpretations as poets, see: J.G. Gutensohn and J. Thürmer, *Decorazioni a fresco e a stucco nelle chiese e nei palazzi d'Italia dei Secoli XV e XVI*, a publication began by Gutensohn and Thürmer and completed by Gruner (London, 1844).

27 Lilius, "Gli Affreschi," 130.

tion Leo X's ascension to the papacy had been facilitated in part by Chigi.[28] The elephant's tenure in Rome was unfortunately brief—it died two years after its arrival—but its celebrity was such that Raphael had been tasked with creating a commemorative fresco in the animal's honor. This work was never realized, yet it seems that some portion of its preparation made its way into this Villa Lante cycle. This might be seen as giving too much weight to a small element in the overall visual program. It is noteworthy nevertheless, though, as elephants are not frequent characters in such works. Recall once again, though, the appearance of the creature in the Doric frieze within the Palazzo Baldassini's courtyard—and this inclusion becomes quite deliberate.

5 The Grand *Salone*

From these anterior *sale* one would continue into the grand *salone*, once the masterpiece of fresco work in Turini's villa. This is the room, however, that has been most heavily modified since the bishop's lifetime. Turini lived in his Janiculum abode until his death in 1543, at which point the villa entered a succession of owners who increasingly disregarded its legacy. In 1551, Turini's heir sold the property to the sons of Michele III Lante (1490–1550), who at the time already possessed a large *vigna* on the Janiculum. The Lante family maintained ownership of the villa until 1817, when a series of financial difficulties forced the sale of the property to Camillo Borghese.[29] Specifically, Carunchio outlines the major phases of the building's modifications between its sixteenth-century creation and the first restoration projects in the 1950s, the most relevant of which was the 1817 purchase of the property by Camillo Borghese, namesake of sixteenth-century Cardinal Camillo Filippo Ludovico Borghese (1775–1832), who also served as patron of the Palazzo Borghese near the Ponte Cavour. Like his ancestors, the eighteenth-century Camillo Borghese was similarly enamored with art appreciation and collection, a testament to which was his commissioning of Antonio Canova's famed *Pauline Bonaparte as Venus Victrix* (1805–1808; Galleria Borghese), as Pauline Bonaparte was Camillo's wife.[30]

Camillo, though, most likely had very little time to enjoy ownership of the Villa Lante, because soon after his purchase he was forced to flee to Florence

28 For more on Hanno and his legacy, see: S.A. Bedini, *The Pope's elephant* (New York: Penguin, 2000).

29 S. Örmä, "I propreitari e la vita nella villa," In T. Carunchio e S. Örmä, *Villa Lante al Gianicolo: Storia della fabbrica e cronaca degli abitatori* (Rome: Palombi Editore, 2005), 151–154.

30 Carunchio, "Villa Lante," 75–76; G. Borghezio, *I Borghese*, Roma, 1954.

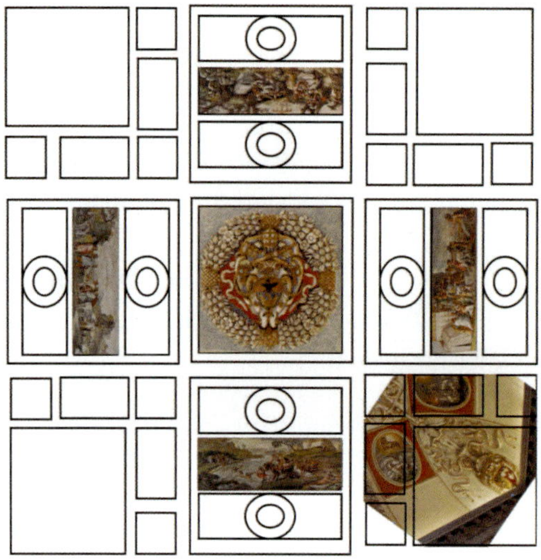

FIGURE 32 Diagram of grand *salone* ceiling as currently installed
AUTHOR'S IMAGE

as he had been disgraced both by his wife and by his allegiances to Napoleon. Camillo died in Florence in 1834, leaving his brother, Francesco Borghese-Aldobrandini (1776–1839) to inherit his estate, which included the Villa Lante. Francesco moved to Rome and threw himself into a variety of projects—archaeological excavations on the grounds of his family's property, philanthropy, an aqueduct in Frascati, to name a few—all of which offered perhaps too much distraction to keep the villa in his possession. Thus, Francesco facilitated the sale of the villa in 1837 to Madeleine Sophie Barat, who was a founding member of the Suore del Sacro Cuore, and, according to popular lore, they were so aghast at the themes of the frescoes in the villa's grande *salone* (Fig. 32)—somehow disregarding the similar timbre of the frescoes and stucco work elsewhere in the villa—that, under permission of the pope, they had the main frescoes removed for storage at the Palazzo Borghese.[31]

31 Lilius, "Gli Affreschi di Villa Lante," in n T. Carunchio and S. Örmä, *Villa Lante al Gianicolo: Storia della Fabbrica e cronaca degli abitatori* (Rome: Institutum Romanum Finlandiae, 2005), 77. Fiorella Sricchia Santoro, "Villa Lante: La Decorazione del Salone, Problemi di Attribuzione," in E.M. Steinby, *Ianiculum—Gianicolo: Storia, topografia, monumenti, leggende dall'antichità al rinascimento* (Rome, 1996), 225. The modern convent of the Suore del Sacro Cuore sits at the bottom of the Janiculum, directly below the Villa Lante. This narrative of the fresco's removal, however, seems far from plausible, particularly given the

Later, in 1892, when the Borghese family officially declared bankruptcy, these same orphaned frescoes were auctioned to Henrietta Hertz, who was at the time amassing what would become one of the most impressive connoisseur collections of early twentieth-century Rome.[32] These extricated frescoes were carefully installed in the main dining room of Hertz's new Roman home in 1906 and thus have been well-preserved over the past century within the Palazzo Zuccari, however there is no record as to whether or not this reinstallation maintained the same organization as the original chamber, a point revisited later.

Hertz's purchase guaranteed the preservation of the panels, making them some of the best-preserved works from the villa (much of the modern frescoes have been heavily restored) and thus also some of the most studied. Lilius has published extensively on the topic of these frescoes as well, working diligently to reassemble a coherent narrative while also examining the various influences at play in each scene. While Lilius' interpretations of the narratives depicted are at times speculative, one can use his observations as a basis for examining this language of visual vocabulary as it continued in this space.

The grande *salone* would have originally been a relatively complex suite of narratives that nevertheless demonstrated unity with the other decorated rooms of the *piano nobile*. Serving as the connecting chamber between the three previously-discussed frescoed rooms and the elegant loggia overlooking the Tiber and the city of Rome, the *salone* today bears at its apex a ceiling panel

---

fact that the Pagan references of the ceiling were still in situ with the small square frescoes left behind, the themes of which are still writ large in the loggia.

32 Records suggest that "the frescoes by Giulio Romano from the Villa Lante" were bought for 20,000 lire by Jean Paul Richter working as emissary for Henrietta Hertz, as recorded in: *Catalgoue des objets d'art et d'ameublement qui garissent le grand appartement au premier étage du palais du Prince Borghese à Rome* (Rome: Imprimerie Éditrice Romana, 1892); ASV, Archivio Borghese, vol. 56, fasc. 1163; F. Curti and L. Sickel, *Dokumente zur Geschichte des Palazzo Zuccari 1578–1904* (Munich: Hirmer Verlag, 2013), 263, 1892/1; J.P. Richter, *La Collezione Hertz e gli affreschi di Giulio Romano nel Palazzo Zuccari (con una prefazione di Robert Mond)* (Leipzig, 1928); G. Steinmetzer, *Der Palazzo Zuccari in Rom. Bau-Umbau-Neubau* (PhD diss., UB Salzburg, 2001), S. 239; E. Kieven, *100 Jahre Biblioteca Hertziana, Max-Plank-Institut für Kunstgeschichte: Der Palazzo Zuccari und die Institutgebäude 1590–2013* (Biblioteca Hertziana, Max Plank-Institut für Kunstgeschichte, 2013), 428. For more on Hertz, see: Kieven, *100 Jahre Biblioteca Hertziana*; also see G. Wolff Metternich, "Die Biblioteca Hertziana und der Palazzo Zuccari zu Rom." *Arbeitsgemeinschaft für Forschung des Landes Nordhein-Westfalen* (Cologne: Westdeutscher Verlag, 1950); C.L. Frommel, "Der Palazzo Zuccari und die Institutsgebäude." *Biblioteca Hertziana—Max-Planck-Institut* (Max-Planck-Gesellschaft. Berichte und Mitteilungen, 40.3), Munich 1991, S. 36–51; Jean Paul Richter, *La Collezione Hertz e gli affreschi di Giulio Romano nel Palazzo Zuccari (con una prefazione di Robert Mond)* (Leipzig, 1928); Curti and Sickel, *Dokumente*, 267, 1904/VI.

revealing the Papal insignia and the crest of the Borghese family (from, recall, the subsequent owners of the property). Of greater importance, however, are the remaining components of the once-fully frescoed panes of the vaulted ceiling. One can see, for example, how the artists at work in the Villa Lante carried forth the motif of the portrait roundel by incorporating freestanding sculpted busts in circular niches around the room, very similar to those conjured for the decorative program of the Villa Madama. In addition, each corner features paired *imprese* that repeat around the room. Clement VII's is that which bears the Latin phrase, "Candor illesus," and is accompanied by a central luminescent orb that appears to be capturing the rays of the incandescent sun and using this power to set a nearby tree ablaze. The neighboring panel bears the motto "Altore alto it fides altius" and depicts the characteristic hound of the Turini family *stemma* who gazes intently upward at a serene, majestic lion that draws direct reference to Pope Leo X.[33] These busts and the *stemme* were once paired with the since-removed fresco cycle—in total, four large rectangular frescoes, eight square scenes, and sixteen smaller rectangular vignettes—now installed at the Palazzo Zuccari and implied at the Villa Lante only in the remaining miniature *sgraffitto* frescoes that once framed each scenes and still grace the ceiling.

Lilius analyzes these vignettes using the reinstalled program at the Palazzo Zuccari to interpret the four main panels as scenes derived from the mythological origins of the Janiculum, recounted here most briefly: *The Meeting of Janus and Saturn on the Janiculum; The Escape of Clelia; The Liberation of Clelia*; and *The Rediscovery of the Tomb of Numa Pompilius* (Fig. 33). He then goes on to identify the smaller square panels as parallel narratives: with *The Meeting of Janus and Saturn*, he identifies *Janus Praying to Peace to Destroy the Armor* and *Jupiter and Saturn* (*Castration*); *The Escape of Clelia* with *Horatius Cocles on the Bridge* and *Mucius Scaevola; The Liberation of Clelia* he pairs with *Fame* and an *Equestrian Statue of Clelia*; and finally *The Rediscovery of the Tomb* with *Numa Pompilius Sacrificing to Vesta* and *Construction of a Temple to Janus*. This array of imagery is further complemented by small panels of what Lilius identifies as depicting Ceres, Victory, Neptune, Pluto, Europa, Bacchus and Silenus, as well as Galatea, along with *amorini* in various riding in chariots led by an assortment of exotic animals.

Lilius' analysis of these scenes is extensive; however, it is not without difficulty. He even admits that two of the central scenes—*The Meeting of Janus and Saturn on the Janiculum* and *The Liberation of Clelia*—have virtually no visual

33 T. Gestrin, "The *Stemma* of Baldassarre Turini."

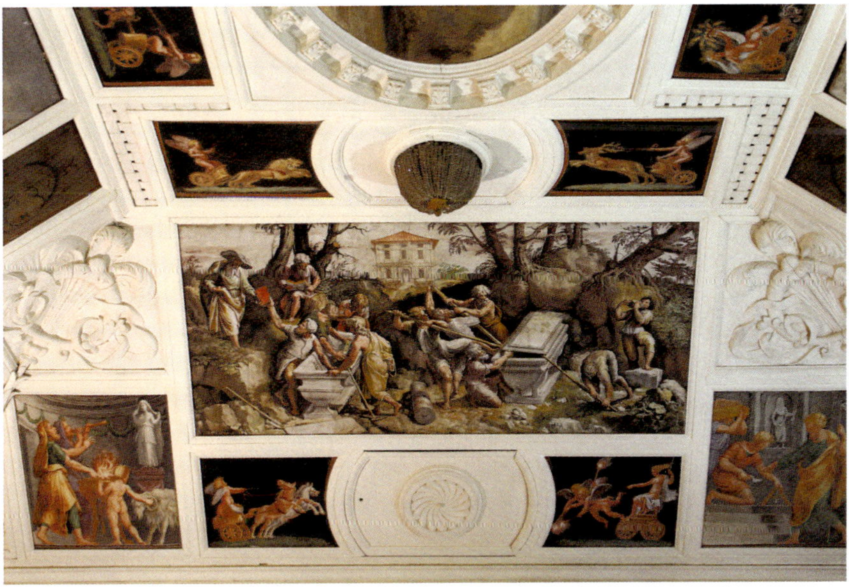

FIGURE 33 Portion of the salone frescoes from the Villa Lante al Gianicolo, showing the *Discovery of the Tomb of Numa Pompilius*
AS INSTALLED AT THE BIBLIOTECA HERTZIANA, ROME—AUTHOR'S PHOTO

precedents, and the precursors he cites for the remaining two are far from substantial. In addition, it seems clear that modifications have been made to these frescoes at some point since their creation. A close look at the proposed figure of Saturn in *The Meeting of Janus and Saturn* reveals that his scythe—a common attribute of his representation—is missing and perhaps has been removed (as evidence in the *intonaco* layer suggests modifications). The building façade that appears in the background of *The Rediscovery of the Tomb of Numa Pompilius* is also suspect, as its sketched treatment seems out of place compared to the definition seen in the remainder of the scene. Moreover, the façade that is presented is somewhat confusing as it is not the eastern façade, which one would expect to see if looking up at the villa as it is perched atop the Janiculum. Rather, it shows the western (frontal) façade of the villa, which skews the viewer's understanding of the context of the scene.[34] Furthermore, Lilius has based his analysis on the manner in which the frescoes were installed in

34 James F. O'Gorman attributed this oversight to Polidoro, suggesting that he "rotated the villa in his painting perhaps in order to show its most characteristic façade facing east, so the painting cannot be used as a document for the relationship between the building and its site." (O'Gorman, 133). Visual observation, though, reveals that it is more likely that this façade was added after the fact.

Palazzo Zuccari, which proves potentially problematic in that there is no record that these panels were maintained in the same organization as they originally appeared in the Villa Lante.[35] The 1892 inventory that noted that not all of the fresco panels are of the same dimensions: while two of the four larger rectangular panels measure 0.98 by 2.19 meters (38.5 by 86.2 inches), the other two span 0.93 by 2.36 meters (36.6 by 92.8 inches). These variations are small but adequately significant to suggest that dimensions varied depending on placement inside the *salone*.

This first set of measurements aligns correctly (that is, the two matching measurements fall on opposite sides of the room from each other in their current display), but this alignment falls apart in consideration of the eight smaller square compositions. Four of these—*Temple of Janus, Numa Sacrificing, Janus Praying for Peace*, and *Fame*—all bear the same dimensions of 0.80 by 0.75 m (31.5 by 29.5 inches). The other four bear slightly varying dimensions, however they all are similarly within range of 0.85 by 0.80 m: *The Equestrian Statue* measures 0.87 by 0.80 (34.25 by 31.5 inches); *Saturn and Jupiter* measures 0.86 by 0.80 (33.9 by 31.5 inches); *Mucius Scaevola* measures 0.95 by 0.78 (37.4 by 30.7 inches); and *Horatius Cocles* measures 0.85 by 0.82 (33.5 by 32.2 inches). This variation suggests that, just like the larger rectangular frescoes, these smaller squares bore specific sites on the four sides of the ceiling vault, yet the consideration of these measurements challenges the current arrangement.

Looking more closely at past documentation reveals, however, that the current arrangement is by no means identical to the original. In her comprehensive monograph on the Biblioteca Hertziana, Elisabeth Keiven notes that the current ordering of the frescoes was most likely guided by Professor Moritz Meurer from the German Artists Association of Rome at the time of their installation in 1906.[36] The accuracy of this order, again according to Keiven, is confirmed from a nineteenth-century watercolor by Giuseppe Maria Perrone that depicts the ceiling (Biblioteca Hertziana, Graphiksammlung, Inv. Nr. 10246), however this offers no legitimate connection to the original sixteenth-century arrangement of these scenes.

What this means is that perhaps one can disentangle the narratives being shown here by rearranging the fresco panels into an assortment more in line with their original placement. It bears mentioning that the 1892 catalogue that

35 *Catalogue des objets d'art et d'ameublement qui garnissent le grand appartement au premier étage du palais du prince Borghese à Rome. La vente aux enchères aura lieu au palais Borghese dans l'appartement même du Lundi 28 Mars au Samedi 9 Avril 1892*. (Rome: Imprimerie Éditrice Romana, 1892), 26–27.

36 Keiven, *100 Jahre*, 255–258.

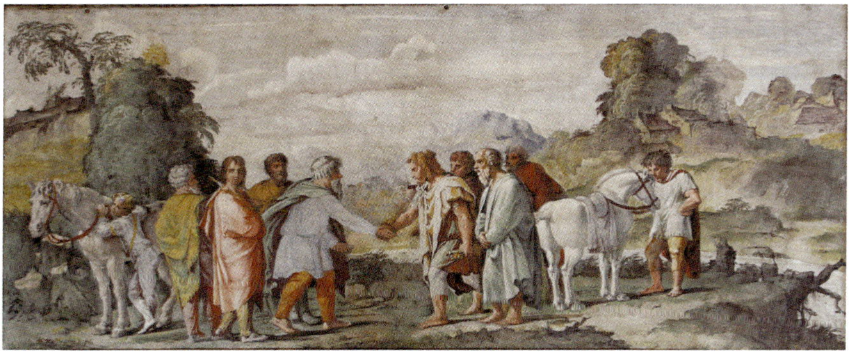

FIGURE 34 Portion of the salone frescoes from the Villa Lante al Gianicolo, showing the *Meeting of Janus and Saturn*
AS INSTALLED AT THE BIBLIOTECA HERTZIANA, ROME—AUTHOR'S IMAGE

recounts these panels for sale identifies them as different subjects. Specifically, this sale inventory identifies Lilius' *The Rediscovery of the Tomb of Numa Pompilius* instead as *The Discovery of the Sibylline Books*.[37] It also deviates from Lilius' proposal by suggesting *The Meeting of Saturn and Janus* was rather *Janus Establishing Latium*, which might reflect the same moment simply under a different title but might also imply the union of Janus and Camese as original co-founders of the region. The final modification that this inventory presents for this program is in the scene that Lilius identifies as *The Liberation of Clelia*. In the 1892 account, this scene is labeled simply as *Servius Tullius Giving Order to the Roman People*. Keeping these alternative readings in mind and returning to the various frescoed panels, one can see how these differences in dimension and interpretations might adjust the ordering of the narrative at hand.

First, in the interest of simplicity and in preparation for the verbal deconstruction of this ceiling into its various component scenes, let us streamline the nomenclature for the four main fresco panels. The scene of Janus, alternately identified as *The Meeting of Saturn and Janus* and *Janus Establishing Latium* (Fig. 34), from here will simply be identified as *The Foundation*, as both of these previous interpretations, though citing different characters, nevertheless relate to this central concept. Adjacent *The Escape of Clelia* will be shortened to *The Escape*; the *Liberation of Clelia*, also seen as *Servius Tullius Giving Order to the Roman People* will be known as *The Liberation*, and, finally, in the composition referred to as *The Rediscovery of the Tomb of Numa Pompilius* and also *The Discovery of the Sibylline Books*, will from this point be called *The Discovery*.

37 For more on these titles and descriptions, see: *Catalogue des objets d'art*, entry no. 193.

In addition to this simplified series of titles to make the following discussion more palatable, this also lays the groundwork for a new interpretation of this cycle not simply as the key rulers of ancient Rome but a framework mapped by the tensions of conquest and power: discovery, for example, leads to the creation, or foundation, of empires just as it does ideologies; escape and liberation, meanwhile, present the counter forces of control versus submission, or adoption versus rejection when it comes to the implications of those political or intellectual dogmas. Setting this line of inquiry aside for a moment, let us return to the issue of dimensions and orientation of this suite of images.

Given these measurements of each fresco, it would seem that the manner in which the four main panels have been installed follows their original installation. Both the scene of the *Escape* and *The Discovery* measure the same parameters of 0.98 meters by 2.19 meters, while the companion *The Foundation* (1.06 meters by 2.35 meters) and *The Liberation* (0.93 meters by 2.35 meters) scenes measure nearly the same as each other as well. Conveniently, these paired images appear across from each other in their current placement and thus seem to ascribe to the original layout of the *salone*'s visual program. A look to the smaller, approximately square frescoes, however, reveals that this neat alignment does not hold, implying that the manner in which they have been reinstalled is not how they would have originally appeared.

Again, a bit of tedious math: applying the dimensions provided for these smaller frescoed scenes reveals a natural pairing between most of them. *Sacrificing Of Arms* and *The Building of the Temple* both have dimensions of 0.80 meters by 0.75 meters, as do the scenes of *Fame* and *Sacrificing to Vesta* (this latter panel deviates slightly in its measurements of 0.80 by 0.76 meters). A similar pairing occurs between *The Equestrian Monument to Clelia* and *The Castration of Uranus*, both of which measure 0.87 by 0.80 meters and 0.86 by 0.80 meters, respectively. The final two vignettes in this series, *Horatius Cocles* and *Mucius Scaevola*, are the only two that do not align so perfectly, the former being 0.85 by 0.82 meters, while the latter totals 0.95 by 0.78 meters. If one begins with the panels that so closely align—that is, the scenes of *Sacrificing of Arms, The Building of the Temple, Fame*, and *Sacrificing to Vesta*—one could assume that these might be the four panels to accompany the shorter of the two larger rectangular panels, those of *The Escape* and *The Discovery*, and yet a look to the current arrangement reveals no such alignment. While *Sacrificing of Arms* and *The Building of the Temple* appear below and adjacent to *The Discovery, The Escape* is instead paired with the larger scenes if *Horatius Cocles* and *Mucius Scaevola*.

If one attempts to reorder these smaller panels in light of these distinctions of dimension, however, an interesting narrative can emerge. One can begin with *The Discovery* panel, which arguably would have been the first in the series for viewers to interpret. Accompanying this frame would have been *Sacrificing to Vesta* and *The Building of the Temple*. This is a minor modification from Lilius' original arrangement (essentially swapping two scenes of sacrifice), however it seems likely as it is clear that the regal figure in this sacrifice scene is posed such that he gazes up and out of the frame, a clever device to lead the viewer to the starting point of the narrative (and that had been used prior in instances such as Polidoro's frescoed frieze for Baldassini). In the next pane, *The Castration of Uranus* and *Horatius Cocles* would be paired with *The Foundation*, perhaps alluding to the inherent war and peace that establishment of Rome would bring. Below *The Escape* one would find *Fame* and *Sacrifice of Arms*, this pairing designed to allude to the notion of fame as it applied to both the Etruscan king, Lars Porsenna, and his captive, Clelia, who was able to escape his grip. Finally, below *The Liberation*, one would find the panels of *Mucius Scaevola* and *The Equestrian Monument of Clelia*. Though *Mucius Scaevola* might seem better suited to appear below the earlier panel—as he was captured by Lars Porsenna in the midst of an assassination attempt—the fact that Lars Porsenna eventually liberated him makes it a fitting complement to both this liberation scene and to the adjacent smaller scene of Clelia's equestrian monument.

This adjusted order is proposed not only to better pair these panels based on their recorded dimensions; it also reveals the potential that these pairings were designed to encourage the eye to keep moving through these complex narratives. Juxtaposing the mortal and the divine as well as the ruler and the subjugated, these smaller panels offer a parallel contemplation to that seen in the larger scenes and thus would have originally added substantial richness for those originally in attendance at one of Turini's elegant dinners.

Even without this readjustment of the fresco panels, it is clear in the overall visual program created in this space that the team of artists at work incorporated a rich series of references to the compositional styles and figural types that had been used in their earlier work alongside Raphael. Echoes of the shared study of antiquity, for instance, can be teased out throughout the four main rectangular fresco scenes. Lilius noted the resemblance of *The Foundation* to a portion of the frieze that encircled the Column of Trajan, a ripe sourcebook for this cohort of artists. He also cites figures as borrowed from the Vatican stanze: the young male nude at far right and the figure adjacent to Janus showcase a visual connection with characters in *The School of Athens*. Finally, Lilius draws a parallel with the horseman at far left, who bares an undeniable parallel to a similar horseman that appears in Baldassarre Peruzzi's *Presentation of the*

Virgin at the Temple, which would have been completed for the Roman Church of Santa Maria della Pace nearly simultaneously with this *salone* suite.[38]

The same connections can be drawn in the scenes of *The Escape* and *The Liberation*. Here too Lilius notes parallels not only with antique examples—for instance, *The Escape*'s likenesses borrowed from the Arch of Constantine—as well as *with* Peruzzi's *Presentation* one again.[39] This continued quotation of Peruzzi's work perhaps reflects the prominent role of Polidoro in the creation of these scenes, as he was arguably the most closely aligned with Peruzzi during these years as they explored the potential of the frescoed façade. Nevertheless, what these observations by Lilius reinforce is that these artists were consciously recalling figures and compositional elements taken from their study of antiquity as well as from their work under Raphael's guidance and recombining them into new works. This visual quotation continues throughout the suite and extends even to the small *fondo nero* frescoes that appear in this chamber depicting Neptune as he charges forth on his water chariot. This inclusion is noteworthy because it borrows the paddlewheel as was used, recall, for Raphael's *Galatea* at Chigi's villa, a reference that has been noted as the first of its kind.[40] This same paddlewheel motif appears again in the nearby version of Galatea that is also part of this *fondo nero* portion, suggesting that these elements serve as yet another motif that was borrowed repeatedly across commissions. The rendition of *Fame* (Fig. 28) is also a direct quotation of da Udine's stucco relief of *Victory* in the Vatican Loggia, wherein a roundel depicting the narrative of Mucius Scaevola, as well as a likeness of *Pax*, appears. These two latter images could easily be considered the key source for the depiction of the *Sacrificing of Arms* at Turini's villa.

What this amounts to is that these artists at work at the Villa Lante were still deeply embedded in the practice of a visual language first employed during Raphael's lifetime, and it is in Turini's chambers that one can note their increased range of reference. Beyond emulations of antique forms and examples from Raphael, the workshop artists here began to add to that language and its varied meanings with the quotations they incorporated. The work at the Villa Lante, then, becomes a prime space in which this innovation can occur, and the result was a series of images that built on these types

38 Lilius, "Gli Affreschi." 78–79.

39 Ibid., 80.

40 For more on this innovation, see earlier chapter on Raphael's work at Chigi's villa; also see Millard Meiss, "Raphael's Mechanized Seashell: Notes on a Myth, Technology and Iconographic Tradition," *The Painter's Choice: Problems in the Interpretation of Renaissance Art* (New York: Harper and Row, 1976), 203–211.

to create a novel visual program that nevertheless bore valuable reference to outside works to invoke an artistic conversation.

So far this discussion of the Villa Lante has overlooked the magnificent suite of stuccoed relief panels executed by Giovanni da Udine to decorate the loggia that framed the overlook onto Rome. This absence is deliberate, as these panels were the last of the visual program to be completed at the Villa Lante. This work most likely occurred in the early 1530s, as a letter from Sebastiano del Piombo dated 7 July 1533 critiques da Udine's work with Michelangelo at the New Sacristy of San Lorenzo as "more closely [resembling] the vault of his *vigna* than that of Messer Baldassarre from Peschia."[41] This later dating means that this portion of the Villa Lante's visual program dated to after the Sack, which Nicole Dacos and Caterina Furlan have noted perhaps impacted the overall design. "When one observes the loggia of the Villa Lante," they note, "the mural of mythological placed in the middle of the panels within the pergola, all in stucco bianco, one gets a sense of the rigidity and coldness almost Neoclassical in nature, a sense that would have been foreign to [Giovanni]."[42] In other words, the aesthetic of Turini's villa had shifted by the time the loggia was complete, as had the artistic atmosphere in Rome. Thus, while visual parallels can be drawn between this striking stuccoed loggia and the imagery of the rest of the villa, they will not be expounded upon here. What Dacos and Furlan's words reinforce is the dramatically different atmosphere of the city following the Sack of Rome, serving as another reminder of how much the visual program of the Villa Lante has been modified over the years. Despite these challenges, the evidence of this recombinative artistic practice, where now individual artists nevertheless continued to collaborate extensively on their work, is clear.

---

41 Lilius proposes a date 1531 for these stucco additions of 1531 (Lilius, *Villa Lante*, 299–347), a dating with which Nicole Dacos and Caterina Furlan agree (Dacos and Furlan, *Giovanni da Udine*, 122); for full text of letter, see: Lettera di Sebastiano del Piombo in Roma a Michelangelo in Firenze, Archivio Buonarroti di Firenze, IX, 500.

42 N. Dacos and C. Furlan, *Giovanni da Udine*, 122–123.

CHAPTER 6

The Fetti Chapel

On the heels of projects like those as the Palazzo Baldassini, Polidoro da Caravaggio had enjoyed advancing acclaim in Rome. This was thanks to, among other projects, his concurrent work alongside Baldassarre Peruzzi and close associate Maturino da Firenze in the development of elaborate frescoed and sgraffitoed facades across the city. Amid those successes, though, Polidoro was tasked with another commission that would prove even more influential in the construction of his Roman legacy: decorations for a private chapel in the Church of San Silvestro al Quirinale (Fig. 35). Completed between roughly 1524 and 1527 for the Dominican Fra Mariano Fetti, this chapel would become one of the final projects on which Polidoro and Maturino would work together, as Maturino purportedly perished during the Sack of Rome. Here too, just as seen in earlier space, one can find Polidoro's powers of recombination at play, as he conjures scenes that invoke a wide array of visual references. Moreover, Polidoro conceptualized the landscape anew in this chapel, as he both upholds elements of antiquity while breaking with other visual traditions. Striking in this space, though, is that this recombination of visual phrases assumes a much more theoretical tone, as if Polidoro was contemplating larger questions about the very practice of painting beyond the conversations of visual forms shared between artists. The result of these ruminations is a visually novel fresco series that showcased Polidoro's abilities as an artist and foreshadowed the potential to come, making this a fitting capstone to Polidoro's and Maturino's years of collaboration.

1 Fra Mariano Fetti (d. 1531)

Fra Mariano Fetti was a Florentine Dominican friar who enjoyed an elevated status in sixteenth-century Rome thanks to his associations with Pope Leo X. Noted by contemporary historian Vincenzo Marchese as a former associate of the infamous Savonarola (1452–1498), Fetti developed an allegiance to the Medici family in the later years of the fifteenth century and grew from humble roots as a barber to Lorenzo il Magnifico to become a close confidant of the prominent Florentine family.[1] He ingratiated himself to the Medici clan in

1 Vicenzo Marchese notes that Fetti took his Dominican habit from Savonarola in 1495 (V. Marchese, *Lives of The Most Eminent Painters, Sculptors & Architects*, trans. by Father Marchese

 | DOI:10.1163/9789004430488_008

part through his recorded buffoonery, and his early years in Rome were marked by similar comical antics.[2] Noted, for instance, were his shenanigans at Pope Leo X's 1513 Roman carnival; while the exact nature of those caprices escaped chronicle, it is clear that his role as a humorous prankster endured. Raphael's curtain designed for the 1519 theatrical performance of *I Suppositi* performed at Castel Sant'Angelo, as an example, depicted Fetti in a humorous mode to the delight of the audience, and, when Leo X met his end in 1521, pasquinades joking that Fetti was indeed next in line for the papal throne abounded.[3] Perhaps as a counter to his reported buffoonery, though, Fetti also put great stock into his heightened Roman social stature. To be a close associate of the pope was a decided advantage and often meant special privileges. Fetti was no exception, as, thanks to his connections with Leo X, he garnered the prestigious post of *piombatore*—the keeper of the papal seal—in 1514 following the death of former bearer Donato Bramante.[4] Cynthia Stollhans has also argued for his important role in the patronage of the arts, which can be seen in his patronage at the church of San Silvestro al Quirinale.[5]

In early 1507, the Dominicans of Rome needed a home as their headquarters, the church of Santa Maria sopra Minerva, was undergoing renovations. Given the need for a new space, Pope Julius granted San Silvestro al Quirinale and its associated complex to the order through a papal bull. As part of this transfer, Fetti was put in charge with the expectation that he would transform the adjoining resident complex—complete with dormitories as well as a cloister and gardens—into a more substantial landmark for the Dominican presence

(Dublin: James Duffy, 1852), (Florence, 1846), II: 83–84); for a more complete biography of Fetti, see: A. Zucchi, *Roma Domenicane* 4 vols (Florence, 1938–1943) 2: 16.

2 Cynthia Stollhans, "The problem of two saints named Catherine in the Fetti Chapel, " *St. Catherine of Alexandria in Renaissance Roman Art: Case Studies in Patronage* (UK: Ashgate, 2014), 115. Stollhans later notes that Fetti enjoyed so close of a relationship with Leo X that he was present at his deathbed (Stollhans, *St. Catherine*, 116; Gnoli, "La Capella,"126);

3 Stollhans, "The problem," 115–116; Gnoli, "La Capella,"126. For a full text of the pasquinade, see: *Pasquinate Romane del cinquecento. 1.* Pasquinate Romane Del Cinquecento / a Cura Di Valerio Marucci, Antonio Marzo E Angelo Romano; Presentazione Di Giovanni Aquilecchia. (Roma: Salerno, 1983), I: no. 254; a full text translation appears in: Stollhans, "Fra Mariano, Peruzzi and Polidoro da Caravaggio: A New Look at Religious Landscapes in Renaissance Rome." *The Sixteenth Century Journal*, 23 (3) (Autumn, 1992), 509.

4 This transfer of title is noted in a letter scribed by Baldassarre Turini, which states that "yesterday morning Bramante has died and Fra Mariano now holds his position as *Piombatore*." (Stollhans, *St. Catherine*, 117; Gnoli, "La Capella," 117; Gnoli, "Raffaello alla corte di Leone X," *Nuova Antologia* (1888); 585).

5 C. Stollhans, "Fra Mariano," 506–525.

in Rome. These grander plans were never realized, but Fetti did maintain residence within the Quirinal complex until his death in 1531.[6]

For someone who appreciated the perks of his elite social standing, Fetti had perhaps knowingly moved into one of the most envied and affluent locales in the city of Rome by choosing to take up residence at San Silvestro. The future Pope Leo X lived nearby, for example, as did Federico II Gonzaga, who was at the time being held hostage by Pope Julius II.[7] Perhaps inspired by these illustrious associates, Fetti's time in residence at the church complex, which itself was complete with splendid gardens, coincided with the development of his art collection. It was also at this time that Fetti called in the service of Peruzzi, from whom he commissioned a likeness of *Saint Bernard of Clairvaux in a Landscape* to be displayed across one of his garden walls adjacent to the church.[8] This image, which is now lost but known through later drawings, revealed the figure of Saint Bernard prostrate in front of his book as he gazed upward to acknowledge the Madonna and child in the upper right quadrant of the scene. This moment of visitation is set against a lush "labyrinth" of foliage.[9] Pier Liugi de Castris has suggested that Polidoro and Maturino aided Peruzzi in the execution of this complex chiaroscuro landscape, performing their contributions so masterfully so as to secure for themselves Fetti's commission for his private chapel.

2 A Complicated History

Understanding the full significance of such a commission for an artist like Polidoro is muddled by the fact that, like other spaces considered in this book, this chapel has experienced substantial changes since the sixteenth century, with no complete account as to the original decorative plans for the chapel. For example, it can only be said with certainty that Polidoro crafted the central zone of imagery that spans the chapel, with Maturino stepping in to aide with the creation of the lower socle grisaille compositions. The remainder of

6 For more on this papal bull, see: Zucchi, *Roma Domenicane*, 2: 198–199; E. Iezzi, *S. Silvestro al Quirinale* (Rome: Fonticoli e Biagetti, 1975), 10. Stollhans points out that, while the exact date of Fetti's death is undocumented, it seems that his death can be confirmed by at the very latest the end of year as "on December 4, 1531, the artist Sebastiano del Piombo received this office [of piombatore] from Pope Clement VII" (Stollhans, "Fra Mariano," 512, n. 20); also see: Graf, *Attraverso*, 317.

7 For more on this hostage situation, see: Alessandro Luzio, "Federico Gonzaga ostaggio alla corte di Giulio II." *Archigio della società Romana di storia patria* 9 (1886): 549.

8 Vasari, IV: 596; Baglione (1642), 396; Marabottini (1969, 143).

9 M. Armellini, *Le Chiese di Roma dal secolo IV al XIX* (Rome: Ruffolo, 1942), II, 1448.

the marble decoration as well as major portions of the visual program, including the elaborate vault decoration, are credited to the later work of Cavaliere d'Arpino (1568–1640) under restorations ordered by Cardinal Giacomo Sannesio (1557/1560–1621).[10]

The altarpiece, which depicts the *Enthroned Madonna and Child with Saints Catherine of Alexandria and Mary Magdalen*, is also most likely not of the period and has generated its own controversy as there is substantial debate over its authorship and dating, particularly given the lack of documentation of the chapel's evolution.[11] It is also not clear when the chapel was devoted to Saint Catherine, who features prominently in Polidoro's designs. An inscription included along one of the pillar bases within the chapel records a 1518 visit to the chapel by Pope Leo X, at which time he paid homage to an image of the Madonna, while another inscription dated to 1530 documents this devotional commemoration (SACELLUM HOC CATHARINAE). What happened in the chapel, what led to this dedication, and the order of these events over this twelve-year time span is largely open to debate.

Beyond the chapel, the church itself has experienced rather dramatic changes: the entire façade of San Silvestro al Quirinale was modified in the 1870s to account for the expansion of the nearby via Nazionale.[12] This adjustment resulted in the demolition of the first two chapels of the church, which meant that the Fetti Chapel, only the second chapel from the original main entrance, was barely spared. While such a transformation might suggest that Fra Mariano's chapel was now in a more prominent place, one must also note that these changes to the main façade also precipitated a modified entryway that transformed what would have been the chapel's prominent placement near the main portal of the church into a somewhat overlooked corner distant from the main altar apse.[13]

---

10 D. Gnoli, "La capella di Fra Mariano del Piombo in Roma," *Archivio storico dell'arte* IV (1891), 117; A. Marabottini, *Polidoro da Caravaggio* (Rome: Edizione dell'elefante, 1969), 136.

11 The altarpiece of an *Enthroned Madonna and Child with Saints Catherine of Alexandria and Mary Magdalene*, as Stollhans has noted, is stylistically distinct from the adjacent panels and thus must be attributed to another artist (Stollhans, *St. Catherine*, 118; Vasari attributes the painting of "S. Dominic, S. Catherine of Siena, with Christ marrying her, and Our Lady" to Mariotto Albertinelli (*Lives*, 1: 685); Gnoli, "La Capella," 123–124). Stollhans notes the potential presence of the thirteen-century *Madonna di Catena*, which may have been moved into Fetti's chapel specifically for the pope's visit and then later replaced by the *Enthroned Madonna* composition later, perhaps even after Fetti's lifetime. For more, see: Stollhans, *St. Catherine*, 120–122.

12 Gnoli, 18; Marabottini, 135.

13 For an extended discussion of these two lost chapels, dedicated to the Alicorni and Pennelli families, respectively, see: F. Cugi, "San Silvestro al Quirinale: Le cappelle perdute e qualche ipotesi sulle pitture del coro." *Bolletino d'Arte* 7 (97) (2012), 35–144.

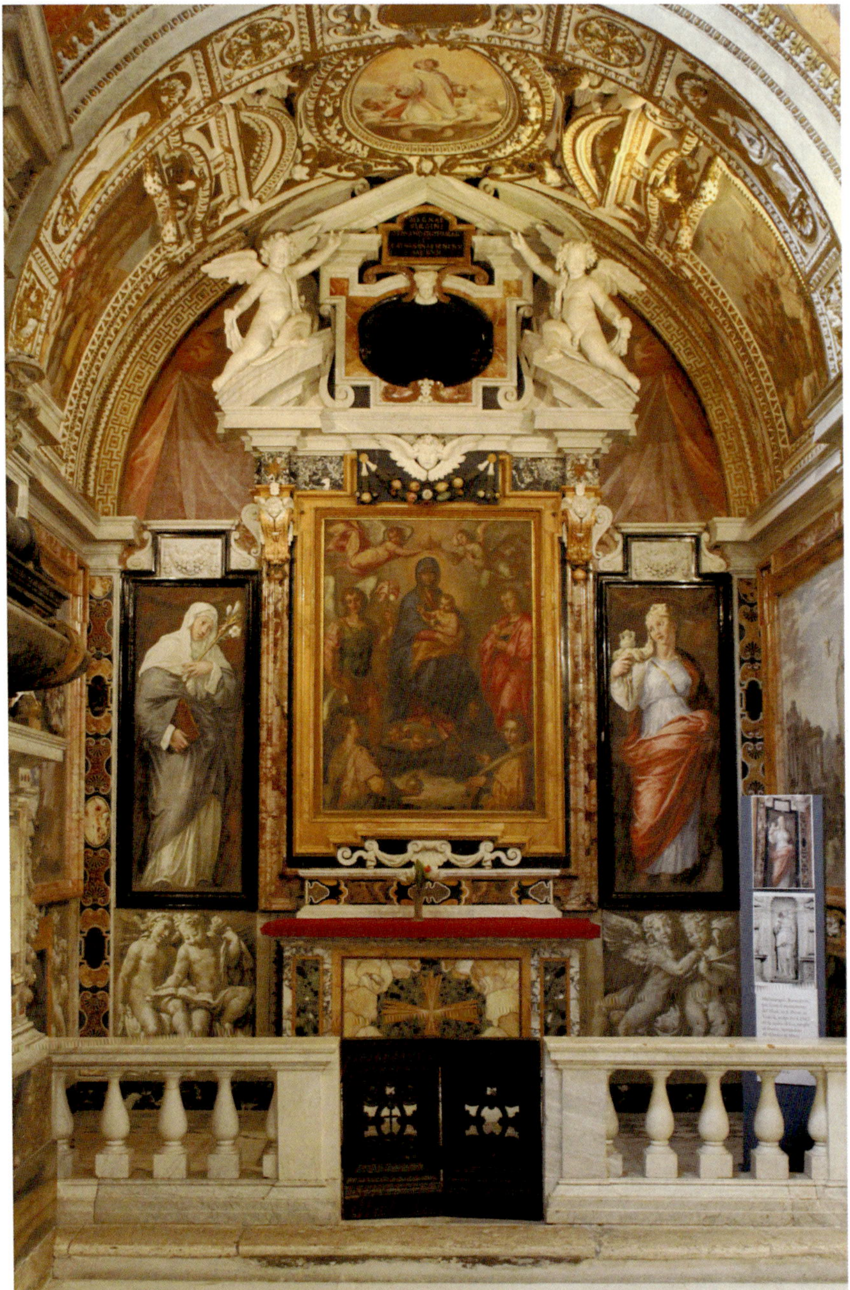

FIGURE 35 The Fetti Chapel
SAN SILVESTRO AL QUIRINALE, ROME—AUTHOR'S IMAGE

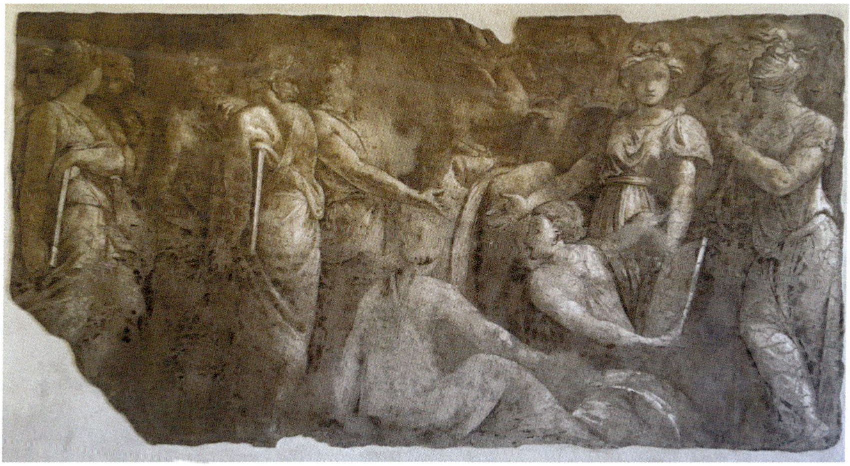

FIGURE 36 Polidoro da Caravaggio, *Muses, Poets, and Pegasus*, from the Casino del Bufalo, c. 1525. Detached fresco
MUSEO DI ROMA/PALAZZO BRASCHI—AUTHOR'S IMAGE

While this chapel has lost some of its pride of placement with the redesign of the church, it nevertheless is still indicative of an exciting moment in Polidoro's development, one that is reflective of his time within Raphael's circle but also of his growth among the workshop members and associates in the years since Raphael's death. Perhaps the most significant influence in this domain was his contributions alongside chiefly Peruzzi and Maturino to the developing field of the frescoed façade.

3 Peruzzi, Polidoro, and Painted Illusion

Since Chigi's decision to emblazon the façade of his lavish *villa suburbana* with an array of frescoed scenes (of which, as has been intimated, only a few survive in sketch form), the notion of the decorated façade had become *en vogue* across the city of Rome. Having mastered the technique, Polidoro and Peruzzi capitalized on this rising trend by developing a collaborative practice of designing facades embellished with an array of fresco and *sgraffitto* ornaments. Some of the best surviving examples of Polidoro's work include fragments from the previously mentioned frescoed casino façade for the *vigna* del Bufalo completed around 1525 and depicting scenes such as *Muses, Poets, and Pegasus* (Fig. 36) that were no doubt also aimed at encouraging associations with the del Bufalo *vigna* as a "new Parnassus."[14] One can also still see Polidoro and Peruzzi's

14 For more, see: Kultzen, Rolf, "Die Malerei Polodoros da Caravaggio im Giardino del

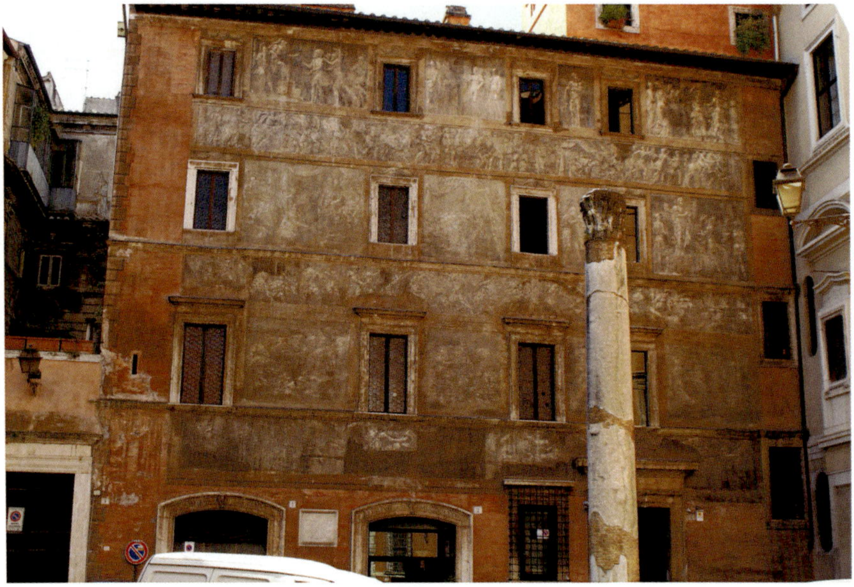

FIGURE 37 Remnants of frescoed façade by Peruzzi, Polidoro, and Maturino
PALAZZO MASSIMO ISTORIATO, ROME—AUTHOR'S IMAGE

extensive program on the secluded façade of the Palazzo Massimo Istoriato (Fig. 37).[15] Hundreds of these painted faces once enlivened the streets of Rome; today, only fragments of a handful of them still survive.[16] Despite this loss, a brief sojourn into the realm of these frescoed facades is valuable as it can be seen as another avenue in which these artists continued to pursue a language of artistic recombination, particularly within the realm of fictive landscapes and scenographic design. Thus, to examine the chapel means to begin—however briefly—with the frescoed façade.

Bufalo in Rom," *Mitteilungen des Kunsthisorichen Institutes in Florenz*, 9 (2) (Feb. 1960), 99–120.

15 Vasari notes that Perino del Vaga also worked on at least one frescoed façade "by the example of Polidoro and Maturino—which opposite to the house of the Marchionness of Massa, near Maestro Pasquino, executing it great boldness of design and with supreme diligence" (Vasari, *Lives*, II: 159). Vasari also noted that one of Polidoro's earliest successes in the realm of the frescoed façade was on a dwelling opposite to San Silvestro (Vasari, *Lives* I: 890).

16 The most complete account of these frescoed facades in Rome published to date can be found in: C.P. Ridolfini, *Le case romane con facciate graffite e dipinte* (Rome: Amici dei Musei di Roma, 1960). For a more substantive review of Polidoro's contribution to the legacy, see: Alessandro Marabottini, *Polidoro da Caravaggio* (Rome: Edizione dell'elefante, 1969).

Figures like Polidoro and Peruzzi were breaking new ground with their exploration of the frescoed façade that resonated with the passion of the day for all things antique. As has been discussed earlier, Rome of this period was awash with revivals of *all'antica* themes, from collections of antiquities and spoliated materials to, as discussed in past chapters, elaborate visual programs that could be seen as anchoring the new citizens of Rome to the city's vast history.[17] Given this context, the frescoed façade seemed a natural extension: an extravagant faux finish that could envelope the face of one's residence in frescoes rendered in a style reminiscent of ancient relief-carved sarcophagi and retelling stories often derived from Classical lore. Rather than a mere column capital or fragmentary inscription, Peruzzi and Polidoro's frescoed façades afforded patrons a more complete showcase: narrative vignettes paired with at times fictive sculpture niches and at others scrolling motifs to develop an all-encompassing *all'antica* revival that appeared to broadcast dynamic tales from the Classical and mythological world for all passersby.

To execute such sweeping programs required ample study of antiquity, but, as has been hopefully illustrated thus far, both Peruzzi and Polidoro were its avid students.[18] Sketches examining the intricacies of relief-carved sarcophagi and sculptures became the visual building blocks for many of these facades. From this perspective, one can also see how the development of these decorated faces could occur as a natural outgrowth of the practice of recombination that had so influenced both Peruzzi's and Polidoro's development. In these frescoed facades, fragments of antiquity could be recombined into new compelling suites of imagery that were both of the past and the present, meeting in visual conversations that engaged a contemporary audience on many levels.

On the other hand, and perhaps one of the most brilliant elements of these faces, was the play of artifice. These frescoed facades played with the surface of these structures to imitate the multilevel surface of a relief carving, using the element of shading to convey to the viewer at street level the illusions of various elevations of the surface. This element of illusion undoubtedly ties into, at the very least, Peruzzi's concurrent interest in theatrical scenography, an art form that had only just been introduced to Rome. It would seem that perhaps Polidoro also had a flair for the scenographic, as he became equally expert in the conjuring of an array of *all'antica* references across some of Rome's most

17 For more, see: M.Y. Hara, "Emphatic Presence: Architectural *Chiaroscuro*." In C. Lehmann et al., *Chiaroscuro als ästhetisches Prinzip: Kunst und Theorie des Helldunkels 1300–1550* (Berlin: De Gruyter, 2018), 351–352.

18 According to Vasari, so too was Maturino, though little visual evidence survives to support such a claim. As he noted in the life of Polidoro: Maturino "was held to be an excellent draftsman of antiquity" (Vasari, *Lives* I: 890).

prominent palazzi, including, as was discussed earlier, the Palazzo Baldassini. Thus, it seems safe to suggest that Polidoro thrived in creating such illusionistic scenes that afforded him license to innovative and experiment, and he carried that energy with him to his work in the Fetti Chapel at the behest of Fra Mariano.

4 Illusions of Landscape in the Fetti Chapel

While problems of chronology and authorship plague an understanding of much of the Fetti Chapel today, certain in this space are the contributions by Polidoro and their impact, as Stollhans has noted, as "key to the development of religious landscape painting in Renaissance Rome."[19] Polidoro's designs within this chapel include two fictive painted niches that flank either side of the central altarpiece. These niches are filled with renderings of Mary Magdalene and St. Catherine of Siena, respectively. Painted to appear as if they are dimensional polychrome sculptures supported within these illusory recesses, these holy figures consume the remainder of the main wall. Both figures angle their heads and turn inward such that it creates the sensation that they are both maintaining a gaze with each other as well as with the central altarpiece between them. Polidoro—assuredly with the aid of Maturino—supported these fictive niches from below with chiaroscuro scenes. This lower socle is in fact filled with grisaille variations—six in sum—featuring coupled putti conjured by Polidoro and Mariano to create the illusion of artfully carved relief panels that wrap around the sanctuary. Paired with the scenes above, these grisaille scenes contribute a sense of historical grounding while also alluding to pious devotion, as some of these diminutive cherubs hold books open in their laps to imply hymnals or prayers books in use.

It is with these cherubic vignettes that one can begin to see the continued use of recombined visual elements borrowed from both past and present. First, one can note Polidoro's partnered *putti* as an allusion to ancient sources, and one can imagine the myriad of carved reliefs from antiquity displayed around the city that might have served as inspiration for these scenes. It would be most satisfying to link, for instance, these posed putti to those that appeared in the Codex Wolfegg's illustration of an ancient sarcophagus relief that bears the inscription "monte chavallo in chasa de mestro andrea scarpelino" and that also served as inspiration for colleague Giulio Romano.[20] Other sources could

19 Stollhans, "Fra Mariano," 506.

20 A. Aspertini, Codex Wolfegg, ff. 34^{v}–35, as illustrated in: P.P. Bober, *Drawings after the*

of course be at play, but regardless of exact sources one can be sure he is deliberately recalling ancient artists with such paired figural groupings.

Beyond these recollections of antiquity, the grisaille socle scenes Polidoro conjured also connect to the legacy of his own past work. Recall, for example, how Polidoro accented the grand *salone* of the Villa Lante with *amorini* with the attributes of various divinities in the *fondo nero* panels. He also paired *putti* with his grouping of vignettes in the studio at the Palazzo Baldassini to engage the audience and commence the cycle of viewing. Is this perhaps Polidoro's efforts to insert himself into the larger conversation of sixteenth-century art, not as directly as Raphael's paired self-portraits in the Stanza della Segnatura, but metaphorically as bold? The theme of the *putti* is perhaps too omnipresent in *cinquecento* design to validate such a claim, but there are additional elements that Polidoro incorporated here that do suggest he was blending themes and references in an effort to broadcast a more theoretical commentary.

Polidoro's frescoed grisaille panels as well as his imagery of Saint Catherine and Mary Magdalene do call upon the artistic language of others. For example, Stollhans has drawn a parallel between Polidoro's *putti* and the various *ignudi* that appear across Michelangelo's ceiling in the Sistine Chapel.[21] Michelangelo's Sistine *putti* are similarly paired; however they appear to labor under the weight of the column capital that emerges overhead. In comparison, Polidoro's *putti* assume a much more relaxed presentation, and it would seem that, if his intention was a parallel with Michelangelo, it was at most a general one. More direct, however, are the connections between his representation of Mary Magdalene and Michelangelo's figure of *Leah* (1515) that later became part of the Tomb of Pope Julius II at San Pietro in Vincoli. Both sculpted and frescoed figures reveal a similar contrapposto stance with right arm raised to the shoulder and head tilted inward. Even the drapery of Polidoro's Magdalene echoes that of Michelangelo's Leah—though not exact, the cincture at the waist and the mantel draped over the shoulders match perfectly. This parallels Polidoro's confrontation with Michelangelo in these frescoes. At the same time, this reference on Polidoro's part could also be seen as an interjection

---

Antique by Amico Aspertini. Sketchbooooks in the British Museum (UK: Studies of the Warburg Institute, 1957); also see: P.P. Bober and R.O. Rubenstein, *Renaissance Artists and Antique Sculpture: A Handbook of Sources* (UK: Harvey Miller, 1986), no. 21. The Romano drawing from based from this relief is documented in: C. Robert, *Die antiken Sarcophagreliefs* (Deutsches Archaëlogisches Inst., Berlin, 1919) III: *Einzelmythen*: 3. *Niobiden, Triptolemos, Ungedeutet*, 564.

21 Stollhans, *St. Catherine*, 119. Stollhans also notes references to Raphael's work in these putti, however she does not offer specific sources.

into the conversation on the longstanding rivalry between the fields of painting and sculpture in the race for artistic supremacy.

There is also the potential that Polidoro here is quoting the work of his former mentor, Raphael. Years prior, painter Fra Bartolomeo (1471–1517) endeavored to create paintings of *Saint Peter* and *Saint Paul* (both circa 1514; Pinacoteca, Vatican). He began work on them but then left them incomplete, eventually leaving them purportedly to Raphael to finish.[22] Both works feature the figure of the saint as inset into a fictive niche, strikingly similar in composition to Polidoro's Saint Catherine and Mary Magdalene. These two paintings were at some point installed near the main altar of San Silvestro al Quirinale, meaning that they would have been in direct view from the Fetti Chapel. Without knowing exactly when these works arrived at San Silvestro, it seems foolish to read too much into their placement, but it is intriguing to wonder, if the timing aligned, that Polidoro was also here borrowing the male forms of those works in his designs for his female saints in an effort to create an artistic dialog that not only spanned the church but also spanned artistic generations.

In addition to references to Michelangelo (ostensibly a rival) and Raphael (his deceased mentor and collaborator), Polidoro also invokes connections with Peruzzi in the ways in which the illusion of spatial recession within these *putti* scenes runs parallel to the tradition of the frescoed façade. One can note across these smaller socle panels that Polidoro and Maturino worked diligently to convey a strong sense of compositional depth in each scene, with artfully foreshortened limbs and expert shadows used to complete the illusion of dimension. This could be seen as a parallel to his abilities in creating similar illusions on facades across Rome. From this perspective, one might draw links to Polidoro's chapel frescoes and Peruzzi's design for the Ponzetti Chapel (begun 1516) in the way in which Polidoro has structured his various scenes as a melding of artistic—and illusory—approaches.[23]

Thus, what one might be seeing here is evidence of the similar perspective once shared between Raphael and Peruzzi in their mentoring; it might also suggest, however, that Polidoro was transferring this recombinative quotation of his former mentor into a new relationship. This connection is furthered with Polidoro's treatment of the side walls of the chapel, where this previously mentioned spatial recession within the socle scenes are paired above with frescoes

22 D. Franklin, *Polidoro da Caravaggio* (New Haven: Yale University Press, 2018), 28. Franklin comments: "that someone who admired Raphael's style would turn to this particular bottega assistant to execute major work is itself telling about the perception of Polidoro's high promise in Rome after 1520."

23 De Castris, 220.

of sweeping landscapes studded with key narratives from the lives of these Biblical women. To the left, and adjacent to the likeness of St. Catherine, one finds scenes from the life of Saint Catherine of Siena (Fig. 38). Included are vignettes of her Mystic Marriage and the Reception of Catherine and her sisters by Pope Urban VI. On the right appear scenes from the life of Mary Magdalene, including a foreground scene of Christ appearing to Mary Magdalen (the traditional basis for the *noli me tangere* composition) complemented by a midground narrative of Mary washing the feet of Jesus in the House of Simon and a far background rendition of St. Martha praying within a grotto as the manifestation of Mary Magdalene in heaven appears (Fig. 39).

Polidoro enters new terrain in his incorporation of these landscape scenes, not just for their novelty but also for the theoretical questions they can be seen as raising. Rather than the more traditional episodic retelling of such narratives, here Polidoro chooses instead to paint away the wall to give the illusion that the visitor is looking far out into the landscape beyond the chapel walls. Such a *trompe-l'oeil* illusion harkens back to the work of Peruzzi in Chigi's Sala delle Prospettive, but it also could be seen as playing on the work of the previously-mentioned Fra Bartolomeo, who was celebrated for his early exploration of landscape painting. Fetti was friendly with Fra Bartolomeo, so the inclusion of such grand landscape scenes perhaps was desired on Fetti's part as a means to further these association with other prominent artists of sixteenth-century Rome.[24] For Polidoro specifically, it would seem that this emphasis on the landscape also allowed him to embark on artistic innovation, advancing the conversation, as it were, on the potential of these various compositional elements.

A hint of this subtlety of innovation can be seen in Polidoro's sly inclusion of a conflated religious narrative. As Stollhans discovered in her incisive look into these landscape scenes, Polidoro renders the scene of Mystic Marriage as happening between St Catherine of Siena, identifiable thanks to her black and white robes indicative of the Dominican Order, and an infant Christ. This is notable because this blends the two stories of the mystic marriage together: while the tale of Saint Catherine of Siena's marriage involves her union with an adult Christ, that of Saint Catherine of Alexandria, most often shown in elegant, regal dress, shows her marriage to the infant Christ. While Polidoro was not the first to attempt such a dual connotation—Ambrogio Bergognone's paint-

24 For more, see: C. Fischer, "Fra Bartolommeo's Landscape Drawings." *Mitteilungen des Kunsthistorischen Institutes in Florenz* 33. Bd., H. 2/3 (1989), 301–342; and E.J. Olszewski, "Central and Lateral Landscapes in Italian Renaissance Paintings," *Source: Notes in the History of Art*, 17 (3) (Spring 1998), 29–35.

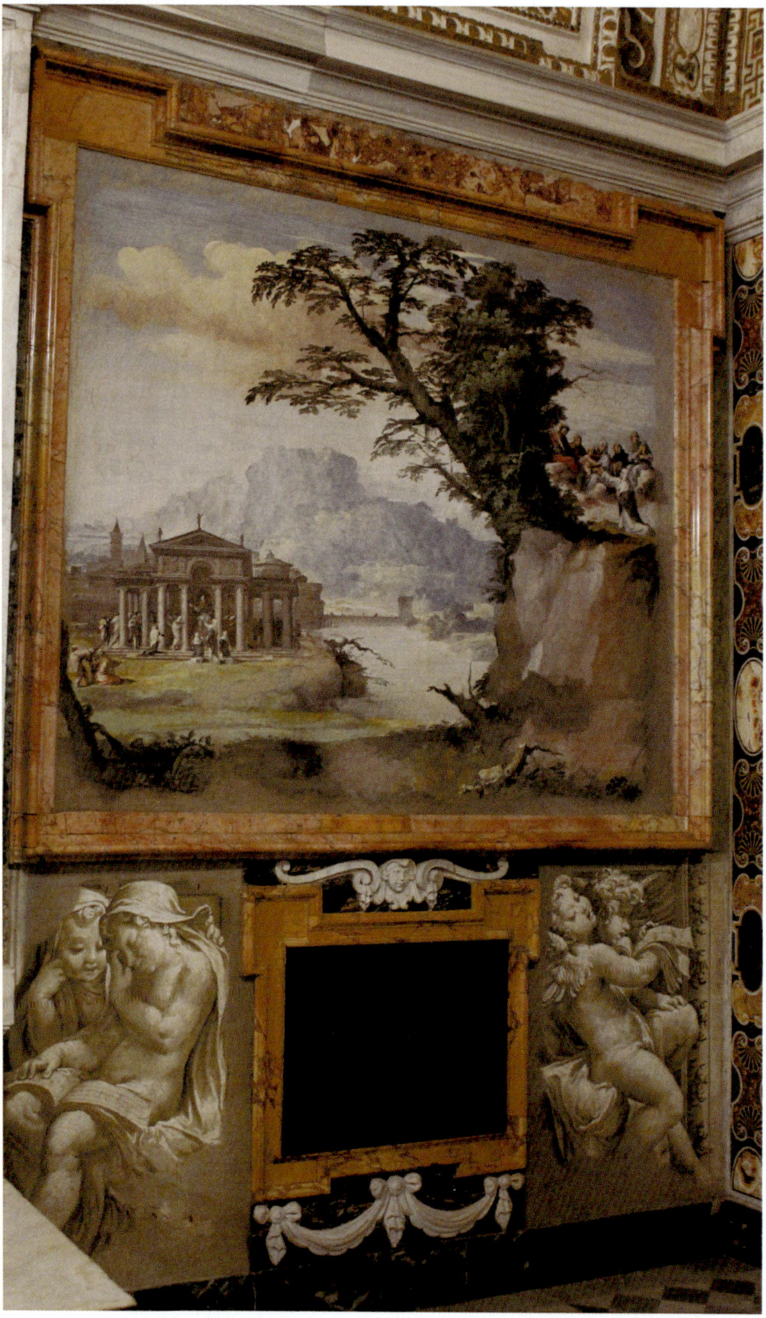

FIGURE 38 View of left lateral chapel wall depicting Polidoro's *Landscape with Scenes from the Life of Saint Catherine*
FETTI CHAPEL, SAN SILVESTRO AL QUIRINALE—AUTHOR'S IMAGE

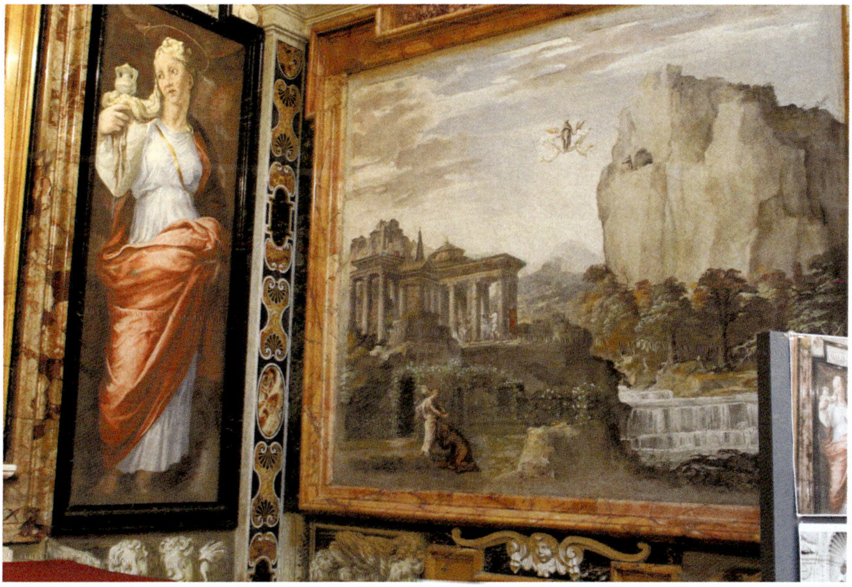

FIGURE 39 View of right lateral chapel wall depicting Polidoro's *Landscape with Scenes from the Life of Mary Magdalen*
FETTI CHAPEL, SAN SILVESTRO AL QUIRINALE—AUTHOR'S IMAGE

ing circa 1490 in London's National Gallery shows an earlier such example—the manner in which he collapses the narratives of the two saints Catherine is both a clever and novel solution.[25]

In addition to conflating the lives of two saintly figures into one, Polidoro also innovates with his compositional space by conflating in each scene three stories into one and dividing them merely by their recession into space. Complementing the illusion of dimension as seen in the accompanying grisaille scenes below, Polidoro's larger landscape thus experiments with the bounds of the illusion of recession and task the viewer with navigating these various episodes independently. In this regard, then, it would seem that Polidoro is tasking the viewer of these landscape to perform their own visual recombination, pulling together these various episodes by weaving together the different spaces he conjured through the illusion of depth. This sweeping depth, which carries the viewer's eye far back into the landscape, transcended the boundary of the wall through effective trompe l'oeil illusion. Polidoro's success in this regard must have come from his study of Peruzzi's trompe l'oeil masterpiece,

25 Stollhans, "Fra Mariano," 521; Stollhans, *St. Catherine*, 119. To conflate these stories and venerate both Saint Catherine of Siena and Alexandria was innovative but also appropriate, as Stollhans notes that both saintly women bore connections to Rome.

the Sala delle Prospettive, wherein Peruzzi successfully transformed a formal reception space for Chigi into a perch that looked out over the Roman landscape. Polidoro does something similar here, by offering to the viewer in each lateral landscape sweeping natural formations along with structures and ruins from antiquity.

To be sure, Peruzzi offers the viewer a clearer topographical grounding by offering identifiable landmarks from Chigi's Rome that are interspersed in his Sala's scenes; Polidoro is perhaps cagier, though, in offering references to the antique that are both clear and yet generic. Each scene offers similar vignettes of Classical architecture: both feature a prominent extended and columnated portico behind which a variety of structures are implied. A circular building, perhaps a reference to the Pantheon or the Temple of Hercules Victor, pops up, as does an obelisk form capped with an orb. One difference to note between these overwhelmingly similar vignettes is the addition in Saint Catherine's landscape of a medieval bell tower, akin to that of the eighth-century Church of Santa Maria in Cosmedin, which might be one clue left by Polidoro to establish the chronology of these two characters' stories.

That Polidoro included these substantial landscapes, truly a landmark in the development of the genre, in his chapel design suggests that he was delving into a new symbolic application of his recombinative approach.[26] The fact that Fetti might select such scenes as an indication of his own interest—or merely as an allusion to his knowledge of these sources or his associations with these artists—follows logically, but what also merits further consideration is the way in which Polidoro so artfully inserted these scenes into the overall chapel program. In doing so, it would seem that Polidoro offered his own revelation of the emerging theories of landscape painting and its potential relevance in a religious context.

The mere fact that Polidoro incorporated such sweeping landscape scenes into his vision for the chapel brings to mind some of the tension that surrounded the genre of religious landscape. Throughout the medieval era, landscapes, particularly rugged, overgrown views of untouched or ruin-dotted nature, had come to be associated with the relinquishing of earthly distractions to encourage a purer moment of religious reflection. As Brian Keene and Alexandra Kaczenski have noted, into the fifteenth century "the wilderness and desert were seen as pure or untouched environments, ... able to test the

26 "To be sure, landscape had been painted before, particularly in a secular context. But rarely had it achieved such monumental treatment, and never in so holy a place." A.R. Turner, *The Vision of Landscape in Renaissance Italy* (New Jersey: Princeton University Press 1966), 153.

religious convictions of those who entered. By Relinquishing the comforts of city life and inhabiting these wild spaces, ascetics and hermits believed they could overcome bodily and worldly desire to achieve a more authentic connection with God."[27] That Polidoro would perhaps be reviving a mode from the medieval world is not beyond possibility, particularly as it has been proposed that his close colleague, Peruzzi, did something similar in his design of the Ponzetti Chapel.[28] At the same time, however, Renaissance sentiment was rooted in ancient ideologies, and from this perspective the landscape took on altogether different connotations.

Scholarly research into the development of the Renaissance sentiment toward the landscape has revealed that, like so many aspects of their cultural understanding, it was rooted in the words of antiquity. Though no single source from the ancient world laid out the parameters for successful landscape painting, it is clear that the practice of illusionistic landscapes was paramount to the rich tradition of ancient Roman wall painting. The principles of such scenes became the roots of the tradition, but it is clear already in these ancient texts that refer to landscape painting that it is considered a pleasurable yet marginal art form.

By the sixteenth century, however, the era that E.H. Gombrich originally credited with the rise of true landscape painting, artists were increasingly aware of the allusions and symbolism that such scenes could relay. Specifically, though, the landscape took on a decidedly feminine connotation. Michelangelo, for instance, likened landscapes to irrational beauty because they fool the eye with their splendors and encouraged a subjective (feminine) escape rather that a rational (masculine) virtue.[29] This perspective was rooted in ancient writings on *parerga*, which translates directly as "beside the work" and was a term used by Vitruvius and interpreted by Renaissance critic Cesare Cesariano to refer to more marginal painterly subjects like landscapes.[30] From the more

27 B.C. Keene and A. Kacenski, *Sacred Landscapes: Nature in Renaissance Manuscripts* (Los Angeles: The J. Paul Getty Museum, 2017), 87.

28 More will be said on this in a subsequent chapter, but in the interim see: C. Stollhans, "Peruzzi's Standing Saint Paul in the Ponzetti Chapel, Santa Maria della Pace: Tradition or Innovation?" *Notes in the History of Art*, 10 (3) (Spring 1991), 18.

29 F. de Hollanda, *Four Dialogues on Painting*. Trans. by F.G. Bell (UK: Oxford University Press, 1928), 15–16.

30 Vitruvius, *De architectura libri deci tructi de latinio in vulgare*, trans. By Cesare Cesariano (Como, 1521), f. cxvii; as quoted in Summers, *Michelangelo and the Language of Art* (1981), 455. For more on Cesariano's influence in the interpretation of Vitruvius, please see: C.H. Krinsky, "Cesariano and the Renaissance without Rome." *Arte Lombarda* 16 (1971): 211–218.

general perspective, the practice of illusionistic landscapes was paramount to the rich and complex fourth-style Roman wall paintings. To be sure, landscape motifs had been popular with others in Polidoro's generation: Giulio Romano's relatively contemporaneous *Holy Family* (*La Perla*) (1518–1520; Museo del Prado, Madrid) and *Stoning of Saint Stephen* (1520–1521), for instance, showcases the artist's early stocking of images with imagined, classical landscapes.[31] What distinguishes Polidoro's landscapes, though, is that he devotes most of the composition to his view of the natural world.

The landscapes included in this chapel were adequately unique to be noted by chroniclers like Vasari and Titi, but they perhaps take on new meaning in consideration of more modern explorations of the landscape's symbolism. Modern scholars such as Karen Hope Goodchild have proposed that the use of the landscape in Renaissance contexts had a gendered intent by embodying the symbolic allusions to the feminine.[32] Vasari further fueled this momentum by sourcing vocabulary connoting the feminine for his description of landscape scenes. In his very description of the landscapes within the Fetti Chapel, in fact, he invokes the "grace" of the paintings, which is equally laudatory and dismissive in its tone but yet reflected not only the gendered difference of the day but also the lesser importance that landscape painting shared among more Classically derived subject matter. Indeed, as Karen Hope Goodchild summarized: "certain Renaissance theorists and writers betray the belief that while any viewer … is qualified to judge how well an artist has counterfeited natural appearances, … only learned viewers can appreciate an artist's inspired conception. Setting this in terms of landscape, painting natural details were suspected of being both too easy to render and too easy to appreciate—so easy, in fact that they were charming even to women."[33] This gendered encapsulation of the landscape seems particularly relevant in the case of this chapel as these scenes are to recall the narratives of two female saints. Perhaps, then, one could argue Polidoro was quite aware of these burgeoning theories of the landscape, thanks to his connections with Raphael and the according links with antiquity and humanist circles.

Thus, while Polidoro's frescoes might not be a literal recombination of earlier ideas, they serve to showcase the way in which Polidoro was unafraid to experi-

31 As Hartt noted: "these structures appear tragic, overgrown with vegetation, illuminated only by sudden shafts of light which leave much of the building in gloomy shadow, constantly threatening collapse." (Hartt, *Giulio Romano*, 1: 6).

32 Karen Hope-Goodchild, "Toward an Italian Renaissance Theory of Landscape" (PhD diss., University of Virginia), 70.

33 Goodchild, 78.

ment with the combination of new ideas as he carried the visual language from Raphael's day forward. The dominance of the landscape in this chapel suggests that Polidoro was exploring the genre as both stage set and symbolic allusion by conjuring views that fooled the eye into thinking it was escaping into a vast wilderness far beyond the chapel and in doing so would pair religious thinking with the combined tensions of Classical thinking and contemporary ingenuity.

Polidoro's landscapes thus served as a landmark in sixteenth century painting and perhaps would have led to even greater acclaim had Polidoro had the opportunity to continue in the tradition; as it were, however, the Sack of Rome would soon after alter the artistic discourse in the Eternal City, and the landscape, though it would return soon after the Sack, would not be the same.

CHAPTER 7

Santa Maria della Pace and a Pastiche by Peruzzi

While these past chapters have made clear the ways in which the artists of Raphael's circle partook in a repertoire of visual phrases or elements that they then recombined into new compositions, a voice that has been somewhat peripheral is that of Baldassarre Peruzzi. Since the culmination of his work for Chigi that reintroduced the ancient *scaenae frons* to Renaissance domestic architecture, Peruzzi had been incredibly busy. Beyond his work at Chigi's villa, one of the central landmarks in Peruzzi's Roman period was his work at the Church of Santa Maria della Pace. He first contributed to the space in his design for a pictorial program for the Ponzetti Chapel (c. 1516), commissioned by Cardinal Ferdinand Ponzetti, who had, similar to Chigi before him, ingratiated himself to the pope by serving as treasurer general for Leo X.[1] Peruzzi's work for Ponzetti would have begun just as his work for Chigi was coming to an end. By that point, however, Peruzzi's prestige was on the rise: in addition to such large-scale artistic commissions, Peruzzi was from 1514 working on designs for St. Peter's Basilica and, as previously discussed, also devoted to the development of the frescoed façade tradition in Rome alongside colleagues like Polidoro da Caravaggio.

His return to the church, then, in the subsequent decade marked a metaphorical bookend to a relatively prolific moment of his professional career. For this later visit, Peruzzi had been tasked with a rather large-scale composition depicting *The Presentation of the Virgin at the Temple*, an intriguing work that has unfortunately been relegated to the periphery in the study of Peruzzi's career in part due to the fact that it has suffered from notable modification (Fig. 40).

When Flavio Chigi ascended the papacy to become Alexander VII in 1655, he embarked upon an impressive campaign to polish the city of Rome, which included the Church of Santa Maria della Pace.[2] What initially began as a solu-

1 For more, see: A. Ferrajoli, *Il ruolo della corte di Leone X (1514–1516)* (Rome: Bulzoni, 1984), 218–221; C. Stollhans, "Baldassare Peruzzi and his patrons: Religious paintings in Rome, 1503–1527" (PhD diss., Northwestern University, 1988), 60–66.

2 It seems significant that, as Frommel has commented, "only Peruzzi's [painting] escaped" Alexander VII's renovations of the church's interior (C.L. Frommel, *Baldassarre Peruzzi als Maler und Zeichner (Vienna: Anoton Schroll, 1967–1968)*, 126).

 | DOI:10.1163/9789004430488_009

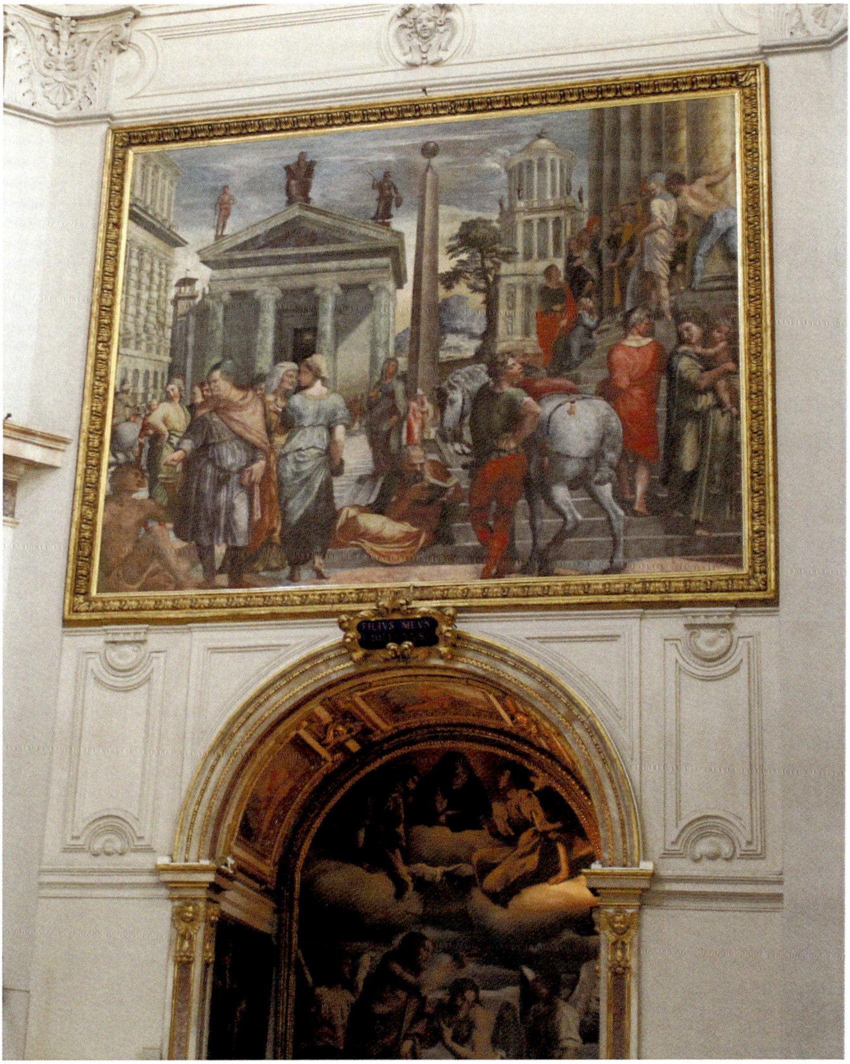

FIGURE 40 View of the tiburio in the modern day showing the placement of Peruzzi's *Presentation of the Virgin* (upper right)
SANTA MARIA DELLA PACE, ROME—AUTHOR'S IMAGE

tion for the traffic congestion that occurred in the church's piazza spread to interior renovation.[3] His plan began with the help of Pietro da Cortona, who in 1658 offered a "decorative dress" of the interior that included renovation of

3 For more on the history and popularity of Santa Maria della Pace, see: P. Burke, "Donec auferatur luna: The Façade of S. Maria della Pace." *Journal of the Warburg and Courtauld Institutes*,

the Chigi Chapel to include new reliefs and sculptures.[4] It also precipitated a reworking of the octagonal tiburio, which had been modified in the exterior work to close off one access point and subsequently create a more substantial egress to the church's octagon at its south-eastern juncture.

These modifications resulted in the work being cut down, thereby obscuring some of its compositional elements. Two drawings (nos. 1410 and 1433, respectively, Louvre Museum) related to this work exist, the first attributed to Peruzzi, and the second to an anonymous figure; both, however, reveal substantial deviations from this finished composition and thus further problematize its analysis. Further muddying the waters of this work's study is the issue of dating: there is little consensus as to what point in the 1520s this work was created. While some have proposed this *Presentation* was conjured as early as 1519–1520, others, like Frommel, stress a later date between 1523–1526 to account for Peruzzi's brief absence from Rome in the early years of the decade to work on the Church of San Petronio in Bologna.[5] This later date is further supported by Piers Barker-Bates, who notes astutely that documents relating to the church's construction confirm that the roof was not completed until nearly 1526.[6] This later date seems more plausible given the progression of events in the space, but one is still left with the challenges of interpretation. Nevertheless, it seems more can be said about this multi-valenced work. Created nearly a decade after Raphael's

---

44 (1981); 238–239; P. Portoghesi, "S. Maria della Pace di Pietro da Cortona," *L'architettura: Cronache e storia*, 7 (1962), 848–851.

4 Cortona's planned for a new façade built on varied references to invoke elements of the antique—Martinelli's guidebook, for example, likened this design to the entryway to the Baths of Diocletian (Portoghesi, "S. Maria della Pace," 847; F. Martinelli, *Roma ricercata nel suo sito e nella scuola di tutti gli antiquari*, Rome 1644, 3rd edition 1658, 176)—along with the contemporary, with echoes of Bramante's Tempietto in the ovoid porch that some scholars have also compared to Peruzzi's Palazzo Massimo alle Colonne (1534–1536) (D.M. Habel, *The Urban Development of Rome in the Age of Alexander VII* (UK: Cambridge University Press, 2002), 308). Coincidingly he also changed the piazza, resulting in what Merz has called "the first formal outdoor space in Rome since Michelangelo's scheme for the Capitoline Hill … [that is] the most stage-like of Cortona's buildings." (J.M. Merz, *Pietro da Cortona: Der Aufsteig zum führenden Maler im barocken Rom* (1991), 174); G. Briganti, *Pietro da Cortona: o della pittura barocca* (Florence: Sansoni Editore Nuova, 1982); A. Lo Bianco, *Pietro da Cortona 1597–1669* (Electa, 1997).

5 Frommel, *Peruzzi als Maler*, 125; Peruzzi was at work in Bologna no later than 1522, as this is the date of his first payment (as noted by: R.J. Tuttle, "The Basilica of S. Petronio in Bologna," in H.A. Millon and V. Magnago Lampugnani, eds., *The Renaissance from Brunelleschi to Michelangelo: The Representation of Architect* (Milan: Bompiani, 1994), 523); he returned to Rome in 1523.

6 For more on these connections please see: P. Barker-Bates, *Sebastiano del Piombo and the World of Spanish Rome* (NY: Routledge, 2017), Chapter 3.

death, and within the context of these various projects that had ensued in the interim, this *Presentation* can be seen as reflective of an enduring spirit of collaboration and of Peruzzi's own talents at artistic recombination that thrived in the years following Raphael's demise.

Peruzzi's selection for his first project at Santa Maria della Pace—that for Cardinal Ferdinand Ponzetti's chapel—was undoubtedly encouraged by the former's friendship with Agostino Chigi. Recall that the Sienese banker enjoyed a remarkable level of social status and must have been pleased with the work of Peruzzi both as architect of and artist within his villa. Contextually, by 1516 when he was granted Ponzetti's patronage, Peruzzi would have completed the elegant astrological ceiling in Chigi's Sala di Galatea and perhaps was already beginning plans for the Sala delle Prospettive as well. Indeed, around the same time as his first work at Santa Maria della Pace, Peruzzi created the striking Sala delle Prospettive. The theatrical quality of this room's design, recall, also spoke to Peruzzi's growing expertise in scenographic design. In addition to designing theatrical apparati for both the *possesso* of Leo X and the confirmation of Roman citizenship on Giuliano and Lorenzo de Medici in 1513, he can also be securely linked to scenograpic designs for a performance of Cardinal Bibbiena's "La Calandria" during the Carnival season of 1515.[7]

This theatrical energy would carry Peruzzi into the next decade, when the artist and architect would return to both to Chigi's villa and Santa Maria della Pace. Remember that in 1518, on the heels of his work on Chigi's Sala delle Prospettive, Peruzzi developed plans for a frescoed façade that would have afforded him further license to explore theatrical themes through the lens of *all'antica* revival.[8] Adding to this landmark design was how Raphael, Peruzzi, and their workshop would have coordinated their visual programs for the façade and adjoining Loggia di Amore e Psiche, allowing both interior and exterior imagery to play off one another to fittingly convey a theatrical framework. The potential of that collaboration, the culmination of over a decades' worth of exchange between Raphael and Peruzzi, was never realized. As a testament to

7 Bibbiena brought his play to Rome for two performances, one in December 1514 for Pope Leo X and Isabella D'Este held at the Vatican, the second during the carnival season of 1515. Peruzzi perhaps contributed to both Roman productions, however this is unconfirmed (C.L. Frommel, "Raffaello e il teatro alla corte di Leone X," *Bolletino del Centro Internazionale di Studi di Architettura Andrea Palladio* 16 (1974), 173–174; also described in a letter by Castiglione to Count Ludovico Canossa, October, 1513; A. Schard, *Beiträge zur Geschichte des Bühnenbildes vom 15. Zum Ende des 17. Jahrhunderts* (Ph.D. diss, Freiburg im Breisgau, 1925), 35). For more on Peruzzi's role in scenography, see: Huppert, *Becoming an Architect*, 100; F. Cruciani, *Teatro nel Rinascimento: Roma, 1450–1550* (Rome, Bulzoni, 1983), 348.

8 For more, see: A.R. Culotta, "The Dramatic Side of Breaking Bad."

their enduring collegiality, though, Peruzzi absorbed several of Raphael's flourishing workshop team members into his subsequent projects and thus Peruzzi carried forth the ideals of Raphael's workshop model while also maintaining his own. This blend is arguably evidenced in this painting of the *Presentation of the Virgin*, a commission that called Peruzzi back to Rome and to Santa Maria della Pace in the early 1520s.[9]

1 Filippo Sergardi (1466–1541)

The patron for this commission, Filippo Sergardi, hailed from Siena but came to Rome to serve as a secretary to Pope Leo X. Complementing his social status from this Papal connection was his close association with fellow Sienese Chigi, whose family had maintained friendships with the Sergardi family for some time.[10] This connection with Chigi is again an essential one, as it was undoubtedly the link to the banker that encouraged Sergardi to solicit commissions from both Peruzzi and Sebastiano del Piombo, who also had worked on Chigi's villa alongside Raphael. One could also assume that these selections were made in part to honor this longstanding friendship, as Chigi's premature death in 1520, nearly simultaneous with that of Raphael, precluded his chance to witness these subsequent commissions. Previous scholarship has done much to reconstruct the motivation behind this commission. Contracts, for instance, from the 1520s determine that at least three works were to be included in a cycle under the main cupola: *The Presentation*, by Peruzzi; *The Visitation* by Sebastiano del Piombo; and *The Assumption* by Francesco Salviati, all in keeping with the theme of the veneration of the Virgin Mary.[11] Peruzzi's composition was the first—and only—to be finished, so it is difficult to determine exactly how his work would have interacted visually with the other two works in the cycle. On its own, though, Peruzzi's *Presentation* contains a fascinating array of references that spoke to his ongoing invocation of visual elements from earlier works.

9 It is important to note that, while this painting was spared during da Cortona's renovations, it was nevertheless trimmed. For more, see: Burke, 238–239; Portoghesi, "S. Maria della Pace." 840–851.

10 Barker-Bates, *Sebastiano del* Piombo; Stollhans, "Baldassare Peruzzi," 99; C. Stollhans, "Peruzzi's Standing Saint Paul in the Ponzetti Chapel, Santa Maria della Pace: Tradition or Innovation?" *Notes in the History of Art*, 10 (3) (Spring 1991), 14–20. Further indicating their connection was the fact that Sergardi assisted Cornelio Benigno with the 1521 inventory of Chigi's estate following his death.

11 For more, see: Stollhans, "Baldassare Peruzzi," 103.

On the one hand, Peruzzi ascribed to conventional representations of this subject. The narrative recounts the presentation of the juvenile Mary by her parents Joachim and Anne at the Temple of Jerusalem as an act of both thanks and of allusory consecration of Mary as the eventual Mother of God. This was a moment depicted in many earlier iterations prior to Peruzzi's painting; for example, one can look to Ghirlandaio's version from the 1480s in the Cappella Tornabuoni in Florence's Santa Maria Novella or Cima da Conegliano's version from the subsequent decade. Given the frequent inclusion of the narrative within Life of the Virgin cycles, Peruzzi was careful to adhere to some of the conventions of iconography exhibited in these earlier versions. For instance, Peruzzi placed the figure of Mary prostrate on the temple steps as she gazed up toward the figure of the priest that reaches toward her from between the temple's columns, a compositional structure seen in both Ghirlandaio's and da Conegliano's versions. A closer look to these steps, however, hints at an early signal of Peruzzi's desire to experiment with his references. A count of these stairs reveals that Peruzzi was so precise in his adherence to the narrative prescribed in the Gospel of Pseudo-Matthew that he included exact count of 15 steps to the temple platform.[12] This exactitude was not a standard convention within this narrative's depiction and thus can serve as an entry point into a more incisive look into the multitude of novel references Peruzzi weaves together in this work.

Stepping back to look at the overall composition, it becomes clear that the life of the Virgin is not Peruzzi's only point of interest here. The narrative is seemingly relegated to a very restricted portion of the composition. Whereas Ghirlandaio's Florentine version, for example, situates the kneeling figure of the version to the center of the composition thus to serve as the focal point, Peruzzi instead abandons the conventional placement of the Virgin's parents, Joachim and Anne, at the bottom of the temple stairs and instead places them in the far end of the stairs at an unusual scale that was out of perspectival alignment with the remainder of the painting. The result of this shift is that the narrative moment is visually isolated to the upper right quadrant of the painting, making Mary and her act of devotion to the Church seemingly peripheral. This secondary status of the Virgin's narrative is further emphasized with, as Stollhans noted, the array of action in the immediate foreground.[13] Equally visually dominant is the architecture that inhabits the background.

12 Ibid., 103.

13 Ibid., 104.

One can also note the overall stage-like setting that this architecturally-grounded composition exudes. As Rosand noted, "the entire spatial setting of Peruzzi's architectural re-creation of antiquity is a full, three-dimensional stage space with a deliberately marked gridwork pattern measuring the recession of the pavement."[14] This allusion to the stage, a point further illuminated by Christoph Frommel in a 1985 hypothetical planimetric diagram of the painting, undoubtedly alluded to Peruzzi's burgeoning specialization in scenography, and his references to ancient architecture are assuredly the product of his diligent study of the antiquity scattered around Rome (Fig. 41).[15] This stage-like structure that underpinned Peruzzi's work thus can be seen as potentially significant on several levels. On the one hand, and in light of the previous chapter's discussion of Polidoro's experimentation with the space of the landscape within his work in the Fetti Chapel, one can wonder if perhaps Peruzzi here was investigating a similar sort of theoretical contemplation. Could, for example, Peruzzi's dramatic cityscape here be a response to Polidoro's expansive landscapes as part of a larger visual conversation on the construction of visual space or the development of scenography? On the other hand, it is possible that Peruzzi here was aiming to exalt his abilities as a scenographer in a more permanent setting. The inherent nature of theatrical scenography was that of transience, with each design demolished with the end of a performance run. By using such a scenographic theme in this composition's design, then, was Peruzzi exploring a space wherein theatricality and religious painting combined?

In addition to these questions, one must also contemplate the cast of characters that Peruzzi included in this packed scene, those which Rosand likened to a "number of independent sculptural units."[16] A closer look to these figures reveals that many of them bear parallels to those found in the work of Raphael. Given these quotations, it would seem that Peruzzi deliberately wished to draw attention to these foregrounded characters as they had been "adopted" from other compositions by his former colleague as yet another instance further reflecting the continuity of the practice of visual recombination over the course of the 1520s.

14 David Rosand, "Titian's Presentation of the Virgin in the Temple and the Scuola della Carità" *Art Bulletin*, 58 (1976), 72 n. 99, 55–84; also echoed in: Huppert, *Becoming an Architect*, 103; also see M.V. Brugnoli, "Baldassarre Peruzzi nella chiesa di S. Maria della Pace e nell "Ucceliera" di Giulio II," *Bolletino d'Arte* LVIII/2–3 (Apr-Sep 1973): 113–122.

15 Christoph Luitpold Frommel, "Baldassarre Peruzzi pittore e architetto." In M. Fagiolo and M.L. Madonna, *Baldassarre Peruzzi pittura scena e architettura nel Cinquecento* (Treccani, 1985), 21–47.

16 Rosand, "Titian's Presentation," 99.

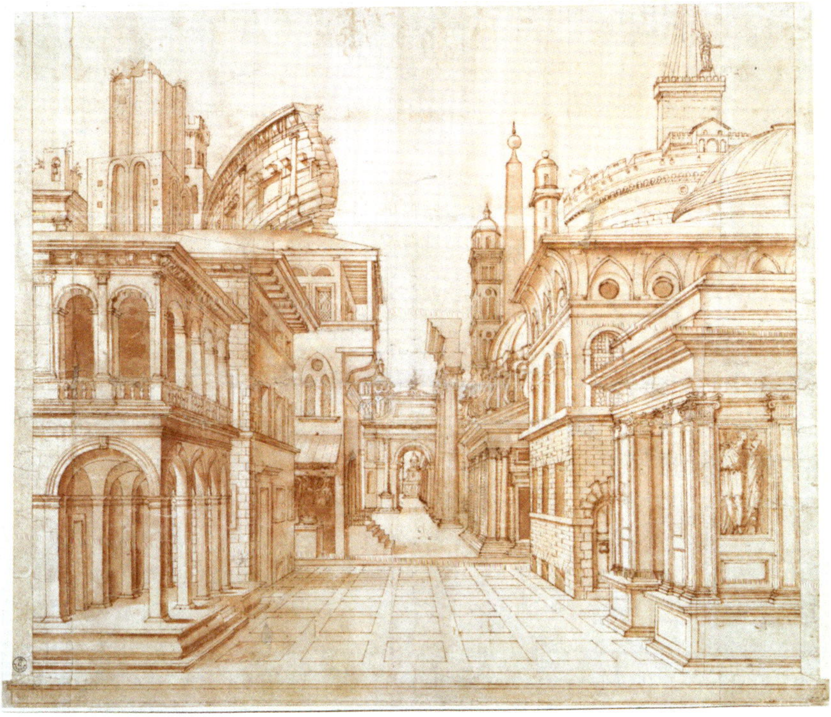

FIGURE 41 Baldassarre Peruzzi, *Theatrical Perspective with the Symbolic Monuments of Rome* (291 A)
GABINETTO DEI DISEGNI E DELLE STAMPE, UFFIZI, FLORENCE/SCALA/ART RESOURCE

Immediately, as has been noted previously, Peruzzi's *Presentation* as a whole is reminiscent of Raphael's *Fire in the Borgo*. Indeed, the foreground figure of the water carrier to the right of Raphael's *Fire* appears in the center foreground of Peruzzi's *Presentation*. She takes a slightly different stance, and yet the muscular bulk of her arm accurately parallels that of the maiden in Raphael's composition.

What makes Peruzzi's quotation so intriguing here is that there is evidence to suggest that Raphael based his *Fire* on a scenographic drawing often attributed to Peruzzi. Recall that Raphael was indeed intrigued by the novel field of theatrical set design and was involved after *Fire in the Borgo* with the set design for the 1519 performance of Ludovico Ariosto's comedy *I Suppositi*.[17] This rein-

17 Golzio, 94; Frommel, "Raffaello e il teatro," 183. Commissioned by Leo X's nephew Cardinal Innocenzio Cibò, Raphael's designs, including a perspectival view of Ferrara, were

forces the spirit of camaraderie between Raphael and Peruzzi as reflected in their previously mentioned collaboration on the *scaenae frons* of Chigi's villa, but it also suggests that the two readily borrowed ideas from each other in the creation of compositions. A similar parallel can be drawn between the architecture witnessed in Peruzzi's *Satirical Allegory*, and undated image originally linked to Peruzzi in Vasari's *Libro di Disegni*, and Raphael's preparatory cartoon for a tapestry depicting *The Sacrifice at Lystra* (1515–1516). Here elements from the *Colossus* in the background to the architectural motifs seem to be shared between artists with relative freedom.

2 A Pastiche of Figures

Furthermore, in addition to these scenographic parallels, one can note that several of Raphael's figures also appear here. Stollhans summarized several of these in her original analysis, including the older lady, whom she connected with Raphael's old sibyl from the nearby Chigi Chapel;[18] the seated philosopher in the center foreground that echoes the figure of Diogenes from Raphael's *School of Athens* (1508); and the figure who swoops in and around the temple column as a parallel to a similar figure in *The Donation of Constantine*, a composition executed by Raphael and his workshop.[19] One can add to these initial observations by noting several other figures that have safely been derived from earlier projects by Raphael. The reclining figure poised at the lower left, interpreted by David Rosand as a beggar seeking alms, is now relatively obscured. A look to Peruzzi's preparatory drawing, however, reveals a figure that seems to blend the classical forms employed by Raphael in two different compositions; the first is that of the previously-mentioned work, *The Judgment of Paris*, that has been passed down in print form by the work of Marcantonio Raimondi. The second reference point is the figure of the semi-reclining deity in Raphael's quadro riportato *Council of the Gods* emblazoned on the ceiling of the Loggia di

used for a performance at the Castel Sant'Angelo (O. Fischel, *Raphael* (London: K. Paul, 1948), vol. 1, 212). So devoted to his designs for this production that he further delayed his promised commissions to Duke Alfonso d'Este of Ferrara, which drew the admonition in early 1520 from the Duke to his agent that Raphael should "think carefully about what it means to give his word" and that the agent should "speak to the most reverend Lord Cardinal Cibò commending us to his Lordship and remind him of the promise he made to manage things so that this Raphael would quickly finish our picture." (Golzio, 105–106).

18 Echoed in: L. Ettlinger, "A Note on Raphael's Sibyls in S. Maria della Pace." *Journal of the Warburg and Courtauld Institutes*, XXIV (1961): 322–323.

19 Stollhans, diss. 105.

Amore e Psiche, Raphael's capstone at Chigi's villa. Though variations occurred in this figure's posture in the painting, the similarity seen between Raphael's fresco and Peruzzi's original drawing suggest that one is taken directly from the other.

Adding to these connections are the two male figures that appear in the composition's lower right corner: the first, who mounts the stairs while turning abruptly to the side and adjacent to the "Raphaelesque" Madonna at the bottom right, and the second, who parallels this figure on the stairs by contorting his figure to look out at the viewer as he tends to his horse. Both of these figures seem to be a variation on a Raphaelesque theme. A relatively close connection, for instance, could be derived from the male form that appears prominently in Raphael's *The Wedding Banquet of Cupid and Psyche*, adjacent to the *Council of the Gods* and thus also from Chigi's villa. If not derived from this source, one could also find a parallel figure in a preparatory drawing executed by Raphael around 1508 for the *La Disputa*—though altered in the final version of the Vatican fresco, it seems clear that yet again similar sources of inspiration are shared between works.

Along these same lines, one could suggest two updates to earlier interpretations of these figures. The first is a modification to Stollhans' identification of the figure wrapped rather precariously around the temple column at center right. Stollhans, recall, connected this figure to one that appears in *The Donation of Constantine*, but this is a potentially problematic link as this fresco was executed between 1520–1524, virtually simultaneous to, or perhaps even after, Peruzzi's *Presentation* was completed. This intertwined figure bears connections to Raphael's work in the slightly earlier *Expulsion of Heliodorus from the Temple*, leading one to surmise that yet again Peruzzi was here looking quite directly to Raphael's figures and perhaps was attempting to draw reference to the role of the temple that plays so prominently in both compositions.

A similar play might be occurring with the reclining figure at the center of the composition previously linked to Raphael's figure of Diogenes in *The School of Athens*. Here too connections could be drawn to the classicizing figures of Raphael's *The Judgment of Paris* or the frescoes from Chigi's villa, but it seems another parallel can be established between this figure and that of Saint Matthew, who appears in one of Raphael's final works, *The Transfiguration*. Though more loosely connected in posture, Peruzzi's reclining figure seems strikingly similar in dress and age, and the fact that he pores over a text, a counterpoint to Raphael's Matthew who is hurriedly abandoning his book to attend to the miraculous moment at hand, suggests that Peruzzi was considering such sources in this figure's creation. Of course, it also fits nicely, given that the narrative of Mary stems from the apocryphal Gospel of Pseudo-Matthew, that Peruzzi might have cleverly included this reference to the figure of Matthew.

3 A Pastiche of Architecture

A similar analysis can be made of the elaborate architecture that looms just beyond these varied figures. It is this architectural backdrop that has received the most scholarly attention, with Christoph Frommel offering one of the earliest interpretations of the space that Peruzzi invokes.[20] In his review, Frommel concluded in his analysis in *Baldassarre Peruzzi als Maler und Zeichner* (1968) that Peruzzi desired an architectural arrangement akin to the classical Roman Forum, with "the emphasis placed on ... confusing variety rather than on clear unity."[21] Susan McKillop echoed this sentiment in her 1974 interpretation, wherein she suggested that the temple of the narrative's focus at right is a version of the Temple of Saturn, situated at the northwest corner of the Roman Forum, and that the unusually tiered structure in the far right background is a variation on the Temple of Vesta.[22] Rounding out these analyses is the observation noted by several scholars of the similarities between the masonry of the fragmentary façade that appears at far left and that of the original design of the facade for the Forma Urbis, identified as a portion of the Church of Santi Cosma e Damiano, a structure that, as Huppert has noted, Peruzzi studied with great detail.[23] Parallel to these antique connections, Rosand subsequently used these forms to draw a parallel between the compositional order and the books of the Bible to surmise that the presence of David, Moses, and Judith along the ridgeline of the anterior temple alludes to the Old Testament, with the New Testament implied by The Presentation of the Virgin, the titular narrative that is nevertheless strangely sequestered in the work.[24]

---

20 Frommel, *Baldassarre Peruzzis*, 128.

21 Ibid. This Forum format was later supported by Susan McKillop, who suggested that the temple that emerges at right (on whose steps the Virgin kneels) is rendered after the Temple of Saturn. She also suggested that the temple at far back right was intended to emulate the Temple of Vesta. For more, see: S.R. McKillop, *Franciabigio* (Berkeley: University of California Press, 1974), 82 n. 80.

22 McKillop, 82.

23 A. Huppert, "Material matters: training the Renaissance architect," in A. Sherman, ed., *Artistic Practices and Cultural Transfer in Early Modern Italy: Essays in Honor of Deborah Howard* (Routledge, 2016), 95.

24 Rosand, "Titian's Presentation," 72 n. 99. Frommel identified Rosand's *David* as Samson, but Rosand disputes this identification.

These are all widely accepted interpretations of the pictorial piazza Peruzzi offers us, but even more considerations can be proffered. The first is in regard to the Ionic Order tetrastyle temple at left that bears these Biblical ridgeline figures. One could propose that Peruzzi is here referencing the Temple of Portunus, known through the Renaissance as the Temple of Fortuna Virilis and one of the best-preserved tetrastyle temples within the cinquecento landscape. This ancient landmark paralleled the plan for the original Temple of Jerusalem, an element reinforced by the presence, as Frommel noted, of the burning oil lamp seen within the open cella or sanctuary doors.[25] It might also have been selected as Peruzzi's muse thanks to the temple's repurposing during the ninth century (around 872) into a Christian church that, in 1492, had been dedicated Santa Maria Egyziaca (Saint Mary of Egypt).[26]

This Medieval repurposing of an antique space might have spurred particular interest for Peruzzi, as he had looked to such medieval connections before. In her 1991 article discussing the Ponzetti Chapel, Stollhans notes that Peruzzi's incorporation of unconventional representations of the conversion of Saints Peter and Paul in the chapel's arches tie to the artist's study of Carolingian narratives that she believes might have been inspired from the prevalent Latin and Greek manuscripts in Rome as well as the patron Ponzetti's fascination with the subject.[27] Thus, for Peruzzi to plumb such medieval transformations of an ancient temple in the nearby *Presentation* painting would not be out of character. The connection to Egypt, though, is also an intriguing one, as it offers a segue into the discussion of the adjacent and quite prominent obelisk at the center of Peruzzi's composition. Some explanation of this obelisk has been made, but none thus far has been fully satisfying. Frommel proposed, for instance, that this device was purely to draw visual attention to Joachim and Anna, who appear unusually out of scale at its base (this is perhaps one of the more unusual elements to this composition wherein Peruzzi's painting falls out of perspectival perfection). Rosand suggests that it was a means to divide the Biblical realms of Old and New Testaments; Stollhans, however, suggests the importance of this obelisk from an antique perspective, and it is from this angle that discussion can advance.

25 Frommel, *Peruzzi als Maler*, 127.

26 J. Osborne, "A Note on the Medieval Name of the So-called 'Temple of Fortuna Virilis' in Rome." *Papers of the British School at Rome*, 56 (1988), 210–212.

27 Indeed, as Stollhans concludes: "Because of Ponzetti's knowledge and interest, one or even many Carolingian or Byzantine manuscripts … may have served as the prototype for Peruzzi's design." Stollhans, "Peruzzi's Standing Saint Paul," 18.

During Peruzzi's day, the art and architecture of ancient Egypt was becoming more widely explored. Discussed in the fifteenth-century writings of theorist Leon Battista Alberti, Egyptianizing themes served as inspiration for the fantastical landscapes in publications such as the *Hypnerotomachia Poliphili* (published in Venice in 1486). Such excitement over these exotic Egyptian motifs spurred a generation of fanatics, with some going so far as to construct a mythological lineage to Egyptian and Near Eastern deities.[28] This fervor continued into the sixteenth century. Pope Leo X, for example, studied in his youth with intellectuals such as Angelo Poliziano, whose *Miscellanea* (published in 1489 in Florence) retells Plutarch's narrative of the syncretic deity Harpocrates.[29] Once elected pope, he maintained a small collection of Egyptian antiquities, and he also developed an extensive literary collection that served as one of the leading collections for Roman humanists from 1508–1527 and included volumes such as Poliziano's *Miscellanea*.[30]

Further fueling this trend was the unearthing of Egyptian obelisks around Rome. Indeed, many scholars have noted the Via Leonina excavation near the modern-day Porta di Ripetta, overseen by Raphael and Antonio di Sangallo in July 1519.[31] This project revealed fragments of one of the obelisks that once graced the ancient Mausoleum of Augustus, and these portions remained exposed in the nearby via di Ripetta until the papacy of Sixtus V (1585–1590). Stollhans argued that Peruzzi undoubtedly studied from these unmoved segments,[32] a point proven not only by the proximity of his concurrent work on the Church of San Rocco's tribuna, but also by Peruzzi's surviving drawings that document these ancient fragments (U 391A*r* and U405A*r*, Gabinetto Diesgni e Stampe, Galleria degli Uffizi, Florence).[33] Thus, one could conclude that

---

28 For more, see: B. Curran et al., *Obelisk: A History* (Cambridge: Burndy Library, 2009), 88–89; I.D. Rowland, *The Culture of the High Renaissance: Ancients and Moderns in Sixteenth-Century Rome* (Cambridge: Cambridge University Press, 2011), 46–53.

29 For more see: K. Giehlow, *The Humanist's Interpretation of Hieroglyphs in the Allegorical Studies of the Renaissance with a Focus on the Triumphal Arch of Maximilian I* (Boston: Brill, 2015).

30 According to sources, he was in possession of a Ptolemaic cup made from sardonyx as well as a likeness of "Isis that reportedly provided the model for the golden image carried in the Carnival procession of 1520" (Curran et al., *Obelisk: A History*, 94).

31 C. Frommel, "Papal Policy: The Planning of Rome During the Renaissance," *Journal of Interdisciplinary History*, 17 (1986), 39–65.

32 Stollhans, "Baldassarre Peruzzi," 109.

33 As noted in: Huppert, "Material Matters," 89–106: also see: V. Zanchettin, "Costruire nell'antico. Roma, Campo Marzio 1508–1523: Peruzzi, la confraternita di San Rocco e i cantieri intorno al mausoleo di Augusto." In *Baldassarre Peruzzi 1481–1536* (Marsilio, 2005), 123–154.

this inclusion was simply an extension of Peruzzi's indebted study of antiquity. While it is unclear the extent to which Sergardi absorbed the Egyptomania of the day, the location for this commission alongside Sergardi's connections to the papacy could explain the inclusion of these Egyptian elements as an allusion to the dominion of Christianity. One could even go so far as to suggest that such study was in part in preparation for this *Presentation*: if one accepts the dating of *Presentation* to between 1525 and 1527, this would make its creation coincide somewhat nicely with the revelation of these via Leonina fragments.[34] Visual evidence suggests, though, that Peruzzi here was not just following trend but rather was yet again entering into a dialogue with his colleagues both past and present. On the one hand, one can find connections to the work of Pinturicchio, who, really, was one of Peruzzi's early mentors; on the other, one can identify how Peruzzi continued to refer to both Raphael and his surviving workshop participants.

The connection with Pinturicchio can be found in his narrative cycle in the Sala dei Santi within Borgia Pope Alexander VI's Apartments at the Vatican created between 1492 and 1495. Pinturicchio's suite of imagery in this chamber channeled the ancient mythologies of Isis and Osiris to recall the Borgia claim of a lineage that stretched to Osiris-Apis and included two representations of Osiris' pyramidal tomb.[35] Such exotic narratives serve as a reminder of the growing popularity of Egyptian lore in Renaissance Rome. As Brian Curran pointed out, "by the last decade of the fifteenth century, the status of the Egyptians as the progenitors of a proto-Christian theology … had become so firmly established that the appearance of a full-blown Egyptian mythological cycle in one of the most important staterooms in the papal residence at the Vatican may not have raised many eyebrows."[36] The prominent cycle that recast these Egyptian deities as part of the Christian legacy was, though accepted, also quite novel and thus makes this suite of imagery an almost guaranteed source for Peruzzi's later composition.

Supporting this connection is the fact that Peruzzi had borrowed from Pinturicchio's work in the past. Peruzzi's connection with Pinturicchio had been established in Siena, when he worked under the Perugian for the motifs created in the Piccolomini Library between 1502 and 1508. Echoes of Pinturicchio's

34 Peruzzi was documented as being in Rome between 1518 and 1520; from 1521–1523, he was in Bologna, though he did return to Rome during that time to complete plans for the Palazzo Fusconi-Pighini; he returned to Rome in 1523 full time to develop the apparati for Clement VII's accession. For more see: H. Wurm, Baldassarre Peruzzi Architekturzeichungen. (Germany: Tubingen, 1984).

35 B. Curran, *The Egyptian Renaissance: The Afterlife of Ancient Egypt In Early Modern Italy* (Chicago: University of Chicago Press, 2007), 117.

36 Curran, *The Egyptian Renaissance*, 107.

Piccolomini program, alongside his work in the Borgia Apartment's *Sala della Sibille* (1492–1499), can be seen in the manner in which Peruzzi later created the fictive framework for Chigi's Loggia di Galatea. It was perhaps this desire to continue this traditional connection that is witnessed in Peruzzi's *Presentation*.

At the same time, one can also propose an additional connection to Raphael, or rather his enduring workshop, in an analysis of these architectural forms. Relatively simultaneous to the proposed completion dates of Peruzzi's *Presentation*, recall, that Giulio Romano and Giovanni Francesco Penni were embroiled in a suite of imagery for the Sala di Costantino (1520–1524). The plans for this large audience hall were only in their infancy when Raphael died—indeed, drawings for only two walls, that depicting *The Vision of the Cross* (or *The Vision of Constantine*) and *The Battle of Milvian Bridge*, had been drafted. In a closer look to the anterior landscape of *The Vision of the Cross* (Fig. 42), one can note the striking similarity in architectural forms as they appear in Peruzzi's *Presentation*. In their research of *The Vision*, Philip Fehl and Vitale Zanchettin identified these structures respectively as the Meta Romuli that once stood on the Via Alessandrina (demolished during the papacy of Leo X) and the Mausoleum of Hadrian (with the obelisk and Mausoleum of Augustus visible on the opposite shore).[37] When compared to Peruzzi's *Presentation*, one can note the similarities of these antique structures, suggesting that Peruzzi had knowledge of and/or exposure to these Vatican frescoes. This link is important because, as Fehl notes in his analysis, these classical references are "entirely an invention of Raphael" and "a springboard for showing off his archaeology."[38] This level of invention, alongside the close similarities between structures seen in *The Vision* and Peruzzi's *Presentation*, suggest that Peruzzi is carefully referencing this collegial association, if not with the deceased Raphael then with his still very active workshop coterie.

One can also note the similarity between Peruzzi's *Presentation* obelisk and that sited in front of the Vatican. This element is distinct from the Vatican *Vision* but compares to Pinturicchio's *Sala di Santi* compositions, wherein Curran noted that the pyramidal tomb bears "the addition of a small globe at the pinnacle that inevitably suggests the Vatican obelisk."[39] While the famed Vat-

37 P.P. Fehl, "Raphael as a Historian: Poetry and Historical Accuracy in the Sala di Costantino." *Artibus et Historiae*, 14 (28) (1993), 9–76; Vitale Zanchettin, "Costruire nell'antico. Roma, Campo Marzio 1508–1523: Peruzzi, la confraternita di San Rocco e i cantieri intorno al mausoleo di Augusto." In *Baldassarre Peruzzi 1481–1536* (Marsilio, 2005), 123–154.

38 Fehl, "Raphael as a Historian," 24–25.

39 Curran, *The Egyptian Renaissance*, 117.

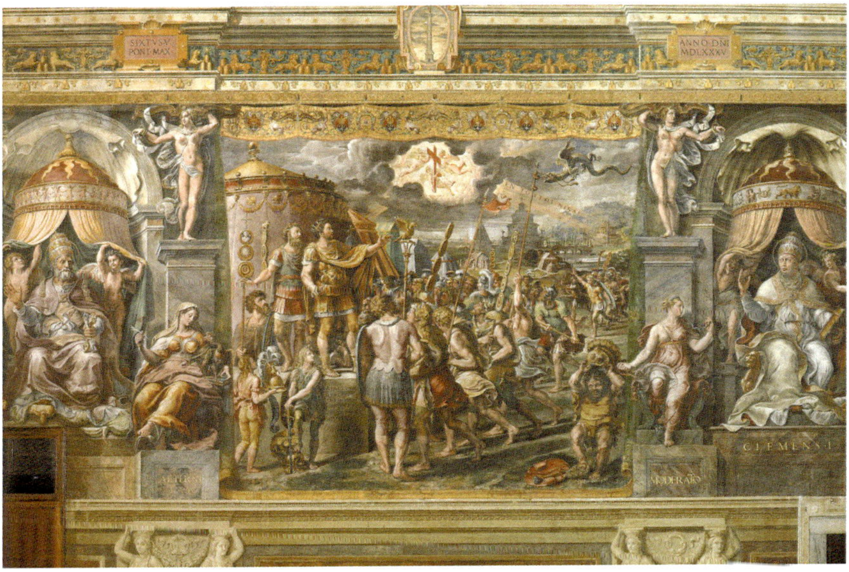

FIGURE 42 Giulio Romano and Gianfrancesco Penni, *Vision of the Cross*
SALA DI COSTANTINO, VATICAN PALACE (PD)

ican obelisk was not yet in its prominent position in front of the new Saint Peter's—Sixtus V would succeed in this task where many predecessors had failed in relocating the Vatican obelisk to the frontal piazza of the New Saint Peters in 1586—it was included as a key reference point many years prior in examples such as Pinturicchio's scenes. Turning to Peruzzi's *Presentation*, one will note that his obelisk also bears this indicative orb, yet one must question whether or not this was an original intention.

The two extant drawings of Peruzzi's *Presentation* noted at the beginning of this chapter, particularly the one assigned to Peruzzi's hand, can give insight into the painting as it exists today. One can note, for example, that several figures change; one can also see that the painting has been trimmed on either side, with scholarship reinforcing that this was done during the previously-mentioned seventeenth-century renovations. In addition, one can observe that, while Peruzzi's drawing reflects a streamlined obelisk profile that is missing this capstone orb, the later seventeenth-century drawing from an anonymous source has added it. This suggests that perhaps this capping orb was a later addition, not part of Peruzzi's original composition (and thereby perhaps aligning it more closely to the Vatican *Vision*) but rather added during these later renovations. Though little clear documentation exists in regard to the work performed on this *Presentation* in the seventeenth century, it seems unquestioned that room for compositional modifications existed.

Despite the complications that this work presents, it seems nevertheless apparent that Peruzzi was able to artfully piece together elements of prior works in an exploration of compositional invention. In other words, what might be seen as disorganized scene lacking unity can take on new life as an inventive contemplation of the works of his colleagues, his mentors, and the masters of antiquity. Peruzzi's pastiche becomes such a contemplation just as it also reflects an innovative take on the subject. It is in this blending that one can see a visual language re-emerge, one that uses the currency of visual memory to further animate the work. As a final indication of this level of connectivity between artists and the motifs they shared among each other, one can look to a letter written in 1570 by Giacomo Barozzi da Vignola to his colleague Martino Bassi. In this correspondence, he notes that Peruzzi inset a wooden armature into the wall, thus making it appear "not as it is painting on the wall but rather rendered on canvas."[40] This notion that Peruzzi was working to create the illusion that the *Presentation* was a suspended canvas or tapestry has been interpreted by Barker-Bates as a signifier of the once unified image planned for the tiburio: "from this description, and a few traces of a fictive tapestry that have emerged during restoration work, it becomes clear that, despite the different artists employed, there was a unifying decorative motif, intended to create a single entity out of the work of different artists."[41]

As a closing point of comparison to underscore the innovative nature of this ongoing use of this recombinative technique, it seems valuable to return briefly to the composition of the *Visitation* tasked to Sebastiano as part of Sergardi's patronage. There is no clear documentation as to when Sebastiano began work on this commission, and knowledge of the composition today is informed only by copies after the work as well as fragmentary portions of the fresco (three such fragments are in the collection of the Duke of Northumberland at Alnick Castle) and accompanying drawings (for example, that in the British Museum, inv. no. 1935,0713.2). It would seem, though, that work on this central scene must have commenced at some point in the 1530s, around the same time that Sebastiano began work on the monumental *Birth of the Virgin* for the Chigi Chapel in Santa Maria del Popolo.[42] What coincided with

40 This letter is documented in: G. Bottari, *Raccolta di lettere sulla pittura, scultura ed architettura: scritte da' più celebri personaggi dei secoli XV, XVI, XVII* (Milan, 1822), I: 499.

41 Barker-Bates, 65.

42 Hirst notes a contract dating to 1530 that restates Sebastiano's commitment to create both works (Hirst, "A Late Work of Sebastiano del Piombo." *The Burlington Magazine*, 107 (745) (Apr., 1965), 178). Sebastiano reportedly worked on *Birth of the Virgin* from 1530 to 1534 but never finished it.

this moment of Sebastiano's career was the dissolution of his relationship with Michelangelo. Hirst noted visual evidence of this fracture in these surviving *Visitation* fragments, observing that the careful articulation of detail, such as seen in his previously-mentioned *Flagellation* for the Borgerhini Chapel within San Pietro in Montorio, was absent from the later *Visitation* drawings. Accordingly, Hirst concluded that there was "no need to invoke the name of Michelangelo as collaborator," as the treatment was the product of Sebastiano's own style.[43]

Given the uncertainty in the dating of both Peruzzi's and Sebastiano's compositions for Santa Maria della Pace, it would be nearly impossible to propose with any certainty if one artist was looking to the other's work, if at all, during the creative process. How marvelous would it be to be able draw parallels here between the visual competition between Raphael and Sebastiano initiated in the early 1510s in the Loggia di Galatea and the "reunion" of colleague Peruzzi and Sebastiano two decades later (in a space, remember, that also feature Raphael's work in another of Chigi's chapels). Setting such flights of fancy aside, it does seem valuable to note Sebastiano's work here as it recalls the enduring element of competition that defined his career. From his early days in Rome he had aligned himself so closely with the rather cantankerous Michelangelo that it would seem he lost touch with the brilliance he had developed during his earlier years in Venice. Though his quarrel with Michelangelo over the use of oil paints in the creation of his Sistine *Last Judgment* (1535–1537) would serve as the official end of their working relationship, works from the earlier years of the 1530s—*Birth of the Virgin*, specifically, and also *The Visitation*, potentially—one can note that the brooding use of somber color serves as stark contrast to Sebastiano's early work. One need only look to his earlier version of *The Visitation* (1518–1519; Louvre Museum, Paris) to see this distinction.

From another perspective, then, these two works by Peruzzi and Sebastiano, respectively, can be seen as showcasing one final instance of the contrast between these working styles within the context of this sixteenth-century moment. Whereas Sebastiano saw collaboration with Michelangelo as part of a rather myopic path to artistic success, Peruzzi, as showcased in his *Presentation* and elsewhere, appreciated the ability of building a wider array of visual references in a more dynamic exchange between colleagues. This invigorated approach to visual recombination, which had taken root in the days of Raphael years before, had fed the artistic innovation of his workshop circle as well as

43 Hirst, "A Late Work," 185.

Peruzzi as a means of ongoing artistic growth. This dynamic play of visual elements, of riffs on each other's visual concepts, seemed to be a practice beyond conceptualization of collaboration as understood by figures like Michelangelo and Sebastiano and thus serves as a new way, as seen throughout this book, of exploring the visual exchange of Raphael and his circle.

Epilogue

Rome in the sixteenth century must have been an overwhelming place. Just as its streets today buzz with the energy of busy citizens and awestruck tourists, sixteenth-century Rome must have deluged the senses with the transformation of the city landscape. From monumental papal projects across the city to the construction of some of the grandest residential palaces ever to have been built lining its main thoroughfares, Rome must have been seen not only as a city on the rise but as a city destined for celebrity throughout, as its moniker implies, eternity.

For the artists and the architects who contributed to these magnificent spaces, Rome presented a different—though equally dynamic—space. In a field then only recently defined as representing a genius beyond a craft, art and its market presented an impossibly steep ascent toward success. Many, who had talent but not connections, achieved modest careers but have been relatively overlooked by history. Those, like Raphael or Michelangelo, however, who achieved acclaim through their immense talent—and also enjoyed the good fortune in securing the right patrons—soon saw themselves overwhelmed with an incredible array of commissions. This success begot more success, as generation after generation held these figures to the highest esteem as virtual paragons of the best that art could create.

Their praise is merited, but if one examines their careers with greater scrutiny one can start to tease out the various factors that contributed to their achievements. For an artist such as Raphael, for instance, his success was undoubtedly predicated upon his workshop. Such *en masse* compositional development was necessary in part because the sheer volume of commissions to which he had agreed required more hands to complete the work. The importance of this workshop goes beyond just volume, though, as these artists were able to work together, despite their desires for individual acclaim, to create the perfection that was known as a "Raphael" composition.

Raphael was not the first artist to have assistants, but, as has been illustrated in prior scholarship and hopefully reinforced here, was novel in the way he approached their development. His cultivation of a visual vocabulary of artistic phrases or forms, culled from antiquity and from his contemporaries, that could be reused and repurposed laid the groundwork for a unique approach to compositional development that encouraged novelty through recombination. Others before Raphael had experimented with a similar vocabulary pulled from past and present, but Raphael advanced this practice into a new, more dynamic, mode of painting. This stood in stark contrast, for instance, to contemporary

 | DOI:10.1163/9789004430488_010

figures such as Michelangelo and Sebastiano who, though engaging with each other as collaborators for a period, nevertheless seemed to have positioned a fluid borrowing of conceptual components as theft rather than as a conversation of forms that ultimately culminated in innovation.

The goal of this book has been to illustrate how this practice took root in Raphael's career, how it evolved over his years in Rome, and how it became central to the artists within his workshop circle. Part of this overarching aim is to celebrate Peruzzi and key workshop figures, from the relatively well-studied Giulio Romano to the somewhat obscure Polidoro da Caravaggio, and to add to the growing interest in their respective oeuvres. Many of these figures have already been pulled out of Raphael's shadow to gain their own recognition, but the hope in this context is to add to the understanding of just how dynamic their involvement was both in upholding the "Raphael" brand in the final years of the artist's life and in the continued development of the artistic ideal of Renaissance Rome in the early decades of the sixteenth century. Having the ability to look back on the period from our modern perspective on the momentum of artistic change through subsequent generations, one might be prone to sweep these figures to the periphery and focus instead on the masters who dominated the decades following the Sack, as art began to transition more rapidly in the Italian peninsula in response to the Reformation and in embrace of new modes of expression. This book, however, has argued for greater attention to his network of artists and their working practice that, had it been saved from the Sack, might have changed the artistic discourse going forward.

The journey this book has taken meandered through a number of Raphael's projects as well as those of his workshop associates to the ways in which this recombinative approach took root and grew, from his student days to his arrival in Rome and his plunge into projects both at the Vatican and at Agostino Chigi's villa—spaces in which Raphael held an enduring presence during his Roman career. Extended focus on his early days in the Stanza della Segnatura and at Chigi's villa afforded the opportunity to better understand how Raphael's visual language advanced through different modes of competition and collaboration. Witnessed within these moments was the development of Raphael's relationship with Peruzzi and the ways in which two incredibly talented figures developed novel ideas in tandem through not just collaboration but rather by borrowing motifs and elements to be used in new ways.

As Raphael's acclaim grew, his workshop became an increasingly important part of his creative process. As the examples illustrated herein supporting the argument that these workshop associates embraced Raphael's approach as a means of building his "brand" as they assumed more substantial control of commissions. Yet, they also saw applications for that same ideology beyond

Raphael's orbit as well. The fact that all of these members enjoyed such prestigious commissions in the wake of Raphael's lifetime speaks to their abilities as artists; how they carried forth this practice of recombination in their compositional development speaks to their true talents as innovators. If one looks to the production of these workshop artists across the spaces highlighted in this book's chapters, then, one can see how this book has helped to advance their narrative.

Shown, for example, is that the workshop cohort did not immediately fall apart after Raphael's death, but rather continued to come together on various projects in new ways and to fit new commissions. Antonio da Sangallo's Palazzo Baldassini, for example, became a space in which Giovanni da Udine, Perino del Vaga, and Polidoro came together to develop a new suite of images that tapped into themes that sampled from the antique and the contemporary in unique ways. The Villa Lante at Gianicolo was similarly inspirational for Romano, Gianfrancesco Penni, and Polidoro, who pulled together quotations of Raphael's art alongside novel narratives to create a compelling visual program that echoed some of the sensibilities seen at the Villa Farnesina. One has also seen that the practice of recombination evolved over the years of the 1520s to make space for these artists to explore new themes, as was showcased in the discussion of Polidoro and Maturino da Firenze's the Fetti Chapel at San Silvestro al Quirinale as well as with Peruzzi's work at Santa Maria della Pace. In these later spaces, Polidoro and Peruzzi, respectively, pushed the bounds of surface and space while also repurposing elements from earlier projects.

One can be sure, though, that these artists in the 1520s were unaware of these impending transformations—artistically, politically, culturally—that would ensue near the decade's conclusion. Attempting to assume the perspective of Romano or Polidoro, then, one might be able to better envision the energy of this moment as one of momentum: building on the ideals that Raphael encouraged among his workshop, these figures were able to contribute to the artistic discourse of their moment by continuing to consider how such a shared artistic language instilled by Raphael could be further developed.

Following the Sack of Rome, each of these figures ended up pursuing various paths. Romano's legacy in Rome ended rather soon after Raphael's passing, as he left for Mantua in 1524. Though he was already remarkably wealthy, Romano's departure was owed to the patronage of the Duke of Mantua (Federico II Gonzaga, 1500–1540), who commissioned from him the iconic Palazzo Tè; though Romano's work on the splendid palace would be completed in 1536, the artist and architect never returned to Rome. As one small indication of this indelible link alongside the enduring artistic ideology he absorbed while in Rome, one can turn to an anecdote shared by Vasari in his biography of artist

Andrea del Sarto (1486–1530), who purportedly had made a secret copy of Raphael's *Portrait of Pope Leo X* as the behest of Ottaviano de' Medici (1482–1546) to be given as a gift to the Duke of Mantua. Vasari recounts a meeting with Romano in Mantua at which he purportedly delighted in sharing with Vasari what he believed to be the original portrait composition; Vasari, however, gently informed Romano that this was indeed not the original but was rather del Sarto's copy of the painting. As Vasari shares: "On hearing this, Giulio turned over the painting, and when he saw the mark, he shrugged his shoulders with these words: 'I don't think any less of it because it's not by Raphael, in fact I think more of it, because it's an extraordinary thing that one excellent man can imitate the style of another so well, and make it so similar.'"[1] Romano remained in Mantua until his death in late 1546.

Penni enjoyed his ongoing work with Romano and their colleagues throughout the 1520s and left just before the atrocities of the Sack of Rome descended on the city. Penni traveled to Mantua in 1526 to assist Romano with compositions for the Palazzo Te but received a cool reception, prompting his eventual departure. He headed south to Naples, where he eventually died in 1528. Da Udine also fled the city with the onset of the Sack, escaping Rome for various projects in Florence, Venice, and his hometown of Udine.[2] He was called back to Rome in 1560 to complete the third floor of the Vatican Loggia and died shortly thereafter.

Perino left Rome to escape the outbreak of the plague that erupted in the city in 1522. He visited briefly in 1528 before moving on to Genoa and returned permanently to Rome in 1536.[3] Perino maintained strong connections with Penni, in part because Perino married Penni's sister, Caterina, and he amassed his own collection of Raphael drawings from Penni's estate when he died.[4] As Joannides has pointed out, he undoubtedly called upon Raphael's *Saint Michael* (Achenbach Foundation, San Francisco) for his *Basadonne Nativity* (1534) and

1 Vasari, *Lives*, I: 845.

2 "Nel clima nuovo che si era venuto creando dopo la morte di Raffaello e che si sarebbe interrotto brutalmente con il Sacco, Giovanni no ha saputo procurarsi uno spazio adequato. A giudicare da un appunto del Peruzzi con il pagamento di giornate di lavoro a diversi artistici e artigiani, fra cui Giovanni da Udine, si può ipotizzare che questi, rimasto solo, pensasse per un momento di lavorare con il Senese … Durante il periodo trascorso a Roma dalla morte di Raffaello al Sacco, non si può dire che Giovanni abbia arricchito la sua cultura né modificato la sua maniera, nel senso di quello che André Chastel ha definito lo stile clementino. Esso fu messo a punto soprattutto da tre pittori, Sebastiano del Piombo, … il Rosso, … [e] il Parmigianino." (Dacos and Furlan, *Giovanni da Udine*, 122–123).

3 B.F. Davidson, *Mostra di disegni*, 4.

4 Joannides, "Some New Drawings by Perino del Vaga," in E. Parma, *Perino del Vaga* (2004), 23.

his study for *Saint Sebastian* (Rijksmuseum).[5] He was appointed court artist to Pope Paul III and even developed his own burgeoning workshop that kept him busy on projects ranging from the Pucci Chapel in Santa Trinità ai Monti to the Pope's Sale Reale until his death in 1547.

Peruzzi also made it out of the city to escape the perils of the Sack. He headed to his native Siena where he worked for several years. He returned to Rome in the 1530s to work on the capstone of his architectural career, the Palazzo Massimo al Colonne (1535), and died shortly thereafter in his mid-fifties. Perhaps the saddest coda comes from the stories of Polidoro da Caravaggio and Maturino da Firenze. Though highly successful during the early 1520s, following the Sack of Rome both artist's careers foundered. It is not clear if Maturino attempted to leave the city, and some sources suggest that Maturino was actually killed during the invasion's proceedings; Polidoro did leave the city and headed to Naples. From there he continued south to Messina, where he continued to work until his unfortunate murder in 1543.

As was mentioned in the introduction, this is not intended as another book about the singular talents of Raphael. Perhaps those who have made it this far might challenge this initial assertion as it cannot be doubted that Raphael features prominently throughout the first half of the text. His role throughout, however, is to illustrate the development of this novel working process: one that navigated the tensions of collaboration and competition through a visual language that could be rephrased or recombined in an effort to achieve a more perfect artistic outcome. Thus, the celebration of Raphael herein is one of his incredibly successful working—and workshop—model that, when paired with his vision and the talents of his workshop associates, fueled his status as one of Rome's leading figures.

There is no doubt that Raphael was a talented artist; it also is without doubt, though, that his success relied upon his workshop, as the increasing demand for his works as the years passed made it impossible for the level of expertise needed for each commission to be upheld by one man alone. Moreover, and as Raphael realized, one person could not master all skills. For an individual who had such a passion for an array of specialties, from the rudiments of color and draftsmanship to the larger fields of architecture and archaeology—Raphael's true genius lay in his ability to recognize the talents of others and to find ways to work together with those masters, whether it was in the form of visual quotations from their work or in direct engagement in collaborative practice. From this perspective, Raphael's workshop can be seen as a group of equals, not one

5 Joannides, "Some New Drawings," 23.

that assumed the more traditional structure of the master and a bevy of apprentices. This is why the effort has been taken in this book to carefully select that language that defined this relationship so as to reinforce that these artists were not simply aping Raphael's style but rather were masters and innovators in their own right.

Why, then, has scholarship been so quick to assume that with the death of Raphael came the end of an artistic era? Perhaps this is a lingering impact of the past pressures toward the periodization of art history, wherein ideas and movements are hemmed in by neat dates and events rather than being allowed to be more reflective of the organic evolution that art more commonly exhibits. Perhaps it is because there was indeed a notable shift in art following the Sack of Rome that, when paired with the loss of Raphael along with other artists who fled the city, never encouraged a new wave of artistic expression decidedly different from what had come before. How, though, is what Romano achieving in this space so divergent from what he accomplished during his earlier Roman years? Of course, Romano is not Raphael; nor is da Udine, Penni, Perino, or Polidoro for that matter. It is precisely this fact, though, that has motivated this book, because it aims to shed light on these figures so adept at Raphael's practice of visual recombination that they have been often overlooked in the years after Raphael's demise.

Did this practice truly end with the Sack of Rome, or with the deaths of the members of Raphael's circle? Perhaps there is evidence that it did not. One can reconsider an observation, for instance, made in Ingrid Rowland and Noah Charney's book, *The Collector of Lives*: *Giorgio Vasari and the Invention of Art*: "when painters as talented as Andrea [del Sarto] or [Peter Paul] Rubens made a copy, these works became masterpieces in their own right: in effect, they are conversations carried out in pigment—an homage, a learning tool, and a means of competition, demonstrating that the later artist's skill is comparable to that of the great master of the original work."[6] While this excerpt illuminates the various facets that the specific art of copying had for other masters, particularly those like Rubens who were active into the seventeenth century, it is also, in essence, outlining the nature of the earlier artistic dialogue occurring within Raphael's circle. Within Raphael's network, the copy or quotation of a given phrase or phrases served as the beginning of a visual conversation. Such quotations served as the foundation of the workshop members' practice and grew, as has been shown, into an even wider array of visual references to

6 I. Rowland and N. Charney, *The Collector of Lives: Giorgio Vasari and the Invention of Art.* (W.W. Norton & Co Inc., 2017), 167.

showcase their individual talents beyond Raphael's day. This is perhaps why Vasari chose to include his anecdote in the life of del Sarto with the attempted hoodwink of Romano with a replica Raphael portrait. In sharing this tale, and its ultimate resolution—wherein Romano declares its extraordinary status for being so fine an imitation—Vasari might have been alluding to continued thriving of Raphael's methodologies. Given these links between the working practice of Raphael's circle and the nature of repetition that Rowland and Charney describe, perhaps it is possible that this method developed by Raphael and carried forth by his workshop associates did not come to an end with the Sack of Rome; perhaps it lingered in the ways artists like del Sarto or Rubens conceptualized the copy. This book hasn't the room to make such far-reaching links, but the hope is that this examination encourages such a cross-chronological reevaluation of these relationships. A closer look to the work of these figures, though varied in commissions, reveal that the art of recombination was still thriving well beyond Raphael's death.

Thus, while Raphael was indeed a crucial voice in early *cinquecento* Rome, the chords of his practice lived on in harmony with his colleague Peruzzi and his workshop artists, and it was the ability of these figures to uphold that tradition while also charting their own careers that made the art of Rome from roughly 1510 to 1527 all the more captivating. The practices of his workshop are still being uncovered, and there are substantial aspects for which full understanding might never be attained. What this examination has hopefully encouraged, though, is a new way of looking at this moment of artistic production that contributed to one of the richest decades of art history.

Bibliography

Ackerman, James S., "The Tuscan/Rustic Order: A Study in the Metaphorical Language of Architecture." *Journal of the Society of Architectural Historians*, 42 (1) (Mar., 1983), 15–34.

Ackerman, James S., "The Villa as Paradigm." *Perspecta*, 22. Paradigms of Architecture (MIT Press, 1986), 10–31.

Alberti, Leon Battista, *On the Art of Building in Ten Books*, trans. by J. Rykwert, N. Leach, and R. Tavernor (Cambridge, MA: MIT Press, 1988).

Alberti, Leon Battista, *On Painting and On Sculpture: The Latin texts of De Pictura and De Statue*. Trans. by Cecil Grayson (London: Phaeton, 1972).

Alcuni palazzi demaniali in Rome: il Quirinale, Palazzo Madama, Montecitorio, Palazzo Chigi (Rome: Istituto Poligrafico e Zecca dello Stato, 1995).

Aldrovandi, Ulisse, *Delle statue antiche di Roma* (Rome: 1556).

Alvarez, Frank Joseph, "The Renaissance Nymphaeum: Its Origins and Its Development in Rome and Vicinity" (PhD diss., Columbia University, 1981).

van Amayden, Dirck, *La storia delle famiglie romane* (Rome: A. Bertini, 1941).

Ames-Lewis, Francis, *The Draftsman Raphael* (New Haven: Yale University Press, 1986).

D'Ancona, Paolo, *Gli Affreschi della Farnesina in Roma* (Milan: Edizione del Milione, 1955).

Angelini, Alessandro, "Francesco di Giorgio e l'architettura dipinta a Siena alla fine del Quattrocento," *Bolletino Senese di Storia Patria*, 109 (2002), 117–183.

Apuleius, *The Story of Cupid and Psyche from the Golden Asses*. Trans. by E.J. Kenny. (NY: Penguin Classics, 2006).

Aretino, Pietro, *Lettere sull'arte di Pietro Aretino*, ed. E. Camesasca, I (Milan, 1537).

Aretino, Pietro, *Tutte Le Opere di Pietro Aretino. Lettere. Il Primo e Secondo Libro* (Milan: Arnoldo Mondatori, 1960).

Arias, Paolo Enrico, *Skopas, a cura di Paolo Enrico Arias* (Roma: 'L'Erma' di Bretschneider, 1952).

Armellini, Mariano, "Un censimento della città di Roma sotto il pontificato di Leone X tratto da un codice inedito dell'Archivio Vaticano." *Gli Studi in Italia* (1882). 155 pages.

Armellini, Mariano, *Le Chiese di Roma dal secolo IV al XIX* (Rome: Ruffolo, 1942), 2 vols.

Armenini, Giovanni Battista, *De veri precetti della* pittura (Ravenna, 1587; reprinted NY, 1971).

Averini, Riccardo, "Giovanni da Udine, inventore di grotteschi e Stucchi." *Studi Romani*, Anno V (1957), 29–38.

Badt, Kurt, "Raphael's 'Incendio del Borgo,'" *Journal of the Warburg and Courtauld* Institutes, 22 (1/2) (Jan.-Jun. 1959).

Baldassarre Peruzzi, 1481–1981: Commemorazione V Centenario Della Nascita (Sovicille: Commune di Sovicille, 1981).

Bambach, Carmen, "Leonardo and Raphael in Rome in 1513–1516." *Late Raphael*, 26–37.

Barbieri, Costanza, *Le "magnificenze" di Agostino Chigi: Collezionie e passioni antiquarie nella Villa Farnesina* (Rome: Scienze e Lettere Editore Commerciale, 2014).

Barbieri, Costanza, "The Competition between Raphael and Michelangelo and Sebastiano's Role In It." In M.B. Hall, ed., *The Cambridge Companion to Raphael* (NY; Cambridge, 2002), 141–166.

Barkan, Leonard, "The Beholder's Tale: Ancient Sculpture, Renaissance Narratives." *Representations*, 44 (Autumn, 1993), 133–166.

Barkan, Leonard, *Unearthing the Past: Archaeology and Aesthetics in the Makings of Renaissance Culture* (New Haven: Yale University Press, 1999).

Barker, Nicholas, *Aldus Manutius and the Development of Greek Script & Type in the Fifteenth Century* (New York: Fordham University Press, 1992).

Barker-Bates, Piers, *Sebastiano del Piombo and the World of Spanish Rome* (NY: Routledge, 2017).

Barrochi, Paola, ed., *Scritti d'Arte del Cinquecento* (Milano-Napoli: R. Ricciardi, 1971–1977), 3 vols.

Bartalini, Roberto, "Due Episodi del Mecenatismo di Agostino Chigi e le Antichità della Farnesina." *Prospettiva* 67 (1992).

Bartalini, Roberto, *Le Occasioni del Sodoma: dalla Milano di Leonardo alla Roma di Raffaello* (Saggi. Rome: Donzelli, 1996).

Bartalini, Roberto, "Sodoma, the Chigi and the Vatican Stanze". *The Burlington Magazine*. 143 (1182) (2001), 544.

Bartoli, Cosimo, *L'Architettura di Leon Battista Alberti trodotta in lingua fiorentina da Cosimo Bartoli ... con l'Aggiunta de Disegni* (Florence: Lorenzo Torrentino, 1550).

Bedini, Silvio A., *The Pope's Elephant* (New York: Penguin, 2000).

Beloe, William, *Anecdotes of Literature and Scarce Books*. 6 vols. (London: Rivington, 1807–1812).

Beltramini, Maria, Elam, Caroline, and Burns, Howard, eds., *Some Degree of Happiness: Studi di Storia dell'Architettura in Onore di Howard Burns* (Pisa: Edizione della Normale, 2010).

Bembo, Pietro, *Prose della volgar lingua*, ed. M. Marti (Padua: Liviana, 1955).

Benocci, Carla, ed., *I giardini Chigi tra Siena e Rome: dal Cinquecento agli inizi dell'Ottocento* (Siena: Fondazione Monte dei Paschi di Siena, 2005).

Bentvoglio, Enzo, "I Baldassini e le loro case: Il palazzo delle "2 Torre," il palazzo del magone; il palazzo del Card. Enkenvort." *Brevi Note per la storia, la topografia, l'architettura di Roma nel XVI secolo* (Rome, 1986).

Bentvoglio, Enzo, "Per la Conoscenza del Palazzo della Cancelleria: la Personalità e l'Ambiente Culturale del Cardinale Raffaelle Sansoni Riario." *Quaderni dell'Istituto di Storia dell'Architettura: Saggi in onore di Renato Bonelli* (1990–1992), 15–20, 367–374.

Bentvoglio, Enzo, "La Presenza di Baldassarre Peruzzi nei Lavori della Casa di Blosio Palladio." In Marcello Fagiolo and Maria Luisa Madonna, eds., *Baldassarre Peruzzi: Pitture Scena e Architettura nel Cinquecento* (Rome: Istituto della Enciclopedia Italiana, 1987), 193–204.

Bentvoglio, Enzo, "Nel Cantiere del Palazzo del Cardinale Raffaelle Riario (La Cancelleria): Organizzazione, materiali, maestranze, personaggi," *Quaderni dell'Istituto di Storia dell'Architettura*, 174 (1983), 27–34.

Bentz, Katherine M., "Cardinal Cesi and His Garden: Antiquities, Landscape and Social Identity in Early Modern Rome" (PhD Diss., The Pennsylvania State University, 2003).

Berzal de Dios, Javier, *Visual Experiences in Cinquecento Theaters* (Toronto: University of Toronto Press, 2019).

Betts, Richard J., "*Si come dice Vitruvio*: Images of Antiquity in Early Renaissance Theory of Architecture." In Alina Payne, Ann Kuttner and Rebekah Smick, eds., *Antiquity and its Interpreters*. (Cambridge: Cambridge University Press, 2000), 244–257.

Bialostocki, J., "A Broad Humanistic Outlook." *American Art Journal*, 3 (1) (Spring, 1971), 95–100.

Bigot, Charles and Mary Healy, *Raphael and the Villa Farnesina* (London: Trench & Co., 1884).

Bignamini, Ilaria, *Archives & Excavations: Essays on the History of Archaeological Excavations in Rome and Southern Italy from the Renaissance to the Nineteenth Century* (London: British School at Rome, 2004).

Bober, Phyllis Pray, *Drawings after the Antique by Amico Aspertini. Sketchbooks in the British Museum* (UK: Studies of the Warburg Institute, 1957).

Bober, Phyllis Pray and Ruth Rubenstein, *Renaissance Artists and Antique Sculpture: A Handbook of Sources*. Second, rev. ed. (London: Miller, 1987).

Boissard, Jean Jacques, *Romanae urbis Topographiae & antiquitatum, qua succincte, breviter describuntur Omnia quae tam publice quam privatum videntur animadversione digna* (Frankfurt, 1597–1062).

Bolgar, R.R., *Classical Influences on European Culture, A.D. 1500–1700: Proceedings of an International Conference Held at King's College, Cambridge, April 1974* (Cambridge, UK: Cambridge University Press, 1976).

Bonamico, G. Molfetta, T. Porn, "Studio metodologico propedeutico ad un restauro conservative nel centro storico." *Capitolium* 9/10 (1966), 5–27.

Bonito, Virginia Anne, "The Saint Anne Altar in Sant'Agostino, Rome" (PhD Diss., New York University, 1983).

Bonito, Virginia Anne, "The Saint Anne altar in Sant'Agostino: Restoration and Interpretation," *The Burlington Magazine*, 124 (950) (May, 1982), 268–273, 275–276.

Bonito, Virginia Anne, "The St Anne Altar in Sant'Agostino in Rome: A New Discovery," *The Burlington Magazine*, Vol. 122 (933) (Dec., 1980), 805–812.

Bottari, Giovanni, *Raccolta di lettere sulla pittura, scultura ed architettura: scritte da' più celebri personaggi dei secoli XV, XVI, XVII* (Milan: Silvestri, 1822). 7 vols.

Boucher, Bruce, "Bernini e l'architettura del Cinquecento: la lezione di Baldassarre Peruzzi e di Sebastiano Serlio." *Bollettino del Centro internazionale di Studi di Architettura Andrea Palladio* (23) (1981), 27–43.

Boucher, Bruce, *The Sculpture of Jacopo Sansovino*. 2 vols. (New Haven: Yale University Press, 1991).

Brandenburger, Adam, and Barry Nalebuff, *Co-opetition: A Revolutionary Mindset that Combines Competition and Cooperation: The Game Theory Strategy That's Changing the Game of Business*. (New York: Currency Doubleday, 1998).

Brentano, Robert, *Rome Before Avignon: A Social History of Thirteenth Century Rome* (New York: Basic Books, 1914).

Briganti, Giuliano, *Pietro da Cortona: o della pittura barocca* (Florence: Sansoni Editore Nuova, 1982).

Britton, Piers Dominic, "A Peruzzi Drawing and the Nymphaeum at Genazzano." *Notes in the History of Art*, 19 (4) (Summer 2000), 1–6.

Brown, Sterling Scott, *The Lira Da Braccio* (Bloomington: Indiana University Press, 1995).

Brugnoli, Maria Vittoria, "Baldassarre Peruzzi nella chiesa di S. Maria della Pace e nell 'Ucceliera' di Giulio II," *Bolletino d'Arte* LVIII/2–3 (Apr-Sep 1973): 113–122.

Brummer, Hans Henrick, *The Statue Court in the Vatican Belvedere* (Stockholm: 1971).

Bruschi, Arnaldo, *Bramante* (London: Thames and Hudson, 1977).

Bruun, Christer, "Il fregio dorico di Villa Lante al Gianicolo. Un progetto sconosciuto di Giulio Romano?" in E.M. Steinby, ed., *Ianiculum—Gianicolo: storia topografia, monumenti, leggende dall'antichità al rinascimento* (Rome, 1996), 141–162.

de Brosses, Charles, *Viaggio in Italia: Lettere Familiare* (Rome: Laterza, 1973).

Bull, Malcolm, *The Mirror of the Gods: How Renaissance Artists Rediscovered the Pagan Gods* (Oxford: Oxford University Press, 2005).

Burke, Peter, "Donec auferatur luna: The Façade of S. Maria della Pace." *Journal of the Warburg and Courtauld Institutes*, 44 (1981), 38–239.

Burckhardt, Jacob, *The Architecture of the Italian Renaissance* (Chicago: University of Chicago Press, 1985).

Burlingham, Cynthia M., *Perino del Vaga's Designs for the Loves of the Gods* (M.A. Thesis, Oberlin College, 1980).

Burke, Jill, "Inventing the High Renaissance, from Winkelmann to Wikipedia: An Introductory Essay," in J. Burke, ed., *Rethinking the High Renaissance: The Culture of the Visual Arts in Early Sixteenth-Century Rome* (UK: Ashgate, 2012), 1–23.

Burke, Jill, ed., *Rethinking the High Renaissance: The Culture of the Visual Arts in Early Sixteenth-Century Rome* (UK: Ashgate, 2012).

Burns, Howard, "Baldassarre Peruzzi and Sixteenth Century Architectural Theory." In Jean Guillaume, ed., *Les Traités d'Architecture de la Renaissance* (Paris: Picard, 1988), 207–226.

Burns, Howard, "I disegni di Francesco di Giorgio agli Uffizi di Firenze." In F.P. Fiore and M. Tafuri, eds., *Francesco di Giorgio architetto* (Milan: Electa, 1993), 330–358.

Butler, Kim E., "Reddita Lux Est: Raphael and the Pursuit of Sacred Eloquence in Leonine Rome." In Stephen J. Campbell and Evelyn S. Welch, eds., *Artists at Court: Image-Making and Identity*, 1300–1550 (2004), 135–142.

Cafà, Valeria, "Divinità a pezzi: Prove di restauro di scultura antica nei disegni di Baldassarre Peruzzi." In M. Beltramini and C. Elam, eds., *Some Degree of Happiness: Studi di Storia dell'Architettura in Onore di Howard Burns* (Pisa: Edizione della Normale, 2010), 155–171 and 697–702.

Calvillo, Elena, "Authoritative Copies and Divine Originals: Lucretian Metaphor, Painting on Stone, and the Problem of Originality in Michelangelo's Rome." *Renaissance Quarterly*, 66 (2) (Summer 2013), 453–508.

Calvo, Marco Fabio, *Antiquae Urbis Romae cum Regionibus Simulachrum* (Basileae, 1532).

Camesasca, Ettore, *Tutta La Pittura di Raffaello* (Milan, 1956).

Campbell, Ian, "Rescue Archaeology in the Renaissance," in Ilaria Bignamini, ed., *Archives & Excavations: Essays on the History of Archaeological Excavations in Rome and Southern Italy from the Renaissance to the Nineteenth Century* (London: British School at Rome, 2004).

Campbell, Ian, "Scamili Inpares: A Problem in Vitruvius." *Papers of the British School at Rome*, Vol. 48 (1980), 17–22.

Campbell, Stephen J., "Naturalism and the Venetian 'Poesia': Grafting, Metaphor, and Embodiment in Giorgione, Titian, and the Campagnolas" in Alexander Nagel and Lorenzo Pericolo, eds., *Subject as Aporia in Early Modern Art* (VT: Ashgate, 2010).

Campbell, Stephen J., and Evelyn S. Welch, eds., *Artists at Court: Image-Making and Identity*, 1300–1550 (Chicago: University of Chicago Press, 2004).

Caneva, Giulia, *Il Mondo di Cerere nella Loggia di Psiche: Villa Farnesina, Sede dell'Accademia Nazionale dei Lincei* (Rome: Fratelli Palombi, 1992).

Cappellatti, Francesca, "'Sentirsi ospite di un umanista dei giorni sereni di Raffaello': Agostino Chigi e la decorazione della Farnesina 1505–1520." In R. Varoli-Piazza, ed., *Raffaello: La Loggia di Amore e Psiche alle Farnesina* (Milan: Silvana Editoriale, 2002), 31–39.

Cappellatti, Francesca, "La Storia di Psiche, il Mito di Raffaello. In Margine alla Storia dei Restauri Antichi," in R. Varoli-Piazza, ed., *Raffaello La Loggia di Amore e Psiche alla Farnesina* (Milan: Silvana Editoriale, 2002).

Cappellatti, Francesca, "L'Uso delle metamorfosi di Ovidio nella decorazione ad affresco della prima meta del Cinquecento. Il caso della Farnesina." In Hermann Walter and Hans-Jürgen Horn, eds., *Die Rezeption der Metamorphosen des Ovid in der Neuzit: der antike Mythos in Text und Bild. Internationales Symposion der Werner Reimers-Stiftung* (Berlin: Gebr. Mann, 1995), 115–128.

Cartari, Carlo, *Advocatorum S. Consistorii syllabum* (Rome, 1656).

Castagnoli, F., "Il Campo Marzio nell'antichità." *Atti dell'Accademia Nazionale dei Lincei* (ser. VIII, 1.4) (1946), 190–193.

Castiglione, Baldassarre, *The Book of the Courtier*, trans. by George Anthony Bull (Baltimore: Penguin Books, 1976).

De Castris, Pierluigi Leone, *Polidoro da Caravaggio* (UK: Matthieson Fine Art, 2004).

Catalogue des objets d'art et d'ameublement qui garnissent le grand appartement au premier étage du palais du prince Borghese à Rome. La vente aux enchères aura lieu au palais Borghese dans l'appartement même du Lundi 28 Mars au Samedi 9 Avril 1892 (Rome: Imprimerie Éditrice Romana, 1892).

Cavallaro, Anna, "Bottega di Giovanni da Udine," in L. Cassanelli and S. Rossi, *Oltre Raffaello: aspetti della cultura figurativa del cinquecento romano* (Rome: Multigrafica Editrice, 1984), 45–48.

Celio, Gaspare, *Memoria dei Nomi dell'Artefici delle Pitture che sono in Alcune Chiese, Facciate e Palazzi di Roma* (Napoli, 1638), reprinted by Emma Zocca (Milan: Electa, 1967).

Cellini, Benvenuto, *The autobiography of Benvenuto Cellini*, trans. by A. MacDonell (New York: Everyman's Library, 2010).

Census of Ancient Art and Architecture Known to the Renaissance. Bibliotheca Hertziana, Rome and Warburg Institute, London. Cerutti Fusco, Annarosa. "La Restituzione Grafica di Teatri Antichi nei Primi Decenni del Cinquecento: Interese Antiquario, Studi Vitruviani e Invenzioni." *Quaderni dell'Istituto di Storia dell'Architettura* (1–10) (1983–1987), 301–312.

Cerri, A., "La traduzione omerica di Angelo Poliziano (gli epiteti degli dèi e degli eroi)," *Acme* 30 (1977), 143–174.

Cesariano, Cesare, *Di Lucio Vitruvio Pollione de Architectura libri dece Traducti de Latino in Vulgare Affigurati: Cōmentati: & con Mirando Ordine Insigniti* (Como: Gotardo da Ponte, 1521).

Chapman, Hugo, Henry, Tom, Piazotta, Carol, Nesselrath, Arnold and Penny, Nicholas, *Raphael: from Urbino to Rome* (London: National Gallery, 2004).

Chastel, André, ed., *"Il se Rendit en Italie": Études Offertes à André Chastel* (Paris: Elefante, 1987).

Chastel, André, *Raffaello a Rome: Il Covegno del 1983* (Rome: Edizioni dell'Elefante, 1986).

Chastel, André, *The Sack of Rome, 1527. The A.W. Mellon Lectures in the Fine Arts, 1977,*

The National Gallery of Art, Washington. D.C. trans. by Beth Archer (Princeton, NJ: Princeton University Press, 1983).

Chastel, André, "Raffaello e Leonardo," in Micaela Sambucco Hamoud and Maria Letizia Strocchi, eds., *Studi su Raffaello: Atti del Congresso Internazionale di Studi (Urbino-Firenze, 1984)*, 2 vols (Urbino, 1987), vol. 1, 335–343.

Chatzēnikolau, Nikos, *Alexander the Great in European Art: 22 September 1997–1911 January 1998* (Thessaloniki: Organisation for the Cultural Capital of Europe, 1997).

Chigi, Agostino, *The Correspondence of Agostino Chigi (1466–1520) in Cod. Chigi R.V.c.* Annotated by Ingrid D. Rowland. (Città di Vaticano: Bibiloteca Apostolica Vaticana, 2001), *Studi i Testi* 399.

Chigi, Fabio, *Chisiae Familiae Comentarij* (Biblioteca Vaticana, MS Chigi a. 1.1, 1618).

Christian, Kathleen Wren, "The De' Rossi Collection of Ancient Sculptures. Leo X, and Raphael." *Journal of the Warburg and Courtauld Institutes*, 65 (2002), 132–200.

Christian, Kathleen Wren, *Empire without End: Antiquities Collections in Renaissance Rome, c. 1350–1527* (New Haven: Yale University Press, 2010).

Christian, Kathleen Wren, "Raphael's 'Philemon' and the Collecting of Antiquities in Rome," *The Burlington Magazine*, 146 (1220) (Nov., 2004).

Cieri, Claudia, "Sala delle Prospettive: Via, Storia e Funzione della Sala." In Sergio Rossi and Luciana Cassanelli, eds., *Di Luoghi di Raffaello a Roma* (Rome: Multigrafica Editrice, 1983), 66–73.

Claudian, *Claudian*, ed. by Maurize Platnauer (London: W. Heinemann, 1922).

Clay, Diskin, "Dante's Parnassus: Raphael's Parnaso." *Arion: A Journal of Humaniteis and the Classics*, 22 (2) (Fall 2014), 3–32.

Coarelli, Filippo, *Roma*. Guide Archeologiche Laterza (Rome: Laterza, 1997).

Cogotti, Marina, and Gigli, Laura, *Palazzo Baldassini* (Rome: L'erma di Bretschneider, 1995).

Coffin, David R., *Magnificent Buildings, Splendid Gardens* (Princeton, NJ: Princeton University Press, 2008).

Coffin, David R., "The Plans of the Villa Madama." *The Art Bulletin*, Vol. 49 (2) (Jun., 1967).

Coffin, David R., *The Villa in the Life of Renaissance Rome*. Princeton monographs in art and archaeology, 43 (Princeton, N.J.: Princeton University Press, 1979).

Cola, Maria Celeste, "Palazzo Baldassini," in F. Cappelletti and C. Cieri, eds., *La cultura artistica nelle dimore romane fra Quattrocento e Cinquecento: funzione e decorazione* (Università Degli Studi Di Roma "La Sapienza", Facoltà Di Lettere E Filosofia, Istituto Di Sotria Dell'Arte, 1991), 55–63.

Cole, Michael and Pardo, Mary, eds., *Inventions of the Studio, Renaissance to Romanticism* (Chapel Hill, NC: University of North Carolina Press, 2005).

Colonna, Francesco, *Hypnertomachia Poliphili*. trans. By J. Godwin. (London: Thames and Hudson, 2005).

Comes, Natalis, *Mythologiae sive explicationis fabularum libri decem, in quibus omnia prope Naturalis & Marlis Philosophiae dogmata contenta fuisse deomonstatur* (Padua, 1616).

Connors, Joseph, "Borromini and Roman Urbanism," *AA Files* 2 (July 1982), 10–21.

Cortesi, Paolo, *Tres libri De cardinalatu at Julium Secundum Pont [ifem] per Paulum Cortesium Protonotarium Apostolicum* (Castel Cortesi: Symeon Nardi, 1510) Craveri, Piero, "Baldassini Melchiorre," in *Dizionario Biografico degli Italiani* 5 (1063).

Cremona, Alessandro, *Felices Procerium Villulae: Il Giardino della Farnesina dai Chigi all'Accademia dei Lincei* (Rome: Accademia Nazionale dei Lincei, 2010).

Cropper, Elizabeth, "Introduction," to Craig Hugh Smyth, *Mannerism and Maniera* (Vienna, Austria: ISRA, 1992), 12–21.

Crowe, J.A. and Cavalcaselle, G.B., *A History of Painting in Italy, Umbria, Florence and Siena from the Second to the Sixteenth Century* (London: J. Murray, 1903–1914). 6 vols.

Cruciani, Fabrizio, *Teatro nel Rinascimento: Roma, 1450–1550* (Rome, Bulzoni, 1983).

Cugi, Francesca, "San Silvestro al Quirinale: Le cappelle perdute e qualche ipotesi sulle pitture del coro." *Bolletino d'Arte* 7 (97) (2012), 35–144.

Cugnoni, Giuseppe, *Agostino Chigi il Magnifico* (Rome: A cura della Società Romana di Storia Patria, 1878).

Culotta, Alexis, "A Novel Nymphaeum: Raphael's Inaugural Architectural Commission in Rome Reconsidered." *Rutgers Art Review*, 31 (Summer 2015), 4–19.

Culotta, Alexis, "The Dramatic Side of Breaking Bad: Raphael, Peruzzi, and a Remarkable Revival of Vitruvius' *Scaenae Frons*." In J.C. Fischer, ed., *Breaking with Convention in Italian Art* (UK: Cambridge Scholars Publishing, 2017), 48–71.

Culotta, Alexis, "Baldassarre Peruzzi and the Architecture of Painting," *Sixteenth Century Journal*, 51 (1) (Spring 2020).

Curran, Brian A., "Ancient Egypt and Egyptian Antiquities in Italian Renaissance Art and Culture." (PhD Diss., Princeton University, 1997).

Curran, Brian A., *The Egyptian Renaissance: The Afterlife of Ancient Egypt In Early Modern Italy* (Chicago: University of Chicago Press, 2007).

Curran, Brian A., et al., *Obelisk. A History* (Cambridge: Burndy Library, 2009).

Curti, Francesca, and Sickel, Lothar, *Dokumente zur Geschichte des Palazzo Zuccari 1578-1904* (Munich: Hirmer Verlag, 2013).

Dacos, Nicole, *Le Logge di Raffaello, Maestro e bottega di fronte all'antico* (Rome: Istitutoe poligrafico e zecco del Stato, Libraria dello Stato, 1986).

Dacos, Nicole, *The Loggia of Raphael: A Vatican Art Treasure*, trans. Josephine Bacon (New York: Abbeville Press Publishers, 2008).

Dacos, Nicole, "Ni Polidoro, ni Peruzzi: Maturino," *Revue de l'Art*, 57 (1982).

Dacos, Nicole, "Peruzzi. Dalla Farnesina alla Cancelleria. Qualche Proposta per la Bottega della Pittore." In Marcello Fagiolo and Maria Luisa Madonna, *Baldassarre*

Peruzzi: Pittura, Scena, e Architettura nel Cinquecento (Rome: Enciclopedia Italiana, 1987), 469–490.

Dacos, Nicole, "Per la storia della grottesche: la riscoperta della Domus Aurea." *Bolletino d'Arte* 1–2 (V) (1966), 43–49.

Dacos, Nicole and Furlan, Caterina, *Giovanni da Udine 1487–1561* (Friuli-Venezia Giulia: Cassamassima 1987).

Daley, J., "The Vault Decoration of Raphael's Loggie" (PhD diss., New York University, 1962).

Danti, Ignazio, *Le Due Regole della Prospettiva Pratica* (Rome: Francesco Zannetti, 1583).

Davidson, Berenice, ed., *Mostra di disegni di Perino del Vaga e la sua cerchia* (Firenze: Leo S. Olschki Editore, 1966).

Davidson, Berenice, "A Study for the Farnesina 'Toilet of Psyche.'" *The Burlington Magazine*, 129 (1013) (Aug., 1987), 510–513.

Denard, Hugh, "Virtuality and Perfomativity: Recreating Rome's Theatre of Pompey," *PAJ: A Journal of Performance and Art*, 24 (1) (Jan., 2002), 25–43.

Dionisotti, Carlo, ed., *Pietro Bembo: Prose e rime* (Turin, 1960).

Di Teodoro, Francesco P., *Raffaello, Baldassar Castiglione e la Lettera à Leone X* (Bologna: Nuova Alfa, 1994).

Dollmayr, Herman, "Raffaels Werkstätte," *Jahrbuch des Allerhöchsten Kaiserhauses*, XVI (1895).

Dorigny, Nicholas, *Favola di Amore e Psiche* (Rome: Istituto Nazionale per la Grafica, 1693).

Du Pérac, Etienne and Lafréry, Antoine, *Nova Urbis Romae Descriptio* (Rome: Antonius Lafreri, 1577).

Dussler, Luitpold, *Raphael: A Critical Catalogue of His Pictures, Wall-Paintings and Tapestries* (NY: Phaldon, 1971)

Dussler, Luitpold, *Sebastiano del Piombo* (Basel: Holbein-Verlag, 1942).

Egger, Hermann, Hülsen, Christian, and Michaelis, Adolf, *Codex Escurialensis: ein Skizzenbuch aus der Werkstatt Domenico Ghirlandaios [1449–1494]* (Vienna, 1906).

Ettlinger, Leopold D., "The Emergence of the Italian Architect during the Fifteenth Century." In Spiro Kostof, ed., *The Architect: Chapters in the History of the Profession* (New York: Oxford University Press, 1977), 96–123.

Ettlinger, Leopold D., "A Note on Raphael's Sibyls in S. Maria della Pace." *Journal of the Warburg and Courtauld Institutes*, XXIV (1961).

Fabricius, Georg, *Roma* (Basel: per Ioannem Oporinum, 1550).

Fagiolo, Marcello, *Natura e Artificio: L'Ordine Rustico, le Fontane, gli Automi nella Cultura del Manierismo Europeo* (Rome: Officina Edizioni, 1979).

Fagiolo, Marcello and Maria Luisa Madonna, eds., *Baldassarre Peruzzi: Pitture Scena e Architettura nel Cinquecento* (Rome: Istituto della Enciclopedia Italiana, 1987).

Falomir, Miguel et al., eds., *Late Raphael.* Proceedings of the International Symposium (Madrid: Museo Nacional del Prado, 2013).

Fane-Saunders, Peter, *Pliny the Elder and the Emergence of Renaissance Architecture* (UK: Cambridge University Press, 2016).

Fantoni, Marcello, Matthew, Louisa C., and Matthews-Grieco, Sara F., *The art market in Italy 15th–17th century = Il mercato dell'arte in Italia secc. XV–XVII* (Modena: Franco Cosimo Panini, 2003).

Farago, Claire J., *Leonardo da Vinci's* Paragone: *A Critical Interpretation with a New Edition of the Text in the* Codex Urbinas (NY: E.J. Brill, 1992).

Fehl, Philipp P., "Imitation as a Source of Greatness," in Görel Cavalli-Björkman, ed., *Bacchanals by Titian and Rubens* (Stockholm: Nationalmuseum, 1987) 107–132.

Fehl, Philipp P., "Raphael as a Historian: Poetry and Historical Accuracy in the Sala di Costantino." *Artibus et Historiae*, 14 (28) (1993), 9–76.

Felletti Maj, B.M., "La Tetide della Stazione Termine," in *Archaeologica Classica*, 1 (1949), 46–68.

Ferrajoli, Alessandro, *Il ruolo della corte di Leone X (1514–1516)* (Rome: Bulzoni, 1984).

Fermor, Sharon, *The Raphael Tapestry Cartoons: Narrative, Decoration, Design* (UK: Scala, 1996).

Fischel, Oskar, *Raphael* (London: K. Paul, 1948).

Fischer, Chris., "Fra Bartolommeo's Landscape Drawings." *Mitteilungen des Kunsthistorischen Institutes in Florenz* 33. Bd., H. 2/3 (1989), 301–342.

Fiore, Francesco Paolo, "Il complesso chigiano de 'Le Volte'." *Rilievi di fabbriche attribuite a Baldassarre Peruzzi* (Siena: Ministero per I Beni Culturali e Ambientali, 1982), 97–119.

Fiore, Francesco Paolo, "La Villa Chigi a 'Le Volte'" e il linguaggio architettonico peruzziano nella tradizione di Francesco di Giorgio," in M. Fagiolo and M.L. Madonna, *Baldassarre Peruzzi: Pitture, scena e architettura nel Cinquecento* (Rome: Istituto della Enciclopedia Italiana, 1987), 133–167.

Fiore, Francesco Paolo, "Villa Chigi a Le Volte," in F.P. Fiore and M. Tafuri, eds., *Francesco di Giorgio architetto* (Milan: Electa, 1993), 318–325.

Fiore, Francesco Paolo and Manfredo Tafuri, eds., *Francesco di Giorgio architetto* (Milan: Electa, 1993).

Fletcher, Jennifer, "Marcantonio Michiel: His Friends and Collection." *The Burlington Magazine*, 123 (1981), 453–467.

Fogelmark, Staffan, "The Anonymous Rome 1522 Chrysoloras: A Newly Discovered Greek Press." *The Papers of the Bibliographic Society of America*, 97 (1) (March 2003), 5–42.

Forster, Kurt W., "Discussion: The Palazzo Rucellai and Questions of Typology in the Development of Renaissance Architecture," *The Art Bulletin*, 58 (1) (Mar., 1976), 109–113.

Förster, Richard, *Farnesina-Studien: ein Beitrag zu Frage nach dem Verhaltnis der Renaissance zur Antike* (Rostock: Stiller, 1880).

Fosi, Irene, "Fra Siena e Rome: Famiglie, Mercanti, Pontefici, fra Cinquecento e Seicento." In C. Benocci, ed., *I Giardini Chigi tra Siena e Roma dal Cinquecento agli Inizi dell'Ottocento* (Siena: Fondazione Monte dei Paschi, 2005), 13–38.

Foster, Phillip, "Raphael on the Villa Madama: The Text of a Lost Letter," *Römisches Jahrbuch für Kuntsgeschichte* 11 (1967), 111–122.

Francesconi, D., *Congettura che una Lettera Creduta di Baldessar Castiglione sia di Raffaello* (Florence, 1799).

Franklin, David, *Polidoro da Caravaggio* (New Haven: Yale University Press, 2018).

Freedman, Luba, "Apollo's Glance in Raphael's 'Parnassus.'" *Source: Notes in the History of Art*, 16 (2) (1997): 20–25.

Freedman, Luba, *Classical Myths in Italian Renaissance Painting* (Cambridge, UK: Cambridge University Press, 2011).

Freedberg, Sydney J., *Painting in Italy: 1500–1600* (New Haven, CT: Yale University Press, 1993) 74.

Freedberg, Sydney J., *Raphael, Michelangelo, and Others: Raphael and His Contemporaries in Rome* (NY: Vassar College, 1983).

Frittelli, Ugo, *Albero genealogico della nobil famiglia Chigi, patrizia senses* (Siena: Arti grafiche Lazzeri, 1922).

Frommel, Christoph Luitpold, *Architettura alle Corte Papale nel Rinascimento* (Rome: Electra, 2003).

Frommel, Christoph Luitpold, *The Architecture of the Italian Renaissance* (London: Thames and Hudson, 2007).

Frommel, Christoph Luitpold, *Baldassarre Peruzzi, 1481–1536* (Venice: Marsilio, 2005).

Frommel, Christoph Luitpold, *Baldassarre Peruzzi als Maler und Zeichner* (Vienna: Anoton Schroll, 1967–1968).

Frommel, Christoph Luitpold, "Bramante and the Origins of the 'High Renaissance,'" in J. Burke, ed., *Rethinking the Renaissance: The Culture of the Visual Arts in Early Sixteenth-Century Rome* (UK: Ashgate, 2012), 147–176.

Frommel, Christoph Luitpold, "Bramantes 'Ninfeo' in Genazzano," *Römisches Jahrbuch für Kunstgeschichte*, 22 (1969) 137–160.

Frommel, Christoph Luitpold, *Die Farnesina und Peruzzis architektonisches Früwerk* (Berlin: W. de Gruyter, 1961).

Frommel, Christoph Luitpold, "Giulio Romano e la Progettazione di Villa Lante," In E.M. Steinby, *Ianiculum—Gianicolo: Storia, topografia, monumenti, leggende dall'antichità al rinascimento* (Rome, 1996), 119–140.

Frommel, Christoph Luitpold, Stefano Ray, Manfredo Tafuri, Howard Burns, and Arnold Nesselrath, *Rafaello Architetto* (Milan: Electra, 1984).

Frommel, Christoph Luitpold, "Papal Policy: The Planning of Rome During the Renaissance," *Journal of Interdisciplinary History*, 17 (1986), 39–65.

Frommel, Christoph Luitpold, "Raffaello e la sua carriera architettonica." In Christoph

Frommel, Stefano Ray, Manfredo Tafuri, Howard Burns, and Arnold Nesselrath, eds., *Rafaello Architetto* (Milan: Electra, 1984).

Frommel, Christoph Luitpold, "Raffaello e il teatro alla Corte di Leone X," *Bollettino del Centro internazionale di Studi di Architettura Andrea Palladio*, XVI, (1974).

Frommel, Christoph Luitpold, "Raffaele Riario, committente della Cancelleria." In Arnold Esch and Christoph Luitpold Frommel, eds., *Arte, Committenza ed Economia a Roma e Nelle Corti del Rinascimento (1420–1530)* (Rome: Piccola Biblioteca Einaudi, 1995).

Frommel, Christoph Luitpold, "The Roman works of Giulio," In C. Frommel and R. Schofield, eds., *Giulio Romano* (UK: Cambridge University Press, 1998), 56–89.

Frommel, Christoph Luitpold, *Der Römische Palastbau der Hochrenaissance*, Vol. 2 (Tübingen: Wasmuth, 1973).

Frommel, Christoph Luitpold, "La Villa Farnesina," in C.L. Frommel, G. Caneva, and A. Angeli, *La Villa Farnesina a Roma = The Villa Farnesina in Rome*. Mirabilia Italiæ, 12 (Modena: F.C. Panini, 2003), 2: 9–144.

Frommel, Christoph Luitpold, Giulia Caneva, and Alessandro Angeli, *La Villa Farnesina a Roma = The Villa Farnesina in Rome*. Mirabilia Italiæ, 12 (Modena: F.C. Panini, 2003), 2 vols.

Frommel, Sabine, "Giuliano da Sangallo between Florentine Quattrocento and Roman High Renaissance," in J. Burke, ed., *Rethinking the Renaissance: The Culture of the Visual Arts in Early Sixteenth-Century Rome* (UK: Ashgate, 2012), 195–222.

Fulvio, Andrea, *Antiquitates urbis per Andream Fuluium Antiquarium* (Rome, 1527).

Gaffori, Franchino, *Theorica musicae* (NY: Broude, 1967).

Gagliardo, C. and Packer, J.E., "A New Look at Pompey's Theater: History, Documentation, and recent Excavation," *American Journal of Archaeology*, 110 (1) (Jan., 2006), 93–122.

Gallo, Egidio, *De viridario Augstini Chigii, Patritii Senen[sis]* (Rome: Biblioteca Apostolica Vaticana, Codici Chigi III, 1511).

Gere, J.A., "Two Fresco Cycles by Perino del Vaga: The Massimi Chapel and the Saola Paolina." *The Burlington Magazine* 102 (682) (Jan., 1960), 8–17 and 19.

Gerlini, Elsa, *Giardino e Architettura nella Farnesina* (Rome: Reale Istituto di Studi Romani, 1942).

Gerlini, Elsa, *La Villa Farnesina in Roma* (Rome: La Libreria dello Stato, 1949).

Geymüller, Enrico di, *Raffaello Sanzio studiato come architetto con l'ajuto di nuovi documenti* (Milan: Hoepli, 1884).

Gestrin, Trygge, "The *Stemma* of Baldassarre Turini: Remarks on the heraldry and architecture of Villa Lante al Gianicolo." In O. Merisalo and R. Vainio, eds., *Ad itum liberum: Essays in Honor of Anne Helttula* (Jyväskylä, 2007), 7–12.

Ghetti, Fabrizio Maria Apollonj, "Ancora sul Palazzo Stati (o Cenci Maccarani)," *Urbe* (47) (1984).

Gielhow, K., *The Humanist's Interpretation of Hieroglyphs in the Allegorical Studies of the Renaissance with a Focus on the Triumphal Arch of Maximilian I* (Boston: Brill, 2015).

Gigli, Laura, "Il salone di Perin del Vaga in palazzo Baldassini fra rigore del disegno e immaginazione creativa," *Strenna dei Romanisti: Natale di Roma* (Fondazione Roma Arte-Musei, 2015), 259–284.

Gigli, Laura, "La decorazione di palazzo Baldassini," in M. Cogotti and L. Gigli, *Palazzo Baldassini* (Rome: L'erma di Bretschneider, 1995), 64–75.

Gigli, Laura, "Melchiorre Baldassini *inisgnis Sacri Consistorii Advocatus*," in M. Cogotti and L. Gigli, *Palazzo Baldassini* (Rome: L'erma di Bretschneider, 1995), 5–16.

Gilbert, Felix, *The Pope, His Banker, and Venice* (Cambridge, MA: Harvard University Press, 1980).

Giles, Laura M., "A Drawing by Raphael for the Sala di Costantino." *Master Drawings*, 37 (2) (Summer, 1999), 156–164.

Gill, Meredith J., "The Fourteenth and Fifteenth Centuries." In M.B. Hall, ed., *Artistic Centers of the Italian Renaissance: Rome* (New York, NY: Cambridge University Press, 2005), 27–105.

Giovio, Paolo, *De Vita Leonis Decimi Pont. Ma. Libri IIII* (Florence, 1551).

Giovio, Paolo, *Lettere*, ed. by G.G. Ferrero (Rome, 1958).

Giovio, Paolo, *Pauli Iovii novocomensis episcopi nucerini Elogia virorum literis illustrium, quotquot vel nostra vel avorum memoria vixere* (Basel: Petri Pernae typographie, 1577).

Gnann, Achim, "Peruzzi oder Raphael? Zu den Entwürfen für die Fresken der *Volta Dorata* in der Cancelleria," in C.L. Frommel et al., eds., *Baldassarre Peruzzi 1481–1536* (Venice: Marsilio, 2005), 199–212.

Gnann, Achim, "Raphael's Workshop in Rome," in A. Gnann and M.C. Plomp, *Raphael and his School* (Haarlem: Teylers Museum, 2012), 19–28.

Gnann, Achim, "Zur Beteililung des Polidoro da Caravaggio an der Ausmallung des Salone der Villa Lante." In E.M. Steinby, ed., *Ianiculum—Gianicolo: storia, topografia, monumenti, leggende dall'antichità al Rinascimento*, 237–259.

Gnoli, Domenico, "La capella di Fra Mariano del Piombo in Roma," *Archivio storico dell'arte* IV (1891), 117–126.

Gnoli, Domenico, "Orti letterari nella Roma di Leon X." *Nuova Antologia* 7 (269) (Jan. 1, 1930), 3–19.

Gnoli, Domenico, "Raffaello alla corte di Leone X," *Nuova Antologia* (1888).

Goffen, Rona, "Raphael's Designer Labels: From the Virgin Mary to La Fornarina," *Artibus et Historiae*, 24 (4) (2003), 123–142.

Goffen, Rona, *Renaissance Rivals: Michelangelo, Leonardo, Raphael, Titian* (New Haven: Yale University Press, 2002).

Golzio, Vincenzo, *Raffaello: nei documenti nelle testimonianze dei contemporanei e nella letteratura del suo secolo* (Città del Vaticano: Pontificia insigne Accad. Artistica dei Virtuosi al Pantheon, 1936).

Gombrich, E.H., "'Anticamente moderni e modernamente antichi'. Notes on the critical fortune of Giulio Romano, painter." In C. Frommel and R. Schofield, eds., *Giulio Romano* (UK: Cambridge University Press, 1998), 7–10.

Gombrich, E.H., "The Style All'Antica: Imitation and Assimilation," in *Norm and Form: Studies in the Art of the Renaissance* (NY: Phaidon, 1966) 122–128.

O'Gorman, James F., "The Villa Lante in Rome: Some Drawings and Some Observations." *The Burlington Magazine*, 113 (816) (Mar., 1971), 132–138.

Gouwens, Kenneth, *Remembering the Renaissance: Humanist Narrative of the Sack of Rome* (Leiden, Netherlands: Brill, 1998).

Greene, Thomas M., *The Light in Troy* (New Haven, CT: Yale University Press, 1982).

Greene, Thomas M., "Resurrecting Rome: the Double Task of the Humanist Imagination." *Rome in the Renaissance: The City and the Myth*. Ed. P.A. Ramsey (Binghamton, NY: Center for Medieval & Early Renaissance Studies, 1982), 41–54.

Grimm, Hermann, *The Life of Michelangelo*, 2 vols. Trans. by F.E. Bunnett (Boston: Little, Brown & Co., 1899), 1: 461, 553–555.

Gutensohn G., and Thürmer, J., *Decorazioni a fresco e a stucco nelle chiese e nei palazzi d'Italia dei Secoli XV e XVI*, a publication began by Gutensohn and Thürmer and completed by Gruner (London, 1844).

Habel, Dorothy Metzger, *The Urban Development of Rome in the Age of Alexander VII* (UK: Cambridge University Press, 2002).

Hall, Marcia B. ed., *The Cambridge Companion to Raphael* (New York, NY: Cambridge University Press, 2005).

Hall, Marcia B., *After Raphael: Painting in Central Italy in the Sixteenth Century* (NY: Cambridge University Press, 1999).

Hamoud, Micaela Sambucco and Strocchi, Maria Letizia, eds., *Studi su Raffaello: Atti del Congresso Internazionale di Studi (Urbino-Firenze, 1984)*, 2 vols (Urbino, 1987).

Hara, Mara Yoko, "Capturing eyes and moving souls: Peruzzi's perspective set for La Calandria and the performative agency of architectural bodies." *Renaissance Studies* (October 2016), 587–703.

Hara, Mara Yoko, "Emphatic Presence: Architectural *Chiaroscuro*." In C. Lehmann et al., *Chiaroscuro als ästhetisches Prinzip: Kunst und Theorie des Helldunkels 1300–1550* (Berlin: De Gruyter, 2018).

Hart, Vaughan, and Peter Hicks, eds., *Paper Palaces: The Rise of the Architectural Treatise*. (New Haven and London: Yale University Press, 1998).

Hart, Vaughan, and Peter Hicks, *Sebastiano Serlio on Architecture*. New Haven, Conn: Yale University Press, 1996–2001).

Hartt, Frederick, *Giulio Romano* (NY: Hacker Art Books, 1981). 2 vols.

Hartt, Frederick, "Raphael and Giulio Romano: With Notes on the Raphael School." *The Art Bulletin* 26, no. 2 (1944): 67–94.

Haskell, Francis and Penny, Nicholas, *Taste and the Antique: the Lure of Classical Sculpture, 1500–1900* (New Haven: Yale University Press, 1981).

Haus, J.J., *Riflessioni di un oltramontano sulla creduta Galatea di Raffael d'Urbino* (Palermo: n.p. 1816).

Hayum, Andrée M., "A New Dating for Sodoma's Frescoes in the Villa Farnesina." *The Art Bulletin*, Vol. 48 (2) (Jun., 1966), 215–217.

Hayum, Andrée M., *Giovanni Antonio Bazzi—"Il Sodoma"* (NY: Garland Publishing, 1976).

van Heemskerck, Martin, *Die römischen Skizzenbücher von Marten van Heemskerke.*

Henning, Andreas, *Raffaels Transfiguration und der Wettstreit um die Farbe: koloritgeschichtliche Untersuchung zur römischen Hochrenaissance* (München: Deutscher Kunstverlag, 2005).

Henry, Tom, and Joannides, Paul, eds., *Late Raphael* (UK: Thames & Hudson, 2013).

Hermanin, Federico, *La Farnesina* (Bergamo: Istituto Italiano d'Arti Grafiche, 1927).

Hibbert, Christopher, *Rome: The Biography of a City* (Penguin Books, 1996).

Hirst, Michael, "A Late Work of Sebastiano del Piombo." *The Burlington Magazine*, 107 (745) (Apr., 1965), 176–185.

Hirst, Michael, *Sebastiano del Piombo* (Oxford: Clarendon Press, 1981).

Hobson, A., "'The printer of the Greek editions 'in gymnasio mediceo ad Cabillinum montem'," in F. Barberi, G. de Gregori, and M. Valenti, *Studi di biblioteconomia e storia del libro in onore di Francesco Barberi* (Roma: Associazione italiana biblioteche, 1976).

Hochmann, Michel, *Venise et Rome 1500–1600: deux écoles de peinture et leurs échanges.* (Geneve: Droz, 2004)

Hofmann, Theobald, *Raffael in seiner Bedeutung als Architekt 1, Villa Madama zu Rom* (Zittau: Menzel, 1908).

De Hollanda, Francesco, *Four Dialogues on Painting*. Trans. by F.G. Bell (UK: Oxford University Press, 1928).

De Hollanda, Francesco, *I Trattati d'Arte*, ed. by Grazia Modroni (Livorno: Sillabe, 2003).

Hoogewerff, Goffredo, "Raffaello nella Villa Farnesina." *Capitoleum* (1945), 1–3, 9- 15.

Hope, Charles, "The Tapestries of the Scuola Nuova in the Vatican Museum" (MA thesis, Courtauld Institute, 1968).

Hubertus, Günther, "The Renaissance of Antiquity." In H.A. Millon and V.M. Lampugnani, eds. *The Renaissance from Brunelleschi to Michelangelo: The Representation of Architecture* (New York: Rizzoli, 1997) 259–306.

Hülsen, Christian, *Römische antikengärten des XVI. Jahrhunderts* (Heidelberg: C. Winter, 1917).

Huppert, Ann C., "The Archaeology of Baldassarre Peruzzi's Architectural Drawings." (Ph.D. Diss., University of Virginia, 2001).

Huppert, Ann C., "Baldassarre Peruzzi as Archeologist in Terracina," in Frommel et al., *Baldassarre Peruzzi, 1481–1536* (Venice: Marsilio, 2005), 213–224.

Huppert, Ann C., *Becoming an Architect in Renaissance Italy: Art, Science, and the Career of Baldassarre Peruzzi* (New Haven: Yale University Press, 2015), 51.

Huppert, Ann C., "Envisioning New St. Peter's: Perspectival Drawings and the Process of Design," *Journal of the Society of Architectural Historians*, 68 (2) (June 2009).

Huppert, Ann C., "Material matters: training the Renaissance architect," in A. Sherman, ed., *Artistic Practices and Cultural Transfer in Early Modern Italy: Essays in Honor of Deborah Howard* (Routledge, 2016).

Iezzi, E., *S. Silvestro al Quirinale* (Rome: Fonticoli e Biagetti, 1975).

Janni, Ettore, *Il Signore della Farnesina* (Bergamo: Istituto Italiano d'Arti Grafiche, 1927).

Joannides, Paul, *The Drawings of Raphael: with a Complete Catalogue* (Berkeley: University of California Press, 1983).

Joannides, Paul, "Some New Drawings by Perino del Vaga," in E. Parma, *Perino del Vaga* (2004).

Jones, Mark Wilson, "Palazzo Massimo and Baldassarre Peruzzi's Approach to Architectural Design." *Architectural History*, Vol. 31 (1998), 59–106.

Jones, Mark Wilson, "The Tempietto and the Roots of Coincidence," *Architectural History*, 33 (1990).

Jones, Roger and Penny, Nicholas, *Raphael* (New Haven: Yale University Press, 1983).

Joost-Gaugier, Christiane L., "Ptolemy and Strabo and Their Conversation with Appelles and Protogenes: Cosmography and Painting in Raphael's School of Athens." *Renaissance Quarterly*, 51 (3) (Autumn, 1998), 761–787.

Joost-Gaugier, Christiane L., *Raphael's Stanza della Segnatura: Meaning and Invention* (NY: Cambridge University Press, 2002).

Joyce, Hetty, "Grasping at Shadows: Ancient Paintings in Renaissance and Baroque Rome." *The Art Bulletin*, 74 (2) (Jun., 1992), 219–246.

Katz, Brigit, "Unknown Raphael Paintings Discovered in the Vatican," *Smithsonian*, 10 July 2017.

Keene, B.C., and Kacenski, A., *Sacred Landscapes: Nature in Renaissance Manuscripts* (Los Angeles: The J. Paul Getty Museum, 2017).

Keiven, Elizabeth, *100 Jahre Biblioteca Hertziana, Max-Plank-Institut für Kunstgeschichte: Der Palazzo Zuccari und die Institutgebäude 1590–2013* (Biblioteca Hertziana, Max-Plank-Institut für Kunstgeschichte, 2013).

Kent, William Winthrop, *The Life and Works of Baldassarre Peruzzi of Siena* (New York: Architectural Book Publishing Company, 1925).

Kleinbub, Christian K., "Raphael's *Quos* Ego: forgotten document on the Renaissance *paragone*," *Word & Image*, 28 (3) (July-September 2012), 287–301.

Koortbojian, Michael, "Classical Antiquity: Discovery of Classical Antiquity." *Encyclopedia of the Renaissance*. Ed. Paul F. Grendler. 6 vols. New York: Charles Scribner's Sons, (II) (1999), 1–7.

Krautheimer, Richard, "Alberti and Vitruvius." *Studies in Western Art: Acts of the Twentieth International Congress of the History of Art, II: The Renaissance and Mannerism* (Princeton: Princeton University Press, 1963.), 42–52.

Krautheimer, Richard, *Rome: Profile of a City 312–1308*. (Princeton, NJ: Princeton University Press, 1980).

Krautheimer, Richard, "The Tragic and Comic Scene of the Renaissance," *Gazette des Beaux-Arts*, XC (1948).

Krinsky, C.H., "Cesariano and the Renaissance without Rome." *Arte Lombarda* 16 (1971): 211–218.

Kwakkelstein, Michael W., "The Model's Pose: Raphael's Early Use of Antique and Italian Art." *Artibus et Historiae*, 23 (46) (2002).

Kultzen, Rolf, "Die Malerei Polodoros da Caravaggio im Giardino del Bufalo in Rom," *Mitteilungen des Kunsthisorichen Institutes in Florenz*, 9 (2) (Feb. 1960), 99–120.

Lanciani, Rodolfo Amedeo, *The Golden Days of the Renaissance in Rome, from the Pontificate of Julius II to that of Paul III* (Boston: Houghton, Mifflin and Co., 1906).

Lanciani, Rodolfo Amedeo, "La Raccolta antiquaria di Giovanni Ciampolini," *Bolletino della Commissione archaeologica communale di Roma*, 27 (1899), 101–115.

Lanciani, Rodolfo Amedeo, *The Ruins and Excavations of Ancient Rome* (New York: Benjamin Blom, 1897).

Lanciani, Rodolfo Amedeo, *Storia degli Scavi di Roma e Notizie Intorno le Collezioni Romane di Antichità* (Rome: Edizioni Quasar, 1989).

Landau, David, and Parshall, Peter, *The Renaissance Print* (New Haven: Yale University Press, 1994).

Larmour, S., and Spencer, D., eds., *The Sites of Rome: Time, Space, Memory* (Oxford), 295-322.

Layton, Evro, *The Sixteenth-Century Greek Book in Italy: Printers and Publishers for the Greek World* (Venice: Istituto ellenico di studi bizantini e postbizantini di Venezia, 1994), 318–329.

Leach, Eleanor Winsor, "Polyphemus in a Landscape: Traditions of Pastoral Courtship," in John Dixon Hunt, ed., *The Pastoral Landscape* (Washington, D.C.: National Gallery of Art, 1992).

Lefevre, Renato, *Palazzo Chigi* (Rome: Editalia, 1973).

Lefevre, Renato, *Villa Madama* (Rome: Istituto Poligrafico dello Stato, 1964).

LeSaige, Jacques and Duthilloeul, H.R., *Voyage des Jacques le Saige de Douai à Rome, Notre-Dame-de-Lorette, Venise, Jérusalem, et autres Saints Lieux* (Douai: Adam d'Aubers, 1851).

Letarouilly, Pierre, "Vedute Prospettica dell'interno della loggia," *Édifices de Rome Moderne* (Paris, 1840–1857).

Leto, Pomponio, "De vetustate urbis." *De Roma prisca et nova* (Rome, 1523).

Licht, Meg, ed., *L'Edificio a pianta centrale: Lo sviluppo del disegno architettonico nel Rinascimento* (Florence, 1984).

Licht, Meg, ed., "Elysium: A Prelude to Renaissance Theater," *Renaissance Quarterly*, 49 (1) (Spring, 1996), 1–29.

Lilius, Henrik, "Gli Affreschi di Villa Lante," in n T. Carunchio and S. Örmä, *Villa Lante al Gianicolo: Storia della Fabbrica e cronaca degli abitatori* (Rome: Institutum Romanum Finlandiae, 2005).

Lilius, Henrik, *Villa Lante al Gianicolo: L'architettura e la decorazione pittorica*. 2 vols. (Roma: Acta Instituti Romani Finlandiae, 1981).

Lippincott, K., "Two Astrological Ceilings Reconsidered: The Sala di Galatea in the Villa Farnesina and the Sala del Mappamondo at Caprarola." *Journal of the Warburg and Courtauld Institutes*, 53 (1990), 185–207.

Loh, Maria, *Titian Remade: Repetition and the Transformation of Early Modern Italian Art* (Los Angeles: Getty Research Institute, 2007).

Lucco, Mauro, *L'Opera Completa di Sebastiano del Piombo* (Milan: Rizzoli, 1980).

Lucian, *Herodotus and Aëtion*, trans. by H.W. Fowler and F.G. Fowler (Oxford: The Clarendon Press, 1905).

Mack, Charles Randall, "The Rucellai Palace: Some New Proposals," *The Art Bulletin*, 56 (4) (Dec., 1974), 517–529.

Magister, S., "Pomponio Leto collezionista di antichità: Note sulle tradizione manoscritta di una raccolta epigrafia nella Roma del tardo Quattrocento." *Xenia antiqua*, 7 (1998): 167–196.

Maj, B.M. Felletti, "La Tetide della Stazione Termine," in *Archaeologica Classica*, 1 (1949), 46–68.

Majanlahti, Anthony, *The Families Who Made Rome: A History and Guide* (London: Chatto & Windus, 2005).

Malafarina, Gianfranco, *La Villa Farnesina a Roma* (Modena: Franco Cosimo Panini Editore, 2003).

O'Malley, John, "The Vatican Library and the School of Athens, a Text of Battista Casali, 1508." *Journal of Medieval and Renaissance Studies*, Vol. 7 (1977), 271–287.

Mancinelli, Fabrizio, "The *Coronation of the Virgin* by Raphael." *Studies in the History of Art* 17: Symposium Papers v: Raphael Before Rome (1986), 127–136.

Mancinelli, Fabrizio, "Restauri in Vaticano in occassione del centenario raffaellesco." In M.S. Hamoud and M.L. Strocchi, eds., *Studi su Raffaello* (Urbino: QuattroVenti, 1987), 479–484.

Mandowsky, Erna and Mitchell, Charles, *Pirro Ligorio's Roman Antiquities: The Drawings in MS XIII. B 7 in the National Library of Naples* (London: Warburg Institute, University of London, 1963).

Mansi, G.D., *Sacrorum Conciliorum, nova et amplissima collectio* (Paris, 1902).

Marabottini, A., *Polidoro da Caravaggio* (Rome: Edizione dell'elefante, 1969).

Marchese, Vincenzo, *Pittori, sculptori e architetti Domenicani*, 3 vols (Florence, 1846).

Marini, G., *Lettera al chiarissimo Monsignor Giuseppe Muti Papazzurri già Casali, nella quale s'illustrati il ruolo de' professori dell'archiginnasio romano per l'anno MDXIV* (Rome, 1797).

Mazzochi, Jacopo, *Epigrammatica antiquae urbis* (Rome: Mazzochi, 1521).

Mazzochi, Jacopo, "The Sleeping Nymph: Origins of a Humanist Fountain Type," *The Art Bulletin*, 57 (3) (Sep., 1975), 357–365.

McDougall, Elizabeth, "The Sleeping Nymph: Origins of a Humanist Fountain Type," *The Art Bulletin*, 57 (3) (Sep., 1975), 357–365.

McKillop, S.R., *Franciabigio* (Berkeley: University of California Press, 1974).

Meiss, Millard, "Raphael's Mechanized Seashell: Notes on a Myth, Technology and Iconographic Tradition," *The Painter's Choice: Problems in the Interpretation of Renaissance Art* (New York: Harper and Row, 1976), 203–211.

Menapace, Luigi, *Il Banchiere di Tre Famosi Pontificati: il Magnifico Agostino Chigi* (Milan: Giuffrè, 1970).

Merisalo, Outi, "Baldassarre Turini e la corte unmanistica medicea a Roma." In Tancredi Carunchio e Simo Örmä, *Villa Lante al Gianicolo: Storia della fabbrica e cronaca degli abitatori* (Rome: Palombi Editore, 2005), 151–154.

Meyer zur Capellen, Jürg and Polter, Stefan B., *Raphael: A Critical Catalogue of his Paintings* (Landshut: Arcos, 2001), 3 vols.

Michiel, Marcantonio, *Notizie d'opere di disegno nella prima metà del secolo XVI, esistenti in Padova, Cremona, Milano, Pavai, Bergamo, Crema e Venezia. Scritta da un anonimo di quell tempo. Pubblicata e illustrata da D. Iacopo Morelli* (Bassano, 1800).

Milizia, Francesco, *Memorie degli Architetti Antichi e Moderni* (Parma, 1781).

Montenovesi, Ottorino, *Agostino Chigi Banchiere e Appaltatore dell'Allume di Tolfa*. Archivio della Società Romana si Storia Patria, 60 (Rome: 1938), 107–147.

Montini, Renzo U., *Palazzo Baldassini e L'Arte di Giovanni da Udine* (Rome: Istituto di Studi Romani Editore, 1957).

Montini, Renzo U., "Palazzo Baldassini Restaurato," *Studi Romani*, Anno V (1957), 39–56.

Morolli, Gabriele, *"Le Belle Forme degli Edifici Antichi": Raffaello e il Progetto del Primo Trattato Rinascimentale sulle Antichità di Roma* (Florence: Alinea, 1984)

Nagel, Alexander, *Michelangelo and the Reform of Art* (NY: Cambridge University Press, 2000).

Nagel, Alexander and Wood, Christopher, *Anachronic Renaissance*. (New York: Zone Books, 2010).

Nagel, Alexander and Wood, Christopher, "Towards a new model of Renaissance Anachronism." *Art Bulletin*, 87 (2005), 403–432.

Nelson, J.K., and Zeckhauser, R., *The Patron's Payoff: Conspicuous Commissions in Italian Renaissance Art* (NJ: Princeton University Press, 2008).

Nesselrath, Arnold, "Art-Historical Findings during the Restoration of the Stanza Dell'Incendio." *Master Drawings*, 30 (1) (1992): 31–60.

Nesselrath, Arnold, "Lorenzo Lotto in the Stanza della Segnatura," *The Burlington Magazine*, 142 (1162) (Jan., 2000), 4–12.

Nesselrath, Arnold, "Lotto as Raphael's Collaborator in the Stanza di Eliodoro," *Burlington Magazine* 146 (1220, Raphael) (Nov. 2004), 732–741.

Nesselrath, Arnold, "Raphael and Pope Julius II," in Hugo Chapman, Tom Henry, Carol Piazotta, Arnold Nesselrath and Nicholas Penny, *Raphael: from Urbino to Rome* (London: National Gallery, 2004), 281–293.

Nesselrath, Arnold, "Raffaello Archaeologo." *Bolaffi, Rivista Mensile di Arte, Cultura, Informazione*, 134 (Oct. 1983), 50–51.

Nesselrath, Arnold, "Raphael's Archaeological Method," in André Chastel, ed., *Raffaello a Rome: Il Covegno del 1983* (Rome: Edizioni dell'Elefante, 1986).

Neuendorf, H., "The Vatican Discovers New Paintings by Raphael Hidden in Plain Sight—Right On Its Walls." *Artnet News*, 6 July 2017.

von Neumann, John and Morgenstern, Oskar, *Theory of Games and Economic Behavior* (Princeton: Princeton University Press, reprinted 1953).

Nonaka, N., *Renaissance Porticoes and Painted Pergolas: Nature and Culture in Early Modern Italy* (NY: Routledge, 2017).

Novelli, U., "Rome: Palazzo Baldassini," in Tancredi Carunchio, ed., *Ricercha di Storia dell'arte: Propedeutica al restsauro; Techniche di Ricerca, richerche sulla technica*, 31 (La Nuova Italia Scientifica, 1987), 85–87.

Oberhuber, Konrad, "Die Werkstatt Raffaels" (*Künstlerwerkstätten Der Renaissance / Sylvie Béguin ... Hrsg. Von Roberto Cassanelli*, 1988), 257–274.

Oberhuber, Konrad, "Lo Stile Classico di Raffaello e la sua Evoluzione a Roma fine al 1527," in K. Oberhuber, ed., *Roma e lo Stile Classico di Raffaello* (Milan: Electa, 1999), 17–30.

Oberhuber, Konrad, "Perino del Vaga e Raffaello," *Perino del Vaga tra Raffaello e Michelangelo* (Milan: Electa, 2001), 51–57.

Oberhuber, Konrad, *Raphael: The Paintings* (NY: Prestel Verlag, 1999).

Oberhuber, Konrad, *Raphaels Zeichnungen* (Berlin: Gebr. Mann Verlag, 1972).

Oberhuber, Konrad, ed., *Roma e lo Stile Classico di Raffaello* (Milan: Electa, 1999).

Olszewski, E.J., "Central and Lateral Landscapes in Italian Renaissance Paintings," *Source: Notes in the History of Art*, 17 (3) (Spring 1998), 29–35.

Onians, John, *Bearers of Meaning* (NJ: Princeton University Press, 1988).

Oppian, *Halieutica* (Loeb Classical Library, 1928).

Orlando, Saverio, ed., *Poesie Italiane* (Milan: Rizzoli, 1988).

Örmä, Simo, "I propreitari e la vita nella villa," In T. Carunchio e S. Örmä, *Villa Lante al Gianicolo: Storia della fabbrica e cronaca degli abitatori* (Rome: Palombi Editore, 2005), 151–169.

Ortolani, Giorgo, "I marmi e le pitture parietali," in R. Varoli-Piazza, ed., *Raffaello La Loggia di Amore e Psiche alla Farnesina* (Milan: Silvana Editoriale, 2002).

Osborne, J., "A Note on the Medieval Name of the So-called 'Temple of Fortuna Virilis' in Rome." *Papers of the British School at Rome*, 56 (1988), 210–212.

Packer, James E., "Report from Rome: The Imperial Fora, A Retrospective." *American Journal of Archaeology*, Vol. 101 (2) (Apr., 1997), 307–330.

Panofsky, Erwin, *Renaissance and Renascences in Western Art* (NY: Harper & Row, 1960).

Parma Armanti, E., *Perin del Vaga: l'anello mancante* (Genoa, 1986).

von Pastor, Ludwig, *Geschichte der Päpste im Zeitalter der Renaissance und der Glaubensspaltung: von der Wahl Leos X. bis zum Tode Klemens' VII (1513–1534), Vol. 1 Leo X* (Freiburg im Breisgau: Herder, 1907).

von Pastor, Ludwig, *Geschichte der Päpste seit dem Ausgang des Mittelalters* (Freiburg, 1885–1933), vol. 28.

Payne, Alina A., *The Architectural Treatise in the Italian Renaissance: Architectural Invention, Ornament, and Literary Culture* (Cambridge: Cambridge University Press, 1999).

Payne, Alina A., Kuttner, Ann, and Smick, Rebecca, eds., *Antiquity and its Interpreters*. (Cambridge: Cambridge University Press, 2000).

Pellechia, Linda, "The Contested City: Urban Form in Early Sixteenth-Century Rome." In M.B. Hall, ed., *The Cambridge Companion to Raphael* (Hong Kong: Cambridge University Press, 2005), 59–94.

Pezzini, Grazia Bernini; Massari, Stagnia; and Prosperi Valenti Rodinò, Simonetta, *Raphael Invenit: stampe da Raffaello nelle collezioni dell'Istituto Nazionale per la Grafica* (Rome: Quasar, 1985).

Philostratus, *Immagines*. trans. by Arthur Fairbanks (London: W. Heinemann, 1931).

Platner, Samuel Ball, *A Topographical Dictionary of Ancient Rome* (London: Oxford University Press, 1929), 109.

Plesters, J., "Raphael's Cartoons for the Vatican Tapestries: A Brief Report of the Materials, Techniques, and Condition." In John Shearman and Marcia Hall, eds., *The Princeton Raphael Symposium. Science in the Service of Art History* (Princeton, NJ: Princeton University Press, 1990), 111–124.

Poggi, Giovanni, Barocchi, Paola, and Ristori, Renzo, *Il Carteggio di Michelangelo* (Firenze: Sansoni, 1965–1983).

Pon, Lisa, "Marcantonio and Raphael," *Print Quarterly*, 16 (4) (December 1999), 368–370

Pon, Lisa, *Raphael, Dürer and Marcantonio Raimondi: Copying and the Italian Renaissance Print* (New Haven: Yale University Press, 2004).

Pontani, Filippomaria, "From Budé to Zenodotus: Homeric Readings in the European Renaissance," *International Journal of the Classical Tradition*, 14 (3/4) (December, 2007), 374–430.

Portoghesi, Paolo, "S. Maria della Pace di Pietro da Cortona," *L'architettura: Cronache e storia*, 7 (1962) 840–851.

Prandi, Adriano, *Villa Lante al Gianicolo*, with a preface and introduction by T. Steinby (Rome: Edizioni dell'Ateneo, 1954).

Quatremère de Quincy, Antoine, *History of the Life and Works of Raffaello*, trans. by W. Hazlitt from 3rd Parisian edition (London: Bell and Daldy, 1869).

Quednau, Rolf, *Die Sala di Costantino im Vatikanischen Palast* (NY: Georg Olms Verlag, 1979).

Quinlan-McGrath, Mary, "Aegidius Gallus, De Viridario Agustini Chigii Vera Libellus. Introduction, Latin Text and English Translation." *Humanistica Lovaniensia—Journal of Neo-Latin Studies*, Vol. 38 (1989), 1–100.

Quinlan-McGrath, Mary, "The Astrological Vault of the Villa Farnesina Agostino Chigi's Rising Sun." *Journal of the Warburg and Courtauld Institutes*, 47 (1984), 91–105.

Quinlan-McGrath, Mary, "Blosius Palladius, *Suburbanum Agustini Chisii.* Introduction, Latin Text and English Translation." *Humanistica Lovaniensia*, 39 (1990), 93–156.

Quinlan-McGrath, Mary, "A Proposal for the Foundation Date of the Villa Farnesina." *Journal of the Warburg and Courtauld Institutes*, 49 (1986), 245–250.

Quinlan-McGrath, Mary, "The Villa of Agostino Chigi: The Poems and The Paintings" (PhD Diss, University of Chicago, 1983).

Quinlan-McGrath, Mary, "The Villa Farnesina, Time-Telling Conventions and Renaissance Astrological Practice." *Journal of the Warburg and Courtauld Institutes*, 58 (1995), 53–71.

Ray, Stefano, *Raffaello architetto: Linguaggio artistico e ideologica nel Rinascimento Romano* (Rome: Laterza, 1974).

Ray, Stefano, "Opere per Agostino Chigi," in C.L. Frommel, S. Ray, and M. Tafuri, eds., *Raffaello Architetto* (Milan: Electra, 1984), 199–124.

Ray, Stefano, "Il Volo di Icaro," in C.L. Frommel, S. Ray, and M. Tafuri, eds., *Raffaello Architetto* (Milan: Electra, 1984), 47–58.

Redig de Campos, Deoclecio, "La Stufetta del Cardinal Bibbiena in Vaticano e il suo restauro." *Römisches Jahrbuch für Kunstgeschichte*, 20 (1983), 221–240.

Redig de Campos, Deoclecio, "Notizia su palazzo Baldassini," *Bollettino del Centro di Studi per la Storia dell'Architettura*, 10 (Rome: Casa dei Crescenzi, 1956), 3–22.

Redig de Campos, Deoclecio, "Palazzo Baldassini," in *Osservatore Romano* (26 February 1956).

Reilly, Patricia, "Raphael's *Fire in the Borgo* and the Italian Pictorial Vernacular." *The Art Bulletin*, 92 (4) (Dec. 2010).

Reiss, Sheryl, "Cardinal Giulio de' Medici as a Patron of Art, 1513–1523" (PhD Diss, Princeton University, 1992).

Reiss, Sheryl, "Raphael and His Patrons: From the Court of Urbino to the Curia and Rome," in M.B. Hall, ed., *The Cambridge Companion to Raphael* (NY: Cambridge University Press, 2005), 36–59.

Reiss, Sheryl and Gouwens, Kenneth, eds., *The Pontificate of Clement VII: History, Politics, Culture* (London: Routledge, 2017).

Reist, Inge Jackson, "Raphael and the Humanist Villa," *Source: Notes in the History of Art*, 3 (4) (Summer 1984), 13–28.

Repetti, Emanuele, *Dizionario geografico fisico storico della Toscana: contenente la descrizione di tutti i luoghi del Granducato, Ducato di Lucca, Garfagnana e Lunigiana*. 6. Appendice (1846).

Richter, Irma A., *Paragone: A Comparison of the Arts* (NY: Oxford University Press, 1949).

Richter, Jean Paul, *La Collezione Hertz e gli affreschi di Giulio Romano nel Palazzo Zuccari (con una prefazione di Robert Mond)* (Leipzig, 1928).

Ridolfini, C.P., *Le case romane con facciate graffite e dipinte* (Rome: Amici dei Musei di Roma, 1960).

Rijser, David, *Raphael's Poetics: Art and Poetry in High Renaissance Rome*. (Amsterdam: Amsterdam University Press, 2012).

Robert, C., *Die antiken Sarcophagreliefs* (Deutsches Archaëlogisches Inst., Berlin, 1919) III: *Einzelmythen*: 3. *Niobiden, Triptolemos, Ungedeutet*.

Rodinò, S. Prosperi Valenti, *Raphael Invenit: Stampe da Raffaello nelle Collezione dell'Istituto Nazionale per a Grafica* (Rome: Edizione Quasar, 1985).

Rodríguez Mayorgas, A., "Romulus, Aeneas and the Cultural Memory of the Roman Republic." *Atheneum*, 98 (1) (2010) 89–109.

de Rosa, G., "L'Istituto Luigi Sturzo," in M. Cogotti and L. Gigli, *Palazzo Baldassini* (Rome: L'erma di Bretschneider, 1995), 71–75.

Rosenfeld, Myra Nan, *Sebastiano Serlio on Domestic Architecture: Different Dwellings from the Meanest Hovel to the Most Ornate Palace: the Sixteenth-Century Manuscript of Book VI in the Avery Library of Columbia University* (New York: Architectural History Foundation, 1978).

Rosier, Bart, "The Victories of Charles V: A Series of Prints by Maarten van Heemskerke, 1555–1556." *Simiolus: Netherlands Quarterly for the History of Art* 20 (1) (1990–1991), 24–38.

Rossi, Sergio and Cassanelli, Luciana, eds., *Di Luoghi di Raffaello a Roma* (Rome: Multigrafica Editrice, 1983).

de Rossi, Domenico, and Maffei, Paolo Alessandro, *Raccolta di statue antiche e moderne* (Rome: 1704).

Rowe, Colin and Satkowski, Leon, *Italian Architecture of the 16th Century* (New York: Princeton Architectural Press, 2002).

Rowland, Ingrid D., "The Birth Date of Agostino Chigi: Documentary Proof." *Journal of the Warburg and Courtauld Institutes*, 47 (1984), 192–193.

Rowland, Ingrid D., *The Correspondence of Agostino Chigi* (Vatican: Biblioteca Apostolica Vaticana, 2001).

Rowland, Ingrid D., "Cultural Introduction to Renaissance Rome." In *Artistic Centers of the Italian Renaissance: Rome*, ed. by M.B. Hall (New York, NY: Cambridge University Press, 2005), 1–14.

Rowland, Ingrid D., "From Vitruvian Scholarship to Vitruvian Practice." *Memoirs of the American Academy in Rome*, 50 (2005), 15–40.

Rowland, Ingrid D., "Il Giardino *Trans Tiberium* di Agostino Chigi." In C. Benocci, ed., *I Giardini Chigi tra Siena e Roma dal Cinquecento agli Inizi dell'Ottocento* (Siena: Fondazione Monte dei Paschi, 2005), 57–72, 421.

Rowland, Ingrid D., "Raphael, Angelo Colocci and the Genesis of the Architectural Orders." *The Art Bulletin*, 76 (1) (March, 1994), 81–104.

Rowland, Ingrid D., "Render Unto Caesar the Things Which are Caesar's: Humanism and the Arts in the Patronage of Agostino Chigi." *Renaissance Quarterly*, 39 (4) (Winter, 1986), 673–730.

Rowland, Ingrid D., "Some Panegyrics to Agostino Chigi." *Journal of the Warburg and Courtauld Institutes*, 47 (1984), 194–199.

Rowland, Ingrid D., *The Culture of the High Renaissance: Ancients and Moderns in Sixteenth-Century Rome* (New York: Cambridge University Press, 1998).

Rowland, Ingrid D., *The Roman garden of Agostino Chigi: the Thirteenth Gerson Lecture held in Memory of Horst Gerson (1907–1978) in the Aula of the University of Groningen on the 17th of November 2005* (Groningen: Gerson, 2005).

Rowland, Ingrid D., "The Vatican Stanze." In M.B. Hall, ed., *The Cambridge Companion to Raphael* (NY: Cambridge University Press, 2005), 95–119.

Rowland, Ingrid D., and Charney, Noah, *Collector of lives: giorgio vasari and the invention of art* (W.W. Norton & Co., 2017).

Rowland, Ingrid D., and Howe, Thomas Noble, *Vitruvius: Ten Books on Architecture* (NY: Cambridge University Press, 1999).

Rubin, Patricia Lee, *Giorgio Vasari: Art and History*. (New Haven: Yale University Press, 1995).

Rubin, Patricia Lee, "Il Contribuo di Raffaello allo sviluppo della Pala d'Altare Rinascimentale," *Arte Cristiana*, 737–738 (March-June, 1990), 169–182.

Sacré, Dirk, "Notes on Fabio Chigi's Chigiae Familiae Commentaria," *Humanistica Lovaniensia—Journal of Neo-Latin Studies*, vol. 54 (2005), 371–379.

Sadoletus, Jacobus, *Epistolai quotquot extant* (Rome: Salomonius, 1760)

von Salis, Arnold, *Antike und Renaissance: Über Nachleben und Weiterwirken der alten in der neueren Kunst* (Erlenbach-Zürich: E. Rentsch, 1947).

Samaltanou-Tsiakma, Ekaterini, "A Renaissance Problem of Archaeology," *Gazette des Beaux Arts*, 78 (1971).

Sankovitch, Ann-Marie, "Anachronism and Simulation in Renaissance Architectural Theory." *RES: Anthropology and Aesthetics*, 49/50 (Spring-Autumn 2006), 188–203.

Sannazaro, Jacopo, *Arcadia & Other Piscatorial Eclogues*. trans. by R. Nash. (Detroit, Michigan: Wayne State University Press, 1966).

Santoro, Fiorella Sricchia, "Villa Lante: La decorazione de salone. Problemi di atttribuzione," in E.M. Steinby, ed., *Ianiculum—Gianicolo: storia topografia, monumenti, leggende dall'antichità al rinascimento* (Rome, 1996), 225–236.

lo Sardo, Mara, "Raffaello e l'odometro," *Rivista on line di storia dell'arte*, 1 (2004), no page numbers.

Saxl, Fritz, *La fede astrologica di Agostino Chigi: interpretazione dei dipinti di Baldassarre Peruzzi nella sala di Galatea della Farnesina* (Rome: Reale Accademia d'Italia, 1934).

Scandiani, Giuseppe, ed., *Sebastiano del Piombo, 1485–1547*. (Milan: Motta, 2008).

Schard, Alfred, *Beiträge zur Geschichte des Bühnenbildes vom 15. Zum Ende des 17. Jahrhunderts* (Ph.D. diss, Freiburg im Breisgau, 1925).

Schwarzenberg, Erkinger, "Raphael und die Psyche-Statue Agostino Chigis," *Jahrbuch der Kunsthistorischen Sammlungen in Wien*, 73 (1977), 107–136.

Scoppola, Francesco, "Villa Chigi alle Volte," *Rilievi di fabbriche attribuite a Baldassarre Peruzzi* (Siena: Palazzo Pubblico, 1981), 361–433.

Sebregondi, Giulia Ceriani, *Architettura e committenza a Siena nel Cinquecento: L'attività di Baldassarre Peruzzi e la storia di Palazzo Francesconi* (Siena: Aska Edizione, 2011).

Serlio, Sebastiano, *The Five Books of Architecture* (New York: Dover Publications, 1982).

Shearman, John K.G., "Alfonso D'Este's Camerino," in A. Chastel, ed. *"Il se Rendit en Italie": Études Offertes à André Chastel* (Paris: Elefante, 1987), 209–230.

Shearman, John K.G., "The Chigi Chapel in S. Maria del Popolo." *Journal of the Warburg and Courtauld Institutes*, 24 (3/4) (Jul-Dec. 1961), pp. 129–160.

Shearman, John K.G., "Die Loggia der Psyche in der Villa Farnesina und di Probleme der Letzten Phase von Raffaels graphischem Stil," *Jahrbuch der Kunsthistorischen Sammlungen in Wien*, 60 (1964), 129–159.

Shearman, John K.G., "A Functional Interpretation of the Villa Madama," *Römisches Jahrbuch für Kunstgeschichte*, Vol. 20 (1983).

Shearman, John K.G., *Mannerism* (NY: Penguin Books, 1967).

Shearman, John K.G., "Il mecenatismo di Giulio II e Leone X." In Arnold Esch and Christoph Luitpold Frommel, eds., *Arte, Committenza ed Economia a Roma e Nelle Corti del Rinascimento (1420–1530)* (Rome: Piccola Biblioteca Einaudi, 1995).

Shearman, John K.G., *Only connect ...: art and the spectator in the Italian Renaissance*. The A.W. Mellon Lectures in the Fine Arts, 1988 (Princeton, NJ: Princeton University Press, 1992).

Shearman, John K.G., "The Organization of Raphael's Workshop," *Art Institute of Chicago Museum Studies*, 10 (1983), 40–57.

Shearman, John K.G., "Raphael as Architect," *Journal of the Royal Society of Arts*, 116 (5141) (April 1968), 388–409.

Shearman, John K.G., *Raphael in Early Modern Sources* (New Haven: Yale University Press, 2003).

Shearman, John K.G., *Raphael's Cartoons an the Tapestries for the Sistine Chapel* (NY: Phaidon, 1972).

Shearman, John K.G., "Raphael's Unexecuted Projects for the Stanze," in Georg Kauffmann et al., eds., *Walter Friedlaender zum 90. Geburtstag: eine Festsgabe seiner europäieshcen Schüler, Freund und Veherer* (Berlin: De Gruyter, 1965), 158–180.

Shearman, John K.G., "Raphael, Rome, and the Codex Escurialensis," *Master Drawings*, Vol. 15 (2) (Summer 1977), 107–146.

Shearman, John K.G., *The Vatican Stanze: Functions and Decoration* (London: Oxford University Press, 1971).

Smyth, Craig Hugh, "Mannerism and *Maniera*." In *the Renaissance and Mannerism*, ed. by M. Meiss, R. Krautheimer, G. Kubler, R.W. Lee, R. Wittkower, and I.E. Rubin (Princeton, NJ: Princeton University Press, 1963).

Sowerby, R., "Early Humanist Failure with Homer," *International Journal of the Classical Tradition*, 4 (1997–1998), 37–63 and 165–194.

Springer, Anton, *Raffael und Michelangelo*, vol. 2 (Leipzig: Seemann, 1895).

Sricchia Santoro, Fiorella, "Villa Lante: La Decorazione del Salone, Problemi di Attribuzione," in E.M. Steinby, *Ianiculum—Gianicolo: Storia, topografia, monumenti, leggende dall'antichità al rinascimento* (Rome, 1996), 225–236.

Steinby, E.M., *Ianiculum—Gianicolo: Storia, topografia, monumenti, leggende dall'antichità al rinascimento* (Rome, 1996).

Steinman, Ernst, "Amor und Psyche, ein Freskenzyklus aus der Schule Raffael's in der Engelsburg zu Rom," *Zeitschrift für Bildended Kunst* 13 (1902), 86–93.

Steinmetzer, Georg, *Der Palazzo Zuccari in Rome. Bau-Umbau-Neubau* (PhD diss., UB Salzburg, 2001).

Stenius, G., "Baldassarre Turini e le sue case romane sulla base dei documenti." *OpIRF*, 1 (1981, 71, nn. 1,3).

Stinger, Charles L., *The Renaissance in Rome* (Bloomington: Indiana University Press, 1998).

Stollhans, Cynthia, "Baldassare Peruzzi and his patrons: Religious paintings in Rome, 1503–1527" (PhD diss., Northwestern University, 1988).

Stollhans, Cynthia, "Fra Mariano, Peruzzi and Polidoro da Caravaggio: A New Look at Religious Landscapes in Renaissance Rome." *The Sixteenth Century Journal*, 23 (3) (Autumn, 1992), 506–525.

Stollhans, Cynthia, "Peruzzi's Standing Saint Paul in the Ponzetti Chapel, Santa Maria della Pace: Tradition or Innovation?" *Notes in the History of Art*, 10 (3) (Spring 1991), 14–20.

Stollhans, Cynthia, "The problem of two saints named Catherine in the Fetti Chapel," *St. Catherine of Alexandria in Renaissance Roman Art: Case Studies in Patronage* (UK: Ashgate, 2014).

Stollhans, Cynthia, *St. Catherine of Alexandria in Renaissance Roman Art: Case Studies in Patronage* (UK: Ashgate, 2014).

Stumpo, E., "Prima e Dopo il Pontificato di Alessandro VII: I Chigi, Famiglia Senese tra Roma e Firenze." In C. Benocci, ed., *I Giardini Chigi tra Siena e Roma dal Cinquecento agli Inizi dell'Ottocento* (Siena: Fondazione Monte dei Paschi, 2005), 39–56.

Summers, David, *Michelangelo and the Language of Art* (NJ: Princeton University Press, 1981).

Tagliolini, Alessandro, *I Giardini di Rome: Foclore, Poesia e Storia della Città Attraverso l'Evoluzione delle «Isole Verdi»: la Riscoperta di una Rinascimentale Belezza in un'Idealesintesi tra Natura e Arte*. (Rome: Newton Compton, 1980).

Talvacchia, Bette, *Raphael* (London: Phaidon, 2007).

Talvacchia, Bette, "Raphael's Workshop and the Development of a Managerial Style." in M.B. Hall, ed., *The Cambridge Companion to Raphael* (NY: Cambridge University Press, 2005) 167–185.

Tantillo, Alma Maria Mignosi, "Restuari alla Farnesina," *Bolletino d'Arte*, 57 (1972), 33–43.

Tarr, Roger, "Brunelleschi and Donatello: Placement and Meaning in Sculpture." *Artibus et Historiae*, 16 (32) (1995), 101–140.

Tavernor, Robert, *On Alberti and the Art of Building* (New Haven: Yale University Press, 1998).

di Teodoro, Francesco P., *Raffaello, Baldassar Castiglione e la Lettera a Leone X* (Bologna: Nuova Alfa, 1994).

Tempesti, Anna Forlani, *Rafaello e Michelangelo* (Florence: Casa Buonarroti, 1984).

Temple, Nicholas, *Renovatio Urbis: Architecture, Urbanism, and Ceremony in the Rome of Julius II*. (Abingdon, UK: Routledge, 2011).

Tessari, Cristiano, *Baldassarre Peruzzi: il progetto dell'antico* (Milan: Electa, 1995).

Thoenes, Christoph, "Note sul 'ninfeo' di Genazzano," *Studi Bramanteschi* (Rome, 1974), 575–583.

Thoenes, Christoph, "Renaissance Saint Peter's," in W. Tronzo, ed., *St. Peter's in the Vatican* (NY: Cambridge University Press, 2005), 64–92.

Thoenes, Christoph, "Zu Raffaels Galatea," in Lucius Grisebach and Konrad Renger, eds., *Festschrift für Otto von Simson zum 65. Gerburtstag* (Vienna: Propyläen Verlag, 1977), 231–244.

Tizio, Sigismondo, *Historiae Senenses*. (Rome: Istituto Storico Italiano per l'Età Moderna e Contemporanea, 1510).

Trachtenberg, Marvin, "An Antique Model for Donatello's Marble David." *The Art Bulletin*, 50 (3) (Sep., 1968), 268–269.

Tuckerman, B., *Planetary, Lunar and Solar Positions, A.D. 2 to A.D. 1649* (Philadelphia, 1964).

Turner, A. Richard, *The Vision of Landscape in Renaissance Italy* (New Jersey: Princeton University Press 1966).

Tuttle, Richard John, "The Basilica of S. Petronio in Bologna," in H.A. Millon and V. Magnago Lampugnani, eds., *The Renaissance from Brunelleschi to Michelangelo: The Representation of Architecture* (Milan: Bompiani, 1994), 522–527.

Ubaldini, Federigo, *Vita di mons. Angelo Colocci.* ed. by Vittorio Fannelli (Città del Vaticano: Biblioteca Apostolica Vaticana, 1969).

Vacca, Flaminio, *Memoriae di varie antichità trovate in diversi luoghi della città di Roma* (Rome, 1594).

Vahland, Kia, "Sebastiano and Raphael," in Giuseppe Scandiani, ed., *Sebastiano del Piombo, 1485–1547* (Milan: Motta, 2008), 133–139.

Valtieri, Simonetta, "La Fabbrica del palazzo del Cardinale Raffaelle Riario (La Cancelleria)," *Quaderni dell'Istituto di Storia dell'Architettura*, 174 (1983), 3–26.

Varoli-Piazza, Rosalia, "Il Fregio nella Sala delle Prospettive. Un'ipotesi per la Bottega del Peruzzi." In Marcello Fagiolo and Maria Luisa Madonna, eds., *Baldassarre Peruzzi: Pittura, Scena, e Architettura nel Cinquecento* (Rome: Istituto della Enciclopedia Italiana, 1987), 363–398.

Varoli-Piazza, Rosalia, "Un Esempio di Concinnitas," in Rosalia Varoli-Piazza, *Raffaello: La Loggia di Amore e Psiche all Farnesina* (Cinisello Balsamo, Milan: Silvana, 2002).

Varoli-Piazza, Rosalia, *Raffaello: la loggia di Amore e Psiche alla Farnesina* (Cinisello Balsamo, Milan: Silvana, 2002).

Varoli-Piazza, Rosalia, "Peruzzi e Beccafumi alla Farnesina," *Quaderni di Palazzo Venezia*, 1 (1981): 60–64.

Vasari, Giorgio, *Lives of the Painters, Sculptors and Architects*, trans. by Gaston du B. de Vere (NY: Alfred Knopf, 1996), vols. 1 and 2.

del Vecchi, Pierluigi, *Raphael* (New York: Abbeville, 2002).

Venturi, A., *Storia dell'arte italiana*, XI (I) (Milan, 1938).

Vermeule, Cornelius, "Sarcophagus: Revelers Gathering Grapes," in A. Chong, *Eye of the Beholder* (Boston, MA: Beacon Press, 2003), 12–13.

Vertova, Luisa, "Cupid and Psyche in Renaissance Painting before Raphael," *Journal of the Warburg and Courtauld Institutes* 42 (1979), 104–121.

Visconti, P.E., *Lettera sulla Antichità di Roma Scritta da Raffaello d'Urbino a Papa Leone X* (Rome, 1833).

de Vos, Mariette, "I monumenti rinvenuti nel giardino della villa rinascimentale di Agostino Chigi: la villa romana della Farnesina," in C.L. Frommel, G. Caneva, and A. Angeli, *La villa Farnesina a Roma = The villa Farnesina in Rome.* Mirabilia Italiæ, 12 (Modena: F.C. Panini, 2003), 2: 155–162.

Vout, Caroline, *The Hills of Rome: Signature of an Eternal City* (UK: Cambridge University Press, 2012).

Vout, Caroline, "Sizing up Rome or theorising the overview," in S. Larmour and D. Spencer, eds., *The Sites of Rome: Time, Space, Memory* (Oxford), 295–322.

Warburg, Aby, *The Renewal of Pagan Antiquity: Contributions to the Cultural History of the European Renaissance.* Trans. by David Britt. (CA: Getty Research Institute for the History of Art and the Humanities, 1999).

Weiss, Roberto, *The Renaissance Discovery of Classical Antiquity*. (Oxford: B. Blackwell, 1969).

Whitcombe, Christopher L.C.E., "The Chapel of the Courtesan and the Quarrel of the Magdalens." *The Art Bulletin*, 84 (2) (Jun., 2002), 273–292.

Williams, Robert, *Raphael and the Redefinition of Art in Renaissance Italy* (UK: Cambridge University Press, 2017).

Winternitz, Emanuel, "Archaelogia musicale del Rinascimento nel Parnaso di Raffaello," *Reondiconti della pontificia Accademia roman di archeologia*, XXVII (1952–1954).

Winternitz, Emanuel, "Il Parnaso di Raffaello," *Gli strumenti musicali e il loro simbolismo nell'arte occidentale* (Turin, 1982).

Wittkower, Rudolf, *Born Under Saturn* (NY: Norton, 1963).

Wivel, Matthias, *Michelangelo & Sebastiano* (New Haven: Yale University Press, 2017).

Wohl, Hellmut, "The Eye of Vasari." *Mitteilungen Des Kunsthistorischen Institutes in Florenz*, 30 (3) (1986), 537–568.

Wolff Metternich, G., "Die Biblioteca Hertziana und der Palazzo Zuccari zu Rom." *Arbeitsgemeinschaft für Forschung des Landes Nordhein-Westfalen* (Cologne: Westdeutscher Verlag, 1950).

Wolk-Simon, Linda, "Competition, Collaboration, and Specialization in the Roman Art World, 1521–1527." In S. Reiss and K. Gouwens, eds., *The Pontificate of Clement VII: History, Politics, Culture* (London: Routledge, 2017) Kindle edition. Chapter 14.

Wolk-Simon, Linda, "Studies in Perino del Vaga's Early Career" (PhD diss, Ann Arbor, 1987).

Wolk-Simon, Linda, "Two early fresco cycles by Perino del Vaga: The Palazzo Baldassini and the Pucci Chapel," *Apollo*, CLV (481) (March 2002), 11–21.

Wrede, Henning, *Der Antikengarten der del Bufalo bei der Fontana Trevi*. Trierer Winckelmannsprogramme IV (Mainz am Rheim: Philip von Zabern, 1983).

Wrede, Henning, "Perseus als Heros der del Bufalo," in Franz George Maier, ed., *Alt-Paphos auf Cypern* (Mainz am Rhein: Phillip von Zabern), 52–54.

Yuen, Toby, "Illusionistic Mural Decorations of the Early Renaissance in Rome" (PhD Diss., New York University, 1972).

Ziefer, Anka, "*Marte e Venere sorpresi da Vulcano*: la fortuna iconografica di un affresco perduto di Baldassarre Peruzzi per la Villa Farnesina a Roma," in M. Beltramini and C. Elam, eds., *Some degree of happiness: Studi di storia dell'architettura in onore di Howard Burns* (Pisa: Scuola Normale Superiore, 2010), 207–233.

Zanchettin, Vitale, "Costruire nell'antico: Roma, Campo Marzio, 1508–1523: Peruzzi, al confraternità di San Rocco e i cantieri intorno al Mausoleo di Augusto." In C.L. Frommel, *Baldassarre Peruzzi, 1481–1536* (Venice: Marsilio, 2005), 123–153.

Zimmerman, T.C.P., *Paolo Giovo: The Historian and the Crisis of Sixteenth-Century Italy* (Princeton, NJ: Princeton University Press, 1995).

Zucchi, Alberto, *Roma Domenicane* 4 vols (Florence, 1938–1943).

Index

The bold page references indicate that an illustration appears in relation to that entry.